"I am glad that David Hartline's occasional writings on the present life of the Church have borne fruit in this book. It is a reasoned account of what led up to present circumstances for Catholics in our culture and the probable course of things. The author does not confuse hope with vacuous optimism, and he does indeed make a good case for sensing that the spiritual struggle of the present time will set the stage for a stronger Church. The increased volume of opposition to the Church's voice, tending to shout down logic with irrational anger, is a good indication that prophetic figures beginning with Benedict XVI, are making a difference. Hartline describes the scene well."

—Father George William Rutler, best-selling author and host of EWTN's **Christ in the City**

"When Catholicism seems under siege in Europe and now also in the USA, David Hartline's upbeat and positive message is a great encouragement. His straightforward presentation of the success of the World Youth Days and (from my own perspective) the Pope's visit to Britain calls us to action inspired by the virtue of hope, trusting in God's providence for his Church."

—Father Tim Finigan, UK's leading Catholic blogger, **The Hermeneutic of Continuity**

"*The Catholic Tide Continues to Turn* shows the world that despite the attacks the Catholic Church is under, many of the Church's faithful, both clergy and laity, are shining a light of faith on a world that so desperately needs to see it. This book will bring hope to all who read it."

—Karyme Lozano, leading Latin American actress, recently appearing in **For Greater Glory**

"*The Catholic Tide Continues to Turn* is a riveting update to *The Tide Is Turning Toward Catholicism,* containing insider versions of the news relating to the culture wars. From papal visits to the US to presidential elections, Hartline's detailed research and analysis provide encouragement for the Church Militant as she gears up for the coming battle: the HHS mandate showdown and the 2012 election. Even if you read the blogs and watch Fox News as I do, this book will surprise and encourage you as you work against the culture of death in America."

—*Leticia Velasquez,* **Catholic Media Review**

"In *The Catholic Tide Continues to Turn*, author Dave Hartline has written an exemplary account of a resilient Church that continues to confound skeptics. The Church is not just growing, she is in full bloom, receiving converts and vigorously defending the dignity of man worldwide.

"What is astonishing is that around the world, especially here in the United States, the mainstream media fails in their responsibilities as journalists in reporting balanced stories, if they report on her at all. Hartline fills this gap exceptionally well as he thoroughly and diligently explains how the tide continues to turn for Holy Mother Church.

"Thanks to Dave Hartline's eloquent writing and command of contemporary Church history, he concisely visits many neglected areas of reporting or misreporting and unveils the truth behind today's issues and conflicts. He points to the triumphs of Pope Benedict XVI's global visits, the brutal culture wars in the West, the internal struggles of the Church, the frailty of the megachurches, and everything else in between.

"I would recommend this book for anyone who wants to know why the gates of hell continue to fail in turning the tide against the Church in the 21st century."

—*Tito Edwards, blogger,* **National Catholic Register,** *The American Catholic, and BigPulpit.com*

The
CATHOLIC TIDE
Continues to Turn

DAVID J. HARTLINE

Copyright © 2012 Catholic Report. All rights reserved.

With the exception of short excerpts used in articles and critical reviews, no part of this work may be reproduced, transmitted, or stored in any form whatsoever, printed or electronic, without the prior written permission of the publisher.

Scripture verses contained herein are from the *Revised Standard Version of the Bible,* Catholic Edition, copyright © 1965, 1966 by the Division of Christian Education of the National Council of the Churches of Christ in the United States of America.

This is a joint effort between Catholic Report and Aquinas and More. Catholic Report retains all publishing and financial rights while Aquinas and More is the distribution arm of this effort. For book orders, please contact Aquinas and More at:

Aquinas and More
4727 N Academy Blvd Suite A
Colorado Springs, CO 80918
(866) 428-2820
aquinasandmore.com

Catholic Report
P.O. Box 775
Worthington, OH 43085
www.CatholicReport.org

Cover design: Ted Schluenderfritz
Author photo: Kay Cubberly
Interior layout and design: Claudia Volkman

Printed in the United States of America

ACKNOWLEDGMENTS

Acknowledging those who have helped you along the way with a major book project may be the toughest part of the writing process. How do you adequately say thank you to those who have helped you? This all starts with my wife Theresa—she put up with another book project and continued to give me her love and understanding. I can honestly say none of my writing endeavors would be possible without her support. My children, while they are too young to realize it, gave me energy to finish what I had started. My editor, Joel Torczon, gave of his time and meticulously thought through everything I was attempting to write. A big thank you to Ian Rutherford of Aquinas and More for seeing the wisdom of this project and for his eagerness in getting this book released; to Claudia Volkman, who did a masterful job with the layout; and to Ted Schluenderfritz, whose beautiful cover design speaks for itself. In addition, Catholic bookstores, Catholic radio, EWTN, *National Catholic Register*, and editor Dave Garick at the *Catholic Times* in Columbus, Ohio, have all been a big help to me.

I owe a great debt of gratitude to Catholic bloggers like Tito Edwards, Amy Welborn, Mark Shea, Jay Anderson, Father John Zuhlsdorf, Father Tim Finigan, Leticia Velasquez, the Curt Jester (Jeff Miller), the Anchoress (Elizabeth Scalia), David and Jonathan Bennett, Michael Brown, and many others like Michael Barone who have shown me the way through the years. The late Michael Dubruiel helped me get started in this crazy writing racket and introduced me to Tom Craughwell, whom he dubbed the smartest man alive—and who could doubt him after reading any of Craughwell's

Catholic books or viewing his History Channel masterpiece, *Stealing Lincoln's Body*. Thanks, Tom, for your advice through the years.

A big thank you to Father George Rutler, who not only praised a past article I had written but also took the time to read the manuscript and send in the first endorsement of this book. Father Willy Raymond, CSC, of Family Theater in Hollywood and the young people at this famous Hollywood studio founded by the late Father Patrick Peyton, CSC (the Rosary priest) give us all hope.

Others in the film world who have been a big help to me include Christian Peschken, Cary Solomon, Chuck Konzelman, Tim Watkins, and Carlos Espinosa. A big thank you goes out to Karyme Lozano who, in the midst of her busy acting career, found time to read my manuscript and endorse the book. Tom Loarie by chance read my first book and went out of his way to help me make the right contacts. I am deeply grateful for my parents, my late sister, my extended family, my friends, and all of those who taught and nurtured me through the years, especially those in my childhood hometown and parish of St. Mary's and Marion Catholic High School in Marion, Ohio.

Finally, to all birth mothers who choose life and give adopted parents and their families the greatest gift one could give. May God abundantly bless you all.

TABLE OF CONTENTS

INTRODUCTION 9

ONE | The Tide Is Still Turning   23

TWO | Pope Benedict XVI Visits the United States   39

THREE | A New Breed of Men and Women Religious   58

FOUR | The Number of Converts Keeps Increasing   82

FIVE | You Can't Keep a Good Church Down   112

SIX | The Culture of Life Will Prevail   132

SEVEN | Who Says the Catholic Church
Has No Political Clout?   162

EIGHT | The Growing Number of Faithful Colleges   189

NINE | The Church Stands Up for Traditional Marriage   196

TEN | The Catholic Church Keeps Growing
and the Media Can't See Why   202

ELEVEN | The Catholic Church and Islam:
An Interesting History   219

TWELVE | A German Pope Triumphs in Britain   237

THIRTEEN | The Impact of Catholic Media   242

FOURTEEN | The Catholic Church, Agnostics, and Atheists   255

FIFTEEN | *"Non Latine Liceat Hic"*
(No Latin Allowed Here")   263

SIXTEEN | The Church Draws Famous Athletes and Coaches   **276**

SEVENTEEN | The Disintegration of Liberal Christianity   **282**

EIGHTEEN | The Perils of Thinking We Know Better Than Our Predecessors   **294**

NINETEEN | The Coming Crash of the Megachurches   **314**

TWENTY | The Catholic Church Marches On   **322**

APPENDIX | A Brief Introduction to Basic Catholic Beliefs   **337**

NOTES   **348**

INDEX   **362**

INTRODUCTION

One would think from listening to mainstream media reports and taking the pulse of pop culture's talking heads that the Catholic Church is in crisis mode or a virtual free fall. Yet the Catholic Church continues to grow, and vocations have been on the increase since 1995. This is part and parcel of the "Springtime of the New Evangelization" preached first by Bl. John Paul II and now his successor, Pope Benedict XVI.

Among others, their clear teaching has resonated with young people. This partly explains why greater numbers of them are drawn to vocations, while many of their friends are attracted to a strictly secular worldview that experience and sociological studies show cannot provide contentment in life.

Perhaps it would be helpful to travel back some 40 years to see how the Catholic Church got into this crisis, how the crisis was averted, and how tide has begun to turn.

Surviving the Seventies

For most of the 1970s, the Catholic Church stared down a series of tsunami-like offensives against that which she had traditionally taught, practiced, and believed. Many simply saw this as a proper reading and the logical consequence of the Second Vatican Council. Meanwhile, many of the more orthodox or traditional members of the Church were appalled at how a growing number of priests and bishops claimed that their dissenting views were actually in accord with what the Council Fathers wanted, even though there was nothing in the actual documents to prove this. The justification for these clerics' claims was that their changes were done in the "spirit of Vatican II," which claimed that everything was open to debate and possible alteration.

It was starting to become all too much for Pope Paul VI in 1972. Seeing the dissent, the constant diminution of vocations to the priestly and religious life, not to mention the thousands of letters on his desk from priests and religious asking to be dispensed from their vows, the Pontiff marked the ninth anniversary of his coronation by uttering those famous words, stating: "The Smoke of Satan has entered the Church."[1]

By the end of the 1970s, thousands of young people had left the Church. Around the same time in the United States, a non-denominational movement began which stated that the apostolic succession (i.e., such as that held by the leadership of the Catholic Church) wasn't important, and neither was church attendance at only Catholic churches. God didn't care where you worshipped on Sunday, went this thinking, so long as you worshipped.

True, this movement often took as many from mainline Protestant communions as it did the Catholic Church. Nonetheless, that so many Catholic and Protestant youth bought into the notion that being part of a denomination almost wasn't legitimate if its services weren't hip and cool, or that so many Catholics readily believed the sacraments were no big deal proved disheartening and bewildering for many.

How could this happen in such a short space of time? Well, for one thing, it wasn't new. Some 2,000 years earlier Jesus mesmerized the crowds eager to hear a clear, compelling message. The crowds loved Jesus because he spoke with authority, and he spoke the truth (see Matthew 7:28-29). He didn't give his audiences wishy-washy, "I'm OK, you're OK" self-esteem seminars.

Sadly, instead of responding with the very thing that would draw people back—with authority and truth—the Catholic Church and many mainline Protestant churches often tried to provide an echo to the non-denominational movement rather than an alternative voice.

Introduction

Undoubtedly, those who started the non-denominational movement had the best of intentions. After all, it's precursor, the Jesus Movement, was founded by those in Evangelical congregations who had seen—often firsthand—the negative spiritual effects of the hippie movement. Those young men and women had had either a spiritual awakening or found their way back to the religion of their youth, only with a different twist. They often brought Catholics along with them, for some believed the Catholic Church had begun to drink of the excess of the times. And, let's just be honest here, in some places it had.

However, these well-intentioned young people had little theological training and a scant knowledge of Catholicism. Later some would steep themselves in theology, not only reading the Scriptures but also the writings of the early Church Fathers. Some would come to the Catholic Church. One such person was the singer John Michael Talbot. He had been part of the up-and-coming rock group Mason Profit. They opened for the likes of Janice Joplin, Black Oak Arkansas, the Doobie Brothers, and others.[2]

At one point Talbot was hailed as the next great guitar hero. He would never achieve that status, however, because he chose to step away from the rock 'n' roll scene. Like so many before him, Talbot first entered the Evangelical world before his biblical and early Church studies brought him to what he believed was the one true Church, the one Jesus founded on Peter, with whom he entrusted the keys of leadership. Today Talbot lives in community with other laypeople in a rural Arkansas setting. He continues to play music and live a simple life, as did the early Christians.

Another returnee from the exile of the 1970s is Francis Beckwith. A cradle Catholic, Beckwith left the Church in his teens when guitar Masses where all the rage. Beckwith wanted something deeper. It's not that Beckwith wasn't a big fan of rock and folk. He was Rather, he wondered why he needed to listen to cheap imitations of his favorite music at Mass when he could have the real thing at a nearby concert. Shouldn't worship music be, well, worshipful? If it was designed to help us convert our hearts and thus get us into the next world, heaven, shouldn't it be otherworldly?

Beckwith also was turned off by milquetoast homilies. To him it appeared priests desperately wanted to fit in with the modern world and be liked rather than simply preach the gospel and let the chips fall where they may.

After Beckwith left the Church and became an adult, he eventually became a leading theologian, even rising to the presidency of the Evangelical Theological Society, one of the most coveted positions in the Evangelical world. However, in his avocation as theologian and scholar, Beckwith became increasingly disconcerted by what he read in the writings of the early Church Fathers. He was learning what Bl. John Henry Cardinal Newman had so famously said in the 19th century, that "to go deep into history is to cease to be Protestant." As a result, in 2007, Beckwith shocked the evangelical world by announcing his reversion back to the Catholic faith.[3]

There have been and will continue to be many reversion stories like Beckwith's, some more, some less dramatic. On the "more" side is the reasonably well-known story of Scott Hahn. As a young man—in high school, college, and graduate school—he proudly called himself anti-Catholic. After finishing his Master's degree and finding himself on the path toward a meteoric rise in the Presbyterian denomination, Hahn did something dangerous: He began to read Catholic theology from a Catholic perspective (as opposed to reading what his fellow Protestants *said* the Church teaches). To paraphrase C.S. Lewis, an anti-Catholic can't be too careful about what he reads.

He resigned his pastorate and began taking further graduate courses at Marquette University. Having never once attended a Catholic Mass, he crept into the university chapel crypt one day during lunch. With his immense knowledge of Scripture, as he listened to the Mass and, knowing the Scriptures as well as he did, he realized that he was beholding the Lamb's Supper foretold in the Book of Revelation.

He increasingly began asking Evangelical colleagues questions

Introduction

about the Protestant stumbling blocks to Catholicism. No one he queried could give a convincing rejoinder to Catholic teaching about John 6:34-69 (the Bread of Life discourse), Luke 22:14-20 (the Last Supper), 1 Corinthians 11:23-30 (St. Paul on the seriousness of the Eucharist), John 20:19-23 (Jesus institutes the sacrament of confession), and Matthew 16:16-20 (the handing of the keys to Peter and the beginning of the papacy.)

Eventually, Hahn began to pray the Rosary in secret, hiding this even from his wife. Some men hide affairs from their wives; Hahn hid his budding Catholic beliefs. At first Hahn's wife Kimberly would have none of it. Some in her family even thought he had become possessed by the devil. However, through the power of the Holy Spirit, Kimberly began to agree with her husband's beliefs. She is now one of Catholicism's strongest defenders.[4]

Each convert and or revert to the Faith has his or her own story. What they all have in common is that they are part of a growing legion of converts. Each year, Catholicism sees 19 million new believers worldwide. That means that the Church is bringing in more additional members every decade than exist in the total membership of some worldwide denominations (e.g., the Anglicans). Just a few years ago the Archdiocese of Baltimore received a record 984 people into the Church.

This isn't to ignore the bleaker parts of the picture, however. The Center for Applied Research in the Apostolate (CARA), a Georgetown University-based Catholic research group, released a study post-Easter in 2011, reporting, "In each of the past three years the number of people entering the faith (of any age) has dropped below one million. Since 1947, during only one other period, from 1973 to 1979, did the annual number of new US Catholics number less than one million."

It goes on to say that the beginning of the drop—200—predates the clergy sex abuse scandal, but one has to believe that had a major impact. Still, there are 19 million global converts per year, including people such as Allen Hunt, a prominent American radio personality who used to pastor the nation's third largest megachurch and converted in 2008, the number of yearly conversions coming from The King's College, an Evangelical college in New York City, and prominent national figures such economist Lawrence Kudlow, former Speaker of the House Newt Gingrich, current Governor of Kansas Sam Brownback, radio talk show host Laura Ingraham, and many more. So, yes, every sea has choppy waters, but it is irrefutable that the tide *has* begun to change.

The Beginning of the Beginning

The first sign that the tide began to turn came with the election of Karol Cardinal Wojtyła of Kraków, who took the name Pope John Paul II, following Pope John Paul I who died a mere 33 days after taking possession of the keys given to St. Peter by Jesus.

The new Polish Pontiff's dramatic appearance on the balcony in St. Peter's Square after his election made everyone sit up and pay attention. Not only was his delivery and appeal to the Italians dramatic, but he wore a Marian stole at a time when the Blessed Mother had somehow grown out of favor with much the "spirit of Vatican II" crowd who had gained the upper hand following the Ecumenical Council.

As Fr. Richard W. Gilsdorf described in *Signs of the Times: Understanding the Church since Vatican II*, a first major step was the Fifth Ordinary General Assembly of the Synod of Bishops, better known as the Synod on the Family, out of which came Bl. John Paul's apostolic exhortation *Familiaris Consortio*. Then, in an unrelenting series of "bend them, don't break them," His Holiness implemented this encyclical here, that apostolic letter there, made a pastoral visit to some part of the world, gradually approved the appointment of a cadre of more faithful bishops, so that by the time of his death in 2005, the Church looked much different than it did upon his ascendency to the See of Peter in 1978.

The second sign the tide was turning was a big one, and it occurred at 1993 World Youth Day in Denver. Many of the United States Conference of Catholic Bishop's bureaucrats had warned the Holy See that crowds might be small, since they were certain most American kids would have no interest in attending. Some US prelates had the same belief, since their diocesan staffs could hardly fathom young people traveling to Denver for such an event. Fortunately, both the Holy Father and then-Archbishop James F. Stafford knew better, and the success of the event made one wonder where all the dismal warnings of failure had come from.[5]

The third sign was the huge crowds that came to see the funeral of Pope John Paul II and the election of Joseph Cardinal Ratzinger, who became Pope Benedict XVI. Some five to seven million came to Rome during the momentous events of April 2005. Many of these attendees were young. They had never known another pope. More to the point, however, had Bl. John Paul and "God's Rottweiler" Cardinal Ratzinger really been the bête noirs the conventional wisdom would have us think they were, why would so many people have turned out for these events? The millions who came to Rome both for John Paul's funeral and Benedict's election *love* these men. Despite a never-ending deluge of negative press, the truth of these men's message—the hope and dignity all mankind can have in Christ Jesus—got through. And the reason? Precisely because it *is* the truth, and the truth is attractive.

A fourth sign, as is evident for all to see, is that the Catholic Church has held firm to her teachings. In a 1999 interview in *Catholic World Report*, then-*The Catholic Answer* editor Fr. Peter Stravinskas observed, "My guess is that both the Holy Father and Cardinal Ratzinger and others are of a mind that the most critical thing they can and should do at the moment is to enter the truth into the record. This way the future will know that in 1999, the Catholic Church still taught this and expected that. At that level, a very important primary goal is achieved." The fact that this has been achieved in spite of the withering cultural onslaught that started, as we will show, well before the Second Vatican Council is certainly worth noting and lauding.

If the Catholic Church is the "true Church," and if liberal (or, as Cardinal George defines them, "relativist") ideas were what constituted the authentic the Catholic religion, then it follows that the 1970s should have seen a boom in vocations instead of a bust, but it didn't. Also, many called for a "spirit-led" picking-and-choosing of which aspects of historical Christian belief one would embrace. If this was a valid way forward for the Church, then the mainline Protestant communions who blazed the trail in this respect would have seen their pews overflowing instead of rapidly emptying and graying.

Take, for example, the worldwide Anglican/Episcopalian Communion. In 1900, Britons made up 82 percent of worldwide Anglicanism's numbers, whereas only 1 percent of adherents were found in sub-Saharan Africa. Today, Great Britain has 33 percent of the worldwide Anglican Communion's members, but that number looks better than it is because the Pew Research organization says that "according to the Church of England's own numbers, average Sunday church attendance during this decade has dipped to approximately one million, or about 4 percent of the country's Anglican population." Furthermore, "the decline of Anglicanism in the US and Britain has occurred not only in relative but also in absolute terms; in recent decades there has been a decrease in the overall numbers as well. Britain has 26 million Anglicans today, which is three million fewer than in 1970; and the United States has two million Episcopalians, which is one million fewer than in 1970, according to the World Christian Database."[6]

Consider that England once had one of the highest percentages of church attendance in the western world. Now, even though the Anglican Communion has done what the pundits say Catholicism should do—that is, buy a supposedly mainstream theological and social agenda whole hog—it has one of the lowest. As a result, it is estimated that in England more people attend Friday prayers at their local mosque than attend Anglican Church services on Sunday morning.

Because of this continuously deteriorating situation, many Anglicans—clergy and laity—have decided to come home to Rome. So many, in fact, that in November 2009, His Holiness created what is called the Anglican Ordinariate. An ordinariate is a body within the Church that allows Anglicans who have converted to Catholicism to maintain some aspects of their Anglican identity. This will help the potentially thousands of Anglicans who want to return to the Church of their ancestors and yet keep the splendid beauty of their music, Mass, and other liturgies.

And yet, for true believers on the left, hope springs eternal. They sincerely thought that the stunning leftward turn in the 2008 US general elections heralded an anti-traditionalist religious renaissance. That hasn't happened. For instance, there been no increase in vocations of men and women who claimed to espouse more liberal views. However, one could contend that because the Church has held firm to her teachings, those entering seminaries and religious orders have become even more conservative, as attested since at least 1994 by more left-of-center outlets such as *National Catholic Reporter* and *The New York Times* since at least 1994. This is the trend even in places such as Great Britain and Australia, neither a hotbed of orthodox Catholicism. And yet the young men there use Bl. John Paul II as their touchstone and not theologians such as Rahner, Schillebeeckx, Bultmann, et al.[7]

I also base this contention on my interviews with several seminary rectors. One priest—not a rector—related that some priests told him he was the most conservative priest to have been ordained in his diocese in many years when he received Holy Orders in 2005. Now he says those same priests call him a moderate in relation to those ordained since then.

This is not to say that things are all peaches and cherries in the Catholic Church. According to CARA, "In 1973, the Catholic retention rate was 84 percent. The current 68 percent estimate is identical to the Pew Religious Landscape study in 2007. If the current rate of decline continues, the Catholic retention rate is expected to be 54 percent in 2050."[8]

This means that for every two Catholics the Church retains, she loses one. Some go to Evangelical churches, some to mainline Protestant communions, some to other faiths, and still others to no faith at all. This last group is the most difficult, because their defection reflects the poor and/or incomplete catechesis of the last 40-plus years.

However, despite many things working against her, the Catholic Church is still growing in ways "visible and invisible," to quote the Nicene Creed. Furthermore, the chances for further growth are limitless. This is because of what blogger John Allen, Jr., calls "Evangelical Catholicism," which he defines in terms of three pillars:

- A strong defense of traditional Catholic identity, meaning attachment to classic markers of Catholic thought (doctrinal orthodoxy) and Catholic practice (liturgical tradition, devotional life, and authority).
- Robust public proclamation of Catholic teaching, with the accent on Catholicism's mission *ad extra*, transforming the culture in light of the Gospel, rather than *ad intra*, on internal Church reform.
- Faith seen as a matter of personal choice rather than cultural inheritance, which among other things implies that in a highly secular culture, Catholic identity can never be taken for granted. It always has to be proven, defended, and made manifest.[9]

As long as the Church continues this momentum set in motion by many of the new bishops, priests, religious, and laity, there is no reason to believe the retention rate trend mentioned above won't change. Perhaps this can best be seen on the Internet. The Catholic blogosphere has but a handful of dissenting websites and blogs. Those of any import could be counted on one hand. Compare this to the hundreds of widely read websites and blogs that hold fidelity to the Church's teachings and the Pope as essential.

These are sites such as The Hermeneutic of Continuity, American Catholic, and the BigPulpit. These sources are where Catholic writers and commentators like Allen and Weigel turn when they want to take the pulse of the active and concerned "evangelical" laity.

Introduction 19

Speaking of Allen, I attended a lecture he gave at Ohio Dominican University a few years ago. In it, he told the crowd that Third World Catholics did not share the views of many Western liberal Catholic opinion makers on moral issues. For all their talk of diversity and tolerance, the former deeply resent the latter's condescending assertions that Africans are culturally backwards on issues like women clergy and same sex marriage.

And yet these Brahmins of what Allen calls the "global North" have to seriously consider what he writes in his book, *The Future Church*:

> In broad terms, Southern [i.e., Third World] Catholics are robustly orthodox. They're not interested in metaphorical interpretations of the Resurrection or the Eucharist, they have no problem with belief in miracles, and they don't get hung up over whether liturgical texts say "man" or "person." One consequence of this orthodox tide will be to push Catholicism into a more traditional position on two questions that often define the "culture wars" in the West—abortion and homosexuality. Combined with the rise of evangelical Catholicism, to be discussed in the next chapter, this reality means that prospects for reconsideration of traditional Catholic teaching on these points are virtually zero....
>
> As [Nigerian Archbishop John Onaiyekan of Abuja has said, Africans resent] "the virulent and currents [in the North] that have tried to push... a non-traditional view of sexuality.... It's not only the Africans who are complaining, but it's the Asians, too, and the Latin Americans. We are the mainstream, not them. The onus lies upon them to explain why they are doing something new. It's a very heavy onus to explain how it is that for 2,000 years the Church somehow did not understand what Jesus meant."[10]

Once again, it's illustrative to look at what happens when denominations become beholden to a militantly activist worldview. As described in journalist Dave Shiflett's 2005 book, *Exodus: Why Americans are Fleeing Liberal Churches for Conservative Christianity*, it is precisely this pushing of a moral agenda radically opposed to two millennia of constant Christian belief and praxis that has caused many mainline Protestant communions to lose nearly half of their members in the last fifty years.

By 2007, so many disaffected Anglicans felt that they had no home that they petitioned the Vatican to accept them *en masse* into the Church. As explained before, this, in turn, led Pope Benedict XVI to approve three personal ordinariates for Anglicans. In the UK, the Our Lady of Walsingham Anglican Ordinariate has attracted over 60 clergymen (including five former bishops), 30 parishes, and 1,000 laymen in the United Kingdom. Some 22 parishes, 100 priests, and 1,400 laymen have either entered or applied for its US counterpart so far.[11] On January 1, 2012, US bishops approved the Personal Ordinariate of the Chair of St. Peter, and on May 11, 2012, the Australian bishops approved the the Personal Ordinariate of Our Lady of the Southern Cross to be erected on June 15, 2012, under the patronage of St. Augustine of Canterbury.

Far more Anglicans have put themselves under the jurisdiction of more traditional African bishops or have formed their own dioceses. Given all of this, one has to feel a certain pity for the Anglican Church primate, Archbishop Rowan Williams, who is trying to keep the Church of England and its satellites intact. After all, who wants to go down in history as the man under whom a nearly 500-year-old denomination disintegrated?

A particularly effective illustration of the sort of confusion and malaise that has beset mainline Christianity can be seen in *Time* magazine's Q&A interview with Episcopalianism's presiding prelate, Bishop Katharine Jefferts Schori, the very model of a major modernist. She gave the interview not long after she took over the reins of Anglicanism's US counterpart, the Episcopalian Church, in 2006. In it, she shows why it is so important for the Catholic Church to not follow the same road.

Introduction

> ***Time***: What will be your focus as head of the US church?
>
> **Jefferts Schori**: Our focus needs to be on feeding people who go to bed hungry, on providing primary education to girls and boys, on healing people with AIDS, on addressing tuberculosis and malaria, on sustainable development. That ought to be the primary focus.
>
> ***Time***: What is your prayer for the church today?
>
> **Jefferts Schori**: That we remember the centrality of our mission is to love each other. That means caring for our neighbors. And it does not mean bickering about fine points of doctrine. [12]

Did you catch what she *didn't* say? Jefferts Schori believes she is a bishop. As Our Lord and Sts. Peter and Paul repeatedly make clear, the foremost duties of a bishop are to "preach" and "teach" (see John 21:15-17; Acts 6:2-4; Romans 10:14; 1 Corinthians 1:7; 1 Timothy 3:2). What are they to preach and teach? They are to preach the gospel of Jesus Christ.

What is the gospel, "the good news," they are to preach and teach? Before 2006, it was generally believed to have been that God so loved mankind, he sent his only begotten to suffer and give his life for the life of his Body and Bride, the Church. In doing so, he restored communion with us and offer us all the possibility of "our salvation, so that we might live through him" (1 John 4:9). God "loved us and sent his Son to be the expiation for our sins" (1 John 4:10) and "the Father has sent his Son as the Savior of the world," (1 John 4:14), and "He was revealed to take away sins" (1 John 3:5). Furthermore, "whoever believes in him should not perish but have eternal life" (John 3:16).

After 2,000 years, however, we now know the truth. A bishop's primary focus ought to be "on feeding people who go to bed hungry, on providing primary education to girls and boys, on healing people with AIDS, on addressing tuberculosis and malaria, on sustainable development."

As for Jefforts Schori's second point, yes, we must love one another as per Luke 10:27-28, but—and this, granted, is a judgment call—shouldn't a bishop's prayer be to lead as many souls as possible to Christ and a life of holiness and thus salvation? And doesn't the desire that we won't bicker "about fine points of doctrine" go precisely against a bishop's first duty to preach and teach"? After all, haven't schisms and heresies both come out of and been resolved by "bickering about fine points of doctrine"?

In one *New York Times* interview, Jefferts Schori strongly implied Catholics had more children than Episcopalians because they are less educated and because Episcopalians cared more for the environment.[13] Not surprisingly, the interview received little negative attention.

Again, Catholicism in a Western world beset by rampant secularism, materialism, and consumerism may not be making the strides it once did in Europe and North America. However, we certainly are not enduring the same situation as the Archbishop of Canterbury, the ELCA, the PCUSA, or the UMC. Rather, the Catholic Church is a relatively thriving organism is precisely because her teachings do not change.

The reason? To paraphrase Edwin Cardinal O'Brien, people are attracted to truth, not to a question mark.

ONE
THE TIDE IS STILL TURNING

Ever since his assuming the papacy in April 2005, Pope Benedict XVI has drawn record crowds, not only in his international trips, such as his 2008 visit to the United States, but at his general audiences and Angelus addresses in St. Peter's Square.

How do we explain this, though? After all, one only has to barely scan any article written about him, any blog combox comment made about him, or any television news report or commentary spoken about him to know that the mavens of our culture don't think too highly of him. And yet average people of all walks of life, of all faiths, and of all ages come to see him—particularly the young, whom polls tell us have widely different views than his.

Consider this: World Youth Day 2003 in Toronto, the last attended by Bl. John Paul II, drew 450,000 pilgrims. Before the next WYD 2005 at Cologne, in the Holy Father's native Germany, many were curious. How could this "out-of-touch" "hard-liner" hold a candle to Pope John Paul II's charismatic appeal? How would he handle the smaller crowds that would inevitably gather? And what a small crowd it was, too. The final number was that the event drew 1,000,000 (remember, Toronto, easily accessible by US, Canadian, and Mexican pilgrims drew less than half that). Six years later, WYD 2011 in Madrid, Spain, attracted 2,000,000 visitors. At both events, youth wore T-shirts that proclaimed, "I love my German Shepherd." This man's teaching of foundational, solid, and historic Catholic doctrine is not repelling the young. If anything, it is attracting them. But why are so many young people admiring an aging German "doctrinaire" Pope?

Catholic columnist, NBC commentator, and *Newsweek* columnist George Weigel said in a 2008 editorial for the magazine:

> The tag line in some Roman circles is that "People came to see John Paul II; they come to hear Benedict XVI." That contrast is too sharply drawn, but Benedict's skills as a teacher have certainly touched a significant 21st-century yearning for solid religious food. His first two encyclicals, on love and hope, were consciously framed to speak to the fears of a deeply conflicted world by reminding the world of Christianity's basic message.[1]

Then there was his address in early fall 2005 in St. Peter's Square to children who had recently made their first Communion. As Weigel recounts in the same piece:

> Benedict's catechetical skills with children are also striking. Six months after his election, he met thousands of Italian eight- and nine-year-olds who had just made their first communion [sic]. One of them asked how Jesus could be present in the consecrated bread and wine of the Eucharist when "I can't see him!"
>
> To which the Pope replied, "No, we cannot see him; there are many things we do not see, but they exist and are essential ... We do not see an electric current; yet we see that it exists. We can see that this microphone is working, and we see lights. We do not see the very deepest things, those that really sustain life and the world, but we can see and feel their effects ... So it is with the Risen Lord: we do not see him with our eyes, but we see that wherever Jesus is, people change, they improve, there is a greater capacity for peace, for reconciliation ..."
>
> Another youngster asked why the church urged frequent confession. Benedict answered: "It's very helpful to

confess with a certain regularity. It is true: our sins are always the same, but we clean our homes, our rooms, at least once a week, even if the dirt is always the same ... Otherwise the dirt might not be seen, but it builds up. Something similar can be said about the soul, about me: if I never go to confession, my soul is neglected and in the end I'm always pleased with myself and no longer understand that I must work hard to improve ..."

What the Pope can say so winsomely to children, he [said] to adults during his American pilgrimage: "Look again at the basics of Catholic faith and practice. They exist for a reason. They just may satisfy the hungers of the human heart. Give them a chance."[2]

And therein lies what many self-defined progressives cannot for the life of them comprehend: The power of popes to not only challenge conventional wisdom, the accepted "consensus," as Jefferts Schori has called it, but to get everyone from average, everyday people to movers and shakers to consider their arguments.

The popes change minds. By doing that, they also change hearts and the decisions people make and thereby the way they live their lives. This is a power of persuasion that our culture's primary shapers only wish they had. Actually, they usually do until someone such as a pope comes along and challenges their omnipotence. Then their nature-abhorred vacuum disappears and with it the façade of their tolerance and diversity. In its place is left the aforementioned lack of comprehension.

It is this incomprehension that likely prompted prominent dissenting theologian Fr. Richard McBrien to state before the conclave that if elected pope, Joseph Cardinal Ratzinger would cause Catholics in the United States to "roll their eyes and head for the margins of the Church." And yet neither Americans nor the peoples of any other nation have rejected him (except perhaps, ironically, his own native Germany). If people vote with their feet, Benedict XVI is doing quite well, especially in Third World countries, where the Church is continuing its growth apace. As Allen writes in his book, *The Future Church*, "… [At] the beginning of the twentieth century, just 25 percent of the world's Catholic population lived outside Europe and North America. By century's end, however, 65.5 percent of the Catholic population was found in Africa, Asia, and Latin America."[3]

The same could be said about young adults. It is true that surveys such as those by the Pew Trust find that most Western Catholics aged 18-35 reject the Church's teachings. However, the ever-growing numbers of those who are in the forefront of the aforementioned Evangelical Catholic movement are typically young people.

As Allen notes in an article on WYD 2011, their elders rebelled against what they saw as a stuffy, constricting Church. Today's generation rebels against the very things for which their autumn year elders fought so long and hard. Instead of wanting a Church that gradually molds itself into the age, they want a Church that is distinct, one that is a choice, not an echo.[4]

This effort was started by John Paul II with his 1979 apostolic exhortation, *Catechesi Tradendae*, which focused on right catechesis. This was followed two years later by another apostolic exhortation, the aforementioned *Familiaris Consortio*. This document detailed the many problems facing the family and the Church's prescriptions for these. It continued throughout his pontificate, particularly through his Theology of the Body discourses given at every General Audience between 1979 and 1984. It also saw fruit in his proclaiming the dignity of every human person and the authentic purpose of man. Such a basic message, and yet it alone started the process that ended with the collapse of the Soviet Union and European communism and thus the Cold War, which had threatened world peace since 1948.

Yes, the human rights stance of such leaders as British Prime Minister Dame Margaret Thatcher and US President Ronald Reagan had an impact, as did the US's huge military buildup and economic boom of the 1980s. Without the Pope's preaching and outright support of Poland's Solidarity movement, however, Soviet communism might still be a force today.

Following communism's general collapse, Bl. John Paul released his pontificate's major economic statement, *Centissimus Annus*, which gave a fiscal road map for the post-communist future. Then there was his encyclical on the compatibility of faith and reason, *Fides et Ratio*, another on objective truth, *Veritatis Splendor*, his vision for the unity of all Christians in one Church, *Ut Unum Sint*, and his majestic reflection on the sacredness of life, *Evangelium Vitae*.

This short list merely scratches the surface of the impact he had, and it doesn't even touch on UN conferences where the Holy See and sympathetic Muslim, African, and Central American countries thwarted the ability of cultural revolutionaries to enshrine abortion as a basic human right and such.

When Benedict XVI assumed the papacy, much noise was made about his being "God's Rottweiler," a member of Hitler's Youth (which every young German boy had to join), and a soldier in the Nazi army (for which he was conscripted, never fired a shot, and purposely sought capture by an Allied unit so he could become a POW). Many observers thought he and his pontificate would be a joke. Many of the early headlines certainly seemed to predict this.

Since then, a funny thing has happened. His Holiness has steadily built a record that could make him even more consequential than his beatified predecessor. We can see an indication of this in the previously cited quotations. His supposedly disastrous Regensburg speech saw him making comments that, taken out of context (as they were), could be seen as offensive to some Muslims. And yet the kerfuffle produced a dialogue that has borne much fruit. People have taken to listening to him and mulling over what he says.

He has made trips to his native land, Austria, Africa, the United States, the Holy Land, Mexico, Cuba, Croatia, the Czech Republic, Brazil, Poland, Spain, France, Australia, Turkey, Malta, Portugal, Cyprus, Benin, San Marino, Lebanon, and the United

Kingdom. These trips made news—when they did at all—not because he did something loopy for which he was roundly criticized. Rather, it was because of the things he *said* that people sat up and took notice.

For instance, consider these comments by British Prime Minister David Cameron at the farewell ceremony following the Holy Father's pastoral and state visit to the UK in September 2010:

> For many, faith is a spur to action. It shapes their beliefs and behaviour [sic]; and it gives them a sense of purpose. Crucially, it is their faith that inspires them to help others. And we should celebrate that. Faith is part of the fabric of our country. It always has been and it always will be. As you, your Holiness, have said... faith is not a problem for legislators to solve... but rather a vital part of our national conversation. And we are proud of that.
>
> But people do not have to share a religious faith or agree with religion on everything... *to see the benefit of asking the searching questions that you, Your Holiness, have posed to us*... about our society and how we treat ourselves and each other. *You have really challenged the whole country to sit up and think, and that can only be a good thing.* Because I believe we can all share in your message of working for the common good... and that we all have a social obligation each other, to our families and our communities."[5]

This assessment happened despite a blitzkrieg of relentless negative publicity in the news media and entertainment sectors prior to the Pope's visit.

When Bad Ink Is Deserved

The Church has always gotten a lot of negative publicity in the United States. Up until recently, though, one would be hard-pressed to have said any of this was deserved. Well, recently some of it was

The Tide Is Still Turning

most assuredly deserved. For instance, take the clergy sexual-abuse scandal.

In journalism, the reality has always been, "If it bleeds, it leads." And for the media, the abuse of or affairs with young teen boys (in most cases) by men of the cloth who have dedicated their lives to serving a God of love is too juicy of a story to neglect. Newspapers, magazines, TV and radio stations, and their Internet counterparts are all businesses. As long as a story continues to produce advertising revenue and sell copies, they will keep that story alive.

The clergy sex-abuse scandal was the gift that kept on giving. Even now, it seems as though the next sordid revelation must surely be around the corner. "Catholic Church Promises to Keep Minors Safe, Fails" will blare the headline.

Were we as Catholics upset and embarrassed by this several-years-long laser-like focus on a shameful problem? Yes. Were we right to be angry that the percentage of Catholic clergy and religious who abused was made to sound higher than abuse perpetrated by those in other fields when it wasn't? Surely. Do many believe that it was not so much that Catholic clergy did these criminal acts but that the Church requires celibacy for them, thus giving the media and some opinion makers a convenient belt with which to whip magisterial teaching? Absolutely.

There is so much that was and is frustrating about this situation. However, one thing that was particularly hard was that the scandal drowned out some really fantastic stories. For instance, even during this time, many dioceses saw more ordinations taking place. Indeed, more young men and women were discerning a call to the priestly or religious life.

Furthermore, lay people were not only attending youth conferences but also men's and women's conferences in numbers not seen since the 1960s Rosary Crusades promoted by Fr. Francis Peyton, CSC. Yet, juxtapose a picture of several thousand orthodox-minded Catholics attending a men's or women's conference in the midst of a severe snowstorm compared to a handful of protestors asking for both women's ordination and an openly gay clergy. Granted, good news ordinarily doesn't sell newspapers. Still, does one have to ask which received more media attention?

Perhaps one of the most unreported Catholic stories of the last five years was the rise of the men's and women's conferences across the United States. In 2000, there were 10 men's and three women's conferences in the United States. In 2012 there will be close to 80 men's conferences and over 40 women's conferences. Attendees hear some of the Church best speakers talk of how to build the kingdom of God in spite of the world resisting this in all sorts of ways.

The presenters at these events represent a cross section of Catholic charisms. For instance, long-time apologist Patrick Madrid shows people how to answer the questions about Catholicism asked by those of other faiths, or how to refute the accusations and misconceptions such people occasionally have. Matthew Kelly and Johnnette Benkovic motivate their audiences by getting them to think and calling them to action. Former pro-football star Danny Abramowicz draws people to a closer understanding of what Christ can do for them as he relates his experience of being a driftless alcoholic and the toll it took on him and his family. His alpha male approach is a big hit at men's conferences.

Jesse Romero's highly charged speaking style is possibly the most unique. One might initially mistake the former Los Angeles deputy sheriff for a Pentecostalist preacher. He practically was one during the time he fell away from the Church. During this time, he tried evangelizing people out of our holy Catholic Faith. Now he does just the opposite. In addition to reaching out to fundamentalists, he also reaches out to dissenting Catholics, agnostics, and atheists.

Major conferences are not the only place where Catholics are growing in their faith. They are also embracing similar but smaller parish and diocesan events. Fifty or even 10 years ago, if one had heard the question "Did you hear about the fantastic Catholic Bible study at St. Pat's?" most likely one would have thought it was the lead into a really good joke, probably involving some stereotype of Irish overdrinking.

And yet it isn't a joke at all. With the great Bible studies provided by publishers such as Word on Fire, Ascension Press, Catholic Scripture Study, and the Institute for Applied Biblical Studies, many parishes have experienced a boom in Bible and Catechism studies.

For many Catholics, these experiences have been a revelation because they have shown that our Faith, far from being a dull bunch of oppressive teachings foisted on an unwilling laity by old white men in pointy hats actually has meat behind it, is intellectually stimulating (read: fun), and, what's even better, exciting! St. Augustine wrote, "Our hearts are restless until they rest in Thee." Tens of thousands of Catholics in weekly groups of five to 2,500 have had the scales not just drop but plummet from their eyes and have been awakened to the special truth of Augustine's insight because of these Bible studies.

This is especially true for those who came of age between the mid-1960s and the 1980s, when religious education in Catholic schools and CCD programs left many not knowing the basics of Catholicism. Now, through these studies, these individuals have a chance to learn their Faith, take it from being some cultural or anthropological ritual they go through because their parents did it and their parents did and their parents did it and so on, and make it their own. They have found that not only is learning about the Faith really "cool," but a) they don't have to be brainiacs to do learn this stuff and b) it is awe-inspiring to be connected intellectually to the same Faith as their ancestors, the Faith handed down to them by the apostles. Truth be told, some have often embraced these educational opportunities because they fear their children are more knowledgeable about the Faith than they are.

This is a great sign for the Church, isn't it? All of these people, and none of them shrugging their shoulders and saying, "Oh, well. Too bad. I guess my time has come and gone. I'll never know why we do what we do or why we believe what we believe." These people—moms and dads, doctors and lawyers, coaches and caretakers, plumbers and factory workers—are pouring their all into trying to grasp what they missed some 20 or 30 years ago. That is fantastic!

Not surprisingly, the increase in interest in learning one's faith has brought with it an increase in developing a deeper relationship with Our Lord Jesus Christ through a deeper prayer life, and this has led to an increase in devotions. Many parishes are engaging in regular and even perpetual Eucharistic Adoration and Marian devotions such as the Rosary and the Divine Mercy chaplet, to name just a few of the options.

What is possibly the most surprising development of this increased piety—and it is by no means widespread, but it is by no means unusual, either—is the attraction and interest of young people in aspects of the Traditional Latin Mass (TLM).[6] For some it's simply an interest in the beauty of Gregorian chant and the polyphony of Palestrina, Cererols, etc. For many others, however, the attraction is to the beauty of the prayers and the exquisite sacred choreography of the Roman Catholicism's most ancient liturgy. Most don't know Latin, of course, but that isn't a problem if you can read and you have a Missal, is it?

These young adults say what the Church now calls the extraordinary form of the Latin rite inspires in them awe, increased devotion, and thus a greater desire to be a saint. Even if Latin isn't your cup of tea, I think we can all agree that having more people motivated to be saints is a good thing.

The media, however, doesn't like it, not one bit. Its downright hostility to good news in the Church could be summed up by one event in Lincoln, Nebraska, in June 2007. The group Call to Action had announced to the media that they were planning a protest in front of Bishop Fabian Bruskewitz's residence in Lincoln because His Excellency had excommunicated members of Call to Action and other dissident groups for their open opposition to Church teaching. Keep in mind, he had done so in March 1996. The Vatican announced that it upheld the excommunications on December 8, 2006.

The media ran stories of the planned protest for a few days before the Sunday event was to take place. It seemed as if the media was prepared for a showdown of the "people verses the bishop." Well a crowd did show up. However, it was not the people that the media seemed intent on seeing. Nine Call to Action supporters squared off against 100 supporters of Bishop Bruskewitz, who many consider to be America's most orthodox bishop.

While the Lincoln media did cover the story and the large support for Lincoln's popular bishop, many other papers who were prepping their readers for a showdown never mentioned the positive conclusion. The events in Lincoln were another sign that the tide was turning, and yet few outside of the Catholic media or blogosphere were told about it.[7]

Does It Have to Be *Latin*?

There is a reason that the release of Pope Benedict's 2007 *motu proprio* titled *Summorum Pontificum* was one of the pontificate's most highly anticipated and controversial moves. Bl. John Paul II had issued two requests to local bishops to generously make the pre-Vatican II rites more available to those who wanted them.

However, the majority of bishops had let that request die a benign neglect (and sometimes the death was not so benign, if we are to be honest). Maybe it was because they didn't want to encourage people they believed were trying to turn back the clock on the Council. (Indeed, there is an element in any TLM congregation that would like to do just that.) Maybe these had bad memories or associations with the improperly named "Tridentine" rite (so-called because it was codified by the Council of Trent). Maybe they believed they had genuine pastoral reasons to deny making the old Mass more readily accessible to those who loved it and wanted it.

Whatever the case, the generosity requested by Benedict XVI's predecessor starting in 1984 was not forthcoming to any great degree. Well, to hardly *any* degree, actually. Indeed, until *Summorum*

Pontificum, one could not licitly celebrate the extraordinary form ,even in St. Peter's Basilica.

For these reasons, many had for decades asked the Vatican to loosen the restrictions on the extraordinary form. Benedict, who is known to have a fondness for this form of the rite, freed it. Then, when certain bishops sadly tried to make *Summorum Pontificum* say things it clearly didn't, he issued *Universae Ecclesiae*, an instruction on the *motu proprio's* proper implementation.

We must ask, why did the Pope insist on making the extraordinary form more available? With all of the numerous concerns before the Church, many believe the cardinal electors chose Pope Ratzinger as pontiff primarily because of his acute analysis of just how bad the crisis of faith in Europe and the West had become. The fundamental reason for this is the erosion of Catholic identity over the last 60 or so years, which was quickened by questionable liturgical theories before the Council and, as the Pope has articulated, an inadequate post-conciliar liturgical reform.

To change this, we need to, in a sense, go back to the future. The Church has always taught *lex orandi, lex credendi* (loosely translated: as we pray, so we believe). With this in mind, reestablishing a strong and positive Catholic orthodoxy (the *credendi* part) will only come from fostering a strong Catholic identity. And historically the best way to accomplish this has been to have an authentic liturgical renewal that practically makes us imbibe our tradition to such an extent that it inebriates us. In this way, it is hoped that we will experience the Faith, not in any way apart from how our ancestors lived it but as its been lived for over two millennia.

The Good News Is Here, There, and Everywhere!

Another story that seems ignored is what is happening in Africa. Since the turn of the 20th century, the continent has seen a Catholic and Protestant explosion. In the last 100 years, Africa has experienced a 6,708 percent increase in the number of Christians.

For Catholics in particular, there were 2,000,000 of us there in 1900. By 2000, that population had grown to 130,000,000.[8]

There are so many young men training for the priesthood that many of them are sent to seminaries in Europe and North America. The same goes for young women religious. The same sort of growth is also occurring in parts of Asia. Indeed, China is moving toward becoming a majority Christian nation. Within a very short period of time, Asia as a whole will have more Christians than Buddhists. And all of this is happening despite persistent communist efforts to suppress Christianity in places such as Vietnam and China.

Some skeptics say, "Well, we could say the tide is turning toward Islam, as well as the Pentecostal movement, given their growth, especially in Africa." This is true, and it presents a pressing pastoral challenge for Catholicism. After all, as Fr. Gerard Chabnon, a missionary in Tanzania, notes, the Catholic Church is not going to promise everyone they will become rich or be cured of a variety of diseases through their own special miracle, unlike many non-denominational churches.

However, as history clearly shows, this sort of sugar rush spirituality cannot sustain itself in the long run.[8] Curtis Martin, founder of the Fellowship of Catholic University Students (FOCUS), uses the analogy of hummingbirds. He says that he likes to sit on the back porch of his parents' home and watch the hummingbirds take their fill from the feeder, which his mother has filled with sugar water. He notes, however, that if one took out the sugar water and replaced it with, say, saccharine water, the hummingbirds would still drink their fill because the similar taste would fool them. However, they would eventually die because saccharine has no nutritive value. Given how many calories they need, only something nutritious will keep them alive.

Martin says it's the same between true and false or at least less than complete spiritualities. People want substance. They want real meat. Without it, they will spiritually whither. Catholicism gives them that real meat, that substance that nourishes. That is why the

Church still has a positive growth rate despite the admittedly alarming attrition rate she faces year in and year out.

Of course, this leaves some people quite unhappy, even from within her own ranks. It's not the tide turning toward the Church or the good things happening on the barque of Peter that makes them sad. It's that the tide is not turning toward the vision they thought would win the day. Once upon a time, they were young and full of an idealistic vision of a radical overhaul of Catholicism. They were in the vanguard and leading the Church—in the Spirit, we were always assured—into a glorious New Age.

In fact, just the opposite has happened, so you can understand their dismay, discouragement, and even disgruntlement. Speaking, to this point, the late Fr. Richard John Neuhaus recounts in his book *Catholic Matters* how far Christianity had come in two to three decades, from a state of almost anything goes to a robust and resurgent orthodoxy. To show the contrast between then and now, he mentions a press conference given in the mid-1980s by the dissenting theologian Hans Küng, who stated "we" dominate and control all of Catholicism's major organs of power. They were the future, and anyone wanting a position of influence in the Church had better get on board the train or get left behind. "It was a clean sweep," wrote Fr. Neuhaus. "All that was left were a few details.... It was a memorable speech, and the circumstance he described is today mainly a memory."[9]

That was then. To show the now, he used Fr. McBrien as an example. As Fr. Neuhaus said in his book, "I apologize for mentioning him again, but he is irresistible."

Fr. Neuhaus further writes of the theologian's behavior in the days following the death of Bl. John Paul II:

> He was trotted out again ... for a column in the *International Herald Tribune*. He opined that all of the *papabili* are distressingly indifferent to the alienation of major constituencies of the Church—gay activists, proponents of women's ordination, and what he

described as the more liberal "middle-aged and elderly clergy."[10] What would the Church be without them? We can only try to imagine. [The] same Fr. McBrien [went] on the tube complaining about the regressive influence of John Paul II. Finally, the interviewer asked whether he was not impressed by the four or five million people, most of them young people, who came to the funeral. Not at all, he replied. Those, he explained, were the young people the Church already had. What about the millions who did not show up? ... To such cantankerousness are the old unstoppables now reduced. But I digress.[10]

And so do I. However, it does bring up a good reminder of what happens when we change the words of the Lord's Prayer from "Thy will be done" to "My will be done." People who call themselves "progressive" do this, and people who call them "orthodox" do this. We all do it at some point. That's not the way to sainthood, though, is it?

It is the way of spoiled children, but somehow I think that's not the type of child Our Lord had in mind when he told the apostles, "Truly, I say to you, unless you turn to become like children, you will never enter the kingdom" (Matthew 18:3). Instead, he had in mind children who are trusting, who are humble, docile, and obedient to their parents and teachers. Servant of God Fulton Sheen quotes St. Thérèse on this point:

> The secret of spiritual childhood is to make yourself nothing.... This then is, as simply as I can put it, the story of becoming little as Our Lord did. If you have a box that is filled with salt, you cannot fill it with pepper, can you?
>
> Well, if we are filled with our own self and our own ego, God can't get in! We often wonder, for example, why it is there is no room for God in certain hearts. He can't get in! There's no vacancy. But the more empty we are, the more he can fill us with His grace. As a matter of fact, we

were made from nothingness, and only when we get back close again to nothingness do we ever get to God.[11]

The point to all of is that the tide is turning in all facets for the Church, and it will keep turning as long as each of tries to stay close to Christ and constantly work on becoming a saint. Then we will see even greater things from the Church than we are seeing even now. Though she may be knocked off course now and then, the promise of Christ is that the gates of hell will not prevail against her (see Matthew 16:16-20).

As Msgr. Charles Pope, a pastor and blogger in the Archdiocese of Washington, DC, wrote in August 2011:

> What would happen to the Church tomorrow if every Church-going Catholic pledged to bring one fallen away family member or friend back to communion with the Church in the next two years? Well, of course our numbers would nearly double. A few of us might not be successful, but, if we really worked at it, we'd probably come close to doubling. And the Lord would surely be pleased and also reward our efforts. The answer is not really so difficult, but it is hard work. Yet, we do not need to go to a mountaintop to get the answer. The answer is staring you in the mirror: Go make disciples. If you need to, grab a partner and work on two people together. But get started. It goes without saying that you ought to have something approaching a relationship with the Lord to be a good evangelizer.... But for now, don't wait to be perfect, just get started.

TWO
POPE BENEDICT XVI VISITS THE UNITED STATES

In early 2008, it was announced that Pope Benedict XVI would travel to the United States that April. The reason for the visit revolved around an invitation the Holy Father received to speak to the United Nations. As soon as the Holy Father accepted the invitation and began to prepare for his visit to New York and Washington, DC, many in the news media prophesied a gloomy scenario of an aging German man who would not be able to connect with an American Catholic audience. They believed this because of their conviction that US Catholics were more liberal in their religious beliefs than Benedict. Furthermore, they still missed Pope John Paul II, who had died in 2005.

It seemed the media had a short memory, as many were being far more kind to Bl. John Paul now than when he was alive. In addition, many practicing US Catholics had long looked to Rome, unhappy about how their local ordinary or the national bishops' conference seemed stuck in the political and social world of the 1960s and 1970s. This discomfiting feeling was accompanied by a mutual lack of understanding between those who tried hard to be faithful to the Magisterium and fellow Mass-attending, practicing Catholics who practice dissent on an awful lot of Church teachings, it seems. Having Bl. John Paul would have been great, but having Pope Ratzinger ride into town—to have anyone come and in a highly visible, vigorous way affirm their orthodoxy—was good news for the former group.

As plans for His Holiness' trip moved along, people began to get a clearer appreciation for the different gifts the current successor to Peter and his predecessor brought to the papal office.

For instance, in Peggy Noonan's weekly column for *The Wall Street Journal,* printed just prior to the Holy Father's arrival on American soil, she recounted a Vatican reporter saying that "John Paul was the perfect pope for the television age, 'a man of images.' Think of the pictures of him storm-tossed, tempest-tossed, standing somewhere and leaning into a heavy wind, his robes whipping behind him, holding on to his crosier, the staff bearing the image of a crucified Christ, with both hands, for dear life, as if consciously giving Christians a picture of what it is to be alive." Benedict, however, "is a man of the word. You download the text of what he said, print it, ponder it."[1]

Of course, even with the development of a more positive attitude about the Pope, many still clung to the old stereotypes. For instance, the *Washington Post* ran this headline in its March 14th edition: "Catholic College Leaders Expect Pope to Deliver Stern Message." Anyone who knew anything about this Pontiff—any reporter who had simply done his or her job by simply picking up the phone and calling someone who knew anything about this Pontiff—could have easily related that "stern" is not a word one associates with this gentle, humble man. Now, some of the Catholic leaders did perhaps need a strong lecture. However, while the Holy Father made his point very clear about what a Catholic institution of higher learning should be, it was far from a stern lecture.

The broadcast and cable news channels brought in their own experts to decipher the upcoming trip of the Holy Father. The very liberal MSNBC cable network's *Morning Joe* show is hosted by Joe Scarborough, one of the cable channel's few relatively conservative hosts. Discussing the papal trip with him was Rick Stengel, the editor of *Time* magazine. While this man spoke highly of Pope Benedict, he still called the Holy Father Bl. John Paul II's "hatchet man" because of his work as prefect of the Congregation for the Doctrine of Faith (CDF).[2] "Hatchet man" seemed an odd choice of words. The CDF is responsible for promoting and safeguarding the Catholic faith's authentic doctrine concerning faith and morals.[3] It is also responsible for grave crimes against the Eucharist, and in 2001, it received jurisdiction over priestly sex-abuse cases. While it has many functions, it is best known for censuring dissenting theologians such as Fr. Charles Curran, Fr. Hans Küng, and others.

This sort of thing only occurs, however, after much deliberation back and forth, and once many opportunities are given to the offending theologian to both explain his or her position—and, when these explanations don't suffice, to make requested corrections to their work. For instance, Fr. Curran made his first notable statement of dissent against orthodox Catholic teaching in 1968. That is when he led the rebellion by American theologians against the Servant of God Paul VI's last encyclical, *Humanae Vitae*. This document simply reaffirmed Catholicism's unbroken stand against artificial means of contraception.

Then, throughout 18 years, Fr. Curran continued to teach and publish various attacks on the Church's moral teachings, particularly on masturbation, homosexuality, abortion, pre-marital sex, and much else. The formal case against him was actually initiated on July 13, 1979, when Franjo Cardinal Seper, then head of the CDF, informed Fr. Curran in a letter that his writings were under investigation for what Seper called "principal errors" in them. At the time, Cardinal Ratzinger was serving as Archbishop of Munich and Freising, so he wasn't even involved in the case. By 1983, however, he had replaced Cardinal Seper as the CDF's prefect. He continued the back-and-forth observations between the Congregation and Curran. In some of these, the professor was quite open about his dissent from magisterial teaching.

In late 1984, Cardinal Ratzinger wrote Fr. Curran that the Church had the right to safeguard the integrity of authentically Catholic doctrine taught in Catholic institutions of higher learning. To do otherwise would be a disservice to the school's students, not to mention those in the laity who might take scandal from teaching that was in error. He continued:

> This freedom of the Church likewise implies the right to choose for her theological faculties those and only those professors who, in complete honesty and integrity, recognize themselves to be capable of meeting these requirements.

He closed the letter by encouraging Fr. Curran to reconsider his published positions. This was followed by more correspondence and even meetings in Rome early in 1986 between Cardinal Ratzinger and Fr. Curran, during which the latter proposed a compromise.

The compromise was this: He would agree to no longer teach about sexuality in his morality classes. In return the Church would allow him to remain a theologian in good standing. This missed the issue, however, because it left untouched the things he wrote in his books, which he refused to refute or retract.

On April 1, 1986, Dr. Curran wrote His Eminence that he had not changed his mind, that he would never change his mind, and then proposed his compromise once again. In response, Cardinal Ratzinger met with the rest of the Congregation at one of its biennial assemblies. Keep in mind, the CDF is not a small group. For instance, today it is made up of the prefect, the secretary, the undersecretary, 27 members consisting of cardinals, archbishops, and bishops, and 28 consultors (mostly academic theologians).

Following that meeting, His Eminence wrote Fr. Curran on July 25, 1986, informing him the CDF had met and determined he was no longer a theologian in good standing with the Church and could not teach theology in a Catholic university. Catholic University of America confirmed the CDF's decision on August 18, 1986, by firing him. Thus, after seven years and much discussion and debate, Curran was censured for his refusal to teach Catholic teaching as a professed Catholic theologian. Fr. Küng was censured even before Cardinal Ratzinger was called to Rome by Bl. John Paul, and his case took even longer to resolve. It started in April 1967, and his status was not determined until July 1979.

The term "hatchet men" is most often used to describe a political operative sent to verbally attack an opponent through ruthless and behind the scenes moves. The work of Pope Benedict when he served as prefect of the CDF hardly seems to fit that description. Yet, few outside of the media watchdog website NewsBusters.org even took notice of the slight.

The same day the Holy Father arrived in the US, *CBS Evening News* anchorwoman Katie Couric called the Holy Father "extremely conservative." Couric also wondered if the visit would, for some unexplained reason, force the Church and Pope Benedict to rethink its teachings on ordaining women priests and artificial birth control. NewsBusters.org's Tim Graham said, "It's fascinating to observe how anchors complain that subjects like women's ordination are not up for debate at the Vatican, and then they fail to debate them on their programs. Instead they merely cite them as markers of progress the Church is sadly failing to meet."[4]

More of this silliness continued up to the Pope's plane touching down, with the media showing not only their ideological biases but their evidently desperate lack of originality and inventiveness vis-à-vis their vocabulary. CBS's *Early Show,* ABC's *Good Morning America,* the same network's *World News Sunday,* and the *NBC Nightly News* all aired segments where the anchors or reporters repeatedly used descriptors such as "hard-line doctrine" and "hard-liner."

In the end, the news media only displayed their ignorance of religion in general and Catholicism in particular. It also exposed their perception that religion and thus religious truth should be subject to democratic deliberation, even though truth as such never changes. Sadly, this shows how little reporters often do to familiarize themselves with the subject they are covering.

One interesting and ultimately beneficial example of this can demonstrated by the following. The day before the Holy Father arrived, National Public Radio reporter Michele Norris began a segment by citing a Georgetown University study, which stated that the

Catholic Church had experienced a 60 percent decrease in seminary enrollment since the 1960s. While that statement is accurate on its face, it ignores the truth below the surface. Yes, seminary enrollment severely dropped after 1968, but this is partly because many of those men who were already enrolled likely left and never graduated. A Catholic boy born in 1945 would have been 20 by the Second Vatican Council's end in 1965, and only 25 by the end of the decade. At that point, droves of already ordained priests were abandoning their vows. We will concede that the following is only logical speculation, but it is reasonable to presume that this also led many to abandon the seminary.

Furthermore, demographic figures show there were far more men under 25 in the 1960s than today, due to the size of the average family having decreased. Indeed, consider that Irish and American Catholics, particularly those who had not been indoctrinated in college, were the longest to hold out against artificial birth control. In one survey, 42 percent of regular Mass attending American Catholic women absolutely disapproved of contraception, versus only 25 percent of regular Mass attenders.

Of sporadically practicing Catholics on the other hand, the ratios were flipped. Fifty-six percent approved of any means necessary to limit the size of a family, while only 17 percent of those who infrequently attended Mass rejected contraception as an option. This all changed because of three factors:

1. The introduction of the Pill in the early 1960s

2. The artificially inflated expectation that the Church would change its teaching on birth control during the same period

3. The assurance given by many priests to married couples and those in the confessional that Paul VI had gotten it wrong when he issued *Humanae Vitae*

Eventually, Catholics contracepted at the same rate as their Protestant and secularist countrymen. The result is a greatly reduced birthrate. In 2011, it was reported that the nation's birthrate had dropped for the third year in a row.[5] At 1.9, it is now below the replacement level of 2.1. Even Hispanic women saw a decline from 3.0 to 2.4 over the last few years. Compare this to post-World War II years, when the average American Catholic family had 4 children.[6]

Put another way, between 1945 and the late 1950s, Catholic infant baptisms averaged roughly 35 per 1,000 Catholics. Today, infant baptisms average just 12.7 per 1,000 Catholics. This corresponds with a drop from a high of 15.1 marriages per 1,000 Catholics in 1947 to 2.7 marriages per 1,000 Catholics in 2009.[7]

This isn't just an American phenomenon, either. Between 1900 and 1960 in the Netherlands, for instance, the country's fertility rate was 3.55. With the growing acceptance of birth control early in the 20th century, the Protestant birthrate had already dropped well below that. It was two Dutch Catholic provinces that kept the nation's numbers as high as they were. While this started to drop with the advent of the Pill, even by the late 1960s, the average for these Catholic areas was still 1.9. This was still higher than the national average. By the 1970s, however, the Catholic fertility rate had plunged below that of the nation's Protestants. Fewer people equals fewer potential seminarians.

Regardless, anyone tuning into the aforementioned programs must have thought the Church under Benedict must be in terrible straits. However, it couldn't be farther from the truth. Despite the drop in birthrates and the rise in only-child families, many seminaries across the country were reporting an increase in the number of young men enrolling. As proof of this, the number of seminarians jumped 4 percent last year over the previous one. Furthermore, it has risen 13.7 percent since the 1997-98 academic year, when the number of graduate seminarians was its nadir. In addition, the growth in pre-theologate programs has been tremendous (these are discernment and formation programs that do not get their degree from a college seminary). From a little under 200 when CARA started tracking these students, there are now 835 at last count, an increase of 76 percent-plus.[8]

Furthermore, the number of priestly ordinations has gone up 5 percent.[9] In 2010, for instance, the Archdiocese of St. Louis had its largest ordination class in over two decades.[10] More substantively, however, these men have by-and-large put much greater stock in being in line with Church teaching than it seems those ordained in the immediate post-conciliar period did.

The increases aren't huge, to be sure. No one is pretending the vocations crisis is over. Also, this is not to say there are not still huge problems facing the Church. There absolutely are. What this does say is that the two markers routinely used to assess the Church's health indicate the Church in the United States may have possibly turned a corner. If nothing else, it has stopped the hemorrhaging, and that is a good thing.

"Let the Sunshine In, Let the Sunshine In…"

Despite the maelstrom of cynical and downright negative spin that characterized most of the Fourth Estate's coverage prior to the Pope's arrival, some rays of light did manage to shine through.

For instance, shortly before His Holiness' arrival, the *Washington Post* ran a story titled, "We Live It Every Day."[11] The story looked at the phenomenon of young Catholics living in and around Washington, DC, who embraced the teachings of the Church. Some were even regular attendees of the TLM.

"I love Pope Benedict," the story quoted wife and mom Karen Hickey saying. "He's done so much good in the little time that he's been there." Karen, of course, was and is not alone. Opinion polls show it is the young (i.e., those under 30) who most support the Church's teachings and are even more pro-life than their grandparents. Putting it mildly, this leaves many who report and comment on the news aghast.

Enter Pope Benedict

The successor to St. Peter arrived in the United States on Tuesday, April 15, 2008. Upon landing at Andrews Air Force Base, he was personally greeted by President George W. Bush, who during his by-then-seven years in office had never greeted another world leader at the airport.

The following day the Holy Father was received at the White House with a welcoming ceremony attended by a record crowd of 13,000 that showed President Bush's affection and esteem for the Pope, despite their differences over the Iraq War. The United States Army Marching Band and Choral Group offered His Holiness a stirring rendition of "The Battle Hymn of the Republic," and Kathleen Battle sang the Lord's Prayer. Friend and foe alike agreed it was an impressive welcome for the Supreme Roman Pontiff.

During their addresses to the assembled guests, both Benedict XVI and President Bush used similar language to speak of human and religious freedom. Several commentators expressed the view that each could have given the other's speech. Each man focused on God-given and thus immutable truths. Because of this alone, the ceremony was a welcome respite for many Christians from the dictatorship of relativism that has become more and more prevalent in the United States.

Rush Limbaugh, arguably the nation's leading talk show host, was so impressed with the event that he was still speaking about it two days later. When President Bush called into the program to thank him for his kind words, Limbaugh told him, "That ceremony, sir, was ... We're in a presidential campaign, and by definition, during a presidential campaign, candidates are telling us what's wrong with the country. And that day, you and the Pope brought ... God Bless America ... *God* to Washington—on *public property*. It was just amazing. I just wanted to thank you for it, because it was so uplifting. It was so timely."[12]

Thursday saw the Holy Father celebrate Mass at the new Nationals Park, and it showcased him at his best. Just one day after his 81st birthday, His Holiness spryly moved around the stadium. That's not what impressed people, though. Rather, it was the blueprint for the continued growth and vitality of the Church that he laid down for the United States in his homily. For that reason, it is worth quoting *in extensio*.

He started off by noting that the Mass was taking place on the anniversary of "the division by my predecessor, Pope Pius VII, of the original Diocese of Baltimore and the establishment of the Dioceses of Boston, Bardstown (now Louisville), New York, and Philadelphia." And while it was fitting to commemorate that anniversary, he indicated his real purpose was:

> ... to confirm you, my brothers and sisters, in the faith of the apostles (see Luke 22:32) ... the inseparable link between the risen Lord, the gift of the Spirit for the forgiveness of sins, and the mystery of the Church.... as a visible, structured community which is at the same time a spiritual communion, a mystical body enlivened by the Spirit's manifold gifts, and the sacrament of salvation for all humanity (see *Lumen Gentium*, 8). In every time and place, the Church is called to grow in unity through constant conversion to Christ ...
>
> I pray, then, that this significant anniversary in the life of the Church in the United States, and the presence of the Successor of Peter in your midst, will be an occasion for all Catholics to reaffirm their unity in the apostolic faith, to offer their contemporaries a convincing account of the hope which inspires them (see 1 Peter 3:15), and to be renewed in missionary zeal for the extension of God's kingdom.
>
> The world needs this witness! Who can deny that the present moment is a crossroads, not only for the Church in America but also for society as a whole? It is a time of great promise, as we see the human family in many

ways drawing closer together and becoming ever more interdependent. Yet at the same time we see clear signs of a disturbing breakdown in the very foundations of society: signs of alienation, anger, and polarization on the part of many of our contemporaries; increased violence; a weakening of the moral sense; a coarsening of social relations; and a growing forgetfulness of Christ and God.

The Church, too, sees signs of immense promise in her many strong parishes and vital movements, in the enthusiasm for the faith shown by so many young people, in the number of those who each year embrace the Catholic faith, and in a greater interest in prayer and catechesis. At the same time she senses, often painfully, the presence of division and polarization in her midst, as well as the troubling realization that many of the baptized, rather than acting as a spiritual leaven in the world, are inclined to embrace attitudes contrary to the truth of the Gospel....

We have heard St. Paul tell us that all creation is even now "groaning" in expectation of that true freedom which is God's gift to his children (see Romans 8:21-22), a freedom which enables us to live in conformity to his will. Today let us pray fervently that the Church in America will be renewed in that same Spirit, and sustained in her mission of proclaiming the Gospel to a world that longs for genuine freedom (see John 8:32), authentic happiness, and the fulfillment of its deepest aspirations!

Here I wish to offer a special word of gratitude and encouragement to all those who have taken up the challenge of the Second Vatican Council, so often reiterated by Pope John Paul II, and committed their lives to the new evangelization. I thank my brother bishops, priests and deacons, men and women religious, parents, teachers, and catechists. The fidelity and courage with which the Church in this country will respond to the challenges raised by an increasingly secular and materialistic culture will depend in large part upon your own fidelity in handing on the treasure of our Catholic faith.

Young people need to be helped to discern the path that leads to true freedom: the path of a sincere and generous imitation of Christ, the path of commitment to justice and peace. Much progress has been made in developing solid programs of catechesis, yet so much more remains to be done in forming the hearts and minds of the young in knowledge and love of the Lord.

The challenges confronting us require a comprehensive and sound instruction in the truths of the faith. But they also call for cultivating a mindset, an intellectual "culture," which is genuinely Catholic, confident in the profound harmony of faith and reason, and prepared to bring the richness of faith's vision to bear on the urgent issues which affect the future of American society.

... Let us trust in the Spirit's power to inspire conversion, to heal every wound, to overcome every division, and to inspire new life and freedom. How much we need these gifts! And how close at hand they are, particularly in the sacrament of penance! The liberating power of this sacrament, in which our honest confession of sin is met by God's merciful word of pardon and peace, needs to be rediscovered and reappropriated by every Catholic. To a great extent, the renewal of the Church in America and throughout the world depends on the renewal of the practice of penance and the growth in holiness which that sacrament both inspires and accomplishes.

"In hope we were saved!" (Romans 8:24). As the Church in the United States gives thanks for the blessings of the past 200 hundred years, I invite you, your families, and every parish and religious community to trust in the power of grace to create a future of promise for God's people in this country. I ask you, in the Lord Jesus, to set aside all division and to work with joy to prepare a way for him, in fidelity to his word and in constant conversion to His will. Above all, I urge you to continue to be a leaven of evangelical hope in American society, striving to bring the light and truth of the Gospel to the task of building an ever more just and free world for generations yet to come.

Those who have hope must live different lives! (see *Spe Salvi*, 2). By your prayers, by the witness of your faith, by the fruitfulness of your charity, may you point the way towards that vast horizon of hope which God is even now opening up to his Church, and indeed to all humanity: the vision of a world reconciled and renewed in Christ Jesus, our Savior. To him be all honor and glory, now and forever. Amen![13]

Reading this, you can really see what writer Peggy Noonan meant when he told her, "You download the text of what [the Pope] said, print it, ponder it."

As popular as the Holy Father's visit to Washington, DC, was, his visit to New York City was the real surprise for many. This city has a reputation of being one of the most secular and relativistic cities in the world. Therefore, it might not be a place one would expect a generous outpouring of affection for the Holy Father from all quarters, and yet that's exactly what happened.

Arriving Friday evening on the day before the start of Passover, His Holiness traveled to Manhattan's Upper East Side. There he paid a visit to Park East Synagogue, one of the city's more historic places of Jewish worship. The synagogue's Chief Rabbi Arthur Schneier, an Austrian immigrant and Holocaust survivor who spoke to him in German, warmly greeted Benedict XVI, as did a Who's Who of the city's Jewish community.

Furthermore, all of the city's television stations carried the event live, and each had its own experts on Catholicism and Judaism chiming in with their almost uniformly positive assessment. Especially refreshingly was the fact that not a single said the "H" word: hard-liner.

The synagogue visit, along with his visit in general, was start of the Pope's trip being the talk of the town. It certainly was the talk of the guests at my hotel. When my wife and I arrived back from a visit to St. Patrick's Cathedral, we were surprised to find so many of the hotel's guests watching the event in a large room near the lobby. Most were not from the US, and it was quite interesting to hear their questions and discussion. It was obvious the visit had engaged them. I doubt any of them expected this.

The following day, *il Papa* celebrated Mass at St. Patrick's Cathedral for a select group of priests and religious. Following Mass, the Successor of Peter was driven up Fifth Avenue in the popemobile to his next appearance, which was a rally for youth at St. Joseph's Seminary in Yonkers, located just north of Manhattan.

During the trip, all along the way, onlookers and well-wishers crowded the sidewalks of 5th Ave., sometimes up to 15 people deep, just to catch a glimpse of this grandfatherly German man who was not at all the terror they had been told to expect. All of this was captured not only on EWTN and the New York area television stations, but on the national cable news channels, CNN, FOX, and MSNBC as well.

At this time, the events on the grounds of St. Joseph's were well underway. For example, a nonstop lineup of religious and secular musicians performed for the attendees, who came from all over the United States. There was the Evangelical rock group, Third Day, who more than once mentioned how honored they were to be asked to perform at such an historic event. There was also *American Idol* winner Kelly Clarkson.

As Clarkson wrapped up her set, all eyes were on the video screen as Pope Benedict XVI made his way onto the grounds. After blessing children with disabilities inside the chapel, the Pope made his way to the event stage where a cacophonous applause greeted him.

In the longest address of his US visit, he gave an impression of what one might have seen in the early days of the Church when St. Peter was Pope. In my mind's eye, I could easily imagine what it must have been like for the former Simon bar Jonah to address his flock from a grassy perch the audience, many of whom had never heard a compelling explanation of the gospel, listened in rapt attention.

The urgency of Benedict's message was not lost on this spiritually hungry crowd. Whenever the Pope said something that conventional wisdom would have us believe is controversial or that the young audience would reject, guess what happened? The crowd cheered! As the crowd cleared the field at the conclusion of his address, I could see a sea of thoughtful faces. People were quiet. Reporters weren't bantering like they often do after an event has wrapped up. Maybe they or some Doubting Thomases were walking away quietly mulling over their prejudices about the much-maligned Pope. What made this event a stunning spiritual success is that by his eloquence, *Papa Ratzi* had preached the gospel in a way some had never heard it. I know I felt a stirring in my heart, and I am sure he got other people thinking of certain issues in ways they never had before, too.

Doing commentary in the lead up to Benedict's talk, Fr. Neuhaus, who served as a commentator for EWTN's broadcast of the event, had grumbled over the logistics and his dislike of some of the musical acts. Afterward, however, he could only talk about how he was moved by the scores of young people who saw him after the event who had told him how the Pope had moved their hearts. Several hundred young priests, young women religious, seminarians, and young men and women exploring a vocation were positioned in front of the stage. They were visibly moved and conveyed this to all who would listen, including both mainstream and Catholic media.

Two final events awaited the Holy Father: His visit to Ground Zero, site of the September 11, 2001, terrorist attacks, and Yankee Stadium, where the Holy Father would conclude his trip by celebrating Mass at the famed "House That Ruth Built." This would be one of the last non-baseball events at the stadium before it was replaced by the new Yankee Stadium. What was striking about the Ground Zero event is how simple, stark, even Spartan it was, but how pitch-perfect that was. Afterward, the media again all agreed it was a moving event.

Upon arriving, His Holiness went to a *prie-dieu* set before a lit Paschal candle meant to suggest hope in the Resurrection, not to mention God's ability to bring goodness out of evil. Then Benedict joined a group of 9/11 survivors and relatives of the deceased in the four-story crater, a seemingly apt symbol for the hole that still lingered in the hearts of so many even years after that tragic day.

And ever since that terrible morning when more than 3,000 lost their lives and those they left behind lost a part of the souls, many had asked how healing for them would ever come. While no one can pretend to say that the Pope's visit had definitively brought that, maybe it did for the 24 people who were there. This isn't hard to imagine when we consider the words he prayed with them:

> O God of love, compassion, and healing, look on us, people of many different faiths and traditions, who gather today at this site, the scene of incredible violence and pain.
>
> We ask you in your goodness to give eternal light and peace to all who died here—the heroic first-responders: our fire fighters, police officers, emergency service workers, and Port Authority personnel, along with all the innocent men and women who were victims of this tragedy simply because their work or service brought them here on September 11, 2001.
>
> We ask you in your compassion to bring healing to those who, because of their presence here that day, suffer from injuries and illness. Heal, too, the pain of still-grieving families and all who lost loved ones in this tragedy. Give them strength to continue their lives with courage and hope. We are mindful as well of those who suffered

death, injury, and loss on the same day at the Pentagon and in Shanksville, Pennsylvania.

Our hearts are one with theirs as our prayer embraces their pain and suffering. God of peace, bring your peace to our violent world: peace in the hearts of all men and women and peace among the nations of the earth.

Turn to your way of love those whose hearts and minds are consumed with hatred. God of understanding, overwhelmed by the magnitude of this tragedy, we seek your light and guidance as we confront such terrible events.

Grant that those whose lives were spared may live so that the lives lost here may not have been lost in vain. Comfort and console us, strengthen us in hope, and give us the wisdom and courage to work tirelessly for a world where true peace and love reign among nations and in the hearts of all.

When the Pope arrived at Yankee Stadium, he found 57,000 people waiting for him, 1,000 shy of full capacity. For over 80 years, countless extraordinary baseball players, as well as some football and boxing stars, had graced these storied grounds. In addition, two popes—Paul VI and John Paul II—had said Mass there.

It was a beautiful, liturgically sound Mass that began with the cessation of the morning's persistent sprinkle and the bursting forth of the sun. In his homily, *il Papa* gave the faithful a timeless takeaway. He encouraged them to not content themselves with being "Sunday-only" Catholics. That, he said, "means overcoming every separation between faith and life, and countering false gospels of freedom and happiness. It also means rejecting a false dichotomy between faith and public life."[14]

Afterward, the verdict rendered by 15-year-old Katherine Kiriakos was: "The Pope is adorable. I like the way he explained the Gospel."

Once the Mass had concluded, secular and sectarian news outlets both sang the praises of Pope Benedict XVI. He found a way to get across his message in a way that was both effective and inspiring. It wasn't Bl. John Paul II's rousing, almost Pentecostalist style, but His Holiness had been so pitch-perfect the entire visit, it didn't have to be.

For the next week, words of praise poured into network news programs, secular and Catholic newspapers, as well as the Catholic blogosphere. The Catholic media and blogosphere captured the faithful's attention with story headlines like "Benedict in America: He Came, He Saw, He Conquered"[15] and "The Shadow of Peter Fell Across America Last Week."[16] All seemed to emphasize the German Pontiff's teaching prowess given his ability to help the average listener grasp deep subjects by giving them a clear, easily understood message.

It is true that the coverage was not all glowing. Some gave only grudging respect to His Holiness, with *Newsweek* saying, for instance, that he "connected better than expected." However, you can also say that piece rendered a split decision, for in addition to a few snarky and frankly not well thought out comments, the piece's author Daniel Stone wrote, "Leading masses for more than 100,000 people and offering blessings to faithful crowds ... clearly had an invigorating effect on both the [Pope] and the crowds."[17] Furthermore, a piece by *Washington Post* staff writers Michelle Boorstein and Jacqueline L. Salmon was very complimentary.

In an *Inside Catholic* article titled "The Face of Pope Benedict," Deal Hudson noted, "It was predicted that John Paul II's successor could never match his charisma, his ability to attract and engage large crowds around the world. No one who watched the Pope mobile travel up 5th Ave. or the Holy Father's entrance into Yankee Stadium on Sunday could doubt he has won the heart of America."[18] What Hudson wrote is absolutely true, but that wasn't the evidence of the tide turning. No, the proof for that lay in the fact that for six days—April 15-21, 2008—a German man with a particularly thick accent, who wore what many called "funny clothes," a man whose face is not particularly attractive and thus easily caricaturized (do a Bing search for +Images Benedict XVI Emperor to see for yourself), who was called a Nazi, a bulldog, a Rottweiler, a hard-liner, and any number of other names, this very same man left the toughest, most cynical city in the world duly impressed.

And he didn't do it by following pundits' suggestions that he bend Church teaching and discipline. Rather, he impressed the United States and many onlookers around the world in the same way he had since his election in 2005 ... with simple words artfully put so that everyone could understand them. Because of this, for six beautiful spring days in 2008, the "Capital of the World" (as NYC is sometimes called) heard the gospel, full, unadulterated, and nonstop.

Now, *that* is the tide turning.

THREE
A NEW BREED OF MEN AND WOMEN RELIGIOUS

For years, the many Western Catholics who followed the Church's teachings were upset about the large number of their nation's bishops who seemed to either ignore or challenge the magisterial authority of the Vatican. In the post-conciliar period, only one bishop from a very small Australian diocese comes to mind who was removed for doctrinal dissent—and that only happened after 18 years of his leading who knows how many souls away from the teachings of true Catholicism.

Catholic scholar George Weigel has noted that a large number of the American bishops consecrated during the 1960s and 1970s and who grew up in the cities or suburbia—and that is the greater portion of them—came out of the so-called "Catholic ghetto."[1] This phrase refers to enclaves in which Catholics lived as a group. There were Irish Catholic ghettos, Italian Catholic ghettos, Polish and German ghettos, and so on. Sometimes there were even mixed ethnic Catholic ghettos. The point is, Catholics did not live in the same neighborhoods, by and large, as their Protestant or Jewish schoolmates.

Fr. Tony Oelrich says, "The Catholic population in the US lived as a minority population that held together strongly by means of clearly defining itself over and against the rest of American culture. Catholics did not eat meat on Friday, they had large families, they did not date Protestants and never went into a Protestant church, they sent their children to Catholic schools, and they never missed going to Sunday Mass. Catholics, living within the ghetto mentality, were responsible citizens but more or less stuck together and did not see themselves as called to influence the culture around them."[2]

In the first chapter of his 2004 book *Letters to a Young Catholic*, titled "Baltimore and Milledgeville—Acquiring the 'Habit of Being,'" George Weigel reflects that these ghettos represented our nation's "seemingly last moment of intact Catholic culture." He claims it made many experience an "intense sense of belonging to something larger than ourselves, something beyond ourselves that somehow lived inside us, too."[3] While many relished growing up in such a milieu, many also regretted it for the separation it enforced between Catholics and their fellow countrymen. This separation represented a lot of things, not the least of which was that many Americans considered Catholics aliens, beholden to a foreign power, and second-class citizens. Thus, it is understandable why many, even bishops, regretted and resented the ghetto period in our nation's life.

Upon achieving episcopal rank (and sometimes beforehand) and to throw off that background, too many prelates threw themselves into the urbane lifestyle of the glitterati in their dioceses. Visiting Friday night fish fries were out and hobnobbing with movers and shakers at the opera was in.[4] It was one thing to regret the lack of engagement with the larger culture that was inarguably part of the Catholic ghetto experience. It was another, however, when many of these bishops distanced themselves from the good things of that period simply because they were associated with that period.

As Weigel writes in *God's Choice: Pope Benedict XVI and the Future of the Catholic Church*, the Catholic ghetto experience was part of the much larger age fixed between the end of World War II and the beginning of Vatican II. Of this time in the Church, many of a certain age will insist it was nightmarish—without putting forth much evidence for that, but that's another story.

As any period does, it had much that was bad and good in it. However, the good was very good. Writing of the Pope, the author reports it "was a time in which Catholic intellectual life convinced him that 'that which is Catholic cannot be stupid, and that which is stupid cannot be Catholic.' Pre-conciliar Catholicism ... was anything but stale: it was bracing, vital, and intellectually vibrant. At the same time, theology was done as a self-consciously ecclesial discipline, a way of thinking with the Church."

He then quotes from the former Cardinal Ratzinger's memoirs. In them, the future Supreme Roman Pontiff recounts a discussion between German Lutheran and Catholic theologians about the then-rumored proclamation of Our Lady's assumption into heaven by Pius XII as a dogma of the Christian faith.[5] One of the men, then-Fr. Gottlieb Söhngen, "held forth passionately against the possibility of [the definition of the dogma of Mary's assumption]....

"In response, Edmund Schlink, a Lutheran expert on systematic theology from Heidelberg, asked Söhngen point-blank: 'But what will you do if the dogma is nevertheless defined? Won't you then have to turn your back on the Catholic Church?' After reflecting for a moment, Söhngen answered: 'If the dogma comes, then I will remember that the Church is wiser than I and that I must trust her more than my own erudition.' I think that this small scene says everything about the spirit in which theology was done [in those days]—both critically and with faith."[6]

Ironically, this sort of thinking began to go out of style at roughly the same time. For instance, during this period, Fr. Tielhard de Chardin, SJ, had many of his works censured by the Vatican. It was said that his "works abound in such ambiguities and indeed even serious errors as to offend Catholic doctrine." Furthermore, his superiors banned him from teaching philosophy or writing. Being a good Jesuit, he abided by these orders. That did not stop his followers, however, from mimeographing his manuscripts and disseminating these views, even though the Holy See said they should never see the light of day.[7] This is how his erroneous views on original sin came to have the influence they did at the Second Vatican Council.

The sort of loyalty showed by Msgr. Söhngen gradually came to be considered an anachronism of the past. Many bishops gave lip service obeisance to traditional Catholic doctrine, pushing themselves just up to the line of heterodoxy without quite crossing it. All the while, they either turned a blind eye toward or actively encouraged moral relativism. Perhaps the nadir (low point) of this phenomenon came during the 1980s when Seattle's Archbishop Raymond Hunthausen was relieved of certain duties due to some questionable and even objectionable actions by him and his curia.[8]

The archdiocese, for instance, allowed Catholics who had divorced but not received an annulment to have "a subsequent Church marriage ... or even after they have received a negative" response to their request for an annulment. If Catholics had divorced and their subsequent marriage was merely a civil one, they were allowed to receive the sacraments. Contraceptive sterilization was allowed until March 1984. And if we were to catalog all the aberrations against the Holy See's authentic teachings concerning doctrine and discipline here, it would without exaggeration take up several pages. To begin the process of restoring order, Bl. John Paul II named Fr. Donald Wuerl as "auxiliary bishop with special faculties" of Seattle in 1985, and he gave him "complete and final decision-making power" in areas such as sexual morality and marriage.

Bold, Brave Bishops

By 2005, however, this situation had changed, by and large, as many younger, more orthodox bishops had been consecrated to lead the United States' dioceses (the same could not be said of other English-speaking nations). Since his ascendency to the papacy, Benedict seems to take more time in naming new bishops to empty sees. He even has impromptu meetings on occasion to learn how things were going.

A case in point occurred in spring of 2006. The then-newly appointed bishop of Saginaw, Michigan, His Excellency Robert Carlson, was leading a pilgrimage to the Eternal City, when the Holy Father summoned him for a meeting.

Since coming to Saginaw from a successful tenure as ordinary of the Diocese of Sioux Falls, South Dakota, Bishop Carlson had experienced a robust start to his new assignment. There were only two men from his diocese studying to become priests when Bishop Carlson assumed his duties. One year later, there were 15. One of his first acts had been to appointed himself vocations director, and he went around his diocese meeting prospective candidates, which encouraged many to enter the seminary.

"The Holy Father had some questions for me about our vocations. We have had some successes, and he was interested in them. I found Pope Benedict extremely knowledgeable about what was going on in the realm of vocations and in the seminaries. I felt truly blessed to have had the meeting," said Bishop Carlson.[10]

In 2010, Bishop Carlson became Archbishop of St. Louis when Benedict appointed him to fill the slot vacated when he named Archbishop Raymond Burke as prefect of the Apostolic Signatura.[11] Archbishop Burke was soon appointed Cardinal, and among other duties, he received a top appointment to help fill vacant episcopal posts. After receiving Holy Orders from Servant of God Pope Paul VI, His Eminence spent the next 29 years flipping back and forth between assignments at the Vatican and in his home diocese of La Crosse, Wisconsin. He became bishop of that See in 1994.

Around the same time Cardinal Burke was settling into his new duties in Rome, His Holiness moved Bishop Robert Baker in 2007 from the Diocese of Charleston, South Carolina, to Birmingham, Alabama, home of EWTN, the Eternal Word Television Network, an international Catholic media concern. Bishop Baker brought with him a fantastic reputation in that the Charleston diocese grew by nearly 40 percent to just under 175,000 souls during his tenure.[12]

A New Breed of Men and Women Religious

On September 8, 2011, the Feast of Our Lady's Nativity, after 14 highly successful years in Denver, Archbishop Charles Chaput was installed as the ordinary in Philadelphia. He has been a leading figure in what some call the "affirmative orthodoxy" movement, which seeks to restore and maintain Catholic identity in a world that is all too keen on the latest religious trends. In Fr. Neuhaus' book *Catholics Matters*, he recounts a *New Yorker* article by Peter Boyer, in which Boyer quoted Archbishop Chaput as stating:

> "Whenever the Church is criticized, she understands herself better and is purified. And when she is purified, she better serves the Lord. We're at a time in our country when some Catholics—too many—are discovering that they've gradually become non-Catholics who happen to go to Mass. That's a sad and difficult, and a judgment on a generation of Catholic leadership. But it may be exactly the moment of truth the Church needs."[13]

As Fr. Neuhaus stated, Archbishop Chaput was sadly reminding us that "many of the most talented in that earlier generation of leadership wanted to 'demystify' the Church. They ended up by abandoning the mystery. This de-theologizing and de-sacramentalizing of our understanding of the Church is now widespread."[14]

It isn't just the bishops who have moved sees that encourage hope, either. While it has made few headlines, the Pope has appointed more and more new bishops who have embraced Catholic orthodoxy and fidelity to the Holy See where some their predecessors may have held their noses to it.

Take, for instance, the 2006 appointment of Bishop David Choby, who grew up in his see, the Diocese of Nashville. This diocese has a small but growing Catholic population. Some believe its crown jewel is the Dominican Sisters of St. Cecelia (aka the Nashville Dominicans), a vibrant community of women religious who are making their mark on the Church.

In addition to being eagerly welcomed by locals, Bishop Choby let it be known that he wanted the Church's teachings and traditions to be loved and understood. He joined a growing chorus of newer bishops who eagerly accepted Pope Benedict's *Summorum Pontificum*, the *motu proprio* by which the Pope made clear that those who wanted to attend the extraordinary form of the Roman rite could do so without restrictions or episcopal interference.

Since coming to the Archdiocese of Saint Paul-Minneapolis in 2008, Archbishop John Nienstedt has served as another good example of courageous orthodoxy. His Excellency came to the Twin Cities from the nearby Diocese of New Ulm, Minnesota, where he succeeded one of the Church in America's most liberal prelates ever, Bishop Raymond Lucker.

Bishop Lucker was a man who thought catechesis in the post-conciliar era was just fine, even when presented with evidence of just how poorly young Catholics knew their faith. "Bishop Ray," as he liked to be called, once placed a rural parish under interdict until each registered member got psychological counseling. The reason? The parishioners didn't like the catechist he had appointed because this woman was teaching their children New Age doctrine and had replaced the sanctuary crucifix with—and I only wish I was making this up—a "cosmic pillow."

It should, therefore, surprise no one that he dissented from Church teaching on issues large and small. St. Paul's *Pioneer Press* reported that Bishop Lucker stated that Catholics should have dialogue about the ordination of women and married priests and should review the Church's stance on the morality of same-sex unions.

After taking office, Archbishop Nienstedt took an unusual step for a bishop by criticizing his predecessor. According to a 2004 story in the *National Catholic Reporter*, His Excellency urged his diocese's Catholics not to read a book containing those views "'as though it reflects Catholic thinking.' ... 'As a whole,' wrote Nienstedt (pro-

A New Breed of Men and Women Religious   65

nounced "nine-stedt"), the book, published by Orbis Press in 2003, 'challenges the church's [sic] own understanding of herself as being authoritatively charged under the guidance of the Holy Spirit to teach in the name of Jesus on matters of faith and morals.' He referred the matter to the doctrine committee of the US bishops' conference, asking them 'to render a statement on the content of the book.'"

This brought a fiery response from *Reporter* editor Thomas Roberts. "It was a really unnecessary and deep insult to a man who had recently died, a man who had given his life to the church," said Roberts. "Just months after a person has died, and you come into a diocese and declare him theologically suspect?"

At the risk of hurting people's feelings or causing offense (which is sincerely not the intent), Mr. Roberts' words remind one of the scene from the 1966 movie, *A Man for All Seasons*, where St. Thomas More is speaking with Will Roper, the man who wants to marry one of his daughters. Sir Thomas has just pronounced Roper a heretic, to which the fiery young man replies: "That's not a word I like, Sir Thomas!"

"It's not a likeable word," replies More. "It's not a likeable thing."

Bishop Lucker had been in eternity for three-and-a-half years when Bishop Nienstedt made his comments in the New Ulm diocesan newspaper. Furthermore, it must have been very difficult for His Grace to make these comments given that Monsignor Lucker had governed that diocese for 25 years and was reputedly very well-liked. And when you factor in the poor level of the laity's familiarity with authentic Church teaching because of Lucker's catechetical ideology, one can surmise that many in the New Ulm see were likely bewildered by what their new ordinary had to say.

Nonetheless, he stuck by his guns. One would therefore imagine, based on his previous and subsequent comments, that he took this stand because he takes quite seriously the bishop's primary job of promoting and upholding an accurate presentation of doctrine and fighting counterfeit notions of what Catholicism holds and believes. He evidently does not believe a bishop's job is to be popular.

In New Ulm, then-Bishop Nienstedt also stopped churches holding joint ecumenical services because these often caused confusion about the centrality of the Catholic Church in the economy of salvation and contributed to a syncretic, "it doesn't matter how you worship, you'll still get to heaven" mentality. He also barred female pastoral administrators from leading prayers at semiannual leadership events. Additionally, His Excellency also barred cohabitating couples from being married in the Church.

Given the Church's current condition, this naturally caused clashes between the bishop and some of his priests. As he prepared to move to the Saint Paul-Minneapolis archdiocese, the *Pioneer Press* quoted New Ulm diocesan priest Fr. Kenneth Irrang as saying, "I expect disaster [in his new see]. I don't think those priests are going to accept him. He's a micromanager. He has to control everything. He hews the line from the Vatican without any question whatsoever…"

While that quote probably concerned those with a "spirit of Vatican II" mindset, those who wanted unadulterated Catholicism were probably uncorking champagne bottles to learn that their next leader actually would take a figurative bullet for what the Church believes. And that is what makes the hubbub over the appointment of bishops such as Nienstadt so befuddling. After all, they do not going beyond what the *Catechism* teaches, but neither will they give short shrift to what the Church has always and in all places held as true.

There is an interesting dichotomy at work here. In April 2012, CARA released "Same Call, Different Men: The Evolution of the Priesthood since Vatican II," a study on the difference between priests who were born between 1943 and 1960 (i.e., roughly during the Baby Boom) and those born before or after that period. It labeled the Baby Boomers "Vatican II" priests. Others call them *Gaudium et Spes* priests, after the conciliar document whose English title is "Joy and Hope" (aka "Constitution on the Church in the Modern World"). They desire dialogue on what the Church says are closed issues (e.g., women's ordination, clerical celibacy, contraception, etc.). They want ecumenism, but one that minimizes rather than tries to resolve sticky differences. They also want more ecclesial involvement in some modern issues that have not typically fallen under the Church's main competency, which is to save souls.

For instance, the *National Catholic Reporter* characterized the perspective of one such priest from Australia as wanting the Church to focus on "global involvement in issues from social justice and technology to economics and ecumenism." Such clerics also tend to be relativistic and not much different than many social libertarians in their approach to sexuality. Perhaps most tellingly, they claim to value dialogue and discussion. As an example of this, the *Reporter* quotes the aforementioned Australian priest as saying, "Priestly celibacy, despite being highly contentious, was reasserted by Paul VI in 1967 without discussion."

Most importantly, however, such priests want the liberty to change doctrine as it suits the times. That in a nutshell is the heresy of modernism, which Pope St. Pius X (1903-14) called the "synthesis of all heresies." Either what the Church teaches about, say, the Eucharist or stealing or contraception is true in all ages or it never has been true because objective "truth" as "truth" never changes. However, those "Vatican II" priests and their fellow travelers in the culture who attacked Archbishop Nienstedt would have us think that to believe this is lunacy.

In response, perhaps His Excellency said it best: "I believe what the Church believes. And unfortunately, in this day and age where there is such pluralism and individualism in our society, a person who believes in a creed, as we do as Catholics, is somehow considered hard-line or a fanatic—a zealot, if you will—because they believe ... what the Church believes."

In 2009, then-Archbishop Timothy Dolan was moved from Milwaukee to New York. The larger-than-life, gregarious man rolled into town and quickly won the hearts and minds of many New Yorkers, Catholic or no. In the homily he gave at his installation Mass, he recounted his desire to travel to Emmaus while in the Holy Land. In it, he asked his fellow New Yorkers to help him find the lost Emmaus by walking with him to uncover holiness from the smallest side street in Gotham to the largest thoroughfare. The sermon was supposedly so powerful that those who were there still remember it today.

Around this same time, the CBS news program *60 Minutes* interviewed Archbishop Dolan, who deftly batted away the usual questions a Catholic prelate faces from the media, which boils down, really, to one question: Why won't the Catholic Church adapt to this, that, or the other change in our culture? His firm but polite answers won over still more people, even the most cynical of hearts simply through his attractive and affirmative orthodoxy. People were used to hearing Catholic leaders preaching, "Thou shalt not ..." What his Excellency did was state what the Church was for rather than what it was against.

The questions on *60 Minutes*, however, were nothing compared to the firestorm Cardinal Dolan received over same sex unions because of his strong, unflinching defense of traditional marriage. Perhaps the most galling aspect of this was not what His Eminence had to endure, but hearing New York's Governor Andrew Cuomo compare himself to St. Thomas More upon his signing the bill legalizing same sex "marriage" in the Empire State.

While taking some pretty heavy punches comes with the territory for orthodox churchmen, perhaps no living Church prelate has received as much withering criticism as Raymond Cardinal Burke, one of Pope Benedict XVI's most trusted confidants. An expert on canon

A New Breed of Men and Women Religious 69

law and the liturgy, Cardinal Burke has long been in the crosshairs of those who don't like what one could call *Catechism* Catholicism. This became especially true after he said US Senator John Kerry (D-MA) could not receive Communion if he traveled within the St. Louis archdiocese during the 2004 presidential campaign.

Then, in April 2007, the Cardinal Glennon Children's Medical Center had decided to hold a charity benefit. As a board member, Archbishop Burke was invited and planned to attend. However, he refused to do so when it came to his attention that popular rock singer Sheryl Crow would be one of the headliners at the benefit.

Citing the *Catechism* no. 2284, His Excellency noted that if he said nothing about Crowe's appearance, it "could call into question in the minds of the faithful the commitment of the medical center and the archdiocese to the cause of life. Ms. Crow is well-known as an abortion activist. She has lent her celebrity status to the promotion of legislation, such as Missouri's Amendment 2 [a state ballot initiative], that creates legal protection for human cloning and the destruction of human beings who are embryos.... Her appearance at a fundraising event for Cardinal Glennon Children's Medical Center is an affront to the identity and mission of the medical center, dedicated as it is to the service of life and Christ's healing mission."[15] His Excellency then resigned from the hospital board.

Perhaps it is needless to note, but during the event, this good man was horribly mocked. Famed St. Louis native and NBC sports announcer Bob Costas emceed the event and said, "Crow was appearing for three reasons; to help children, put on a good show, and get me excommunicated." Comedian Billy Crystal stooped to such yuckers as, "I respect his right to choose—his right to choose not to be here."[16]

The next in this series of unfortunate events came just one week later when the archbishop prevented US Senator Clare McCaskill (D-MO) from delivering the commencement address at her daughter's Catholic high school. The reason, again, was the scandal this might cause the faithful since the senator is well-known for her anti-Culture of Life position.[17]

Then in January 2008, St. Louis University head basketball coach Rick Majerus addressed a presidential campaign rally for then-US Senator Hillary Clinton (D-NY). Majerus admitted he had always been a proponent of abortion rights as well as embryonic stem-cell research. Naturally, Archbishop Burke wasted no time in saying it was not proper for a Catholic "leader" to express such views:

> I'm concerned that [he] made these comments. It can lead Catholics astray. I just believe that it's of the essence for people to understand as a Catholic you just cannot hold these beliefs.[18]

After His Excellency asked the coach's Jesuit employer to take action against him, the school responded through a spokesman said Majerus was stating his views and not that of the Church.

A month after this incident, people were again grumbling about Archbishop Burke. This time it was because St. Patrick's Day fell on the Monday during Holy Week, which is ordinarily supposed to be a penitential time and not one for celebrating the Irish in all of us with green beer. Archbishop Burke simply asked local Catholic organizations what all other bishops had asked, that festivities be moved from Monday to sometime during the week prior.

Many cities celebrated the Feast on the previous Friday or Saturday. His Excellency was absolutely correct in acting as he did—indeed, as every other diocesan bishop did. Nonetheless, in a culture where many people pay more attention to the headlines than to the actual facts surrounding salacious stories, much of this was lost.

Two incidences, however, proved the archbishop was on the right track. In June 2008, a man whom he had excommunicated for schismatic activities publicly announced he had erred and was coming back to the Church. He even said he was grateful for the excommunication, for without that stern warning, he would have continued in the error of his ways. That same month, the archdiocese welcomed its largest ordination in almost 30 years. The numbers of seminarians were growing, and it was because they were attracted to His Grace's firm leadership. However, why did the His Eminence take such an unrelenting stand, which must have caused him no small amount of heartache?

The answer comes in his June 2012 book, *Divine Love Made Flesh: The Holy Eucharist as the Sacrament of Charity*. Actually, it comes in the book's very title. So deep, so profound, so—I hate to use the word, but I can't think of another—so chivalric is his love for Our Lord's Real Presence, that Cardinal Burke will let nothing—absolutely nothing—denigrate it if he can help it. He is an earl whose devotion to his King is such that, during battle, he would gladly die in his defense. And battles are exactly what he faced for over a year as archbishop of St. Louis.

Another firm new leader is Archbishop Joseph Naumann of the Archdiocese of Kansas City, Kansas. Upon assuming the mantle as his see's 10th leader, he immediately began making changes. In late 2008, I interviewed him for Zenit News. He spoke passionately of what called him to faith and the changes he saw during turbulent 1960s and 1970s.

He told me, "The 1960s and 1970s were in many ways an exciting time in the Church and society. Like many young Catholics, I was inspired by John F. Kennedy and his challenge to 'ask not what your country can do for you, but what you can do for your country.' I was inspired by the civil rights movement and the efforts to bring about in law and society equality for people of all races. The changes in the Church, resulting from the Second Vatican Council, were also exciting. I experienced the reform of the liturgy as an effort to make the Eucharist more accessible to God's people.

"Yet in time I began to see another side to some of the cultural changes around me. The disastrous consequences of the drug culture and the sexual revolution became more and more apparent. At the time it was issued, I did not appreciate the courageous and prophetic nature of *Humanae Vitae*.

"In time, I began to appreciate the heroic leadership of Pope Paul VI in protecting the authentic meaning of our sexuality, as well as the meaning of marriage. In the liturgy, I also began to realize, for all of our good intentions with the renewal, some of the experience of the sacred had been diminished."[19]

Prior to our talk, and following the April 15-21, 2008, visit of Pope Benedict XVI, Archbishop Naumann related that the visit had moved him. So inspired was he by the Holy Father's admonition to fearlessly witness to our faith, he decided to take an uncomfortable and unwanted but necessary defense of Church teaching.

The previous August, with the consent of his brother Kansan bishops, he had sent then-Governor Kathleen Sebelius a letter reviewing her unfailing and uncompromising pro-abortion record over 30 years in Kansas politics. In light of this, he then asked her to refrain from receiving the Eucharist. After all, to take the Bread of Life when one so manifestly supports the Culture of Death is a perfect illustration of the seriousness of 1 Cor 11:27-29.

He also wrote her a second letter, probably following her public reception of Communion sometime in March. On April 21, the day after the Pope's departure, Sabelius vetoed the Comprehensive Abortion Reform Act. This legislation would have made the language in Kansas' partial-birth abortion law match that of the 2007 Supreme Court decision *Gonzales v Carhart* that upheld the Partial-Birth Abortion Ban Act. Significant majorities in both chambers of the Kansas Legislature had passed the bill.

It was in the wake of this that Archbishop Naumann made public his previously private efforts with regards to Governor Sebelius' receiving the Eucharist.[32] It was a big story, one that gained even more traction than it ordinarily might have because many at the time were mentioning her as a possible running mate for then-US Sena-

A New Breed of Men and Women Religious 73

tor Barack Obama (D-IL), who would soon receive the Democrat Party's presidential nomination.

The usual suspects, of course, derided the Church for its pro-life stance and for allegedly violating the boundaries of Church and State. In the end, though, the bottom line was this: Archbishop Naumann was one of 70 bishops that presidential election year to emphasize the scandal and confusion caused when pro-abortion politicians supporting the Culture of Death receive the Bread of Life (see John 6:32-63), which is Our Lord's Body, Blood, Soul, and Divinity.

Here is why this is a sign the tide is turning: In decades past, when their predecessors in the episcopate had faced a similar problem, a significant number of bishops chose to practice verbal gymnastics when they weren't being outright and dishearteningly silent. Contrast that with our current situation where so many of today's bishops stand so publicly and courageously against the evil of abortion and the sanctity of life. It is thrilling.

It's not that no bishop stood up for life in the immediate years following the *Roe v. Wade* decision in 1973, but it took 11 years for the first to prominently do so. That was during the 1984 presidential campaign, when the late John Cardinal O'Connor of the Archdiocese of New York became the first to make such a public stand. Since, then, though, many have. What impact that has had is open to debate. One could argue, "Not very much."

There are two answers to this, however. The first is that God does not call us to be successful; he calls us to be faithful, for it is he who can and will bring good out of every situation. The second is that these men are bishops; their job is to teach and tend the flock. By maintaining silence, they do neither. Thank God that these men are living up to their vocations and working with the graces God is giving them.

In August 24, 2008, the day before the opening of the Democratic National Convention, then-Speaker of the House Nancy Pelosi (D-CA) made the incredible claim to NBC's Tom Brokaw on *Meet the Press* that the Catholic Church has never really been able to define when human life begins. She also said, "This is an issue that I have studied for a long time," and that while she was an "ardent" Catholic, she believed in abortion on demand.[20]

As a result, her own archbishop and the bishops of Sioux City, Iowa, Denver, Washington, DC, New York, Colorado Springs, Pittsburgh, La Crosse, Baker, Oregon, 17 other diocesan ordinaries, and even the entire US episcopate through a statement from the United States Conference of Catholic Bishops publicly refuted what she said. All noted that the Church has always been pro-life and against abortion.[21]

As I noted at the time on my website, CatholicReport.org, I can't remember the US Catholic Bishops ever responding so quickly to a doctrinal error such as this on the part of someone so prominent. It was great to see such unity among the bishops, not to mention the encouragement many rank-and-file Catholics took from this. And that was because comments such as those by Speaker Pelosi were no longer being ignored or swept under the rug. They were being challenged and, most importantly, corrected.

The Plight of the Papist Priest Takes a Turn

For years, many within and without the Catholic Church harped on the need to end the celibacy rule for priests and nuns. "It's is driving away potential vocations," we were told (endlessly), and only the requirement's elimination would keep vocations from completely disappearing. This chorus only grew louder after the clergy sex-abuse scandal surfaced. What could you expect, we were asked, from virile men who had no outlet for their sexual urges?

This ignored the fact that other denominations and religions with no celibacy rule experienced roughly the same rate as was found in the Catholic priesthood, as was also the case in respected professions such as medicine and law. For faithful priests who understood what it truly meant to be a Catholic cleric, this was only the latest in a long line of demoralizing incidents. The morale engendered by this was perhaps best captured in a *cri de cœur* and 1981 *Homiletic & Pastoral Review* article by the late Green Bay diocesan priest, Fr. Richard Gilsdorf, titled, "The Plight of the Papist Priest."[22] In it, Fr. Gilsdorf painfully demonstrated how difficult it was to remain a priest who was trying to remain loyal to the Roman Pontiff and his teachings, while at the same time serving diocesan bishops who often taught the exact opposite. Such priests had been treated like pariahs by their brother priests and bishops for remaining true to the Magisterium, and now they were receiving the same treatment from society at large because a small number of their fellow clergy had perpetrated what the Pope has called "this filth."[23]

The sorts of things that contributed to the existence of such circumstances slowly started to turn around in the 1990s, however. Seminaries around the US and other parts of the Western world began noticing a marked change in the number of seminarians and their theological worldview. They would be dubbed "Generation John Paul" for their reflection of the resurgent emphasis on traditional Church teaching, devotions, and identity promoted by Bl. John Paul II.

As you would expect, this alarmed many who had worked hard and invested their lives and hopes on building a radically different Church, on achieving a revolution, really. Others simply derided the new breed of seminarians. For instance, a highly patronizing and thus disappointing 1999 *Commonweal* editorial asked, "Can seminarians who believe there is some 'supernatural element' to priestly garb or who talk blithely about guardian angels and fawningly about the pope's every utterance, make themselves heard by an educated and questioning laity? They're going to give it the old seminary try!"

What both groups had in common was a fear that these priests would turn back the clock on Vatican II, or, as the same *Commonweal* editorial put it, "What the seminarians confidently proclaim to be 'the future' of the church looks and sounds a great deal like the past—the 1950s to be precise."[24]

Neither faction could consider the possibility that their reading of the conciliar documents had been wrong, and that thus their vision of Catholicism was hopelessly skewed. If we want evidence of their faulty appraisal, however, it exists quite amply in the precipitous drops in every indicator of the Church's health, not the least of which was the number of young men entering seminaries.

And now that number is finally starting to climb, yet another sign that the tide is turning. Granted, the numbers aren't huge. Indeed, in a world of one billion Catholics, they're a drop in the bucket. Nonetheless, there are 5,000 more Catholic priests in the world in 2009 than there were in 1999.

Many African and Asian seminaries are bursting at the seams, and their students are often sent to Europe and North America. In European countries where the new orthodoxy has been slower to emerge, we see a crisis in vocations. However, where orthodoxy is embraced as in the Diocese of Regensburg, Germany, there, too, we see vocations rising. Even France saw a slight increase in the number of ordinations there, with 106 in 2011 versus 96 in 2010. That is very much needed in a nation where half of diocesan priests are over 75 years old.[25]

In that same period the number of French college-level seminarians increased by 10 to 312, although the number of graduate seminarians fell by 32 to 398. This is the diocesan picture, however. Groups that adhere to historical Catholic belief and praxis are doing better. For instance, the St. Martin Community had 60 seminarians in 2011 with eight priestly ordinations.

Sadly, the number of French women religious has not seen such good fortune. Their numbers continue to drop, with a total of 28,000 in 2010, which is a drop of 20,000 within just a decade.

It's Hip to Be Square

In *The Tide Is Turning Toward Catholicism*, I mentioned the disparity in vocations in those dioceses with a strong attachment to a more traditional Catholic identity, largely seen as passé and almost rube-like, compared to those where the bishop, chancery, priests, and laymen (or all of the above) continued to act as though the Second Vatican Council was a radical break with our shared Catholic past. How to explain the difference? Archbishop Edwin O'Brien neatly summed up the reason for this when he said that a man will give his life for a mystery but not a question mark.[26]

The purveyors of both liberal Protestantism and Catholicism have no doubt been sincere and hardworking in their pursuit of a different form of Christianity than that which history has ever held as orthodox (literally, "right believing"). For decades now, however, the unfortunate end of all that hard work has been leaving people leaving those churches in droves.

Consider the following: Mainline communions once had the majority of American Protestants, with their numbers peaking sometime before 1959. Between 1960 and 1988, however, membership in these denominations dropped by nearly 20 percent to 25 million. By 2005, that number had plummeted another 16 percent to 21 million, totaling a loss of 10 million people in just 45 years. No longer are they American Christianity's dominant force. Instead, they are the minority.[27]

The hemorrhaging has not stopped, either. From 2010 to 2011, the United Methodist Church lost an additional 1.01 percent of its followers, the main body of Lutherans in the US dropped from their rolls an additional 1.96 percent, the Presbyterians declined by 2.61 percent, and the Episcopalians fell by 2.48 percent.[28]

We have also seen situation befall Catholicism in certain parts of the US, particularly the Northeast, which was once the bastion of our holy religion in this land. Today, however, the Church there is on life support, with that region having lost more Catholics than any other in the United States.

A report by the Program on Public Values at Trinity College, in Hartford, Connecticut, says that, during the 1990s, "New England had a net loss of one million Catholics. Big losses in both the number of Catholic adherents and their proportion occurred also in Massachusetts, and in Rhode Island, the nation's most heavily Catholic state, where the proportion of Catholics dropped from 62 percent to 46 percent. New York State lost 800,000 Catholics, and they dropped from 44 percent to 37 percent of the adult population." The report's director said, "The decline of Catholicism in the Northeast is nothing short of stunning."[29]

This is made manifest in ordination numbers, particularly 64 to 6 and 14 to 4. What do I mean by that? When writing my first book in 2006, I noted that even though the Diocese of Rochester had more Catholics than the dioceses of Lincoln and Omaha combined, Rochester had six men studying for the priesthood while Lincoln and Omaha had a combined total of 64. That same year, the Archbishop Chaput-led Denver archdiocese had 14 young men ordained to the priesthood (11 in May, and three earlier in the academic year), while the more doctrinally flexible Archdiocese of Los Angeles had four.

This is a staggering statistic when one considers that the Archdiocese of Los Angeles has 4,300,000 Catholic residents compared to just 385,000 Catholics for the Archdiocese of Denver. In 2006, Los Angeles and Rochester were led by Roger Cardinal Mahony and Bishop Matthew Clark respectively, neither of whom could be accused of demanding a close adherence to the *Catechism* or a strong Catholic identity. At the same time, doctrinally authentic bishops led the other three sees.

The last available year for statistics was 2011, also the last year for Roger Cardinal Mahony of Los Angeles. That year, the Archdiocese of Los Angeles had a Catholic population of 4.2 million Catholics and 50 seminarians. The Diocese of Albany had a Catholic population of 334,000 with six seminarians, while the Diocese of Rochester had a Catholic population of 310,000 with eight seminarians. Juxtapose that with Denver, a more conservative archdiocese, which had 541,000 Catholics and 78 seminarians; Wichita, Kansas, with a Catholic population of 114,000 and 46 seminarians; and Lincoln, which had a Catholic population of 95,000 and 39 seminarians.

The statistics say a mouthful concerning the role of orthodox teaching, Catholic devotions, and a rigorous defense of the faith taught in these dioceses. Denver, Wichita, and Omaha are hardly outlier locations. For example, Arkansas has only 131,000 Catholics in the entire state, the smallest per capita in the nation, yet it has 35 seminarians. Mobile, Alabama, has only 66,000 Catholics in its diocese; it has 21 seminarians. The list could go on and on, but let me give you just a couple of more examples: Lafayette, Indiana, has only 95,000 Catholics but 28 seminarians, while Nashville has only 75,000 Catholics but 20 seminarians.[30]

All of that said, the most recent analysis shows that of the 20 most vocations-starved dioceses, only three are led by readily recognizable orthodox bishops (or were in 2008, the most recent data available). The rest are either in the Northeast and/or are led by bishops who are in little danger of being considered in league with Cardinal Dolan, Archbishop Chaput, Archbishop Carlson, and the like.

With the 20 most vocation-rich dioceses, on the other hand, practically every one of them is led by a certifiably faithful ordinary, and there is not a wobbler on doctrine in the bunch. Final good news note on this front: Despite poor dioceses and besides large student loans from their post-secondary schooling, an ever-younger group of young men are entering the priesthood. According to the May 2012 CARA study, "The Class of 2012: Survey of Ordinands to the Priesthood," just under 70 percent ordained in 2012 were between the ages of 25 to 34.

This marks the sixth straight year where the United States saw an ever larger percentage of younger men receive Holy Orders. Also worth noting: Of the 2012 class, 6 percent were converts, just under 30 percent were born outside of the US, over 80 percent have at least one parent who is Catholic, and roughly 30 percent have a relative who is a priest or religious. And get this: Prior to becoming a seminarian, about 20 percent attended a World Youth Day. Another big factor for the ordinands? Siblings. Over half of the new priests had more than two siblings, whereas 28 percent had five-plus brothers and sisters.

The Not-So-Blue Nuns

We can draw the same contrast when it comes to orders of women religious. Those that shrugged off a distinctive Catholic identity and/or traditional outward signs of their witness to Jesus Christ (such as a religious habit) 50 or so years ago are really struggling. Indeed, many haven't had a postulant in years.

However, if one wants to participate in Reiki or some other New Age practice or would prefer to pray "Our Mother" during Mass, these convents are the places to go. Mind you, this is not to be uncharitable or snide. Rather, it is based on people's very real experiences at retreat houses run by such orders of sisters.

On the other hand, orders such as the Dominican Sisters of Mary, Mother of the Eucharist, in Ann Arbor, Michigan, have struggles, too, but of a far different kind. Their difficulty is in finding room enough to hold the large number of young women coming to join them. The Ann Arbor Dominicans is not the only such order that is growing, either. The aforementioned Nashville Dominicans (from whom the Ann Arbor sisters spun off), the Carmelite Sisters of the Most Sacred Heart in Los Angeles, and others are experiencing similar growing pains.

In the time since my previous book came out, a variety of stories surfaced in the Catholic media that expanded on the theme that the tide truly is turning on the vocations front. Besides some of the dioceses mentioned above, new centers of vocational upsurges were seen across the country. For instance, take the only Vatican-owned property in the United States, the Pontifical College Josephinum. Located in the Diocese of Columbus, Ohio, it is under the direction of newly appointed rector Fr. Joseph Wehner, who has guided the institution in such a way that it has seen its numbers rise some 53 percent in recent years. As a result, the Josephinum currently has the largest number of young men studying within its walls in some 30 years.

A New Breed of Men and Women Religious

None of this is to whitewash any obvious problems. To ignore certain data and highlight the above information is not to look at the Catholic world with rose-colored glasses. Rather, it is simply to accentuate the positive, because 30 years ago, could we have said any of this about the Church?

Today, however, is a new day. It's a day of hope, the sort of hope Our Lord Jesus Christ always encourages us to have, come what may. There are just so many good things happening for which to praise and thank him, the new breed of bishops, priests, religious, and seminarians being just a few of them.

FOUR
THE NUMBER OF CONVERTS KEEPS INCREASING

They kept coming into the Church, year after year, sometimes over 150,000 of them. Yet this was occurring during the first decade of the new millennium, the same time as the sex-abuse scandal was rocking the Church. And yet still the converts came. Why? After listening to their deep discernment, it is as though the converts are saying "Why *wouldn't* we?"

The converts coming into the Church or those reverting back to their Catholic faith have not taken this decision lightly. They have prayed, studied, and pondered. Often their decision causes consternation among their families. However, after lengthy and serious consideration and prayerful discernment, other options left them cold. A parade of Evangelical heavyweights, many of whom were once openly hostile to Catholicism, have entered the Catholic Church in the last 20 years or so.

As already mentioned, Scott Hahn, PhD, an admitted anti-Catholic in his teenage and college years, came into the Church in the 1980s. He has become a fixture on EWTN and teaches at the Franciscan University of Steubenville. Dr. Hahn loves the Scriptures and the Church's traditions, and heaven help the person who would argue against him.

During the 1980s, along with Scott Hahn came many others who, like him, felt like they were reading some Scriptures for the first time. The sacraments, especially the Eucharist and confession, which

The Number of Converts Keeps Increasing 83

they once had roundly condemned, were now having new meaning with verses like John 6:32-63 and 20:19-23.

For instance, Dr. Kenneth Howell—18 years a Presbyterian pastor and seven years a theology professor—came into the Catholic Church in 1996. A former classmate of Dr. Hahn's, his story became known to those who frequently watch EWTN's *The Journey Home* and/or who attend fellow-convert Marcus Grodi and his Coming Home Network's Deep in History Conferences held annually in Columbus, Ohio.

However, it was Dr. Howell's sudden firing from the University of Illinois that many will remember, for it made the rounds on the various national news outlets. Dr. Howell was fired simply for laying out the rationale for the Catholic Church's teaching on homosexuality while teaching a course on religion. A student objected and, though Howell was later reinstated, the firing spoke volumes concerning political correctness. However, Howell owes his reinstatement to the huge volume of letters, emails, and faxes that bombarded the university, many of which came from students and other young people across the nation. Alumni threatening to withhold donations didn't hurt, either.

Even the Church's teaching authority—established with the Pope and Magisterium, which is often the target of Evangelicals and Fundamentalists, found new meaning in Matthew 16:16-20. It was as if the scales that once were in Paul's eyes now fell from their eyes.

Sometimes God works in ways which at the time seems to have no particular relevance, but only later do we realize his methods and purposes. Dr. Robert Webber was once an evangelical who later became an orthodox Episcopalian, and wrote a landmark book in the late 1980s called *Evangelicals on the Canterbury Trail*.[1]

The book would initially bring many into the orthodox (i.e., Anglo-Catholic) wing of the Episcopal Church through its emphasis on ancient liturgical worship. Two Catholic converts who give some credit for their conversion to Webber's book are Fr. Dwight Longenecker, a graduate of the anti-Catholic Bob Jones University, and Fr. Al Kimel.[2] Additionally, over 1,000 former Campus Crusade for Christ members joined the Orthodox Church, which was documented in the book *Becoming Orthodox*.[3] Some later found their way to Rome and converted to Catholicism.

Why are these points relevant to the tide turning toward Catholicism? Simply put, the reason these people "swam the Tiber" (or the Bosphorus or the Dnieper) was the sacraments, especially the Eucharist, and their attraction to these as engendered by ancient forms of liturgical worship. For others, such as Marcus Grodi, it was the authority Catholics believe Jesus gave to Peter and his successors, as well as to the apostles and those of their successors who teach in union with him. Since the Catholic Church is protected by the Holy Spirit, they have learned that she is the only surety for objective truth in matters of Christian faith and morals.

A Reason to Convert

As the New Millennium dawned, the mainstream media was full of stories about the declining health of Pope John Paul II. Then, when the sex-abuse scandal broke, the stories were all about this admittedly horrific crisis in the Catholic Church. We had an ailing Pope and a tsunami-like devastating scandal: How could the Church not lose members? many asked.

And while it is true that numbers of US converts steadily declined on the whole after 2002 (from its high-water mark in 2000, no less), nonetheless, large numbers of people were and are still coming into the Church. In the UK Church, although the numbers were not large, some very prominent people became Catholic. Lord Nicholas Windsor did so in 2001 and has since become one of his nation's most articulate voices for the Culture of Life (Lord Nicholas' mother, Duchess Katharine of Kent, became Catholic in 1994, becoming the first royal to do so since the deathbed conversion of Charles II). His nephew and heir apparent to the dukedom of Kent, Lord Edward Windsor, entered the Church in 2004, while Edward's sister Lady Marina-Charlotte Windsor did so in 2008.

While many in the media may have seen an ailing Pope, believers like these saw a mighty man who had survived an assassination attempt, helped end communism, proclaimed the truth and led the Church toward a more orthodox path, and who did all in his power—including traveling around the world—to spread the "good news."

On this side of the Atlantic, the Church continued to draw the most unlikely of converts. Consider Michael Cumbie. Raised a Baptist (he calls himself a former pew-jumping Baptist), he eventually became a Pentecostal minister. However, the verses to which he saw Catholics refer—"proof texts," if you will on beliefs such as the Eucharist, confession, and apostolic authority—perplexed him. He acknowledged them—he had to; the evidence was right there in front of him—yet he could barely remember ever encountering those citations. Catholicism could answer the questions he had, and thus another convert was good. (The Church is *really* good about doing that kind of thing, you know.)

One of the more dramatic conversion events to happen in the Catholic Church concerned that of Alex Jones (now Deacon Alex Jones). A successful Pentecostal pastor in a large prominent African-American Church in Detroit, it had bothered him for years that if the Catholic Church was as biblically corrupt as he had been taught, why did God allow Catholicism to survive?

The thoughts troubled him and kept building until he finally placed a call to fellow Michigander and recent convert Steve Ray. Jones thought someone like Ray would be able to understand his plight. After a period of discernment and family bewilderment, Jones, his family, and much of his congregation came into the Church. Jones now travels the country speaking about the Faith.

Different *Papa*, Same Situation

As I noted in the first chapter of my previous book, the death of Pope John Paul II saw some 5 to 7 million people descend upon Rome—a quarter of whom were under the age of 25—a number that left many of the media and the cultural elite befuddled. It was as if they could simply not wrap their minds around these huge numbers and were thinking, 'Hey, you kids, don't you see the amount of trouble Catholicism is in? Don't you recognize how backward/patriarchal/undemocratic/(throw in your own uncomplimentary adverbial) this Pope was? Why would so many of you come?' Some explained it away as a cult of personality sort of thing, since Bl. John Paul was the only pope most young people had ever known.

However, these people came for the same reason that their elder brothers and sisters in the faith came: John Paul was a great man who made an impact and showed what one man can do. Some merely came out of curiosity. For instance, *ABC News* ran a report on a Canadian man in his early twenties who was traveling through Europe at the time. Since he found himself near Rome when John Paul died, he rerouted his itinerary simply to take part in history and the spectacle of it all.

At the beginning of the report, this young man appeared bemused, and he admitted that while Catholic, he knew little about his Faith and practiced it to no great extent. The story then broke away to other interviews, etc. At the end of this piece, the reporter came back to the Canadian. Since the sky in background had the hue of thick twilight, one could tell several hours had passed. The last shot, presented mostly in silence, was of this young fellow on his knees, his head bowed, his fingers working a rosary, and his voice praying along with the others. Remember, this man had admitted knowing little of his faith. John Paul II was evidently still getting converts. It was beautiful.

After Joseph Cardinal Ratzinger's election, the media came to the conclusion that St. Peter's Square would be empty for his installation as Pope. After all, who would have any interest in seeing an octogenarian, German (with not so subtle implications of Nazism), doctrinaire become leader of a rule bound, joy killing, medieval, hierarchical, patriarchal institution that surely would start dying any day now?

Well, we know the rest of the story, don't we? From his installation to this very day, Benedict XVI has drawn record crowds for his Wednesday General Audiences and his Sunday Angelus addresses. *Record drawing* ... as in, he attracts *more* people than Bl. John Paul II, the supposedly better communicator. Benedict is moving people's souls. He is touching their hearts by making them think. That ability has certainly contributed to some fascinating converts.

April 2007 saw the entrance into the Church of the aforementioned Dr. Francis Beckwith. The professor told *National Catholic Register* stated that over time and reading the works of the last two popes, he began to appreciate the Catholic Church. However, it was after reading the early Church Fathers and the writings of the Council of Trent that he could no longer say he wasn't Catholic.

The *Register* interview was a smorgasbord of reasons why people left the Church, why many have returned, and why still more are coming "home." Speaking of the late 1970s, for instance, Dr. Beckwith said that while he appreciated the "hip priests" trying to understand and relate to the youth, he felt that these clerics were missing the point somehow.

Consider also the guitar, or "folk," Masses. While trying to be relevant for the young and draw something then perceived as good from the era, they could never really compete with the times. As Beckwith put it, "We already had Bob Dylan and Neil Young; why would I listen to something at Mass which was a cheap imitation?"[4]

In addition to the already mentioned heavyweights, there were also the bombshell conversions of Norma McCorvey—aka, plaintiff "Jane Roe" of *Roe v. Wade*—and Dr. Bernard Nathanson, founding father of the National Abortion Rights Action League in 1968.

For her part, McCorvey had lived a hardscrabble life during the 1960s. The product of a troubled childhood and a ninth-grade dropout, she ended up in reform school and found herself married at 16. McCorvey's husband often beat her. She left him, returning home pregnant with his child, which her mother later raised.

She got pregnant a second time, and left the father to raise the child per mutual agreement. After that, Norma bounced around doing odd jobs from bartender to carnival barker, all the while getting involved in sexual relationships with both men and women, as well as experimenting with drugs.

After getting pregnant a third time at age 21 and desperately trying to get the baby aborted, she agreed to be part of the 1970 class-action lawsuit challenging Texas' strong stand against abortion (it was allowed only in the case of rape or incest, so McCorvey pled rape, which she later said wasn't true). Two feminist lawyers had been looking for a case with which to challenge the illegality of abortion. With Norma, and after three year of trials and appeals, they had it: the infamous 1973 Supreme Court Roe v. Wade case, which led to legalized abortion across the nation.

By this time, the pregnancy had come to term and Norma put the baby girl up for adoption. Somewhere today, there is a 39-year-old woman who lived so that millions could die. Ironic, no? In any event, McCorvey kept her anonymity but during the 1980s agreed to help the pro-choice forces by coming out of the shadows and doing media appearances for the abortion cause.

In an odd series of events, McCorvey met Rev. Flip Benham of Operation Rescue, whose offices had located near that of a Dallas women's clinic. Benham would politely try to engage McCorvey in conversation. He even got her to visit him at his place of work. While there, McCorvey noticed posters that showed fetal development. Afterward, McCorvey felt abortion was something she could no longer defend. After some time, she agreed to be baptized. She felt comfortable in Benham's church studying about Christianity and the Bible. However, the more she learned, the more she felt the Catholic Church was the one she recognized from her studies.

On August 17, 1998, in a Mass concelebrated by Fr. Edward Robinson, OP, who instructed her, and Fr. Frank Pavone, director of Priests for Life, McCorvey came into the Catholic Church.[5] McCorvey told the Dallas diocesan newspaper, the *Texas Catholic*, that after receiving the Eucharist, she felt "a real sense of inner peace."[6] McCorvey has continued her work of speaking up for the unborn throughout the country.

By his own admission, on the other hand, Dr. Nathanson was ruthless in his pursuit of abortion.[7] He admitted he had a truly evil zest for abortion, once threatening a woman who was carrying his child that if she didn't abort the baby, he would personally find a way to abduct her and do it himself. She consented, and he aborted his own child.

By the late 1970s, with the growing medical data of life beginning at conception as well as the burgeoning use of ultrasound with pregnant women, the burden of what he had done became overwhelming. He began pouring through the philosophers in an endless search for the truth. Providentially, Nathanson found a book by an old professor of his at McGill University in Montreal, the noted psychoanalyst Dr. Karl Stern. To his surprise, Nathanson found that Stern had converted to Catholicism, which became very helpful as Nathanson probed the various thoughts and ideas that would cause someone who was a secular Jew to explore Catholicism.

In addition to the Scriptures, Nathanson was exposed to Catholic writers such as St. Teresa of Avila and other doctors of the Church, which helped him to understand the realities of truth, reason, and the miraculous. The doctor also had Fr. C. John McCloskey to help him through the intellectual minefield that confronts many skeptics on their road to Rome. With the help of this Opus Dei priest, Nathanson became a Catholic in 1996. At the same time, this man who had performed 75,000 abortions did an about-face and joined the pro-life movement, appearing on many pro-life videos and speaking across the country before his death on February 21, 2011.

One would think conversions like Nathanson's and McCorvey's would make for compelling news stories. Two prominent members of the pro-abortion movement came to Catholicism within two years of each other. Ironically, if one checks an Internet search engine for the years 1996 and 1998, one will find more media coverage given to Catholic dissident Frances Kissling and her unequivocal support for abortion, not to mention of her denunciation of the teachings of the Catholic Church, than on the conversion of McCorvey and Nathanson, two towering figures in the pro-choice movement.

One of the most courageous examples of a Benedict-era convert came in the person of Magdi Allam, an Egyptian-born journalist who has worked in Italy since the early 1970s. After pondering the move for years, he was received into the Church by Pope Benedict in the Basilica of St. Peter at the Easter Vigil Mass in 2008. Some in the West took issue with His Holiness and Allam for making the conversion so public and possibly provoking the wrath of radical Islam.

First, Benedict's personal reception of Allam was appropriate because it is Benedict who the journalist most credits with his conversion. Second, the Holy Father and Allam weren't about to be cowed by what a group of violent extremists might do in response to a yearly event that happens in most churches of the Catholic faith, including ones where Islam is the predominant religion. In any event, it was much ado about nothing. So far no harm has come from the situation. Let us pray that none ever will.

World Youth Day

Under-the-radar political or social movements that change history often happen out in the open for all to see. However, those whom society deems as having the power to recognize these changes in society are often busily studying what they believe to be the latest trend, which all too often never materializes or quickly fades into the mists of history.

In the summer of 2008, most of the mainstream media were fixated on then-Senator Obama's tour of the Middle East and Europe. All three network news anchors broadcast live on location.

Yet, half a world away in Sydney, Australia, an event that was truly changing history was taking place, one few besides the Catholic media even bothered to notice. Between 200,000 and 500,000 young people gathered at various World Youth Day events. They came to hear the successor of St. Peter instruct the young on the ways of faith and life. They left changed and fervent to spread the good news of this "New Pentecost," as Pope Benedict XVI had dubbed it.

Pope John Paul II had begun World Youth Day in 1986 as a small Palm Sunday gathering ministering to the youth of the Church.[8] By the end of his pontificate, it would arguably be the biggest promoter of vocations for the young and would push the stereotypes, which suggested that the young had no use for organized religion—especially the Catholic Church—out the window.

World Youth Day would occur every year in Rome. However, every second or third year the event would take place on alternating continents.

The first World Youth Day to take place outside of Rome occurred in 1987 in Buenos Aires, Argentina. This was followed by World Youth Day 1989 in Santiago de Compostela, Spain, and 1991 in Czestochowa, Poland. Then, as we have already discussed, there was the 1993 World Youth Day in Denver.

The script couldn't have been written any better if it were written in Hollywood. Disaster was predicted, enormous success was what actually happened. Some 15 years later, that success is still being measured. Not only were the Catholic media out in force, but even the secular media and the youth-oriented MTV channel were there. Many from the secular media were somewhat perplexed as to why so many Catholic young people would show up to see an elderly man talk about the old, even antiquated, crusty Catholic Church.

Since then, there have been many more World Youth Days and many more perplexed onlookers. There have also been many more young people joyfully experiencing what is by all accounts a fun event and persuasively explaining why they were there. For many it was the chance to learn more about their faith, and for others it was the best way to show gratitude for the Pontiff whose burdens they knew were many.

In *The Tide Is Turning Toward Catholicism*, I demonstrated how the 1993 World Youth Day in Denver was a turning point and indeed one of the three critical dates to which one can irrefutably say the tide had started to turn. As I noted, one such reason was a showdown that occurred between ETWN's Mother Angelica and the bureaucrats at the US Conference of Catholic Bishops. If you watched EWTN that fateful day, you may never forget Mother Angelica's mini-meltdown over the subtle and not-so-subtle ways that US Church authorities tried to push what she clearly saw as a liberal agenda during the Pontiff's visit. Mother Angelica wasn't about to let this happen on her watch.

The Number of Converts Keeps Increasing

For the first time anywhere, a detailed account of the behind-the-scenes showdown can be read here. Michael Barone, who produced the *Mother Angelica Live* show was on hand and provides for us this account:[9]

> "There's always a chain of command for television. There's a pool feed for all of the events that took place at Cherry Park or Mile High Stadium, etc. We were really excited to be able to broadcast wheels-down, wheels-up coverage for World Youth Day. There was a great enthusiasm at EWTN for the Holy Father coming to the United States, and we were dutifully trying to cover everything offered at World Youth Day.
>
> While the Holy Father had retired for the day, the activities went on and the crew was coming and going while the day was winding down. The Fountain Square Fools [stage troupe were] doing their theatrical portrayal of the Stations of the Cross.[1] Somewhere along the early Stations of the Cross it was brought to Mother Angelica's attention that the actor portraying Jesus didn't look like a man.
>
> Mother by nature was slow to anger; she was a kindly grandmother to us all. However, slowly but surely she became angry that people were passing the buck with regard to what was happening.
>
> Mother asked some of the assembled staff to ascertain what was going on, though she didn't seem overly bothered at this point. However, the thought was that if it was a woman, we would just go on to our daily wrap-up, since this would certainly not be something we would be a part of or our audience would want to see.
>
> My guess is the first [people] contacted said they didn't know if it was a woman, and they didn't seem to care if it was. However, more calls were made and finally we were told not to worry; it was a man.

One of the EWTN employees, who wasn't Catholic, said, "I hate to say this to a nun but those are breasts—that's not a man," while still being told by various callbacks from event organizers that the actor portraying Jesus was a man. Mother Angelica became increasingly angered because she knew the hoops Dana [Scallon] had to jump through to get on the air while the organizers were lying to her, knowing the person portraying Jesus was a woman.

Mother felt this was a terrible outrage since so many organizers knew this was a woman, lied to her, and the network along with the viewers, but finally the Pope were all deceived by organizers whose agenda seemed to be women's ordination. Mother Angelica then let her feelings known in a legendary outburst of righteousness:

"You've made your statement: Now I'm making mine. I believe in this Church. I believe in this Pontiff. I believe in what the Church teaches, and I am convinced that unless we follow that light we will be in utter darkness. Total darkness.

"As Catholics, we've been terribly quiet all these years. Those beautiful Vatican II documents that were inspired by the Holy Spirit have been misrepresented and misportrayed [sic]... You have a right before God and this nation to do what you do, but I resent you trying to destroy the Catholicity of the simple and the poor and the elderly by your ways."

Looking back some 20 years later, Michael Barone commented:

For those of us at the network working World Youth Day, it was a little bit of a lag time when you are in the midst of a major event, but Mother knew what was going on; it was intentional deception. The smoke had entered the sanctuary. It was like Jesus in the

Temple; it was righteous indignation. It wasn't personal for Mother; it was that to her the Lord was being mocked and shabbily treated by those with a nefarious agenda. There was no apology to the network from the organizers. Coming to work with EWTN, I had heard about Mother's mystical visions of seeing St. Michael and building the radio network in a area that everyone thought couldn't work and yet it did. The experience reminded of me of St. Catherine of Siena telling the powers that be in her era that they were leading the Church astray; so it was with Mother Angelica at Denver in 1993.

In some ways Mother Angelica's famous and righteous outburst was a turning point for the Church in the US. Not only did many Catholics warmly receive it, but she also took it upon herself to show a more classic view of the religious world.

After this, she decided she wanted her community to return to their roots, and its members began wearing the traditional Poor Clare habit. She also became more pointed in her jabs. For instance, Mother increasingly used phrases along the lines of, "If you want to find a policeman or firefighter, you know what to look for; if a priest or nun looks like everyone else, what does that say about how serious they take their profession?"

The Road Less Traveled

Denver's World Youth Day was a fork in the road for the American church. After this, the radical breaks with Catholicism's past and the innovations of those whom Pope Benedict says look at the Council with a "hermeneutic of rupture" (i.e., who took the catch-all "spirit of the Council" as an invitation to reinvent the Church's proverbial wheel all over again) began to quickly lose steam. At the same time, the good things we have discussed really got into gear and began moving.

The 1990s were an economic boom time for the United States and the rest of the West. It even saw the emergence of Indian and China as budding economic powerhouses. However, these prosperous years also appeared to have brought with them a reversion to a time of unabashed promiscuity. Sometimes this was even promoted through their actions by those who many regarded as being amongst the pillars of society. Between 1988 and 1995, the percentage of teen females engaging in intercourse rose eight points to 19 percent. By the decade's end, more than half of teens aged 15 to 19 claimed they had lost their virginity.[10]

The problem was not just in America, obviously. In 2008, the UK's *Daily Mail* reported that around half of new STD infections were from those under 25 years old, although the group amounts to only 12.5 percent of the population. Indeed, in that same year, 400,000 Britons reported STDs, the highest number since the British government started keeping records in the 1970s. The under-25 cohort had two-thirds of new Chlamydia cases, 55 percent of the genital warts cases, and when all but women ages 16-24 were factored out, these females accounted for 75 percent of new Chlamydia and gonorrhea cases. The same government's statistics show that abortion has soared amongst the young, with a large number of girls having had four abortions by age 18.[11]

Afterwards, young people who had attended 1993 WYD would recognize the toll of the promiscuous 1990s—the "Culture of Death," as Bl. John Paul II called it—and it prompted many to study and promote the "Culture of Life" they had heard so much about at the Denver event. It is no accident that those most involved in promoting not just abstinence but the deeper, richer, and much more fulfilling vision of chastity belong to WYD '93 generation.

The seeds of Denver are also still bearing fruit years later in the number of lay and clerical people currently active in the Church who had attended the event or even simply watched it on television. We also see it in large number of those who went to Denver and realized their vocation there. If we remember the 1993 World Youth Day by the vocations it produced and the growth in youth ministry in America it engendered, then we will remember the 1995 World Youth Day in Manila for its sheer numbers. It was the largest World Youth Day and the largest crowd ever to see a pontiff or attend a Mass.

Some suggest it might have been the largest gathering ever assembled on the planet. Estimates of up to 7 million people have been reported. Granted, most of these people came from the Philippines, the only majority Catholic nation in Asia. Nonetheless, this event showed the strength of the ability of the Faith to hold and attract adherents. If we can take this as evidence of its power to evangelize—whether in lands for which the New Evangelization was born or those that have had a less than full exposure to the gospel—we can tap into something that is nuclear in terms of its supernatural strength. And the thing is that it wouldn't be hard.

However, an event so sinister that to this day it is hard to fathom nearly cost the Holy Father and many others their lives on January 15, 1995, during the event. Prior to the event's opening, a hitherto unheard of group called al-Qaeda had planned a massive attack that would have resulted in the deaths of thousands, including Blessed John Paul II.

Called the Bojinka Plot, it was the demonic brainchild of Khalid Sheik Mohammad, mastermind of the September 11, 2001, attacks. Mohammad planned to use a suicide attack to assassinate the Holy Father (he got the idea from suicide attackers in Sri Lanka). A man dressed as a priest was supposed to get close to the motorcade and blow himself up. Following that, over a dozen airliners with 4,000 passengers returning from Asia to the US were to have been blown from the sky as they left Manila. For the believer, it would seem as if the Holy Spirit intervened to spare the lives of so many, including the Holy Father.

What caused the plan to go awry? By the blessing of Divine Providence, the night before the al-Qaeda terror squad was to have executed its plan, some of the chemicals for the bombs caught fire in the group's rented apartment. With the arrival of police investigators, the operation ended before it came to fruition.[12]

World Youth Day 1997 took place in Paris, and once again over 1 million attended. Some three years later, World Youth Day 2000 came home to Rome, where it had originated. Celebrated in the midst of the Jubilee Year, World Youth Day attendees were surrounded by scenes and images from the dawn of Christianity. There they gathered in the ancient city where St. Peter, with the spiritual keys that Jesus gave him, ruled the Church literally from the underground. They saw the very places where both he and the Church's greatest missionary St. Paul were martyred within a few years of each other.

World Youth Day Toronto in 2003 would be the last for Pope John Paul II. The ravages of Parkinson's Disease had made him exceedingly frail. Everyone knew how hard it must have been for him to travel so far. Yet there he was in their midst, which delighted the jubilant crowd. Many might have secretly thought that this would be his last World Youth Day. Despite the evident toll his disease was having on him, the simple fact that he was there spoke volumes about the fact that suffering was not useless.

As he did with his death two years later, he demonstrated that when suffering is taken with the proper spirit—that is, when we unite our sufferings with those of Jesus on the cross for the salvation of souls—that suffering, far from being some monstrous evil, is salvific and has purpose. John Paul II was teaching the young in attendance as well as the world this terribly important message, one that our world desperately needs to understand but of which it is so dismissive.

After his death in April 2005, some wondered whether the new German pontiff Benedict XVI would even attend. Why this was a question since the event was already scheduled not only in his homeland, but in Cologne, a city where he taught for several years, is admittedly a tad befuddling. Then again, those in the news media can sometimes ask questions just to ask questions, so take it for what it's worth.

When it was announced that he would attend (I'd hate to have been the guy who bet all his dough on Benedict saying "No"), many pundits turned their speculation to the theory that future World Youth Days might fizzle with the party-pooper leadership of this allegedly "authoritarian German Pontiff." However, the young people answered that question with by warmly greeted the new Holy Father by chanting, "Benedetto ... [clap, clap, clap-clap, clap] ... Benedetto ..." Many of the English-speaking pilgrims were clad with shirts that said, "I love my German Shepherd."

Some in the news media even speculated that when the youth got a hold of the oh-so-extreme level of *über*-conservatism in the new Pope, they might turn to the theological Left, by golly. Some of the Church's old-guard liberals and dissidents even circulated talk of starting a Counter World Youth Day in Cologne, Germany, to showcase where they wanted to go. After the idea was mocked by, the dissidents claimed it had *really* never been their intention to stage such an event.

The Holy Father's talks to the young were greeted warmly and, more importantly, they listened to him. Many went home mulling over his astute and thought-provoking words. Some even went on to study them in greater depth. His insights seemed to captivate the young much like the instructions one might receive from a revered grandfather. Cologne's World Youth Day was an overwhelming success, and the smile and look of joy on the face of the man many affectionately call "B16" seemed to say it all.

World Youth Day Australia

In 2008, Pope Benedict XVI, along with several hundred

thousand young people, ventured to Australia for World Youth Day. What is interesting about Australia is that we don't know the name of the Portuguese mariner who discovered her, but we do know the name he gave this rich, in places mysterious, and everywhere beautiful land: *"La Australia de Espiritu Santo"* (The Great Southern Land of the Holy Spirit). How fitting, then, that the theme for this WYD was "You will receive power when the Holy Spirit has come upon you; and you will be my witnesses" (Acts 1:8).

WYD '08 was the first time the event had ever been in Oceania. This meant that, because of the enormous travel distances from Europe and the Americas, crowds would be smaller. However, its location would give those in other parts of Oceania and nearby Asia a chance to see the German Pope.

It was also an interesting test: Many had booked their WYD '05 plans for Cologne because they figured they would see John Paul II. This was the first WYD where Benedict XVI was the indisputable main draw. How would he do?

In the end, he did very well, if we are to judge the event by how well the popes leading them enkindle in the young faithful and their chaperones an awareness of what it means to be authentically Catholic. Indeed, World Youth Day has increasingly been seen as a way for pontiffs to tell large audiences what is on their mind as it relates to the Church's issues and direction.

Before leaving for Sydney, Pope Benedict XVI made it known he would give Communion only to those who would receive it on the tongue while kneeling (the traditional way of receiving the sacrament in the Latin Church for most of its history). While at World Youth Day, the Holy Father presided over an evening Vigil Mass in which he gave a sermon directed at the youth. It concluded with a dusting off of another age-old tradition in the Church: Benediction and Adoration of the Blessed Sacrament after the dismissal. It was no secret that this Holy Father felt the Church should more firmly embrace her traditions, and World Youth Day was a large stage in which to show it.

After a 20-hour plane ride to Sydney, the Holy Father rested at an Opus Dei retreat center on the outskirts of the city, which gave Sydney's Cardinal George Pell the opportunity to celebrate the World Youth Day opening Mass. His Eminence gave a homily that was gripping and displayed something of a more muscular Christianity than would have been seen some years ago. It must have been a stirring homily, as even some of Sydney's admittedly non-religious journalists seemed impressed.

> The gospel parable of the sower and the seed remind you of the great opportunity you have to embrace your vocation and produce an abundant harvest one hundred-fold crop.[13]

Even if the homily didn't impress observers, the overflow capacity crowd of 500,000 must have. After all, many pilgrims were turned away to watch the Mass via closed circuit TV.

Two days after he arrived, Pope Benedict made his World Youth Day appearance. On Thursday, July 17, 2008, the Holy Father traveled by boat to Sydney's harbor, disembarking for a short walk up a hill to a beautiful dockside location in Darling Harbour named Barangaroo, where he was to address the youth for the first time.

The visuals were breathtaking, and more than a few noticed the similarities between this arrival via boat and his arrival in Cologne, when he traveled down the Rhine. Some were convinced that this was fulfilling a prophecy of St. John Bosco, which is known as the "Two Pillar Vision." In this vision, Bosco envisioned a future pontiff arriving by boat to strengthen the Church.[14]

As previously noted, the official theme for WYD '08 was "You will receive power when the Holy Spirit has come upon you; and you will be my witnesses." His Holiness constantly repeated this theme, especially driving it home at the concluding Mass. The Holy Father reasoned that since so many had traveled to this end of the Earth, they would be like the first pilgrims in Jerusalem after Jesus' death and resurrection. Recall that these individuals were greeted with the spectacular presence of the Holy Spirit, and when they returned to their homes and explained the "Good News" to others.

Yet this wasn't the first time he had used the imagery of the first Pentecost to usher in a 21st century Pentecost. While visiting the United States earlier in 2008, the Holy Father used the "New Pentecost" motif in both Washington, DC, and New York.

During the latter days of his pontificate, Bl. John Paul II was fond of speaking about the New Springtime of Evangelization. The Polish Pontiff was simply commenting on what he was seeing around him, especially as it related to World Youth Day. Pope Benedict XVI built upon that theme, telling these ever-faithful young people that they mustn't keep the light under a bushel basket but share it with the world. Those who were at the first Pentecost spread the good news near and far, often under the most trying of circumstances. His Holiness reminded the faithful that, though the world calls one to a life of ease, Christ reminds us that we are to pick up our cross daily. The Gospel is not so much rejected as it is ignored, and the Holy Father encouraged the young that their mission was to remind their peers and even their parents that this is not the path a believer takes.

In the opening paragraph of both his address at the Vigil Mass and his homily at the closing Mass the following day, Pope Benedict XVI quoted from the first chapter of the Acts of the Apostles concerning Christ's great promise about the coming of the Holy Spirit. He implored the young people gathered in Sydney that they must heed the call of the Holy Spirit and spread the Good News to those around them. The message of his homily was even more pressing than that of the Vigil Mass. The Holy Father reminded the young people that he, the successor of St. Peter, has the same duty that they have to spread Christ's Good News to those near and far. He went on to ask them what kind of a world they would like to leave to the generation behind them, asking, "What difference will you make?" He both challenged them and reminded them that some generations have done more with their call than others. The Holy Spirit would give them the power necessary to help bring people to Christ's message, but they must first agree to answer the call.

When World Youth Day began, the Australian media was filled with stories of young people who ignored the Church, claiming the young people came to World Youth Day only because it was a chance to travel and meet new friends. The Australian media also reported on those who were not looking forward to the visit, from dissident groups to patrons of the local horse racetrack who wondered what toll several hundreds of thousands of young people would take on the track. However, as World Youth Day concluded, the mood of the media and the residents of Sydney was nearly unanimous: The event had been a rousing success for the city's spirit. Many reported that the city seemed friendlier as the pilgrims were departing.

Sydney's chief of police reported he couldn't remember when the crime rate had been so low. Not only did the pilgrims behave themselves, but their love was infectious and spread to those who might have tried to take advantage of such easy targets. Even though the young pilgrims had little money to spend and certainly nothing like most conventions would bring, the city seemed happy about the event, so much so that the police chief, who was not Catholic, wished "they could come every month."[15]

The success of World Youth Days also came to the attention of militant secularists. In August 2011, the Catholic youth of the world once again gathered, this time in Madrid. However, already ahead of their arrival, throngs of militant secularists tried to shut down the event with protests and cyber attacks. The mainstream media, and the BBC in particular, seemed to concentrate on the small group of demonstrators rather than the over one million gathered for the event.

World Youth Day Madrid

As previously noted, when the left-leaning UK newspaper *The Guardian* comes to the defense of the Holy Father with regard to the BBC's coverage of World Youth Day, one knows something is terribly amiss. Indeed, by the sheer venom contained in the attacks on the Holy Father and the pious young people who attend World Youth Days, we must be reminded of Jesus' words to the 72 when they came back and reported on what they saw: "I saw Satan falling from the sky" (Luke 10:17-18).

The young people at World Youth Day are taking the message of Christ from the Pope, who is Christ's personal representative on Earth, to the four corners of the world from which they came. The message given by both John Paul II and Benedict XVI to the youth over the years has been one of love, forgiveness of sins, redemption by Christ's sacrifice, and surrender to Christ.

This does not sit well with an increasingly militant and secularized culture that hates this message, for at its core it goes against our age's First Commandment, "Do what thou wilt." And although it was different on the surface from that of the communists, both groups had the same end. It is no coincidence that the 20th century saw more faithful Catholics and Christians of all stripes murdered than had died in all the previous 19. No part of Christianity was left untouched, and the stories of the last 100-plus years' martyrdoms are some of the most horrific we have. They also rank among the most heroic. Read the stories of the martyrs of Thailand, of the Congo, of the Chinese Trappist monks, of the Catholics in North Korea, and so on. They are fantastic, compelling stories that deserve telling.

Yet the secular world ignores them. Occasionally, however, it does celebrate those who killed these martyrs as "freedom fighters."

The Number of Converts Keeps Increasing

The networks have done retrospectives of those from America who fought "for freedom" on the side of the Republicans in the Spanish Civil War. Often mentioned is the cleverly named "Abraham Lincoln Brigade," the support it had from people such as singer Paul Robeson and writer Ernest Hemmingway (whose famed book *For Whom the Bell Tolls* was based on his experiences as a war correspondent during the conflict). Some members of the Brigade (which was really a battalion) were simply trying to check the fascist advance; the Nationalists were led by fascist Generalissimo Francisco Franco).

Many, if not most, however, were diehard American Communist Party members from New York City. Although several veterans of the ALB later became decorated veterans during World War II, so strongly were the ALB soldiers and the Soviets seen as being linked that the US government dictated that no Brigade veteran could serve as a commissioned officer. FBI chief J. Edgar Hoover wanted to make sure none even received a single decoration.[16] Yet has there ever been a network report done on the atrocities done to the Catholic faithful by these "freedom fighters?" The answer is no.

The atrocities committed by those who said they were fighting against fascism and for "democracy" are perhaps the least reported in the modern era. We are not talking about Christians being thrown to the lions in the third century, but something that happened in the lifetime of some of those reading this very book. Indeed, some are old enough to remember newspapers and newsreels featuring stories on the Spanish conflict.

Don McClarey, writing at the popular blog *The American Catholic,* noted the following with regard to the Spanish Civil War and those on the Spanish left who spewed verbal hatred and bile at the young people while they were praying at World Youth Day:

> At the beginning of the Spanish Civil War, forces on the Left in Spain massacred 283 nuns and sisters, 13 bishops,

4,172 diocesan priests, and 2,364 monks, friars, brothers and priests of religious orders. Their deaths were often accompanied with every cruelty and sacrilege the fertile minds of their tormentors could conjure up. There were atrocious massacres on both sides of the Spanish Civil War, but this mass murder of totally innocent men and women of God set the tone for the bitterness with which the War was conducted. Apparently the modern Spanish Left has not fallen far from the hatred of the Church that led to the crimes of their ideological forebears.[17]

According to the Wikipedia article, "Red Massacre in Spain," in Barbastro, 123 of the city's 140 secular priests—88 percent—lost their lives. In May 1931, 100 Church buildings fell victim to arson. Firefighters were on the scene only to make sure that the flames didn't spread to other buildings.

The communists/socialists still hold great influence in Spain (at the time of WYD '11, the socialists controlled the government), and there is still great division within Spanish society. This may help explain why the Church in Spain, as in most European countries, is on life support. To wit, while 94 percent of the nation's 40-plus million people have received baptism, and 54 percent attend only wedding and funeral Masses. Compare this to just 19 percent who go weekly or daily.

Furthermore, polls show there is basically little fidelity to the Church's moral teachings, most particularly among the young. There are also fewer clergy and religious. Since 1975, the number of the nation's priests has dropped 20.5 percent. However, the relatively slight 6.9 percent drop in women religious between 2000-2005 is not so bad, especially when compared to the continued decline in the US and elsewhere.

Perhaps the most compelling figure is that in a continent where secularism is ever on the rise, just 3 percent of Spaniards say the Church's teachings sway their decisions and form their values, versus all of Europe, where the figure is 7 percent.

This could explain why Benedict has visited Spain three times and why he chose Madrid for WYD '11. The Pope's concern for Spain is also a likely reason why the First World Congress of Catholic Universities took place in Avila.

The Congress focused on several themes Benedict XVI has highlighted during his pontificate. These included the need for a greater focus on an authentically Catholic identity at Church-related institutions, as well as the necessity of their showing that faith is not contrary to reason. Indeed, reason without faith and vice versa make either operate like a body with only one lung.

One area participants saw a particular need for this demonstration was in the sciences and the necessity to look at scientific advances in light of philosophical and theological considerations. However, it also would require philosophy and theology to struggle with new questions.

Prior to the event's start, a poll indicated that Benedict was likely very wise in putting so many of his eggs in the Spanish basket. It revealed that 90 percent of the nation's youth who would attend the event believed WYD is an "experience that changes your life." Furthermore, Zenit reported that:

> [N]ine out of 10 young people are looking to "have a new experience" (93%), to "spread the message of Jesus Christ" (92%), to "express their commitment to the Church" (90%), and to "satisfy their own spiritual anxieties" (90%).
>
> Of those interviewed, the majority were under 30, and one out of four had participated in a previous youth day. More than 60% had attended in Cologne (2005), and 44% had traveled to Sydney (2008).
>
> More than 98% of those surveyed who had attended a youth day said they positively value their experience (80% very positive and 18% positive).

> The youth said they also attended the youth days to meet people (87%) and to be with people who have the same values (88%).
>
> On the importance of the faith in their own life, 85% of those surveyed thought that believing in Christ helps to forgive others, 80% thought it contributes to being solidaristic and to helping those most in need, and 7% felt it is necessary to mature and be a better person.[17]

The Holy Father and the 1.5 million young people who gathered in Madrid, therefore, were in stark contrast to the increasingly angry voices coming out of the Spanish media and academia.

The voices of the Holy Father and the young people are those of love, redemption, and forgiveness, something the militant secular Left (a characterization based on the pictures of such folk screaming down WYD attendees who were praying on their knees) found hard to believe. However, what else would you expect? As we see by their words and deeds, they do not or will not believe. If they have been more formed by the culture than by our *Mater et Magistra*, then of course the Church's teachings will seem bizarre, repugnant, and necessary to oppose.

The secular humanists in Madrid seemed particularly baffled as to how an aging pontiff like Pope Benedict XVI could be able to connect with so many young people. After all, this Pontiff hardly possessed the same charisma as did his popular Polish predecessor. The UK's *Catholic Herald* Milo Yiannopoulos explored this phenomenon in some depth:

> John Paul II's Masses were sometimes uncomfortable marriages of prescribed ritual and modern culture, but there's a particular genius about the way the present Pope interprets his role. And observe how, acting

through his master of ceremonies, Msgr. Guido Marini, he stamped his authority—and, at the same time, his personality— on the papal visit to Britain. That authority came across as authentic and compelling. And young people have natural desire to attach themselves to such charismatic figures.

In Benedict XVI, the public and private seem to be in much closer harmony. His ability to blend his own personality with the grandeur of his office seems to be leading young people to feel a personal connection with him that they don't with a faceless diocesan bureaucracy.

His kindliness and grandfatherly demeanour [sic] appeal to them, because they seem more genuine than the cringe worthy attempts to "reach out" that young Catholics are so often made to suffer.

Many of the last few years' liturgical reforms and encouragements, such as the "Benedictine" altar arrangement, have the effect of reducing attention on the celebrant, while adding solemnity to the proceedings with their dramatic symbols and more elevating music.[18]

Perhaps to understand the lessons of World Youth Day, one has to look at the change they helped bring to the host cities and nation's. In the case of Denver, when then-Archbishop James Stafford met Pope John Paul II sometime after the history-making event, the Pope greeted him with the words, "Una rivoluzione." Tim Drake of the *National Catholic Register* delved into the success of Denver's World Youth Day by pointing out the long-term positive effects the archdiocese's youth ministry program has brought forth and the number of young men being ordained into the priesthood and young women entering religious life. Some 20 years later, the fruit continues to be seen.[19]

One certain fruit is that it has irrevocably awakened the Church to the need to engage youth as it never has before. Not in a way that is "relevant" and "hip" as in bygone days, but one that appeals to them, while still forming them with the truth (e.g., *YouCat*, which is a youth version of the *Catechism of the Catholic Church*).

As president of the Pontifical Council for Promoting New Evangelization, Archbishop Rino Fisichella told students taking a 2011 university summer course in Madrid titled "Young People and the Catholic Church: Points for a Youth Ministry for Today," the Church needs to "understand youth and their culture." It also must learn how to speak to a society where faith has been supplanted by a false notion of freedom and a belief that science trumps all.[20]

In Spain, Benedict's visits have given people the courage to express their faith, even though their many secular neighbors look askance at this. Indeed, the previously dormant social conservatives formed a movement and took to the streets with one million people in 2009 and 600,000 in 2010 to show their opposition to the socialist government's weakening of their society on everything from the protection of life in the womb, the role of religion in the public square, marriage, and an anti-Christian, same-sex agenda. These are unprecedented numbers in such a secular state. Both events had explicit backing from the nation's bishops, which was also unprecedented.[21]

Three months less one day after the close of WYD Madrid, a "snap" parliamentary election was called, four months earlier than scheduled. In it, the socialists failed to gain above 30 percent of the vote "for the first time since 1977."[22] Certainly the economic issues plaguing the nation were the key campaign issue. However, many believed the socialists had so often gone out of their way to poke the proverbial stick in the Vatican's eye that this had to have had an effect, as well.

Nothing good in this world will last, however, if it does not actively engage Christ and seek to submit to and then do his will. So when they come, the greatest expected fruits will, therefore, be spiritual. To this end, Zenit reported Fr. Ángel Alba, a Spanish campus minister based in Rome, as saying, "Just think that [WYD '11] is an event that also touches small villages where youth ministry has had no attraction and that, because of this event, because of the possibility of receiving people from other countries, such as Latin America, etc., [we] have seen a particular enthusiasm resurrected."[23]

FIVE
YOU CAN'T KEEP A GOOD CHURCH DOWN

For a host of reasons it seemed that after 2005, the floodgates had opened up against the beliefs Christians have always held. Attacks from atheists, liberal Christians, and folks from all realms left some of the faithful a bit worried. Some in the culture appeared downright exuberant over the onslaught of secular humanist agitprop directed against the Barque of Peter, in particular.

The great news, though? Not only has the Church largely withstood this onslaught, but in some cases, it has caused individuals to not just accept the hype but take a deeper look at the charges against her and judge whether they were valid. Finding that they weren't, they investigated more, and some of those folks have come or are coming into the Church.

That's just about par for the course with Catholicism, which has withstood so much over the last 2,000 years. However, as the following shows, the aforementioned onslaught is not only unrelenting, but things in this regard are going to get worse before they get better.[1]

Take, for example, the discipline of history. In the Internet age, revisionist and conspiracy theory "history" is often viewed with a more than skeptical eye when applied to the past in general. Unfortunately, the same caution is often not seen when it comes Catholic history. From the Last Supper to the Crusades, the Protestant Reformation, and even World War II, Catholicism's story is being rewritten by those who appear to favor an ideological agenda over the factual historical record. The result is that many either don't know what to believe, or a badly misinformed populace—and this includes Catholics—often believe what they are told by revisionists hook, line, and sinker.

The Da Vinci Code: The Synthesis of All Bad, Anti-Catholic History

When the novel *The Da Vinci Code* came out, many knowledgeable Catholics and other Christians were bewildered that so many historical and factual errors made up this best seller. However, when the book's contents made it onto the silver screen, that bewilderment turned into anger and frustration. These negative emotions rose because the secular media left unchallenged many of the book's and film's falsehoods. Indeed, some show hosts and journalists seemed to think the work was gospel truth. This might explain why this industry appeared to be rooting for the film's success.

In any event, because no one in the popular media challenged author Dan Brown's fabrications masquerading as facts, much of the public now believe the falsehoods to be the truth. Pity the poor parish priests, religious education directors, and local Catholic and Protestant bookstore owners whom the less informed faithful barraged with questions as to why no one ever taught them these "truths" about their faith. Case in point: Consider the outrageous assertions that Opus Dei and the Priory of Sion were each hundreds of years old. That could be true—if we're talking dog years.

For its part, Opus Dei was founded in the 20th century, and its founder, St. Jose Maria Escriva, didn't die until 1980. The Priory of Sion was a confirmed hoax created in 1956 by French con man Pierre Plantard, who desired people to believe that he was a king prophesied by Nostradamus. Furthermore, while it did have at one time have members on paper, it no longer does because French law states: "References to the Priory bear no legal relation to that of 1956 and no one, other than the original signatories, is entitled to use its name in an official capacity."[2]

The Da Vinci Code had many more ludicrous, blasphemous points. It claimed Jesus secretly married Mary Magdalene and that Christ's divinity was made up. It also said the heretic Arius' view of Christ was held as "gospel truth."[2] Brown even asserts in his book that the Council of Nicaea had a "close vote" over question of whether Arius had it right. Perhaps the Evangelical leader Dr. R. Albert Mohler, Jr., president of the Southern Baptist Theological Seminary, said it best:

> The Council of Nicaea did not "invent" the divinity of Jesus. This was already the declaration of the Church, claimed by Jesus himself and proclaimed by the apostles. The Council boldly claimed this as the faith of the Church and named Arianism as a heresy and Arians as heretics. A close vote? Only two out of more than 300 bishops failed to sign the creed [affirming Jesus' divinity]. Not exactly a cliff-hanger.[3]

"Why the big deal?" some say. "Isn't it just a story?"

Yes, it is a story, but it's one whose author has claimed that it puts forth irrefutable facts. It's a story whose premise is that Christianity is really a deception founded by a man named Jesus, who, along with his followers, wasn't a messiah or God's community on earth, but a bunch of frauds. Also, don't forget, tell a lie often enough, and people take it as the truth. Today, many people believe Dan Brown more than they do their Church or pastor.

Throw in some bashing of the "hierarchy of the Catholic Church" and, *voilà*, another attack against Christianity makes the general public doubt even more the beliefs handed on to them by their parents, grandparents, churches, and even society. This is especially true for those who never had much of a religious foundation with which to start.

Look at it this way: What would happen if someone wrote a book or made a film whose foundation was the *Protocols of the Elders of Zion*. This anti-Semitic screed was created in Russia and dates to 1903. It purported to show global Judaism's plans for world domination. If some piece of popular entertainment was derived from that pieces of putrid trash, there would rightly be universal outrage. Bookstores and theaters might not carry the work, either because they were concerned they might face boycotts for pushing such a damaging fantasy or out of righteous anger and principle.

Sadly, that sort of sensitivity and analysis was applied by precious few. Some believe that the devil picks those who appear to be wholesome and inviting to do his work. If that is true, he made a masterful stroke in picking Ron Howard to direct the film. No, I'm not saying the beloved actor-turned-director is a professed minion of Satan. However, it's hard to imagine someone so decent taking on a project so patently offensive to a good number of the 77 million Catholics in our nation. Is it unreasonable that some sort of negative force may have subtly and surreptitiously swayed him and his production partner, Brian Grazer, to take on this film?

Howard is a product of TV's Golden Age and then some. He first came to notice in *The Andy Griffith Show* as Sheriff Andy's son Opie, and he played a big part in keeping the show on the air for its eight-year run. He came to even greater notoriety for his role as the adorable, shy, stuttering Winthrop Paroo in the 1962 film version of Meredith Wilson's Broadway smash, *The Music Man*. Many best remember Howard from his days as the wholesome Richie Cunningham, 1950s high-schooler from Milwaukee, Wisconsin, who always did the right thing in the long-running TV series, *Happy Days*. He also starred in what some consider the seminal coming-of-age movie, *American Graffiti*.

While Howard met with many Catholics about the film, they could not persuade him to change the direction of the film. So persistent was Howard that he even refused to put a disclaimer on the film stating that it was fiction.

The Catholic League for Religious and Civil Rights noted that Disney put a disclaimer on the movie *White Fang* stating: "There is no evidence that healthy wolves attack humans in North America." Muslims received a disclaimer in *True Lies* that not all Muslims are terrorists, and homosexuals received similar consideration in the film *Jay and Silent Bob Strike Back*. When the film *Pocahontas II* was released, it had a disclaimer for indigenous Americans. Even the lighthearted *Mr. Magoo* had a disclaimer saying there was no intent offend the nearsighted. However, a film attacking the Christianity, and Catholic Christianity in particular, offered no such courtesy.[4]

When *The Da Vinci Code* was released, a lead character in the film, the famed British actor Sir Ian McKellen told Matt Lauer of the *Today* show that if the film had a disclaimer, "the Bible should have a disclaimer in the front saying that it is fiction. I mean, walking on water. It takes an act of faith, and I have faith in this movie."

Well, there you have it: The equation of the fictional work of one man (Dan Brown) with the Holy Writ, a divinely inspired work of the Holy Spirit. If ever there was a great illustration of the relativist mindset, of the "dictatorship of relativism," McKellen gave it, and all in the space of a short television interview. That takes talent, folks.

However, *The Da Vinci Code* was just the first in a line of other things to come. More films and documentaries that questioned much of what Christianity—and specifically Catholic beliefs—were made. Our Lord in Scripture essentially tells us to take attacks on our faith with a grain of salt because they are to be expected when we profess his Holy Name (see Matthew 5:11, Luke 21:17, Mark 13:13; John 15:21-23). We are to expect "false prophets," even if they come in the guise of fiction authors or moviemakers.

Of course, while some seemed so convinced that this book and movie would result in the Church's losing clout, as in previous cases, it was largely much ado about nothing. Still, how many have been led astray by the damage wrought by Dan Brown and the Howard/Grazer production team?

Rosemary's ... er, *The Da Vinci Code*'s Babies

Following on the heels of *The Da Vinci Code* was the infamous *Gospel of Judas: A Gnostic Gospel*, not only a heretical book but a forgery written in antiquity to lead early Christians astray. It was a failed effort. Most Christians, especially such Church Fathers as Sts. Irenaeus of Lyons and Athanasius of Alexandria, discounted it as fiction.

However, when it came to light and was translated into English in the early 21st century, that didn't stop modern theological dissidents from asserting that this was a major find that would, yet again, wreck traditional Christian scholarship (especially as it related to Catholicism). Despite the fact that the Gospels tell us Judas killed himself and that the early Church despised him, some ancient oddball (or "eccentric" for those who like him), for whatever reason, wrote glowingly about the traitorous former disciple of Jesus. And if some scholars are to be believed, the initial translation of the apocryphal work may have been a hack job because some scholars believe that, far from exonerating Judas as Jesus' best buddy who was doing his friend a favor by getting him arrested, the book actually makes him look worse than ever.

Take the following passage:

> Truly [I] say to you, Judas, [those who] offer sacrifices to Saklas, the great fool, [... exemplify ...] everything that is evil. But you will exceed all of them. For you will sacrifice the man that clothes me. Already your horn has been raised, your wrath has been kindled, your star has shone brightly, and your heart has [been hardened...]

Instead of reading it as though Judas intentionally set up Our Lord, it could be read from a perspective that Jesus was simply telling Judas he knew what was happening and that he was fooling no one. Professor April D. DeConick, who teaches Scripture at Rice University, wrote an op-ed for *The New York Times*, saying the *National Geographic* team (more on them later) mistranslated the Greek word *daimon*, which Judas is called in the book, as "spirit," when even in Gnostic writings, the word always connotes "demon." Therefore, she says, "Judas is not set apart 'for' the holy generation, as the *National Geographic* translation says. [Rather,]he is separated 'from' it." She asks, "Were they genuine errors or was something more deliberate going on?"⁵

The Wikipedia article on the subject further notes:

> André Gagné, Professor at Concordia University in Montreal also questioned how the experts of the National Geographic Society ... understood the role of Judas Iscariot in the Gospel of Judas. His argument rests on the translation of the Greco-Coptic term *apophasis* as "denial." According to Gagné, the opening lines of the Judas Gospel should not be translated as "the secret word of declaration by which Jesus spoke in conversation with Judas Iscariot" but rather as "the secret word of the denial by which Jesus spoke in conversation with Judas Iscariot" (Gospel of Judas 33:1). Gagné's conclusion is that this gospel is the story of the denial of true salvation for Judas.⁶

The press was all aflutter, giving free advertising to the upcoming *National Geographic* documentary special about this major archaeological find. During the broadcast, antiquities dealer Frieda Nussberger-Tchacos said, "I think I was chosen by Judas to rehabilitate him."

The hubris of this statement is almost as laughable as the $1 million that *National Geographic* paid for the rights to do the show. Yet, while this particular codex might have been unknown, it contained the same wording that is found in other Gospels of Judas that were discovered in the Middle East and North Africa and had been known *for centuries*. For instance, in 180 AD, St. Irenaeus, a Church Father, denounced this document. Nor was he the first to do so. Later, prior the establishment by several Church councils and by Pope St. Damasus I in 382 AD of the biblical canon, all sorts of papyrus floated around the Middle East and North Africa.

Early Christians cherished the Gospels and New Testament letters for their ring of truthfulness. Nutty works such as the false Gospel of Judas had practically no following. Therefore, there was no grand conspiracy when the canon of the Bible was put together. The Councils of Hippo (393) and Carthage (397) considered all the books claiming canonicity. Simply put, the Gospel of Judas wasn't even in the running to make the cut, since the councils were simply ratifying what was already accepted.

The writers at the GetReligion blog (www.getreligion.org) were beside themselves with astonishment about an Associated Press story that circulated during the week of *National Geographic*'s documentary release, which coincided with the release of the *The Da Vinci Code* film, which incidentally was on Palm Sunday.

The AP story glowingly talked about the movie and implied that perhaps it was the early Christians and St. Irenaeus who missed the boat regarding this apocryphal gospel. It is a nice luxury to play revisionist history and pretend one knows better than those who were there 1,900-plus years ago.

The writers at GetReligion noted that the AP piece quoted several theologians (a loose use of that term, frankly), and they were elated over the Judas gospel. For instance, Fr. Donald Senior, president of the Catholic Theological Union in Chicago, said, "Let a vigorous debate on the significance of this fascinating ancient text begin."

A similar comment came from Craig Evans of the Acadia Divinity College in Nova Scotia, who said, "Perhaps more now can be said." The document, he said, "implies that Judas only did what Jesus wanted him to do."

If one wanted to learn from the report what the overwhelming amount of theologians who thought the entire affair was so much hooey, one would have been sorely disappointed, for the story only quoted Judas enthusiasts, most especially the gushing remarks from

Princeton University's Professor Elaine Pagels, a Gnostic scholar and sympathizer.

Pagels wasn't only featured in the AP piece. Usually, the calendar permits that for at least a few days of the year, usually around Christmas and Easter, the faithful are treated well by the press. Sometimes, it even gives some accurate historical or anecdotal information that help better form the faithful and all society. But not on Good Friday 2007, which was when, of all days, PBS decided to run a program that essentially portrayed Judas as the first Christian martyr in an effort to help the faithful better understand Islamic suicide bombers.

Moderator Charlie Rose's guests were Dr. Pagels, Harvard University Professor Karen King, and Rev. James Forbes, the successor to Rev. William Sloane Coffin at New York City's famed hub of liberal Christianity, the Riverside Church. A full transcript is truly needed, because for anyone familiar with the historic tenets of Christianity, the thesis of the guests was incompatible with accepted orthodox Christian theology.

For instance, it is hard to understand how an ordained minister such as Rev. Forbes or self-described historians of Christianity such as King and Pagels could regard Judas as Jesus' favorite disciple and the first Christian martyr. In true Gnostic form, Pagels admitted she doesn't even necessarily believe Jesus really rose from the dead, and Rev. Forbes wasn't convinced he had performed miracles.

Granted, such opinions are all too readily found these days. We even find them preached from Catholic pulpits. What makes this over-the-top sad, however, was that all of this sacrilege, blasphemy, and scandal occurred on Good Friday, and nary one person on the PBS panel thought anything was amiss with what was said on that program.

With all the Christian films and documentaries being made, it must be very frustrating for faith-filled filmmakers. After all, they have to sit and watch those who make documentaries with dubious and outright false information that attack our religion and yet seemingly have no trouble getting booked on the most prominent network and cable shows.

Case in point: The documentary film *Bloodline*, which picks up on *The Da Vinci Code's* nonsense claim that Jesus and Mary Magdalene were secretly married. And, hey, if you have a secret marriage, you have to have secret societies like the Priory of Sion, right? Never mind that, as previously noted, the Priory of Sion was a hoax. Nope. Various television programs still booked the film's creator as a guest.

While we can't know his heart or motives, the *Los Angeles Times* film reviewer Gary Goldstein seemed to relish the prospect of the damage *Bloodline* might do to the Catholic Church. Consider the first line of his review of the picture: "If the Catholic Church fumed over *The Da Vinci Code*, wait until it gets a load of *Bloodline*, an ambitious, sharply intriguing documentary exploring the theory that Jesus married Mary Magdalene, had children with her, did not die on the cross, was never resurrected, and was, therefore, not divine. Holy Moly."

Or consider Goldstein's final sentence: "With hands-on assistance from amateur archaeologist Ben Hammott, plus input from theologians, authors, researchers, and even members of the church's shadowy offshoot, the Priory of Sion, [director Bruce] Burgess goes the distance to posit that maybe it's not the proposed Jesus-Mary bloodline that needs defending but, rather, Christian doctrine itself."[7]

You just can't make this stuff up. First of all, what is a theologist? Secondly, remember, the Priory of Sion was a *hoax*.

Sadly, those reading the *Times* may be unaware of how factually fraudulent both the documentary and the accompanying review were. As possibly demonstrated by *Bloodline*, the madness of *The Da Vinci Code* seemed to unhinge every conspiracy theory about Catholicism known to man. For instance, on the heels of *The Da Vinci Code* and the *National Geographic Society's* documentary, *The Gospel of Judas,* came Discovery Channel's *The Lost Tomb of Jesus.*

In this latest effort to turn everything we have been known about Christ's divinity and what the Early Church taught about that upon its head, the documentary's three hosts—Oden Golan, an Israeli antiquities dealer who had been arrested for forgery; James Cameron, director of the movie *Titanic*; and Simcha Jacobovici, host of the Discovery Channel program, *Naked Archaeologist*—displayed a showcase of tidbits that sure did seem designed to leave viewers confused and doubting. Never mind that none of the three men have experience in Scripture scholarship or biblical archaeology. The Discovery Channel took their work as authoritative.

The Discovery Channel and the hosts leading the effort for the Jesus tomb couldn't be happier with the way the *Today* Show reported on the "find." Host Matt Lauer told *Today's* audience that the Discovery Channel program could "rock Christianity to its core"—quite a plug for a program that wasn't on any of NBC's family of networks. Faithful viewers couldn't help but remember how years ago, when the fictional doctor, Marcus Welby, stated that "I'm not a doctor, but I play one on TV," he at least made the distinction. However, with Cameron, Jacobovici, and Golan, this was not the case. They were not experts or scholars but were treated as such in the press.

Catholic apologist and blogger Jimmy Akin skillfully and humorously debunked the whole charade in one deft post on his website. He simply stated that everyone would have known where the ossuary and burial place was for Jesus and his family if he hadn't risen from the dead. Had there been any truth to the Jesus tomb, not only Jewish residents but also the Romans themselves would have known where to look for it. The fact that almost 2,000 years later it is miraculously found seems more than a little ridiculous.[8]

Fortunately, many of the networks and news channels did express some skepticism. Experts on Jerusalem, most of them Jewish, quickly brushed off this tale. They pointed out the sheer number of people named Jesus, Mary, Joseph, and James at the time (these were the names on the ossuary of Jesus Cameron et al purported to find).

They all made mention of the fact that this would have never gone unnoticed in first-century Israel, and a tomb with their names on it was certainly not rare. Jewish archaeologists who had earlier examined the areas where the ossuary was found also declared they most certainly would have seen something as large as an ossuary.

In what must have been quite uncomfortable for Discovery, in the end, the Israeli government labeled it a complete hoax. Yet despite all of this evidence, the *Naked Archaeologist* remained unconvinced and proudly stood by his find. Interestingly, even curiously, for all of the hoopla created during the lead-up to the documentary's airing, the Israeli government's announcement debunking the show's received far less media attention.

Giving *The Lost Tomb of Jesus* a run for its money was one of the most preposterous American network shows to surface in recent years. It was an ABC television special titled *Pope Joan*. The documentary-style show featured an age-old and oft-debunked legend asserting that at one time during the Middle Ages, there was a woman pope named Joan. While the story has been around for centuries, not even a shred of credible evidence exists to support the theory.

One would think that with such potentially game-changing information, the network would have wanted to at least appear objective and dispassionate. That wasn't the way show's host Diane Sawyer played it, though. Rather, she seemed excited about the prospect of a story that would prove the existence of a woman pope (and, incidentally, call into question several teachings of the Catholic Church).

A host of historians and Catholic writers such as Akin, Carl Olson, and Patrick Madrid not only completely debunked the idea, they obliterated it. Akin recalls a phone call he received from a noteworthy producer who was pitching a big-time move project. After a few short minutes with Akin, the producer realized that he had no solid history to back up his film, and it was scuttled. Too bad ABC didn't take the same approach.[9]

Pius XII: A Vilified but Still "Righteous" Gentile

If there was ever proof that the Lord works in mysterious ways, one could make the argument that Ven. Pius XII—vilified for having done "enough" to help save Jews—during World War II—would have as his greatest defenders two very prominent Jews.

Yet this is exactly what happened. Rabbi David G. Dalin's *Righteous Gentile* book dispelled the premise that Pope Pius XII subtly aided Adolf Hitler in rounding up Italy's Jews. At the same time, Jonah Goldberg's book, *Liberal Fascism,* quashed the notion that both Hitler and Benito Mussolini had any sympathies with Catholicism.

For years, books from supposedly reputable authors and television documentaries from networks people implicitly trusted cast a pall over the pontificate of Pope Pius XII. These portrayed him as turning a blind eye to the evil perpetrated by Hitler and Mussolini. However, in one fell swoop and with excellent research to boot, Rabbi Dalin and Goldberg toppled many myths that this saintly man was in any way, shape, or form sympathetic to these two evil rulers. In fact, both showed how Pius and Catholicism were the victims.

While it started with the play *The Deputy* (better translated as *The Vicar*) by Rolf Hochhuth, much of the venom directed at Ven. Pius XII came from two men: John Cornwell, who wrote the book, *Hitler's Pope: The Secret History of Pope Pius XII*, and Daniel Goldhagen, author of the books *Hitler's Willing Executioners: Ordinary Germans and the Holocaust* and *A Moral Reckoning*, not to mention articles such as "Benedict's Sin of Omission."

Many in the news media gave these men's works an uncritical reception. For instance, CBS's *60 Minutes* ignited a firestorm of protest from Catholic groups such as the Catholic League after it ran an episode where its reporter took Cornwell's assertions at face value and interviewed no opposing viewpoints. This was in spite of the fact that Cornwell's work (as with Goldhagen's) contained scores of objectively false "facts" and incorrect assertions that the media never scrutinized.

In the intervening years, Cornwell has retracted many of his claims. Goldhagen never has, however; he says his is more a work focusing on the moral relationship between Catholicism and the Holocaust and not an historical work. Critiquing *Hitler's Willing Executioners*, Rabbi Dalin notes that Goldhagen made error after error on small matters about his own Jewish faith, specifically various dates of Jewish settlement in Europe. It should come as no surprise, then that Goldhagen similarly made serious errors when it came to Catholicism.

He claimed that Bishop Alois Hudal, an Austrian bishop who helped unknown numbers of war criminals and other Nazis escape after World War II, was an "important bishop" in Rome. He also says he was a "close friend and confidant" of Pope Pius XII. Rabbi Dalin notes that while Bishop Hudal was in Rome, he was simply rector of the German College. The-then Eugenio Cardinal Pacelli (who would later become Pius XII) consecrated Hudal as bishop and, given the favor Hudal had early in his ecclesiastical career, is someone he knew but with whom had no close relationship whatsoever.[10]

In fact, in 1937, before the start of World War II and toward the end of Pius XI's pontificate, Hudal published a book that criticized the Holy See's coldness toward National Socialism and said that the Concordat Pacelli had negotiated with the Third Reich (which Hitler began violating before the ink was even dry on the agreement). After that, Pius XI made several attempts at bringing Hudal around to an authentic Catholic view on Nazism. When this proved unsuccessful, however, Hudal became *persona non grata*. After his role in the so-called Nazi "ratline" which enabled those criminals to escape became known in 1947, Hudal was forced to resign. Pius XII was still Pope at the time. So much for a close relationship.

Goldberg's *Liberal Fascism* asserts that Hitler despised the Catholic Church and Christianity in general. Hitler often spoke of his wish that the Muslim armies had not been stopped by Charles Martel at Tours, France, in 732. Hitler longed for the day when Germany would be rid of Christianity and return to her pagan roots. This mirrors the views of both Alfred Rosenberg—the Reich's primary philosopher, and his writings served as the intellectual underpinning of Nazism—and Ernst Bergmann, another prominent German ideologue. Rosenberg in particular wanted to promote Nazi notions of German pagan mythology, the occult, race, and blood to replace Christianity, and he wanted to do so in a way that would rival Nietzche in stoking people's hatred of Christianity.

Perhaps the best example of Hitler's hatred for Christianity and Catholicism in general can be seen in the various songs sung by the Hitler youth. One such song's lyrics are:

> We are the happy Hitler youth;
> We have no need for Christian virtue;
> For Adolf Hitler is our intercessor and our redeemer.
> No priest, no evil one can keep us from feeling like
>   Hitler's children.
> No Christ do we follow, but Horst Wessel!
> Away with incense and holy water pots.[11]

It has been said that the nuns helped build the Church wherever they went. With the help of nuns like Sr. Margherita Marchione, MPF, PhD, of the Religious Teachers Fillippini, perhaps it will be said that they also helped defend the Church from evil lies and distortions. Sr. Margherita is the author of 30 books and is considered to be one of the world's leading authorities on Pope Pius XII. She was 17 years old when then-Cardinal Eugenio Pacelli became Pope Pius XII. She speaks of the admiration her generation had for this man, whose gentleness and holiness were legendary. Perhaps because of these qualities, those who hated the Church saw a great target, for what better way to humiliate the Church than to defame such a pious man?

Sr. Margherita reminds us that on Christmas 1942, *The New York Times* declared in an editorial that "the voice of Pius XII is a lonely voice in the silence and darkness enveloping Europe this Christmas. He is about the only ruler left on the continent of Europe who dares to raise his voice at all."[12]

In a debate with John Cornwell, Sr. Margherita tried to bring up these and other facts, such as the claim by future Israeli diplomat and scholar Pinchas Lapide that "the Catholic Church under the pontificate of Pius XII was instrumental in saving as many as 860,000 Jews from certain death at Nazi hands." Sadly, but not surprisingly, Sr. Margherita was not given a fair hearing. Fortunately, Catholic radio talk show host Al Kresta gave her and Cornwell a chance to continue the debate.

The facts go on and on with the evidence that Pope Pius XII saved countless Jews from certain death, so much so that the chief rabbi in Rome, Israel Zolli, converted to Catholicism due in part to his admiration of Pope Pius XII. At his baptism, he took the Christian name of Eugenio, the Pope's given first name, in order to honor his efforts. When Ven. Pius XII died in 1958, future Israeli Prime Minister Golda Meir gave him a moving eulogy at the United Nations.

Recently discovered records also show that as early as 1917, he was in favor a Jewish homeland, and that he pushed for one with Catholic countries from at least 1944 through the early 1950s. In November 1944, British diplomats appealed to Pius to not speak out about the recent mass deportation of Hungarian Jews, which he ignored when the Vatican joined other neutral nations in calling for a halt to the forced relocations of Jews. And between 1941 and the liberation of Italy in 1944, Pius made it his business to keep tabs on the welfare of Italian Jews, sending aid to those being detained in southern Italy. One former inmate credits His Holiness with preventing their deportation to the concentration camps in Poland.

Albert Einstein's 1940 *Time* magazine quote should be remembered for what he said about the Church saving and defending Jews. It was recorded in the present, which is very important: "Only the Church stood squarely across the path of Hitler's campaign for suppressing truth ... The Church alone has had the courage and persistence to stand for intellectual truth and moral freedom."[13] Sadly, few who denigrate His Holiness have ever paid attention to these words of the person reputed to be the world's smartest-ever man.

With Friends Like These...

Finally, what about all of these sinister secrets that everyone from Catholicism-hating Fundamentalists to supposedly traditional and loyal sons of the Church claim that the Vatican supposedly keeps? It seems if there is a small cottage industry that has grown up to trumpet and propagate around every new Vatican conspiracy theory that comes along.

We have all probably been asked about this a time or two. How does a faithful Catholic deal with such questions? For instance, there are many books concerning the third secret of Fátima, let alone the first two, all of which the Church has deemed as worthy of belief and that they are of supernatural origin. Some say the third secret has been fully revealed. Others argue that the Holy See has a) not released all the message or b) has not released the real message, which it still has hid someplace.

What, exactly, is the third secret?

On June 26, 2000, the Vatican Information Service released the text of the secret, which reads as follows:

> ... we saw an Angel with a flaming sword in his left hand; flashing, it gave out flames that looked as though they would set the world on fire; but they died out in contact with the splendor that Our Lady radiated towards him from her right hand: pointing to the earth with his right hand, the Angel cried out in a loud voice, "Penance! Penance! Penance!" And we saw in an immense light that is God: "something similar to how people appear in a mirror when they pass in front of it"‛ a Bishop dressed in White "we had the impression that it was the Holy Father." Other Bishops, Priests, men and women Religious going up a steep mountain, at the top of which there was a big Cross of rough-hewn trunks as of a cork-tree with the bark; before reaching there the Holy Father passed through a big city half in ruins and

half trembling with halting step, afflicted with pain and sorrow, he prayed for the souls of the corpses he met on his way; having reached the top of the mountain, on his knees at the foot of the big Cross, he was killed by a group of soldiers who fired bullets and arrows at him, and in the same way, there died one after another the other Bishops, Priests, men and women Religious, and various lay people of different ranks and positions. Beneath the two arms of the Cross there were two Angels each with a crystal aspersorium in his hand, in which they gathered up the blood of the Martyrs and with it sprinkled the souls that were making their way to God.

To feed into the curiosity this has stoked, there have been numerous cable television shows on the apocalyptic aspects of the third secret. Who was the pontiff that would die, and were the Freemasons and the Mafia involved? The mysterious death of John Paul I even figured prominently in the last of *The Godfather* trilogy, *The Godfather Part III*, although he died in his sleep of a heart attack and not by bullets and arrows.

Brad Metzler's History Channel show, *Decoded*, claimed the third secret has something to do with a Masonic cabal secretly trying to infiltrate the Vatican which calls itself the "Blackfriars." And since Vatican banker Roberto Calvi was found dead hanging from the Blackfriars Bridge in London in 1982, couldn't there be a connection? Later Metzler, in a Facebook post, noted that John Paul I died on the 33rd day of his pontificate, and 33 is a key number to the Masons.

So what about all of these connections? What should Catholics whose friends believe these sorts of conspiracy theories do if they ask about them?

Much of the doubt about whether the Church has revealed the true text of the Third Secret of Fátima given to Sr. Lucia by the Virgin Mary in 1917 comes from some self-described traditionalist Catholics (although by no means all; let's make that clear). They have convinced themselves that Masons have indeed overrun the Holy See. They think that one cannot believe to one extent or another anything the Vatican says on the matter.

Furthermore, since Masons are dedicated to the Church's destruction, and because they will keep creating humiliation after humiliation for the Vatican, it is only a matter of time until just the right scandal breaks the Church's back, and with it, any moral sway she might retain by that point.

These traditionalists point to some very interesting statements coming from some senior Church officials. Robert Moynihan publishes *Inside the Vatican*, a right-leaning but not traditionalist *per se* magazine. Through his nearly 20 years in business, he has gained intimate access to many senior Vatican officials. One of these was former head of the Vatican Bank, Archbishop Paul Marcinkus.

Dr. Moynihan claims that the archbishop told him that in time, he would tell him truth behind the Vatican banking scandal and all of its twists and turns. His Excellency went on to tell Moynihan that his "hair would curl" when he learned the truth of the matter (which is somewhat amusing since Moynihan's hair is already somewhat curly).[14]

After the archbishop's retirement, the publisher would telephone the aging prelate, who was originally from Chicago but had retired to Arizona. In their last call, Marcinkus told Moynihan that soon he would tell him the truth. Moynihan was ready to fly out to Arizona to hear, as the late Paul Harvey was fond of saying, "the rest of the story." Sadly, His Excellency died shortly thereafter at the age of 84, and "the rest of the story" never came out.

To give more ammunition to conspiracy theorists, Moynihan also related his last conversation with Archbishop Pietro Sambi, the late papal nuncio to the United States who died of surgical complications in 2011. It seems that at the time of his death, His Excellency was reading archtraditionalist Christopher Ferrara's book *The Secret Still Hidden*, one of many on the controversy surrounding the third secret of Fátima. The archbishop told Moynihan that he found the book very interesting, something that Moynihan wasn't expecting. Moynihan figured someone of the stature of the papal nuncio would dismiss out of hand any conspiracy theories surrounding the third secret, especially since the Vatican secretary of state, Tarcisio Cardinal Bertone, SDB, had just written his own book detailing the history surrounding the third secret and why it was finally released in 2000.

Now, you may ask why I am even detailing all of this, since I have made it clear that, by and large, I don't believe in conspiracy theories. The reason I am putting this information out there is to illustrate that evil has always tried to attack and undermine the Church. It was true with the crises prompted by corrupt popes during the Middle Ages, it was true of sexually scandalous pontiffs during the Renaissance, and it is true with our present-day scandals.

Therefore, even if there were evil people in the Vatican, in a roundabout way all of this helps prove whom the Church says she is. After all, wouldn't it stand to reason that evil would attack good and that darkness would attack the light? For example, Satanists don't steal from Protestant tabernacles (or, rather, the cupboards where they keep the leftover communion wafers). Why? Protestants don't have the Real Presence of Christ in the Eucharist. Catholics do, and that is why Satanists get consecrated hosts from our churches.

For instance, in 2009, Carlo Cardinal Caffarra, archbishop of Bologna, suspended the indult (i.e., special permission) for people to receive Communion in the hand at the three principle churches within his see, including the cathedral. The reason? Along with Turin, Milan, and Rome, Bologna has an especially high concentration of Satanists and reports filtered back that the Satanists were taking the hosts and desecrating them or using them in black masses.

Ironically, in all of this we see the tide turning. Our Lord is raising up people of all backgrounds to defend Catholicism's teachings, sometimes even people who don't even belong to the Catholic Church. God does this to honor his word that the gates of hell will not prevail against her (see Matthew 16:16-20).

SIX
THE CULTURE OF LIFE WILL PREVAIL

If you were to look at the title of this chapter and think, "Yeah, right," don't feel bad. It would be hard to blame you. However, a brief review of the facts shows that the notion of the Culture of Life's final perseverance is not as farfetched as it might initially seem.

The Catholic Church has been preaching and teaching about the sanctity of life since its earliest days. In good times and bad, the Church has always let women know that regardless of their marital status, it would welcome any child from an unwanted pregnancy.

Abortion = Forbidden. Period. Always Has Been, Always Will Be. Any Questions?

As proof of the seriousness with which the Church has always taken the value of life, consider the Didache, an early Church document. Some scholars believe it was written even before certain books in the Bible. It states, "Thou shall not murder a child by abortion."

Early Church saints such as Alexander, Ambrose, Basil, Clement, and Jerome all talked about the evils of abortion. Historically, all of Christianity has always been united against abortion. All the leaders of the Protestant Reformation spoke out against it as well as contraception, in particular Martin Luther and John Calvin. The WWII Lutheran martyr, Dietrich Bonhoeffer, a hero to many for the heroic stand he took against Adolf Hitler, was also known for his pro-life views.

However, starting in the late 1960s and continuing through the mid-1970s, every organized church went on record as supporting abortion in one form or another—even the Southern Baptists for a time. The sole exceptions were the Catholic and Orthodox Churches.

Then, a few years after the *Roe v. Wade* decision legalizing abortion in the US, the Evangelical publication *Christianity Today* issued two *mea culpas*, one for using the term "therapeutic abortion" and the second for famed Evangelical leader W.A. Criswell's statements in favor of abortion.[1]

By the late 1970s, groups such as the Moral Majority, the Southern Baptists, and other Protestant communions began to repudiate their support for legalized abortion. As Dr. Mohler has said, "The early Evangelical response to legalized abortion was woefully inadequate."[2]

Contraception: Taking the Gift Out of Giving

For many, it will come as news that it wasn't until 1930 that the first organized Christian communion, Anglicanism, approved the use of birth control. By the early 1960s, Presbyterianism became the last Protestant body to capitulate in allowing its members to use birth control. And by the late 1960s, even the Orthodox churches were allowing contraception within marriage.

It is possible that the last resistance against contraception among Christian denominations came with the invention of the birth control pill in 1960. It certainly was the impetus for many within Catholicism to prod Pope Paul VI into changing the age-old prohibition against it. Thankfully, with release of *Humanae Vitae*, Paul VI said no, but the resulting aftermath probably took him totally by surprise. Look at pictures of him before 1968 and after—there is a discernible difference, and it is likely no mistake that he never wrote another encyclical. One thing that he predicted in *Humanae Vitae* was that it would encourage sex before marriage. Given how his prediction in this and other areas were spot on has led many Evangelicals in recent years to ponder whether the Catholic Church had it right all along.

Once again, Dr. Mohler praised the Catholic Church, no small thing from someone who has made no bones about his lack of use for much of Catholic theology. However, as the breakdown of the social order persisted, Dr. Mohler came to a conclusion, which he wrote about in *The Christian Post*:

> We should look closely at the Catholic moral argument found in *Humanae Vitae*. Evangelicals will find themselves in surprising agreement with much of the encyclical's argument.
>
> As the Pope warned, widespread use of the pill has led to serious consequences including marital infidelity and rampant immorality. In reality, the pill allowed a near total abandonment of Christian sexuality morality in the larger culture. Once the sex act was severed from the likelihood of childbearing, the traditional structure of sexual morality collapsed.[3]

Where There's Smoke, There's Fire

In a society where the people govern themselves and their passions and strive for virtue, abortion and contraception would not be issues. They are the smoke, if you will, that signal that someplace we have a fire we need to extinguish. That fire represents the moral choices each of us make.

And let's be real here, folks: some of sex-obsessed and highly rated programs that give a "wink-wink, nudge-nudge" to the Culture of Death did not gain their popularity without an awful lot of supposedly committed Catholics and Protestants watching them. The late and very prominent Evangelical leader Chuck Colson joined Dr. Mohler when they spoke of the damage many such Top 10 TV shows have had on America's moral fabric. This is not a new phenomenon, obviously. Each of us old enough to do so can probably remember at least one show and maybe several from 50, 40, 30, 20, and 10 years ago that paved the way for the moral sewage that flows into our homes via our Zeniths and Sony flat screens. As a result, many who like Dr. Mohler would once have been hard-pressed to say anything positive about Catholicism have joined Catholics in the battle for our culture. It is what Boston College professor of philosophy Peter Kreeft calls an "ecumenical jihad." Yet few in the mainstream media have paid much heed other than to change the definition of "religious social fundamentalists" to include Catholics.

Maybe in this instance ignoring us is a good thing. After all, given that the fight for a Culture of Life has never been an easy one, we need all the help we can get, especially considering how the venom people with traditional family values now face. This would have been incomprehensible just a few years ago. The change in the cultural winds and the quick way in which this has happened are staggering.

A good exemplification of this mind-numbing swing to becoming so blasé about abortion comes from a former senior editor of *Newsweek*, Melinda Beck, who in 1989 warned of the consequences for those administering self-performed abortion (i.e., RU-486), "Sadly, many home remedies could damage a fetus instead of kill it."[4]

The Church's consistent teaching about chaste living since the earliest of days has historically been admired and lauded by the powers that be. However, the powers she faced at her birth, the Romans, had gone from being a largely socially moral people to those who delighted in all things hedonistic. This transformation followed that of the previous world power, the ancient Greeks. However, that age-old spirit still lives on, as is evident from looking all around us.

Perhaps nowhere better than San Francisco does there exist a better example of a city where religious and cultural norms have changed over the last 50 years. Many today laud the beautiful City by the Bay as one full of tolerance, creative ideas, and energy. One can hardly watch a week of cable television without seeing some program, documentary, or retrospective claiming that the social revolution that incubated in the city's Haight-Ashbury neighborhood and fully hatched during 1967's "Summer of Love" helped change America for the better.

136   THE CATHOLIC TIDE CONTINUES TO TURN

Walk through the city's Golden Gate Park today (assuming one is able to avoid the trash left by the permanent homeless encampment there), and it is hard to imagine this place being the location of any world-changing event. However, on January 14, 1967, the Park played host to the "Human Be-In," which drew 30,000 people. Historians say that this event, which featured open drug use and free love, is where the counterculture really gained the momentum which then exploded into the 1967 Summer of Love.

Only six years earlier, this same park had played host to a massive Rosary rally led by the Servant of God Fr. Patrick Peyton, the famed "Rosary Priest" who founded the radio series, *Family Theater* and is often credited with coining the term "The family that prays together stays together. A world at prayer is a world at peace." He had begun hosting such rallies the world over after World War II after witnessing family discord due to soldiers coming home and dealing with battle stress as well as families coping with absent fathers. The 1961 event drew over 550,000 to the Golden Gate Park in 1961. Yet, how many cable channels have dedicated a single program to this event? None.[5]

While the Summer of Love has often been treated as a liberating event by the media, even being hailed as the doorway to the future, the after effects have been far more sobering. The city has a high homeless population, many unable to recover from years of drug use that started in the late 1960s. The loosening of morals led to a burgeoning prostitution industry, which in turn evolved into pornographic movies and theater productions. While Los Angeles communities such as North Hollywood are today Ground Zero for the nation's pornography business, it was once San Francisco.

Unfortunately, not only were men in trench coats attending these productions in the landmark O'Farrell Theatre, but the city's establishment came to see various pornographic films produced by the Mitchell brothers, Jim and Artie. These two brothers made the pornography business mainstream with their infamous film, *Behind the Green Door*. The 1972 picture featured a young Marilyn Chambers fresh from her image of feminine wholesomeness holding a baby on Ivory Snow soap boxes.

The Mitchell brothers knew the firestorm effect that a film whose lead actress was once viewed to be the epitome of wholesomeness would have on society. The film became the first pornographic film ever featured at the Cannes Film Festival. Men and women, husbands and wives attended *Behind the Green Door* and similar films together. This helped take the pornography business from grainy stag films filmed in seedy hotel rooms to critically acclaimed cinematic works. All of a sudden, the industry acquired a degree of respectability. Young women in San Francisco who were once part of the flower power movement flocked to pornographic studios in the Bay area to actually make money off of their "liberated" ways.

Another result of the metropolis' no-holds-barred sexual mores is that it became the epicenter of the homosexual lifestyle. Over time, this subculture became the mainstream. Drive through town on a Friday or Saturday night, and you'll see men of all different sorts dressed in leather queued to get into some gay bar. Or you might see a guy dressed only in cowboy boots (with spurs, no less), a cowboy hat, and a pair of open-backed chaps walking around as if it's the most normal thing in the world. Middle-aged lesbian lovebirds stop every few feet like adolescents to kiss one another. And then take the annual Gay Pride Parade.

The first cracks in this no-holds-barred way of life appeared in the 1980s when the AIDS crisis gained notoriety in San Francisco and then became known throughout the United States and the world. The reason HIV/AIDS spread so rapidly is due to the great number of partners the average homosexual male cycles through in a year—and in a lifetime. A 1978 study done by Leon McKusich for Public Health Reports was published in Facts About Youth, a website run by the American Pediatric Association. Mr. McKusich's research revealed that 75 percent of self-identified, white, gay men admitted to having sex with more than 100 different males in their lifetime: 15 percent claimed 100-249 sex partners; 17 percent claimed 250- 499; 15

percent claimed 500-999; and 28 percent claimed more than 1,000 lifetime male sex partners.

The AIDS crisis really seems to have put the scare in the homosexual community. Whereas in 1982, the average homosexual man had six-plus partners in a month, that number had dropped to roughly four each month by 1984. Big drop, no?

While no longer at 1978 levels, promiscuity is a huge part of the homosexual lifestyle even today. By 2003, US homosexual men were averaging 27 partners annually. In the same year, a study of Amsterdam men with no partner reported that they averaged 22 bedfellows annually, while those in a relationship averaged eight per annum (with the average committed relationship lasting just a year and a half). In a 2005 Canadian vaccine trial, homosexual men claimed on average seven companions in the past six months. Very often, the partners are anonymous. Also, there is much anecdotal evidence that the number of homosexual men having unprotected sex is on the rise for a variety of reasons.[6]

The result of all this sleeping around? Deaths from AIDS reached a high of 41,700 in 1995 before falling 16,685 in 1997, which is about the same rate as in 1989. Most of these deaths were homosexual men. As of 2002, the number of deaths was just north of 12,000 men. By 2007, the Centers for Disease Control estimated that 583,298 had lost their lives to AIDS, that 1.05 million had the disease, and another 1.106 million were HIV positive.

Read that 2007 figure again: 583,298. Rock Hudson. Keith Haring. Brothers, uncles, husbands, friends. Gone. Free love has its price, and it was something the pornography industry, which had gained such a foothold in the city, helped promote (not that it was called to account for this, mind you).

In a scene right out of the Old Testament, the demise of the Mitchell brothers came to a violent and deadly ending. Their business of vice naturally progressed to drugs and, in 1991, deadly violence, eventually leading Jim to shoot and kill his brother over Artie's mismanagement and drug abuse. However, these two brothers were so influential that none other than former city Mayor Frank Jordan, former chief of police Richard Hongisto, and then-county Sheriff Michael Hennessey wrote letters or publicly raised their voices in front of the judge, vouching for Jim Mitchell's character and asking him for leniency.[7] Jim Mitchell was found guilty only of manslaughter and served three years of a six-year prison.

It is hard to believe that just 30 short years after the 550,000-strong Rosary rally, the city had descended to this point. Yes, I know a lot can happen in 30 years. By the same token, however, nothing significant has to change if men are willing to be men of character and godly leaders, and if women are willing to demand of their men that lead and hold certain standards.

Against this backdrop to the north, people such as a young, San Diego-based Catholic youth minister named Jason Evert would help launch a chastity movement that would grow and grow in the first decade of the New Millennium. During this period, many school districts had to daily deal with the fact that not only were young men attempting to view pornography on the school's Internet link, but also young women were sending nude pictures of themselves via email and cell phones to male classmates they deemed desirable. Evert and his wife Crystalina would be influential in trying to stop the moral collapse of a generation that held so much promise.

No More Going Steady

Starting in the 1990s, a youth-oriented chastity movement started to slowly grow within the Church. This was at least partly in response to school officials reporting a rapid rise in the number of youth engaging in risky sexual practices which these teens and even adolescents believed wouldn't result in losing their virginity or acquiring a sexually transmitted disease. Pretty soon, people were hearing new phrases such "friends with benefits," "hooking up," and "rainbow parties," with the people involved sometimes being in elementary school.

Furthermore, given the ever-mushrooming sexualization of the culture, Evert and others like him had their work cut out for them. By 2010, pop culture would be awash not only in suggestive television programming, risqué hit songs, and revealing clothing, but also in brand-new ways to entice young people.

For instance, until the executive producer was thrown in jail, one could not flip through late-night TV without seeing the titillating infomercial for the *Girls Gone Wild* series, which sold millions of copies. The videos featured often drunken young women in their late teens and early 20s taking off their clothes, acting provocatively, and kissing young men or each other.

What did the young women get for this sad debasement of their glorious and God-given gift of femininity, for allowing themselves to be treated as an object, a piece of meat to be ogled and demeaned for the cheap thrills of drunken college boys in dorm rooms and lecherous, lonely old men in flophouses? A T-shirt. Yes, that's right—for their efforts, they received a sewn piece of cotton with some silk screening on it. Meanwhile, smut mogul and GGW producer Joe Francis received millions in revenues. The plight of these women was synonymous with the after effects of promiscuity in general and of sexploitation in particular: Some were left scarred and penniless, while others financially benefited.

Popular entertainers like Britney Spears and Madonna kissed each other on live television, and reports of young women doing the same increased across the country. It was alarming, to say the least, for many parents. While many young women shrugged off this activity as silliness or experimentation, there were reports of a rampant increase in lesbian experimentation among young women, especially those of college age. It seemed Western society was pushing its young toward the edge.

In the summer of 2007, many in the United Kingdom were shocked by weekend and weekday debauchery that left ambulance services going nonstop. One weekend in particular saw London ambulance services called every 30 seconds each night for reports of young people, often women, passed out due to the effects of alcohol or drugs. The London *Daily Mail* showed a rather depressing picture of young men and women walking through the streets of London, clad only in undergarments, passing other young people who were either vomiting (with nothing left to the imagination) or lying incapacitated on the sidewalk.

In the spring of 2008, Katy Perry's "I Kissed a Girl" reached number one on the United States' pop charts. The daughter of a former evangelical pastor and once a promising Christian artist, Perry changed her name from Katy Hudson and apparently her values along with it when she hit it big at the age of 23.[8]

Given the aforementioned experimentation, the song was part of what became dubbed "lesbian chic," which included songs, books, plays such as *The Vagina Monologues*, and movies about young girls experimenting with lesbianism. This was only the tip of the iceberg, as reports surfaced throughout the country of middle- and high-school boys paying young girls to kiss each other.

Because of all this, faithful young men and women tried to show their peers or those who came to the parish youth group another way. They openly talked of their chaste lifestyle and the joy it gave them. At first these young people and the movement they represented were almost universally greeted with kind words and warmth. However, sometime around 2003 these wholesome young people started to become labeled as odd, freaks, losers, or worse.

The public was then deluged by survey after survey that said abstinence education doesn't work. Some of those pooh-poohing these studies went so far as to proclaim in public speeches that young men and young women could not control their sexual urges in the current permissive climate. Therefore, birth control had to be made available. This was simply the reality, they proclaimed. Face facts, you fundamentalists, and get over it.

For instance, two professors, Peter Bearrman and Hannah Brückner, wrote in the April 2005 issue of *Journal of Adolescent Health* that youth who make virginity pledges are more likely to engage in risky sexual behavior than those who don't.

Of course, many in the media couldn't resist this "Aha! Gotcha!" stick in the eye to the Religious Right, and so leapt on this story with a vengeance. All the evening news programs, as well as NBC's widely watched *Today* show and CBS's *60 Minutes* gave wide coverage to the story. There was just one problem, though: It was all false. In exhaustive research conducted by Robert Rector and Kirk Johnson, PhD, of the Heritage Institute, the conclusions were shown to be bogus. As a matter of fact, they proved that the opposite was true. Did this make all the evening news programs along with *Today* and *60 Minutes*? Well, no.

A 2007 Zogby Poll showed that 80 percent of parents would prefer an abstinence approach to one that focused on safe sex. Smart parents, because condoms fail to protect against disease between 13 to 30 percent of the time, and they do not prevent pregnancy 10 percent of the time. In fact, the ISO standard allows six defects in 1000. Can you say "Russian roulette"?

Furthermore, the respected British medical journal *The Lancet* reported in 2000, "Increased condom use will increase the number of [HIV/AIDS] transmissions that result from condom failure" and "A vigorous condom promotion policy could increase rather than decrease unprotected sexual exposure if it has the unintended effect of encouraging a greater overall level of sexual activity."[9]

Valerie Huber, executive director of the National Abstinence Education Association, told CitizenLink, "There is so much misinformation out there. We were convinced that once parents understood the real content of abstinence education, they would overwhelmingly support abstinence."

In a separate study, Rector found that the US government spent $12 to promote contraception for every $1 spent on abstinence education. This despite studies showing that sexually active teens are more likely to be depressed and attempt suicide compared to those who are

The Culture of Life Will Prevail

not sexually active. In addition, abstinence programs have shown to dramatically decrease out-of-wedlock births and teen sexual activity.

Simply put, the "safe-sex" myth is just that, a myth. Many newer strains of sexually transmitted diseases like the human papillomavirus (HPV) are spread by sweat near the genital area. Abstinence officials have been told that most safe sex organizers don't like to mention this fact because it might cause a public healthcare crisis. Some safe-sex experts theorize that if one can get a disease with a condom, what would be the need for wearing one in the first place? And yet have you ever seen pictures of someone with HPV? People get it on their hands, their feet, their faces ... it is truly horrific.

One is tempted, therefore, to ask why adults would keep silent about something so dangerous. Do they really believe humans can't control their urges? Practically every faith in existence today preaches chastity, and they have done so for up to 10,000 years in some cases. Scores of societies throughout history have worked to make licentiousness the exception and not the rule. Both have traditionally met with a good deal of success, all things considered. How can this be if, as the experts claim, we are simply animals who can't control our base passions?

Perhaps the answer lies in the fall of man. Even the first humans found sin attractive, and we have suffered for it ever since. The fruit from the tree of good and evil looked so juicy and "good to eat." The same could be said of any other temptation, whether it be lust, greed, sloth, or any of the other seven deadly sins.

Sadly, we think we are invincible. "Sin won't rule me. *I'll* rule *it*." But under the control, the sway, of lust or some other attraction, we can become a shell of ourselves, a sad, pathetic mess of what we once were. Our hardened resolve becomes so much mush. Many hate themselves so much for what was done to them that they either try to end their own lives or that of others or they engage in risky behaviors.

Yet that is the great thing about our Christian faith. Our God is a merciful God. He loves us and wants us with him forever. St. Faustina tells us his mercy is unfathomable, and it is ours for the taking if we will just ask for it. Bl. Bartolo Longo was a satanic priest, for goodness' sake. He repented, though. By accepting the redemption Christ won for him on the cross, which is still poured out for us today in the sacraments, he reconciled with God and is today effectively a saint. If God can give his mercy to Bl. Bartolo, why is your sin so special?

Sadly, the awareness of sin, special or otherwise, and the opportunities to stray from God's plan and from his law through sin are so voluminous that in some ways the most miraculous grace God gives us is the ability to sin no more. It used to be that popular culture glamorized the randy James Bond. Now it glamorizes promiscuous women—young and old (witness the introduction of the sexually charged term "cougar" into our culture's lexicon). Is it any wonder that by 2008, health department officials in New York City reported that one in four adults in the city had contracted the herpes virus?[10]

And instead of teaching people how to live by God's law as expressed through Church teaching, we have instead obscene mockeries of all that is good. Take, for instance, a group of abortion operators called the "November Gang." They encouraged their customers to write little Valentines to the babies that they had just aborted. The abortionists believed that if the mothers would write good-byes to their dying children, it would help the mother's adjust to the reality of what just happened. One poem went as follows: "I smile when I think of you, even if I cry. You have given me reason to be strong and wise and responsible. You will always be my baby. I will see you in heaven, sweetheart. Love you! Love always and unconditionally, your mommy."[11]

In 2010, New York City health officials reported that 41 percent of all pregnancies resulted in abortions. *The American Spectator's* headline was "NYC: The Statue of Liberty or the Grim Reaper?" In addition, the report stated that there were more abortions than live births among African-Americans.[12]

A rather chilling website emerged, called *NYC41Percent.com*, in which readers could scroll over certain zip codes and find the abortion rates, which often topped those of live births. The highest numbers were in the poorest areas of Brooklyn and the Bronx, as well as posh Manhattan neighborhoods.

Then-Archbishop Timothy Dolan said the numbers were "chilling and embarrassing." He once again restated the words of the late John Cardinal O'Connor that any woman in the city could come to the archdiocese for free help so her child could live. Oddly, when a group of New Yorkers wanted to put up a billboard stating that more African-Americans were dying in the womb than being allowed to be born, Rev. Al Sharpton scolded those who made mention of this alarming statistic and pressed for the billboard not to be put up.

Another indicator of the problem we have on our hands is the increasing number of out-of-wedlock births. The CDC's preliminary 2010 statistics show out of wedlock births for African-Americans at 72.5 percent, American Indians at 66.5 percent, Hispanics at 53.5 percent, Caucasians at 29.0 percent, and Asians and Pacific Islanders at 17 percent.

Sadly, many of the young women giving birth never get adequate information about the adoption option. Before *Roe v. Wade*, there were about 2 million young women who felt they couldn't properly care for their baby, and there were about 2 million married couples who couldn't have children. The 2 million couples remain and often travel the ends of the earth searching for a child, or they wait on a domestic adoption list for a considerable length of time. The cost can run into the tens of thousands of dollars. It just seems there has to be a better way for all involved.

Where Planned Parenthood Comes In

There is no better way than the status quo for Planned Parenthood, however. The pro-life community has never had any use for the nation's largest abortion provider. However, there was a time in the days following its founding in 1921, when it was known as the American Birth Control League, that most of society reviled it as well (the organization changed its name to Planned Parenthood Federation of America in 1942 upon merging with several like-minded groups).

Regardless of its name or level of popularity, though, few have known how the group's foundress Margaret Sanger not only disliked Catholicism but *all* religions. She also had no use for minority races. She had a cozy relationship with the Ku Klux Klan and Nazi Germany and openly favored eugenics. Yet, outside of the Catholic Church and people such as talk show host Larry Elders, columnist Star Parker, and pro-life activist Alveda King (niece of Dr. Martin Luther King Jr.), few make the connection between Planned Parenthood's racist past and the large number of abortions in the minority communities.

The aforementioned Dr. Bernard Nathanson, who knew a little about Planned Parenthood, stated that the organization's anti-Catholicism still provided its animating force in the 1960s since the Church was the only Christian body that still opposed contraception and the loosening of restrictions on abortion on any level. (Depending on the year, the priest, national affiliation, or any number of other factors, the various Orthodox Churches may or may not oppose contraception.[13])

Since then, Planned Parenthood has moved farther and farther to the political Left. Case in point: In August 2005, Catholic blogger and new convert Dawn Eden was able to quickly download a cartoon from Planned Parenthood's website before the outfit's staffers could delete it. The animated cartoon was entitled "A Superhero for Choice." This lady superhero would traverse the universe, looking for pro-life demonstrators to annihilate with her "condom gun." One graphic scene showed a man holding a sign that said, "Pray for thy sins." The man was then obliterated, to the shock of younger female demonstrators who held signs saying, "Safe is sexy."[14]

The story made the rounds on many politically conservative

websites and showed the disregard Planned Parenthood had for people of faith. Given the Church's work against Planned Parenthood's *de facto* mission and the organization's evident mission to denigrate the Church, both on its own and through its front group, "Catholics for Choice," it seemed quite fitting that a Catholic blogger broke open the case.

Abortion as a "Sacred" Act

In an apparent attempt to take the battle to the Church's ground, Planned Parenthood has offered "Spirituality and Sexuality" weekend retreats for spiritual young people. What greater gift could you give your "spiritual" friends than to co-opt them? Perhaps this retreat would be made complete by the words of Rev. Mark Pawlowski, a Presbyterian minister who often recites the pro-choice credo, "I believe God stands with women as they end pregnancies." One can only imagine a retreat led by people such as Rev. Pawlowski, where abortion is preached as if it is some sort of sacrament.

Some may blanche at that characterization. Yet, isn't that what abortion has become to the secular Left? Obviously, if you are secular (i.e., atheist), you have no sacraments as such. However, you do have substitutes.

The word "sacrament" comes from the Latin *sacramentum*, which in turn is that language's translation of the Greek *mysterion* (i.e., mystery; see Ephesians 5:32). It means to consecrate something. It also has connotations of giving an oath, guarantee, or pledge, a sign of a covenant where God gives us grace and we place our faith in him.

So let's do the arithmetic here: For abortion to be a sacrament for some group or other, it would have to be something that the practitioner does as an act of consecration and of faith to someone or something. Does this work for abortion? Quite possibly.

Satanists say that their initiation rituals require total commitment and the ability to do things which one would otherwise fear to do.[15] It is well known that the highest act in Satanism is human sacrifice.[14] With all of this in mind, it is not unreasonable to call abortion a satanic sacrament, or something that would qualify for one. Whether it equates as such for Planned Parenthood is open to debate. However, one quality of a sacrament—and, indeed, of religion period—is that one will work like mad to defend its tenets and practices.

Aren't Planned Parenthood's and its fellow travelers' unyielding dedication to keep abortion legal—all abortions, any abortions, and abortions at any time—reminiscent of religion and/or sacrament? Furthermore, Aleister Crowly, the man who said he essentially transcribed the *Satanic Book of the Law* from a "spirit," wrote, "'Do what thou wilt' shall be the whole of the Law." Isn't one of the main reasons for keeping abortion legal so that people can "Do what [they] wilt"?

Bl. Teresa of Calcutta once said, "It is a poverty to decide that a child must die so that you may live as you wish." Or put another way, "It is a poverty to decide that a child must die so that you may 'Do what thou wilt.'" Her quote sort of takes on another hue considered in this light, doesn't it?

Even if abortion doesn't rise to the level of sacrament, for many within the abortion movement, the procedure has taken on a religious flavor. For instance, upon being hired as manager of 13 Planned Parenthood locations, one of the company's managers said she felt hers was a "sacred duty." Between March and April 2012, Planned Parenthood even held its own version of 40 Days for Life called "40 Days of Prayer." Suggested prayers were, "We give thanks for the doctors who provide quality abortion care" and "We pray for all the staff at abortion clinics around the nation. May they be daily confirmed in the sacred care that they offer women."

Visit Planned Parenthood's website and you can still find that golden oldie of a bumper sticker for purchase: "Keep your rosaries off our ovaries." How does something so simple as a bumper sticker show the tide is turning? If it weren't, Planned Parenthood wouldn't care about the Catholic Church, and that old bumper sticker wouldn't be available. However, in what this observer sees as its increasing venom directed toward the Church is evidence that the tide is turning. The devil only squawks when you're getting to him.

One person who probably doesn't feel abortion is a sacred act is singer Stevie Nicks, who is both a solo artist and a member of the band Fleetwood Mac. During the band's 1970s heyday, abortion was an easy and accepted option. Women were told that they would be getting rid of a "pregnancy," not killing an unborn child, who, regardless, was simply a blob of unrecognizable tissue.

In his book, *To the Limit: The Story of the Eagles*, Marc Eliot relates the sad circumstances of Nicks' abortion. She had been dating Eagles drummer Don Henley, who it seems had little time for her when informed she was pregnant. As a result, Nicks had an abortion and sometime later wrote an introspective song about the experience entitled "Sara," which became a hit for Fleetwood Mac with the release of its *Tusk* album in 1979.

I can never listen to the words "When you build your house, then call me home" without feeling a deep sense of sadness. The lyrics reference the fact that Henley was building a house and seemed to have little time for Nicks and Sara, which, according to Eliot, is the name for the unborn child. While Nicks hasn't eagerly discussed the true meaning of the song, she did tell *Fox News* that she had regrets from her stardom.

However, Henley did address the true meaning of the song in Eliot's book by stating, "[Stevie had] named the unborn kid, Sara, and she had an abortion." She then wrote the song and, according to Henley, dedicated it "to the spirit of the aborted baby."[15] This is just one sad story out of the approximately 50 million equally sad legal abortion stories in the United States alone. God help us.

Children ≠ Burden; Children = Blessing

It appears that the efforts of Planned Parenthood, the HHS decision, etc., is all part of a growing trend toward seeing children as a burden rather than a blessing. Remember, in Scripture, when God opens the womb and gives a couple a child, it is always a blessing (see Psalms 127 and 128). Furthermore, as we read in Acts 17:24-27, Jeremiah 1:5 and 29:11, and Ephesians 1:3-5, the Lord has a special destiny for every person he wills to come into existence. This is why the crimes of contraception and abortion along with this burgeoning hostility toward children are so troubling. To one degree or another, all thwart God's holy will.

Toward this end, also troubling is the fact that in San Francisco, dogs outnumber children by 45 percent. Maine, Massachusetts, New York, and Vermont, four northeastern states that are deemed to be some of America's most liberal, also have the distinction of having the lowest fertility rates.

None of this is happy news. What is good news is that study after study confirms what most of us already know: Those children who are raised in religiously observant homes are more likely to preserve their chastity until marriage. That means no STDs, no early pregnancies that could derail hopes and dreams, no raising children in poverty as a single mother. This is great proof that God's ways work.

What about all the cool, teen-oriented programming such as one sees on MTV? You know, the videos with women in skimpy outfits, lingerie, and bikinis, or the Spring Break festivals with women in skimpy outfits, lingerie, and bikinis, or the reality shows with women in skimpy outfits, lingerie, and bikinis. Isn't every teen enamored with them?

Actually, one would think MTV offers nothing to many teenagers, since they get the true "reality" programming right in their own schools. Why would they need some corporate entity to "entertain" them in their homes with what they see every day? And did you know that busloads of protesting Catholic college-age kids, rosaries in hand, often come to pray outside the MTV studios in Manhattan? Funny how MTV doesn't show viewers that.

When I was a teen, there were no young speakers going around to junior highs, high schools, and parishes voicing their support for a chaste lifestyle. There were certainly sex talks at my Catholic high school, usually given by well-meaning priests, nuns, and parishioners who were members of the parish, but they often lacked an ability to connect with my peers and me.

Today, however, we have a number of dynamic, engaging, and attractive speakers who crisscross the nation to bring the message that chastity and saving oneself for marriage is a great gift of love. In fact, there are whole speakers' bureaus dedicated to handling requests for booking chastity speakers. This is a truly exciting development for our Church and our society.

Natural Family Planning Is Becoming More Fruitful

Another sign of weakness in the pro-abortion and anti-chastity movements is the fact that the Natural Family Planning (NFP) movement has been gaining converts and respect not only from Catholics but also from believers of every stripe. The groundbreaking work done by Dr. Thomas Hilgers at the Pope Paul VI Institute in Nebraska has had a growing impact on those who have not bought the propaganda concerning in vitro fertilization.

Until the US Supreme Court-decreed Roe v. Wade, there had always been a natural give-and-take between those who found themselves in an unwanted pregnancy and those couples who were having problems conceiving a child. Since 1973, between 2 million and 3 million babies have been aborted in the United States each year, which obviously meant that the natural balance was being disturbed. Couples had to find some way to adopt a child, and often that meant adopting from a foreign nation.

However, even before the adoption process was ever initiated, couples, Catholics included, were being told that in vitro fertilization was their only true option of conceiving a child. Initially, many healthcare professionals scoffed at Natural Family Planning. However, according to data recently provided to various medical journals, couples using NFP have a better chance of achieving a pregnancy than those participating in IVF. The business of babies is becoming big business, and while NFP relies on age-old methods, science and a great deal of marketing are used to lure couples into the IVF program. Sadly, sometimes physicians even recommend the spiritual services of Catholic laypeople or priests who openly go against the teachings of the Church to support the lucrative business of IVF.

By word of mouth, many have noticed NFP effectiveness, which has resulting in more doctors being trained in its methodology. This is happening just in the nick of time, and many NFP physicians are finding their practices getting more crowded. The success of NFP is indicative of the burgeoning Culture of Life.

A more contemporary music example might come from the band Death Cab for Cutie's song, "I Will Follow You into the Darkness." It decries mean nuns dressed in black who attack students. While the group's Ben Gibbard was raised Catholic, it seems he never really knew any nuns in habits, though he claims he was indoctrinated by Catholicism and found truth in Jack Kerouac.

Ironically, Kerouac gave up all of his rambling secular and anti-establishment beliefs for not only a return to Catholicism later in life, but a very orthodox brand of Catholicism. In addition, he also became a conservative at the height of the Vietnam War. It seems Gibbard never got the memo. However, he was not alone, as millions of young adults have heard about mean nuns and rulers from the likes of people who never had such an experience, but didn't hear that Kerouac threw away his "Beat Generation" ways. How many in the hip alternative culture who worship Kerouac have ever heard his famous quote "I don't want to be known as a Beat poet any longer; I want to be known as a Catholic"?

A more hopeful example may come to pass from the final days of reggae star Bob Marley. Even today, his name is treated as if he is some sort of religious figure by some, especially those in the alternative community and drug culture. One would think that the legendary musician went to his death living a life of debauchery, filled with the clichés of sex, drugs, and rock 'n' roll. Yet, in reality Marley lived most of life far from the all-night parties one might expect him to visit in Hollywood Hills. Marley, like many Jamaicans, worked for a time in the United States. He worked an industrial job in Delaware and went back to his beloved island to spend more time playing the music he loved, which would eventually evolve into what we now call reggae.

Marley became closely associated with the Rastafari movement, which is far more complicated in its beliefs than the popular misconception that all Rastafarians believe that Marley and former Ethiopian emperor Haile Selassie are some sort of biblical descendants of King David. Yet, Marley never became a tried-and-true Rastafarian. It might befuddle many that Marley was a member of the Ethiopian Orthodox Church. Abuna Yesehaq, a leader of the Ethiopian Orthodox Church, reported that Marley was never more at peace than in his last days, battling cancer and talking about the benchmarks of Christianity. Yesehaq reported seeing Marley often at the Divine Liturgy, and His Excellency also spoke with him on several occasions. Like Kerouac's return to traditional Catholicism, this information is hardly ferreted away in some remote vault; it is out there for anyone to see if they want to know the truth.

How Did We Get Here?

For years there has been a steady drumbeat of permissiveness coming from the militant secular elites. One might have a forgiving spirit toward those who were raised with such a death-spiral ethos. It had been a long time in the making. In Roger Kimball's tour de force book *The Long March*,[16] he examines many points in what he says is the long march forced upon us by secular humanist activists. He notes that the secular left uses one phrase above all others: sexual repression. He points out this condition's supposedly *ipso facto* connection with religion. Indeed, he says the Left treats these two words as if they were carried down from Sinai by Moses himself.

Rather, the term "sexual repression" was given to us by Herbert

Marcuse of the neo-Marxist "Frankfurt School."[17] Marcuse was a leading figure of the school, which had a profound impact on Western thought. He emigrated out of Germany in the 1930s and went on to teach at a slew of American universities. Several 1960s radicals came under his tutelage. One student in particular, the longtime communist radical Angela Davis, was credited as being his most brilliant.

Marcuse railed against "the repressive order of procreative sexuality" and hailed a society where sexuality would have no bounds and human beings could live in "primary narcissism." Wittingly or unwittingly, this is the man whom many take their cues from instead of from the Scriptures and Sacred Tradition.

If Marcuse's term "sexual repression" was a rallying cry for secular humanists who believed in the need to radically deconstruct society as we know it, Dr. Alfred Kinsey's *The Kinsey Report* gave them the supposed evidence they needed to assert that there was nothing sacred or unique about the marital act and that human beings were sexual animals whose only hope of containment was more sex and lowering the bar on what society had traditionally defined as deviant behavior.

Using rigged data, Kinsey wrote glowingly about the joy of all forms of sexual expression, even if they went against God's law, even if this expression had as its outlet those who weren't of legal age and those who didn't have a choice. How well he had persuaded the world to buy a lie would only be understood decades after his reports on male and female sexuality had become gospel for sex educators, psychologists, and lawmakers alike.

Kinsey's influence is why our culture lives with the assumption that we are basically nothing more than sexual animals from birth and that we will somehow harm ourselves if we don't indulge our fantasies or engage in various forms of experimentation, and that we will scar for life our children if we refuse them birth control or counsel chastity before marriage "since they're just gonna do it anyway." Of course, with this understanding in mind, it goes without saying that the faith of our fathers was "repressive," and anyone who takes their faith seriously will experience terrible sexual hang-ups such as frigidity unless we slough off these "patriarchal" restrictions on our deepest sexual longings and needs.

Well, as Jeff Cavins likes to say, there's an old Hebrew term for this: *Bah-loe-nee.* Sadly, however, too many still believe the depravity and nuttiness that Marcuse and Kinsey have served us.

Perhaps the late Irving Kristol, an influential political writer, best summed up the impact these two have had:

> Sexual liberation is always near the top of a countercultural agenda—though just what form the liberation takes can and does vary, sometimes quite wildly. Women's liberation, likewise, is another consistent feature of all counterculture movements—liberation from husbands, liberation from children, liberation from family. Indeed, the real object of these various sexual heterodoxies is to disestablish the family as the central institution of human society, the citadel of orthodoxy.

We are all paying the price for it.

As we will detail in a later chapter, the presidential candidacy of former US Senator Rick Santorum (R-PA) and the ensuing faux "birth control" argument was a fascinating study of just how far we have come.

At the start of campaigning for the Iowa caucuses, Santorum was so far back in the GOP pack that he took to campaigning in pizza parlors, even when only one person was present and his talk to the prospective voter was interrupted by someman picking up an order. At debates, the former senator voiced his frustration that he was barely given a question. After all, this was a man who had served a total of 16 years in both houses of Congress, who had helped expose the House banking scandal, who was the third ranking Republican in the US Senate for six years, and who led the Senate GOP's welfare reform efforts in the late 1990s. However, who could blame the press when the senator had barely one percent support in the polls?

Providentially, it all seemed to change at the last minute, as Santorum seemed ride an inexplicable surge that came not from any well-heeled advertising campaign but by word of mouth and from a dedicated band of pro-life Catholics and Evangelicals who seemed to coalesce behind the endorsements of pro-life activist Bob Vander Plaats and the Duggar family, who were made famous by the television reality show that featured the family of 21.

The campaign went through a series of losses in New Hampshire, South Carolina, and Florida before coming back with a string of upsets in Missouri, Minnesota, and Colorado. At that point, some thought a victory in Michigan, the boyhood home of Governor Mitt Romney, might turn the Santorum surge into the Santorum stomp.

However, as soon as the surge began, the senator found himself in the crosshairs of not only putative Democrat opponents and the media but even conservatives. Why would his presumed natural allies make such a big deal of his opposition to the HHS mandate? They couldn't understand why anyone would make birth control a campaign issue (this despite the fact that birth control per se was not the issue).

Furthermore, now that he was a serious challenger to the Romney nomination, Senator Santorum found himself unflatteringly portrayed in one story after another in the Romney-supporting and influential *Drudge Report*. Perhaps the crescendo of these attacks came when a story about Santorum's 2008 appearance and speech at Ave Maria University found its way to a banner headline on the *Drudge Report*. In the speech, he opined that Satan had his sights set on the United States because America was a force for good in this world. It wasn't his belief that Satan was targeting the US, but rather that he actually, heaven forbid, believed in Satan. This was a man, the commentators bloviated *ad nauseam*, being seriously considered for the highest office in the land? Gasp! According to CNN's Belief blog:

> The speech came at the beginning of the academic year at the Catholic university in Florida. At that point, the

The Culture of Life Will Prevail

2008 presidential campaign was in full swing. Then-candidate Barack Obama had recently made a statement about abortion and the issue of deciding when life began, which he said was above his pay grade.

Santorum was using the devil-tinged language after explaining Obama's position on abortion. He quoted Bishop Samuel Aquila of Fargo, North Dakota, who said at the time, "Catholics who support so-called 'abortion rights' support a false right, promote a culture of death and are guarded by the father of lies."

"This is not a political war at all, this is not a culture war at all, this is a spiritual war," Santorum said, according to a recording of the speech on the university's website. "And the father of lies has his sights on what you think the father of lies, Satan, would have his sights on. A good, decent, powerful, influential country, the United States of America."

The speech gained a new life this week when it surfaced on the website Right Wing Watch and was then picked up by the Drudge Report and a host of media outlets.

"If you were Satan, who would you attack?" the former U.S. senator asked the students. "There's no one else to go after other than the United States, and that's been the case, for now, almost 200 years."

Santorum went on to explain how he thought the devil had attacked the United States in several areas: its foundations, academia, the Protestant Church and government.

Asked about the speech on Tuesday, Santorum offered no apologies. "I'm a person of faith. I believe in good and evil," Santorum told CNN in Arizona.

"If somehow or another because you're a person of

> faith and you believe in good and evil is a disqualifier for president, we're going to have a very small pool of candidates who can run for president," he said.
>
> "If they want to go ahead and dig up old speeches to a religious group they can go right ahead and do so," Santorum went on. "I'm going to stay on message. I'm going to talk about the things Americans want to talk about."

Interestingly, the story was first seen in a positive light a few days earlier on the influential Catholic website SpiritDaily.net, which is run by former Pulitzer Prize-nominee Michael Brown. A four-year-old story that made many readers of Brown's website nod with approval at someone who spoke to their concerns got a different spin, and all of a sudden, Santorum became cemented in some people's minds as a superstitious Catholic relic from the Middle Ages.

Not surprisingly, faithful Catholics and Evangelicals came to his defense. Conservative opinion makers also defended the senator, noting that at the time of the talk, he was out of office and speaking at a traditional Catholic university saying traditional Catholic things to a traditional Catholic audience.

One of Santorum's most interesting defenders was the aforementioned Dr. R. Albert Mohler, who wrote a glowing defense of the candidate, and used the piece to state his wish that more Evangelical leaders would be so bold.[18]

Nonetheless, as mentioned above, the candidate took "friendly fire" from some fellow conservatives. Indeed, many expressed shock that not only did Santorum not back down in the face of such attacks, he continued on with his social and religious themes (often picking up more votes along the way).

However, this "with friends like these" treatment was relatively limited. Furthermore, for every negative comment, scores of Catholic women from all races and walks of life defended the former Pennsylvania lawmaker and the Church's teachings via Facebook and other social media. They included the growing number of female Catholic bloggers—women such as Ashley McGuire, the Robert Novak Journalism Fellow at Philips Foundation, as well as founder and editor-in-chief of the online women's magazine *Altcatholicah*, radio host Teresa Tomeo, Carrie Severino, a Harvard-trained lawyer chief counsel and policy director Judicial Crisis Network, and Gloria Purvis, an African-American Ivy League-educated woman and pro-life activist who has appeared on EWTN and ABC News.

As the Tufts-educated McGuire put it, the debate over the issue is "increasingly being framed as one between women and religion, women and the Catholic Church, which is very problematic because it's a distraction from the real issue, and it's completely unfair to women who are ... divided about the mandate.... Objecting to the HHS mandate is not an attack on women."

As an aside about the HHS situation, in light of the Obama Administration's forcing Catholic employers to violate their consciences, it is too bad that we couldn't have had a debate between Herbert Marcuse and someone such as Elizabeth Anscombe.[19]

Anscombe was such a formidable debater that after having dispatched C.S. Lewis during a disagreement over a certain theological point, he not only rewrote a chapter in his book *Miracles*, he never again did any strictly theological writing. Although written in 1972, Anscombe's treatise on the ill societal effects of birth control titled "Contraception and Chastity" is possibly more relevant today than what it was published and is a must-read for anyone interested in the topic of birth control. It would have been interesting to see what this remarkable woman would have done with the arguments the administration has used to impose the sophistic tyranny of the HHS decision.

In a *Christianity Today* November 8, 2005, article entitled: "A Hard Pill to Swallow," senior associate writer Agniezka Tennant bared her soul to reveal why an Evangelical decided to leave birth control behind. "Mircette [oral contraceptive] and I became one shortly after my wedding day. In a way, my union with the wallet-sized green box of 28 pills was more complete than the bond I had with my husband." A sobering story that no doubt resonated with many who read it.

Yet, sometimes heroes to the pro-life community can come in the most unexpected of ways. The unexpected death of conservative activist Andrew Breitbart shocked the conservative community. Many pro-lifers were unaware of the outspoken nature of Breitbart, who was not known to be particularly religious and was not raised as such. However, in the last speech he ever gave, which was to a small pro-life youth faction of the Conservative Political Action Committee in Washington, DC, on January 10, 2012, Breitbart poured out his emotions to the crowd. Breitbart told the group that he was adopted and so were many of the children on his cul-de-sac in a trendy Hollywood-area neighborhood, yet it never dawned on him until later what pro-choice meant. He added:

> I became a culture warrior. I am less political than I am about the culture ... I am adopted, I never heard the conservative message because I was surrounded by a pro-abortion culture. The media portrayed the pro-life people as crazy people. I never thought about the issue at all, at all. It (abortion) was something that mattered more than anything in that part of town I grew up in, liberal Hollywood. It was a key card that got you into everywhere in Hollywood. However, there was a seed literally planted in me (crowd laughs). I don't think I would have seen the light if it weren't for people like you that stood up to that, especially young people. Now there are open pro-life people in Hollywood like Patricia Heaton who get jobs, but it is because of people like you ... Stand strong; you inspire me.

Getting back to the subject, women like McGuire are a perfect example of why the Culture of Life will prevail. Because of the depravity of some aspects of popular culture, it might appear on the surface that there is no way the tide could be turning toward Catholicism. Yet more and more studies show that young people are rejecting the Culture of Death the culture has tried feeding them all their lives.

For instance, in 2009, many news outlets, including *The New York Times,* reported the findings of the National Center for Health Statistics. The report showed that young people are waiting longer to have sex than did teens just a few years earlier. The *Times* also reported that many teens are not sexually active.[20]

As a matter of fact, many teens today engage in far less pre-marital sexual activity than did their parents. While there are many reasons for this, more and more Catholics, especially youth and young adults, are embracing the teachings of the Church, even if only in a *de facto* way.

This is not only helping themselves but also helping others by their example.

SEVEN
WHO SAYS THE CHURCH HAS NO POLITICAL CLOUT?

It used to be that, after the unions, the Catholic Church taken as a bloc had arguably the most powerful political voice in the United States. Indeed, recall that the 1960 Kennedy-Nixon presidential contest was very close. With 70 percent of the Catholic vote going to Kennedy, one could make a strong case that without that portion of the electorate, our nation's history and that of the world would be very different. In parts of the country, notable the voter-rich Northeast and Midwest, Democrat leaders would hardly make a move without the tacit sign-off of Church leaders. This may slightly overstate the case, but not by much. The Catholic vote was seen as being that reliable and crucial, much like the African American and Jewish vote is for Democrats today.

The marginalization of the Catholic vote and eventually religion and faith began with certain US Supreme Court decisions in the late 1940s and continued through the mid-1960s (e.g., two 1962 and 1963 decisions by the US Supreme Court to disallow school and/or state-sanctioned prayer in school). However, undermining the presence of religion in the secular square did not change the *realpolitik* electoral situation in which the Church, and thus a religious worldview held sway.

What began changing this was the election of 1972. That is when, building on the work of the McGovern Commission, radical secularists increasingly began their takeover of the Democrat Party.

While the Commission took its name from then-US Senator George McGovern (D-ND), it was really the work of Fred Dutton. He had not only managed Bobby Kennedy's 1968 presidential campaign, he was a major voice of the anti-Vietnam War movement. Dutton wasn't anti-Catholic (his father had been Catholic); rather, he looked at his own politics, saw what he thought was a still-burgeoning youth movement, and thought that the dimensions of *realpolitik* had changed. It was time to reach out to different constituencies. Put in today's jargon, the Commission recommended throwing the Church and a religiously informed worldview under the bus.

When McGovern became his Party's nominee and gave Dutton free rein to implement his vision, he did two things. First, he increased the number of women delegates, primarily because he thought they would increase the number of voices for peace and thus withdrawal from Vietnam. Keep in mind that the Party's 1968 platform was still in favor of an American presence in Southeast Asia. However, as alluded to above, the anti-War movement was just beginning to lose some steam. What was still an active, motivating force for women was feminism. Remember that *Roe v. Wade* decision did not come until January 1973.

According to Mark Stricherz, author of *Why the Democrats are Blue*, the second thing Dutton did was use "other measures to, in effect, help secular, educated elites wrest the party machinery from state and big-city bosses."[1] As pro-life Democrat and former Rhode Island State Senate Majority Leader David R. Carlin writes:

> [P]ro-choice true believers have a tremendous sense of social superiority relative to the average pro-life American. And with good reason – they really are socially superior. They tend to be better educated, wealthier and more privileged than their pro-life counterparts. They drive better cars and live in better houses. They have better taste in coffee, wine, food and music. They are more likely to watch *Mystery*!

> As a rule, socially superior people feel morally superior as well. If they did not, they would have a guilty conscience about their privileges. This tendency to grab a bigger share, then to congratulate oneself on having deserved it, is one of the stronger bits of empirical evidence for the reality of Original Sin.
>
> At any rate, pro-choicers look at pro-lifers with a mixture of disdain and pity. They consider them to be both vulgar and morally offensive—not at all the kind of people whose views need to be listened to, let alone encouraged.

Fast forward to 2006, and in that mid-term election, we saw some of the first signs that religion was openly in the crosshairs of some of the resurgent secularists. With significant gains in Congress and thus greater power, they had now gained a greater ability to foster change. The only thing standing in their way was the veto pen of President George W. Bush. Indeed, all but one of his vetoes came in the last two years of his second term.

The election of 2008 brought more secularist liberals into power on the coattails of Barack Obama, and it seemed to many observers that religion was being pushed into a musty locker in some dank basement, out of sight and out of the way. God, if "she" existed, would not deliver paradise on earth, but mankind (and womankind) would.

The French Enlightenment thinker Voltaire had gleefully predicted that the Catholic Church would be gone by the time the impending French Revolution finished with it. He didn't live to see that, but we can be excused for wondering if his modern day fellow travelers hope for the same result.

We can certainly detect his influence in statements such as President Obama's explanation for the phenomenon of the small town and rural folk across America who "cling" to their religion and guns when times get tough. We can also see it in hindsight with the evidently false outreach President Obama made during his honorary doctorate acceptance speech at Notre Dame and, most infamously, the HHS mandate.

Do these maneuvers fit in with some secular utopian plan of his? After all during the 2008 campaign, he told a congregation in Greenville, South Carolina, "I am confident we can create a Kingdom right here on earth." Left unsaid, of course, is *whose* kingdom? As historian Paul Johnson asks in his book *Modern Times: the World from the Twenties to the Nineties*, shouldn't we have been cautious about such world-changing visions?

Despite the size of his victory, commentator Dr. Fouad Ajami notes that the common people of this nation never bought into the notion that the president is somehow a sort of Messiah who would bring about "hope" and "change."[2] They already believed in the One (God), and the man from Chicago via Honolulu was not him. In his analysis, Dr Ajami drew from his experience in the Middle East where leaders such as Gamal Abdel Nasser promised the sun and moon to their people but could never truly deliver or meet such lofty expectations.

The midterm elections of 2006 and the general presidential election of 2008 were the culmination of decades, if not centuries, of anti-religious machinations and rhetoric in the Western world. If nothing else, one can safely say that the last 50 years fell under the sway of the anti-religious sentiment stoked by the likes of Alinsky and company. Alinsky was far more subtle in his touch than the verbose but honest communists who openly said that religion should be destroyed. Alinsky often used religious figures such as Don Jones, who served as the youth pastor to a young lady named Hillary Rodham (now Secretary of State Hillary Clinton).

In Roger Kimball's aforementioned book, *The Long March*, he delves into the inroads the Far Left made in all areas of our economy, culture, and psyche. It all seemed to come together in the election of 2008. Kimball tells us of a revealing quote made in 1942 by socialist economist Joseph Schumpeter: "Capitalism is being killed by its achievements." Kimball posits that Schumpeter may have been onto something, as some 70 years later religion was slowly being shown the door, and filling the vacuum was the nanny state.[3] Kimball's book was written in 2000, and in the 12 years since its release the secular elites have shown nary a concern about their salvation but quite a bit about their trans fat intake—so much so that New York Mayor Michael Bloomberg led the charge in banning it, along with foods that contained high levels of salt and sugar. Perhaps Mark Steyn has it right when he calls him Nurse Bloomberg. Somewhere Voltaire and Alinsky must be smiling, knowing that the progressive secular elites have created so much angst over trans fats, all the while alleviating any concern over one's soul.

Not surprisingly, it seems that those who disdain organized religion are all aflutter with the talk of secret meetings among Catholics. One only has to witness the delusional *Da Vinci Code* following, complete with European tours to find "the truth," to understand this point. However, in reality, it would appear that it was the liberals who all too often were holding meetings cloaked with secrecy.

A meeting in 1964 in Hyannis Port, Massachusetts, where several liberal theologians convened as guests of the Kennedys, is a prime example. Fortunately, we have the words of one of the attendees, former Jesuit priest Albert Jonsen, professor of ethics (of all things), who eagerly tells us the details. In a January 2009 *Wall Street Journal* story, Jonsen spoke of the 1964 meeting, which was held with several members of the extended Kennedy clan in attendance. In addition to the late Robert and Edward Kennedy, Jesuit priests Fr. Robert Drinan (who later became a congressman from Massachusetts until the election of Pope John Paul II forced him to retire from the House) and Fr. Joseph Fuchs, along with diocesan priests Fr. Charles Curran and Fr. Giles Milhaven, were in attendance. The crux of the meeting was pushing a social agenda highlighted by abortion into the forefront of American politics. What better way for the agenda to be pushed than to have an audience with the Kennedys?[4]

Though abortion would not become legal until 1973, the late Senator Edward Kennedy would surprisingly hold out on the pro-life side for a short while longer before he jumped onto the bandwagon of death with gusto. In 1972 he even famously sent a reply to a constituent who supported abortion in which he stated that, in his view, abortion was horrific and something he could never support. Shortly thereafter the senator from Massachusetts supported abortion wholesale.

In late 2011, the famed Boston College professor and prolific conservative writer Peter Kreeft delivered a eyebrow-raising speech in Wisconsin during which he stated that those priests who steered the Kennedys and others in Catholic America down the abortion path were greater sinners than priests who abused children.[5]

The priests who had called for the unholy conclave had roped their first patsies, and there would be many more doing the bidding of the evil one. In a metaphorical sense, those who convened the gathering took on the persona of the fictional Michael Corleone of *The Godfather* film trilogy. Like the junior Corleone, those priests were once considered to have great potential in the legitimate world. However, also like the younger Corleone, they let their egos get the best of them; one minute they were doing the Lord's work, and the next they were doing the bidding of the evil one—all the while feigning that they were protecting the weak and innocent from dark forces. Those infamous words, "my conscience," were often used by the unholy men at Hyannis Port. They never used the Church's terminology of "a well-formed conscience."

The news media lambasted the comments former Pennsylvania US Senator and GOP presidential candidate Rick Santorum made in early 2012 concerning the September 12, 1960, speech by then-Senator John Kennedy to the Greater Houston Ministerial Association, 1960 at the Rice Hotel in Houston, Texas. The common wisdom focused on the fact that Kennedy had made traditionally anti-Catholic American WASPs feel comfortable that he wouldn't establish a papal theocracy once in the White House.

What many ignored were the most basic of facts as to why this was so. Santorum had simply expressed his outrage that the future president almost seemed to apologize for his Catholic faith. In fact, Archbishop Charles Chaput, arguably the second most important American prelate after Cardinal Dolan, expressed nearly the same sentiments in a speech on March 1, 2010, at Houston Baptist University to mark the 50th anniversary of Kennedy's speech.

Those who took issue with Senator Santorum usually point out that Jesus' mission was to the poor of the world. Yet, Jesus said the poor would always be among us, most likely because he knew that they would always be used by the very people who claim to be helping them. The likes of the unholy alliance at Hyannis Port have supported abortion and Big Government programs in the name of the poor, and yet the poor were being enslaved by a culture of death and a government that wanted them controlled.

Slowly but surely the culture bought into the lies of the men at Hyannis Port, who heard them from the apostle of agitation, Saul Alinsky. He wrote in his most famous work, *Rules for Radicals*, "In the beginning the organizer's first job is to create the issues or problems."[6] This is the same man who penned the following epigraph[7] in *Rules for Radicals*, writing, "Lest we forget at least an over-the-shoulder acknowledgment to the very first radical: from all our legends...the first radical known to man who rebelled against the establishment and did it so effectively that he at least won his own kingdom—Lucifer."

Alinsky's admirers included former first lady and current secretary of state, Hillary Rodham Clinton, who wrote her 1969 senior college thesis on the effectiveness and viability of Alinsky's tactics (she agreed with him regarding empowering people but disagreed with his relativist "end justifies the means" worldview and his conviction that injustice couldn't be changed by those working from inside the system).

His disciples accessed the highest levels of government in 2008 when a former Chicago community activist who was not only schooled in Alinsky's canons and rhetoric but taught them and wrote the fourth chapter of the book, *After Alinsky: Community Organiz-*

ing in Illinois—a chapter that is practically word-for-word *Rules for Radicals*—became president of the United States. Of course, we're talking about President Barack Obama.

Both the president and his secretary of state surely are charming individuals who have lived fascinating lives and would snicker at the assertion that somehow they have been influenced by forces from the dark side. Yet how many other apostles of political activism ever dedicated a book to Lucifer? How many others said the following just two months before their death?

> ... if there is an afterlife, and I have anything to say about it, I will unreservedly choose to go to hell.... Hell would be heaven for me. All my life I've been with the have-nots. Over here, if you're a have-not, you're short of dough. If you're a have-not in hell, you're short of virtue. Once I get into hell, I'll start organizing the have-nots over there.... They're my kind of people.[7]

Evil is subtle. It influences us best when we least realize it. Alinsky didn't believe in over-the-top protests; he believed in subtle takeovers. Being flamboyant in life draws too much attention, making takeover that much more difficult.

Once the Obama administration had been assembled, they constantly faced criticism from a host of conservative commentators. These pundits brought up the names of infamous White House appointees like Van Jones, who mouthed 9/11 conspiracy theories asserting that the government aided and abetted Osama Bin Laden.

They also drew attention to former White House communications director Anita Dunn, who told students—in a church of all places—that "two of my favorite political philosophers" were Bl. Mother Teresa and Mao Tse-tung. She claims she was joking, but whatever her motivations, she seemed oblivious to Mao's possibly not being the best person to quote. After all, he is a man who killed millions of people during his Cultural Revolution, a revolution that in turn killed thousands of Catholics, including priests and even Mother Teresa's fellow nuns.[8] Would she or anyone use Hitler or Stalin as a positive example to make a point? Mao was at least as bad as those two.

As Christians, we should presume good will and take her at her word that she was simply using the founder of Communist China as someone who "chose his own way." However, as we have subsequently seen by the president's support for same sex marriage and his approval of the HHS mandate, when he surrounds himself with people such as Jones and Dunn and then says he wants to fundamentally transform America, it really makes one stop and think, doesn't it?

Anti-Life Politicians Teach the Masses Catholic Theology

The election of 2008 made many pro-life Catholics cringe at the prospects of hearing more of the less then well-formed pontifications from the likes of now-Vice President Joe Biden, who noted he was never a John Paul II guy but a John XXIII guy.

And sitting with an even firmer grip on actual power and influence was the then-Speaker House of Representatives Nancy Pelosi. It was very kind of her to let the Church in on an apparently well-kept secret, namely that Catholic Christianity had never really known when life begins. Pelosi and those advising her must have been taking their theological cues from the likes of the Hyannis Port attendees, since the Church has been in opposition to abortion since the days of Trajan Caesar (if not before), and the Church has always taught that life begins at conception.

It would have been cringe-worthy had Pelosi referred to herself as a "collapsed Catholic," as did *New York Times* editor Bill Keller. However, she referred to herself as a "devout Catholic." The Church—via her bishops, theologians, and animated laymen—mounted a vigorous campaign to show what actual Church teaching was and the history of it.

The midterm congressional election of 2010 brought redemption, as pro-lifers and pro-life Catholics made great gains. For instance, US Rep. Pat Toomey was elected to the US Senate from Pennsylvania and Sean Duffy, who was previously best known as a cast member on the MTV reality show *Real World: Boston* in 1997, was elected to US House of Representatives from Wisconsin.

Sadly, 15 of the relatively small number of pro-life Democrats lost the seats many would have held in the 112th Congress but for their vote for Obamacare in the 111th Congress' waning days. Their ranks include Rep. Bart Stupak (D-MI), the pro-life Democrat who had given President Obama the most cover on the issue of whether his reform plan paid for abortions. Another pro-life Democrat who followed Stupak's lead was Rep. Kathy Dahlkemper (D-PA), whose Republican opponent soundly trounced her. As a result, while Congress is more pro-life as a whole, there are roughly 20 pro-life Democrats left in the House of Representatives, and not a single one in the Senate.

Regardless, with more pro-life legislators over all, the 112th Congress saw more and more vigorous pro-life bills, including ones by pro-life hero US Rep. Chris Smith (R-NJ) and his co-chair of the Bipartisan Congressional Pro-Life Caucus, US Rep. Dan Lipinski. In May 2011, US Rep. Paul Ryan (R-WI), the House GOP's lead on budget issues, exchanged cordial letters on the topic of helping the less fortunate with then-Archbishop Timothy Dolan, president of the US Conference of Catholic Bishops. While the cordial tone of the archbishop's response outraged some on the Left, many tradition-minded Catholics were happy to see that Republicans were no longer treated as agents of Beelzebub because of their differences with the Democrats over how to best help the poor and marginalized of our society.

Rep. Ryan assured Archbishop Dolan that he was indeed adhering to his Catholic faith's teachings on helping the less fortunate. It seemed that both agreed that not only were the poor to be a primary concern if and when Social Security and Medicare were overhauled, but it was indeed the poor who truly suffer when they rely on Big Government solutions to ease them out of life's burdens. Interestingly enough, it was none other than former President Bill Clinton who came to Rep. Ryan's aid when he came under a withering assault by the Leftist pundits, including a commercial that showed an actor playing Ryan pushing an elderly woman over a cliff. Those who saw nothing wrong with such an attack on Ryan then turned their pens on the former president.

As the race for the White House began to heat up, it was a given that Catholicism would somehow become an issue, and a negative one at that. Ironically, the first evidence of this came when some key liberal journalists took issue with Salem Lutheran Church, which US Rep. Michele Bachmann (R-MN) had attended when she was younger. That parish belongs to the Wisconsin Evangelical Lutheran Synod, which does have some old anti-Catholic teachings, although these are hardly mentioned in the modern era.

In reality, most members probably didn't know their Communion's teachings about Catholicism, or that they were once commonplace. For her part, the congresswoman released a statement saying she no longer attended that church. For some onlookers, it seemed more than a bit peculiar that the news media would pay attention to anti-Catholicism, when it often seems to be something at which journalists excel.

However, it was former Speaker of the House Newt Gingrich, a convert to Catholicism, and former US Senator Rick Santorum, a cradle Catholic from Pennsylvania, who seemed to be in journalistic crosshairs because of their religion. Santorum was badgered on the campaign trail and in the debates about his views on traditional marriage and his beliefs concerning contraception. Santorum soldiered on, winning the hearts and minds of orthodox Catholics and others, even as some elite in the culture raised their eyebrows at the fact that he often attended the extraordinary form.

The only indication of Santorum's frustration with this occurred in a post-debate interview when he noted that Google allowed certain militant homosexual websites that equated his name with a certain homosexual sex practice to be front and center on the first page of a search for the name Santorum. At the same time, vile websites using President Obama's name are nowhere to be seen on Google.

Who Says the Church Has No Political Clout? 173

In perhaps the most egregious event of the campaign season, several left-wing, pro-abortion sites ridiculed Santorum and his wife for bringing home their stillborn child Gabriel so that their children could say good-bye to their brother before he was buried. This came to national attention when Democrat talk show host Alan Colmes openly mocked Santorum while on a Fox News live segment with *National Review* editor Rich Lowry. After Lowry lashed out at his fellow pundit for this heartless tirade, Colmes did later apologize. He even did the right thing by personally calling Santorum and expressing his regret. Yet many on the secular Left refused to apologize and follow Colmes on that high road.

The mercurial Gingrich came under a blistering attack not only from the mainstream media but from the GOP establishment. Gingrich's ego, grandiosity, and womanizing were hardly a secret. Yet, the media seemed flummoxed as to why Gingrich, a nominal mainline Protestant, would convert to Catholicism. While the mainstream media seemed more than happy to allow those on the left a chance to repent, those on the right who repented and then became Catholic seemed ludicrous to the media gatekeepers.

Santorum was mercilessly put through the gauntlet when an old audiotape emerged of him giving a talk at Ave Maria University in Florida. In his talk, the former senator mentioned the existence of Satan and the decline in morality so evident in the western world. For starters, it seems some in the mainstream media are so ignorant of religion that although 90 percent of Americans belong to some form of Christianity, Judaism, or Islam, each of which believes evil is manifested through a figure known as Satan, the media still sees fit to mock them. Some in the media seemed to take glee in pouncing on Santorum. He was called a kook, a nut, deranged, a mullah, and an ayatollah, not by nameless posters on left-wing blogs but by famed writers at serious newspapers.

Leading the charge was a woman who just seems as if she was born angry, that maven of militant secularism, Maureen Dowd. She called fellow Catholic Santorum a "mullah" who wants to take "women back to the caves," because, golly, he actually agrees with what is in the *Catechism of the Catholic Church* and Scripture. Senator Santorum shouldn't feel bad, though. She derides anyone who actually believes in the teachings of Catholicism.

Never one to miss a chance at showing what is evidently his bad formation (or maybe it's a rejection of his good formation), MSNBC's Chris Matthews also entered the fray. He claimed the reason Catholicism is growing is due to homophobic converts coming into the Church.[9]

Evidently, Matthews seems not to know about Melinda Selmys, author of the book *Authentic Sexuality*, a Catholic convert, mother of six, and former lesbian. Or Eve Tushnet, an Ivy League graduate and chaste lesbian. Or David Morrison, a chaste homosexual and author of *Beyond Gay*. Then there are SSA blogger "Catholic Boy Richard," Catholic theologian Joshua Gonnerman, and a gentleman named Thad who blogs at "Gay, Catholic, and Chaste!"

Finally, at least for now, there a guy who writes with the penname of Steve Gershom. His "gut reaction" to people like Matthews who say, "How mean the Church is, and how bigoted, because she opposes gay marriage.... How badly she misunderstands gay people, and how hostile she is towards us" is, "Are we even talking about the same church?"

Yep, there's a bunch of homophobic converts and reverts for you.

Mr. Matthews may also be ignorant of groups such as Courage, the apostolate for those who struggle with same-sex attractions and whose ranks are rapidly filling with men and women from all walks of life. Courage and its parent support group, Encourage, help them feel the comfort of and have assurance in God's chaste plan for their lives. *The New York Times,* of all papers, did a favorable story on Eve Tushnet, who is a popular Catholic writer who belongs to the group.[1]

The *coup de grâce* of hate came from David Waldman, who writes for a number of publications. His little nugget makes the Know Nothing Party of the 1840s smile. I will not print his vile and foul-mouthed diatribes in this book, but suffice it to say you can read his scurrilous rant on the Internet.

Who Says the Church Has No Political Clout?   175

And even with Waldman's piece, just when you thought expressions of anti-Catholicism couldn't get any worse, *Huffington Post* columnist Larry Doyle entered the fray with a column titled, "The Jesus-Eating Cult of Rick Santorum." Though it is hard to read without getting extremely angry, I will just include one passage so as to give the article's tone and tenor:

> As a former member of the same sect (an Irish-Catholic, the worst kind), I have read the texts, participated in the rites, and even seen behind the curtain, as it were, as a one-time altar boy, so help me. I managed to escape, but then, Santorum is in much deeper than I ever was. Unlike Christians, Santorum and his fellow Roman Catholics participate in a barbaric ritual dating back two millennia, a "mass" in which a black-robed cleric casts a spell over some bread and wine, transfiguring it into the actual living flesh and blood of their Christ. Followers then line up to eat the Jesus meat and drink his holy blood in a cannibalistic reverie not often seen outside Cinemax.[10]

Mind you, the *Huffington Post* is not only read by its readers but by those with AOL Internet service, as it is their news server. The angry aftermath that followed the anti-Catholic article was carried extensively by Fox News and the new media, but naturally the old media ignored the story. This is telling enough, but the supposed apology issued by Doyle was hardly what one would call an apology.

"It's traditional at this point for me to half-apologize, to say that I'm sorry if anybody was offended, but I really don't mind if anybody was offended," Doyle stated. Again, the smug arrogance is hard to stomach. You know what I love about this, though? It means the Church continues to have relevance. It means that she still possesses influence to sway hearts and souls. No one pays attention to the insignificant. Former Minnesota governor Harold Stassen ran for president 12 times between 1944 and 2000. After 1952, and especially in 2000, he was never more than an afterthought. That is not happening with the Catholic Church, though, is it?

Indeed, the Church can get the likes of Dowd, Matthews, and Waldman to froth at the mouth in an almost Pavlovian way. The simple reason is that she is growing when by their lights she should be not only dying on the vine but shriveling in a complete statistical free fall. You can understand how it would feel if the shoe was on the other foot.

So that they don't have neurological issues down the road, maybe they should just work on accepting what it seems to this observer they simply won't accept now. After all, Catholic women's conferences are growing by leaps and bounds, as are Catholic colleges that rigorously adhere to the teachings of the Church. Catholic young people who go to regularly attend Mass are more pro-life than their grandparents. Notice anything about the two groups I have emphasized here: women and youth?

As the Republican primary season marched on, the former Pennsylvania senator kept grabbing larger shares of each group's vote. He won both in Ohio and then won by even larger margins in Tennessee, Oklahoma, Alabama, and Mississippi. While Senator Santorum didn't win Wisconsin, he did win that state's capital, Madison, which is known even by people outside the Badger State as "the People's Republic of Madison" because of how unrelentingly ... well, liberal is not the word. Many people in Madison think President Obama, arguably the most liberal president in our nation's history, is a DINO ... a Democrat In Name Only. Get the picture? The capital's daily trumpeted a headline that fairly screamed, "How did *this* happen?"

Judging by the reporting and editorials one saw afterward, this bewilderment was pretty much par for the course around the nation where the Pennsylvania native did well. People just assumed that the rich, women, and youth were in the firm grasp of President Obama (or at least the "not as icky as Santorum" Governor Romney). It should not have been a surprise, really. Many women and young people (especially first-time voters), not to mention the elderly, went for Santorum because they were taken with his frank, honest, and sincere approach.

At the same time, reports that Governor Romney had won the Catholic vote in places such as Michigan and Ohio did perplex many. Rick Santorum was so sincerely and authentically Catholic: How could any of his coreligionists vote against him?

To get the answer, one needs to look deep into the numbers. Romney did win the Catholic vote in suburban Ohio and Michigan, particularly areas where Catholic voters make over $100,000 a year and are roughly in the 50 to 70 age group—in other words, Baby Boomers, whose prime concern may have been economic. The economy was an issue on which Romney was, rightly or wrongly, seen as having a better plan than Santorum. Romney, however, lost the Catholic vote in more traditional areas of each state. Indeed, conservative Catholic in Ohio's eastern industrial zone and western Ohio's agricultural heartland easily went for Santorum.

Meanwhile, Back in Washington, DC (or How I Spent My Summer Trying to Remove President Obama from Office)

In January 2012, Secretary of Health and Human Services Kathleen Sebelius (a Catholic), made it mandatory that Catholic employers would soon have a no-conscience clause with regard to the "Obamacare" healthcare law that mandated that everyone provide and pay for abortion and contraception coverage, whether they agreed with it or not. Though this was barely mentioned by the mainstream media, the Catholic media went ballistic. Bishop after bishop and cardinal after cardinal railed against this mandate from pulpit, pen, and computer keyboard. Eventually, every Catholic prelate in America would denounce the measure—something unprecedented in the history of the American Church. Cardinal Timothy Dolan of New York seemed to feel especially taken advantage of because he was assured via a phone call from President Obama, shortly before Secretary Sebelius' announcement, that no such law would be enacted.

The following Sunday, in many dioceses across the country, a letter from the respective bishop of that diocese was read. In the letter, the bishop's flock was told of the egregious nature in which the federal government implemented the dictates of the Obama administration. While the GOP candidates mentioned it in their various Florida primary appearances, it was once again ignored by the mainstream media, even though within several days three-quarters of the nation's bishops had issued a statement denouncing the Obama administration, which led to letters being read at Mass. However, it is events like these that help to spawn political grass fires.

Former Speaker Gingrich helped accelerate the brush fire on the night of January 31, 2012, when, after losing the Florida primary, he railed at President Obama and said the administration had started "a war on the Catholic Church and other religious institutions." The concession speech was carried by all the cable news outlets. Ed Schultz of MSNBC infamously said that Gingrich was making wild accusations "without a shred of evidence," seemingly unaware of the whole issue surrounding the bishops' statements that were read at Catholic Masses across the country.

Former Alaska Governor Sarah Palin chimed in on the controversy with a Facebook post that pondered what the administrators at Notre Dame must have thought after all of the controversy for rolling out the red carpet for Obama and giving him an honorary degree in 2009. Notre Dame would be squarely in the crosshairs for the Obamacare mandate, for it employs thousands of people and would risk either being fined and jailed or foregoing healthcare coverage for their employees altogether.

A *Politico* article, quoting inside sources, seemed to indicate the Obama administration was caught off guard by the uproar from the Catholic clergy and even some on the Catholic Left like liberal *Washington Post* columnist E.J. Dionne, who vigorously supports most of the Obama administration's agenda. Dionne wrote that "Obama threw his progressive Catholic allies under the bus."

The *Politico* article went on to indicate that the reason President Obama took this step concerned his deeply held beliefs on the subject. The same sources felt that conservative Catholics weren't going to vote for Obama anyway. However, even among those Catholics who didn't adhere to the Church's teachings, this—like the overall Obama healthcare initiative—seemed to be a strong-arm tactic that wouldn't sit well even among those who generally supported his ideas.

The article also made mention of US Senator (R-Fla.) Marco Rubio's bill that would reverse the administration's actions. The senator said he adhered to the Church's teachings and none of his four children were planned. He left that up to God, which no doubt sent some liberal militant secularists into a tizzy.

What many pundits and talking heads failed to realize is that while the Obama administration may eventually try to smooth over this crisis before the election by appearing to back down, this leaves their far-left allies feeling emboldened. If the nation's largest church can come under this kind of barrage, what message does that send to other religious bodies and organizations as well as conservative groups? The message is that no one is safe, and a second term could be used to steamroll these groups into giving to the Far Left what they could have only dreamed of: a neutered group of churches and conservative groups ripe for the picking. Yet, if the Church and her allies hold firm, this could be a death knell not only for Obamacare but the entire militant secular agenda that has been the hope of the Left for decades and centuries.

Perhaps the biggest thing mainstream media, and even some elements of the Catholic media, missed was the role of the bishops. Had this occurred some 30 years ago, a few older voices would be raised in protest but relatively few of the newer bishops. Fast-forward to 2012 after years of bishops and cardinals being appointed by Bl. John Paul II and especially Pope Benedict XVI, whose appointments have been far more to the conservative Catholic's liking. This is in sharp contrast to the years when the apostolic delegate to the United States Archbishop Jean Jadot recommended to Pope Paul VI for American episcopal appointments only those who were firmly in the modernist, "spirit of Vatican II" camp.

The new crop of bishops and cardinals are going to get only more orthodox in their orientation and confrontations, if necessary, in defending the Church from sinister forces both in the secular world and within the Church itself. Statements like those from Bishop David Zubik of Pittsburgh, who said the Obama administration's contraception mandate is like telling Catholics, "To hell with you," started to catch the eye of the conservative-oriented media (talk radio, the blogosphere, and Fox News).

Investor's Business Daily ran an editorial entitled "Is Obama Trying to Replace the Pope?"[19] In the days that followed, many religious blogs, especially Evangelical ones, noted that if the administration could do this to the Catholic Church, what might the administration have in store for Evangelicals should the president win a second term? Political commentators like Dick Morris and Dr. Charles Krauthammer said this political ploy was puzzling. They voiced the opinion that this issue was not going to go away and fed into a view that the Obama administration was out to get what it deemed conservative institutions. It did seem especially puzzling in swing states where Catholics are a considerable voting bloc. However, as I noted above, this may well have been well scripted with a wink and a nod to the far Left that if they stuck with the Obama Administration, no institution deemed conservative would be exempt from a modern, state-sponsored liberal overhaul.

Most conservatives have had these sorts of political grass-fire moments in their lives. Like many Catholic families in the industrial Midwest, those in my family were social conservatives who voted Democrat in my childhood. While we became increasingly disillusioned with the state of the national Democratic party, there was always hope that some candidate would help turn things back to the pre-1972 Democratic Party.

I've had a few political wildfire moments in my life. I vividly recall a fellow graduate student and teaching assistant express utter shock that I went to church and held conservative social views. "But you are smart," he exclaimed. Sadly, he admitted that he had no friends outside of his liberal academic social strata, so he believed all that he was told by his liberal elite mentors.

An even more sobering experience lay in wait for me in Washington, DC, in 1994 and 1995, when I worked with the Democratic Leadership Council, a conservative offshoot of the Democratic Party that believed in keeping the party away from the 1972 and 1984 liberal meltdown. I was amazed at how hated we were at certain Washington, DC, social functions, which was populated by the Democratic Party's more liberal operatives. At some events we could have said we worked for Rush Limbaugh and might have been treated better.

I can't get one event in particular out of my head. It was some sort of cocktail party reception, and a woman came over to talk to me. It was apparent that she had not shied away from the wine bar, which perhaps in this instance was very helpful in light of the old Latin saying: "Out of wine the truth flows." This woman asked me about myself and where I was from—the usual conversation-starter material. This led her to ask me about my religion, which isn't normal protocol on Capitol Hill.

When she found out I was Catholic, she said, "Are you one of those good Catholics or bad Catholics?" Sensing the minefield that surrounded that question, I asked her what she meant. She went on a polite tirade (if there is such a thing) about the need to move beyond miracles, saints, and celibacy to relativism, free thinking, and free love. She hardly looked the part of some Age of Aquarius hippie about to take some smoke-filled VW bus back in time to Woodstock, although she was of such an age; rather, she was professionally attired and looked as if she was about ready to argue a case in front of the Supreme Court. In many ways the Left has completely overrun the Democratic Party, as evidenced by the fact that when President Obama was elected, the Left saw to it that the Democratic Leadership Council was put out of business.

Some might point to these last few pages as examples that exhibit anything but the turning tide. Yet, it is exactly the opposite. Though they fail to realize it, the Church has always been a sleeping giant, especially in the United States. Even though there are far too many poorly catechized Catholics, they still attend Mass, even if only occasionally. However—and this is very important—they believe that the teachings of the Church and her message are important guideposts in life and therefore essential to pass on to their children. An attack on the Church from Big Government, which is viewed with suspicion by many churchgoers to begin with, only solidifies the importance of the Church in their lives. The Church not only survived a withering assault from the Left during the Election of 2008, but, as was the case countless times before, providentially made it through the maelstrom stronger than before.

Cardinal Dolan has been known as a master communicator, perhaps the last of the prelates with whom one could seemingly have a beer and talk local sports and in the same breath delve into deep theological questions. Few in any age can pull off this feat, but Cardinal Dolan is certainly one of the best, if not the best in the English-speaking world. Perhaps the only other cardinal in the Western world who could do so is the relatively young 54-year-old German cardinal, Rainer Maria Woelki, the archbishop of Berlin. He has been known, over a beer, to unflinchingly tell Berlin's alternative lifestyle groups the Church's teachings and somehow earn their respect, even as they vehemently disagree with him. His Eminence is also known to wander into German sports bars and talk soccer and the faith with those of the German working class.

Cardinal Dolan quickly became popular in New York, even though much of the city may disagree with the Church's social teachings. He quickly forged the respect, if not the fear, of the city's power structure. This was evident for all the world to see when His Eminence returned to New York City and was greeted with a stroll down Fifth Avenue, where a receiving line of politicians who were liberal, conservative, openly gay, and atheist greeted the conquering hero, red hat in hand. He was the toast of the city. Though many in the city are far to the political and religious left of His Eminence, the city that never sleeps has always had a special place in its heart for organized religion—if nothing else to accommodate the various ethnic groups, especially those that comprise the Catholic Church and Judaism. His Eminence had spoken highly of New York while in Rome and took offense at those who thought of New York as a modern Sodom and Gomorrah.

Many had hoped that the Empire State Building would be lit up in red. It was thought that if the city could honor the Mutant Ninja Turtles, the Kit Kat candy bar, and even the Communist Chinese revolution by lighting the building in their respective colors, surely Cardinal Dolan would be honored as well. Sadly, just like with Bl. Teresa of Calcutta, the powers that be said no. This didn't sit well even with the *Daily News* of New York, which is not exactly a paper known as being friendly to conservatives. The *Daily News* ran an editorial that stated, "The management of the Empire State Building has committed an egregious affront by refusing to light the skyline icon in red to mark Timothy Cardinal Dolan's elevation."[12]

It was a reminder for Cardinal Dolan that lurking just behind him were powerful forces ready for him and the Church to stumble, hesitate, or lose their way, as had countless other churches. The streets of America were littered with the dying structures of once-proud mainline Protestant Churches that have all but disappeared from the religious and political landscape, much to the chagrin of those who once called those churches home. Many have left for Catholic or Evangelical churches that more resemble the creed and beliefs they were once taught.

A few of Cardinal Dolan's statements about President Obama's words to him or those from other White House officials seemed chilling in the political calculus that, like other churches, the Catholic Church would buckle to the whims of the world; at least that's what the White House was counting on.

Some political observers had surmised that the whole HHS

mandate was a strategy concocted by the White House in the hopes of luring single and young married women to the president's side as they tried to paint conservatives, and especially those inside the Catholic Church, as anti-woman, anti-health, and anti-science. This continued with the Sandra Fluke controversy when a large outcry grew over Rush Limbaugh using derogatory language toward the unmarried Georgetown University Law School student. She had lamented that her friends were paying too much for birth control to accommodate their active sex lives at the Jesuit school.

Though Limbaugh did eventually apologize for his remarks, the White House did not return a $1 million pledge to a White House-friendly super PAC from atheist comedian Bill Maher. This apostate Catholic has a habit of not only using extremely vile language to attack conservative women but also using sacrilegious language to attack the Catholic Church, with special emphasis on the Eucharist and confession.

In addition, liberal talk radio host Mike Malloy said he wished Cardinal George of Chicago and Rick Santorum would drink hemlock and die.[13] Many Catholics and conservatives tried to make this an issue as well, but the mainstream media once again barely mentioned the hypocrisy.

Chris Matthews even feared Cardinal George would endorse Rick Santorum, which seemed an odd thing to say. A churchman hasn't endorsed a presidential candidate since President Franklin D. Roosevelt received endorsements in 1932 first from radio priest Fr. Charles Coughlin and then from Fr. James Cox, the first and only Catholic priest to be a party's nominee for president.

Even more peculiar to faithful Catholics was that some liberals surmised Cardinal George was a right-wing conservative. This was news to many of the conservative faithful, who saw His Eminence as a decidedly middle-of-the-road prelate. They did not like that it took him so long to remove the radical activist priest Fr. Michael Pfleger as pastor of St. Sabina Church on Chicago's South Side.

Even if His Eminence is more traditional in his views than he lets on, he is not nearly as outspoken as Cardinal Burke, Archbishop Chaput, or the newly appointed 52-year-old Bishop Alexander Samples of Marquette, a rising star amongst more traditional Catholics.

Reporters and the culture's other opinion makers' lack of knowledge on Catholic issues, particularly moral issues such as contraception, not to mention their seemingly willful inattention to the Church's insistence that birth control was not even the issue per se, appeared to betray an outright contempt by some for Catholicism. This, of course, only added more fuel to the fire.

During the HHS controversy, Cardinal Dolan informed his fellow bishops that some Catholics had sided with the White House, and these people were now suggesting that perhaps the Church should do the same. Cardinal Dolan, who at the time was serving as president of the United States Conference of Catholic Bishops (USCCB) penned a letter to his brother bishops, saying he wasn't having any of it:

> At a recent meeting between staff of the bishops' conference and the White House staff, our staff members [at the USCCB] asked directly whether the broader concerns of religious freedom—that is, revisiting the straight-jacketing mandates, or broadening the maligned exemption—are all off the table. They were informed that they are. So much for "working out the wrinkles." Instead, [Administration staff] advised the bishops' conference that we should listen to the "enlightened" voices of accommodation, such as the recent, hardly surprising yet terribly unfortunate editorial in *America*. The White House seems to think we bishops simply do not know or understand Catholic teaching and so, taking a cue from its own definition of religious freedom, now has nominated its own handpicked official Catholic teachers.[14]

This appalled even many dissenting churchmen. The self-described Catholic liberal Michael Sean Winters, for one, seemed absolutely dumbstruck. Despite assurances he would stand firm on campaign promises such as the Bush tax cuts, the closing of Guantanamo Bay detentions facility for accused terrorists, and the union card check issue, President Obama had folded like an origami crane over all of these. Why, then, couldn't he accommodate the 77 million Catholics in the US, 20 percent of the nation's population? However, the President would not bend on the mandate. Winters vented in the *National Catholic Reporter*:

> I confess I no longer understand Obama. He did not go to the mat to end the Bush tax cuts for the super-rich. He did not go to the mat for comprehensive immigration reform. He did not go to the mat to close Guantanamo Bay. He did not go to the mat for Card Check. He did not go to the mat for a public option in the health care reform. But, he went to the mat over the principle that a Catholic college or charity or hospital is not really religious.
>
> The president not only is the chief magistrate of the land, he is the leader of the Democratic Party. I know I am something of an odd duck by being what I call an "Ella Grasso Democrat." Grasso was the first woman to be elected a governor of her state in her own right, not succeeding her husband. She was pro-labor. She was pro-Israel. She was pro-higher taxes on rich folk. She stood up for the little guy. Unlike other male Democrats—Kennedy and Gore and Gephardt and Muskie—she remained pro-life.
>
> I believe that it is the historic calling of the Democratic Party to stand up to the moneyed interests and say that the common good, not just the individual pursuit of profit, is a moral obligation and a necessity in a free and just society. I am simply not interested in a Democratic Party that is so beholden to the fundraisers at Emily's

List, so consumed with lifestyle politics, that it is willing to thumb its nose at those working class voters who really do care about social justice and for whom that care is a part of their religious beliefs. And, if liberals no longer care about a robust defense of the First Amendment, well, then, we do not deserve the presidency.[14]

As the intrigue continued, US bishops met again in March 2012, and though they expressed their hope for some sort of further compromise from the Obama Administration, the prelates let it be known that they would not back down. Many observers didn't understand why the hierarchy was being so rigid. After all, it was *only* contraception. It's not like (snicker, snicker) those old men in red and magenta dresses (tee-hee) would ever have to worry about using it.

Author and Catholic intellectual George Weigel painted a stark comparison between the US in 2012 and totalitarian Poland in 1953. That was the year the great Stefan Cardinal Wyszynski told the communist authorities that the Church would not acquiesce to the state's choosing members of the ecclesial hierarchy. Picking the successors of the apostles was prerogative of the Holy See, not the regime.

Likewise, Weigel says, by trying to pit dissident Catholics against those who adhere to the Church's teachings, the Obama Administration was attempting to usurp the Church. As Weigel tells it:

> In both cases, an overweening and arrogant government tries, through the use of coercive power, to make the Church a subsidiary of the state. In both cases, the state claims the authority to define religious ministries and services on its own narrow and secularist terms. In both cases, the state is attempting to co-opt as much of society as it can, while the Church is defending the prerogatives of civil society.

Weigel goes on to say:

> In sum, the bishops have rebuffed calls for a tactical retreat; the analysts who have not grasped the sea-change in perspective of the bishops' conference have been confounded; the Catholic Lite brigades have been challenged to think again about the gravity of the theological and constitutional issues involved in the mandate; and those who have supported the bishops thus far have been affirmed in their work.
>
> There will be no compromise here, for there can be no compromise of first principles. Those who understand that will gather their energies and continue to defend both Catholic and American tradition.[15]

Television commentator Glenn Beck, a Mormon, asserted in his program that he had been invited to go to Rome to witness the installation of several cardinals, including Timothy Cardinal Dolan. He said he was struck that the Church realizes that it is not fighting against merely relativism but evil. He went on to say that so many churches have dwindled or disappeared because they had become of the world. Indeed, his witness may be even more powerful than from a believing Catholic, for if he can see what is at stake, then perhaps his testimony will help others see it. He closed by describing a scenario where if the Catholic Church can be attacked, no one is safe. He implored his *GBTV* viewers to understand the consequences by saying, "We are all Catholics now." It didn't end with one simple pronouncement; Beck turned it into a full-fledged campaign and implored his viewers to join him, whatever their faith, in the "We are all Catholics now" campaign.[16] Truer words have rarely been spoken.

EIGHT
THE GROWING NUMBER OF FAITHFUL COLLEGES

Had Notre Dame's President Emeritus Fr. Theodore Hesburgh, CSC, invited the pro-choice President Jimmy Carter to receive an award at Notre Dame in 1979, there might have been scant attention paid.[1]

However, this was 2009, and the pro-life movement was that much stronger. President Obama had already stated on the campaign trail that he didn't want to punish his daughters with children should they unexpectedly become pregnant during their teenage years. Given this and many other comments, many in the pro-life community were shocked when Fr. John Jenkins, CSC, president of Notre Dame, announced that President Obama would be giving the commencement address and receiving an honorary degree.

The firestorm that resulted caused great damage to the university, not only in acrimony but in fund-raising efforts. It caused a rift that wasn't necessary, especially on a campus that was the most orthodox of all the major Catholic campuses (e.g., Georgetown, Boston College, Marquette, and DePaul.) The sheer numbers of bishops openly condemning Fr. Jenkins' decision was over 100, including the prelate of his own Fort Wayne-South Bend diocese, Bishop John D'Arcy, who didn't attend the commencement, as he had always done. Not one major prelate spoke up for Fr. Jenkins, and this fact led many liberal Catholics to bemoan the new orthodoxy of conservatism that had enveloped the Church.

Unlike the aforementioned liberal-skewed campuses, Notre Dame is run by the Congregation of Holy Cross. Unlike some of the major Jesuit-run institutions, the university has always had a strong core of faithful students who take their faith seriously by attending daily Mass and participating in devotions such as the Rosary and Eucharistic Adoration. None other than Cardinal Raymond Burke at the Vatican made clear that any anger directed by the orthodox-minded faithful at the university should not be directed at the university as a whole, since attacking the faithful students would be like throwing the baby out with the bath water.[2]

However, it seemed that far too many Catholic college and universities were hit with the self-absorbed virus in the 1960s. Notre Dame and many other Catholic campuses signed on to the provisions of the Land O'Lakes Conference held in Wisconsin in July 1967, which stated that they would act independently of the Holy See. It was a way for these campuses to state their academic and intellectual independence. Obviously it was more important for them to be liked and respected by the powers that be than adhere to the Church. Jesus warned about the sin of pride and the fact that we can't serve two masters, but it seems to be easiest trap in which to fall.

Actually, when he took the helm at Notre Dame, Fr. Jenkins was viewed very suspiciously by the liberal elites. He initially scrapped plans to show the *Vagina Monologues*, a play that is not only in bad taste but looks in a relativistic way at things prohibited by Church teaching. Thus, it could well be argued such a piece needn't be seen on a Catholic college campus. It appeared that Fr. Jenkins was distancing himself from the Fr. Richard McBrien-wing of the campus.

In doing research for articles and this follow-up book, I made several visits to South Bend. I met with some of the highest officials on campus, including the Holy Cross priests. I was initially told that Fr. Jenkins was quite different from his predecessor, Fr. Edward "Monk" Molloy. Though certainly not as conservative as the new breed of seminarians seen in most orders and dioceses, Fr. Jenkins was going to be different. Sadly, it would appear that being liked by the liberal elites was too much even for him. In fact, the snares of being liked and accepted by those well-entrenched liberal elites would take its toll on others as well.

New leadership often has great ideas, but can it deliver? Case in point: When a new and strong archbishop arrived in Cincinnati—host to Xavier University, which the Catholic college-ranking apostolate, the Cardinal Newman Society, describes as one of the most heterodox in the US—many in the "Queen City" rejoiced. Yet the new leadership did not take on certain priests and officials connected with Xavier University whose occasional homilies and campus programs openly challenged the Church's teachings. In addition, the university regularly hosts groups that openly dissent on Catholic teaching. This raised the ire of popular Catholic blogger and Cincinnati resident Rich Leonardi, who found himself taken off the air by a local Catholic radio station on which he regularly broadcast.

The culprit in his dismissal was an administrator of the Athenaeum, the famed seminary of the archdiocese. Leonardi received support from many Catholics, including seminarians. Yet, it left a bad taste in the mouth for some that those who openly challenge the Church are permitted to preach, teach, and administer the sacraments, while a simple layman is thrown off the air for simply recording the words of those who are dissenting. One must remember that the Church teaches that the sin of omission is just that: a sin; a sin that Leonardi did not commit.[3]

A similar dust-up occurred in the Archdiocese of Detroit when the chancery notified Catholic speaker Michael Voris that he was not allowed to use the word "Catholic" in his apostolate's title, Real Catholic TV. Voris is a lightning rod, and even some orthodox-minded Catholics say his approach can be over the top. However, to ask that he change his ministry's name when hundreds of questionable Catholic institutions from hospitals to educational facilities use the word Catholic and are in open violation of Church teaching seems more than a little perplexing. Yet in some ways, many Catholics who have worked for the Church in various capacities have seen this all before. A liberal chancery official makes a pronouncement that he believes his bishop knows little about; therefore, his actions won't be questioned. Busy bishops can't keep track of everything, so they abdicate their judgment to someone they think they can trust. Sadly, it is the faithful who suffer and the evil one who is the temporary victor.

One might also remember two examples from Church history. The first is that of St. John Chrysostum, who said the floor of hell is paved with the skulls of those ordained who led the faithful astray. Secondly, St. Nicholas of Smyrna (yes, the same jolly old St. Nick we all know and love) once punched Arius the heretic in the face at the Council of Nicaea in 325 AD for leading the faithful astray. St. Nicholas was rebuked and told to leave the council for his rash actions. However, several of the bishops received visions that night of Jesus and his Blessed Mother standing next to St. Nicholas in total support of his actions. The bishops promptly brought St. Nicholas back to the council and profusely apologized for showing him the door.[4] What St. Nicholas did makes Leonardi and Voris look rather tame.

Getting back to Notre Dame, and with regard to Fr. Richard McBrien, I was again told by some of the most senior members of the administration that Fr. McBrien is basically on an island. He has no campus following; the only local followers he has are some old dissident types who live in and around South Bend and nearby Chicago. His biggest following comes from those who read the *National Catholic Reporter* and, of course, those in the mainstream media. As one senior campus administrator put it, "He is more or less a relic of a bygone liberal age, a museum piece."

I was told that Fr. Jenkins and much of his staff were caught off guard by the uproar surrounding the honorary degree that he gave to President Obama. Apparently his staff has some of the same ideological holdovers of the McBrien era. Many, it seemed, didn't understand that few had any objections to the president visiting the campus, but receiving a university honor in light of his egregious stance and statements on abortion was simply unacceptable.

The administration and some at the highest levels of the Holy Cross order simply were taken aback by the national Catholic reaction—particularly those within the order, specifically younger priests and seminarians who came from all races and backgrounds and who were vocal in their protest of Fr. Jenkins. It was a wake-up call for not only their managerial style but most importantly their mindset regarding the state of the Catholic Church, seminarians, and younger priests. Naturally, all of this translates into money, and donations to the university sank like a stone. In the one-year period following President Obama's appearance, the university lost more than $120 million in donations.

Notre Dame officials and those at the bigger Jesuit schools (Georgetown, Boston College, Marquette, DePaul, etc.) expressed utter shock that President Obama's receiving an honorary degree from an officially pro-life institution would cause such an uproar, showing the disconnect that has come to exist between the more liberal universities and Church officials and those of the younger, typically more faithful Catholic population.

Adding to the financial pressure was the economic debacle that was head football Coach Charlie Weis' contract. During his first incredibly successful season, Weis was signed to an unprecedented 10-year contract extension because Notre Dame officials evidently assumed that Weis' first season was the start of a new golden era. Unfortunately, it would fall onto Weis' successor Brian Kelly to see if he could shake up the thunder and bring back the aura that once existed around Knute Rockne, Frank Leahy, Ara Parseghian, Dan Devine, and Lou Holtz.

The controversy surrounding President Obama's award only helped show that the tide was turning. As indicated earlier, had this happened during the Carter administration, nary an eyelash would have been batted. However, this is a new, more orthodox era in the Church, something that still puzzles and angers liberal Catholics, liberal Protestants, and those who hate any religious faith but seem fit to judge from their perches in Manhattan, Washington, San Francisco and Hollywood.

The Cardinal Newman Society suggested some 20 American and two Canadian Catholic campuses for students and parents to consider.[5] They range from very small campuses like the St. Thomas More College of Liberal Arts in Merrimac, New Hampshire, and Belmont Abbey College in North Carolina to somewhat larger campuses like Catholic University in Washington, DC, Providence College in Providence, Rhode Island, Mount St. Mary's in Emmitsburg, Maryland, and Franciscan University in Steubenville, Ohio. In between there are campuses such as Benedictine College in Kansas and Thomas Aquinas College in California. The sheer fact that Catholic University, located in the nation's capital, and Providence College, also located in an urban area and known for its Division I athletic prowess, proves that Catholic colleges can be located in urban settings equipped with all the trappings of Division I sports and still be vibrant campuses living and teaching the Catholic message.

In addition to these growing campuses, there are brand-new colleges like Wyoming Catholic College in Lander, Wyoming, which in addition to faith emphasizes life in the outdoors; students learn to live an outdoor life, complete with horseback riding and marksmanship.

When one speaks of newer Catholic universities, certainly Ave Maria University comes to mind. The brainchild of Thomas Monaghan, founder of Domino's Pizza and former owner of the Detroit Tigers, the university is Monaghan's lifelong dream. There have been many twists and turns in the road. It was originally supposed to be built near Ann Arbor, Michigan, but a mountain of bureaucracy forced Monaghan to look south. He built his campus near Naples, Florida, where once alligators had roamed; now a magnificent Catholic college has emerged from the swamps of southwest Florida.

The Growing Number of Faithful Colleges

There would be many personnel battles, and naturally the mainstream media became apoplectic with Monaghan, who made no bones about the fact that he believed in the teachings of the Catholic Church. They even questioned his adjacent housing project, which some in the mainstream media had surmised would not allow birth control for its residents. The sheer ignorance and the venom the elites spewed only helped to shed more light on why campuses like Ave Maria were necessary. They are needed to bring light to a world so full of self-absorbed beliefs and so bereft of the truths and knowledge of God.

NINE
THE CHURCH STANDS UP FOR TRADITIONAL MARRIAGE

When President Bill Clinton signed the Defense of Marriage Act in 1996, he did so because he didn't want his administration to be tied in with a few homosexual activists in Hawaii who were practically alone at the time in pushing same-sex marriage, something that seemed too radical even for most liberals.

Some 16 years later, most liberals eagerly supported the agenda. Polling data suggested Americans were split. Though religious-oriented Americans were not in favor of this change to marriage, many in the secular world, who a dozen years ago thought same-sex marriage was being pushed by the kook fringe, were now embracing it. Why?

The answer to that question could well have been answered by G.K. Chesterton, the English "Apostle of Common Sense," who a century earlier coined the phrase, "It's not that those who don't believe in God believe in nothing; they believe in everything." Yet even some lukewarm Christians were joining the fray. It isn't too hard to see why. The media's agenda, through their news outlets but especially through popular network programming, made one feel that they were a virtual Neanderthal if they didn't believe in same-sex marriage.

One by one, the dwindling liberal mainline Protestant churches supported the measure. Naturally, the Catholic Church and many Evangelical Churches did not. The Catholic Church, being the largest religious body in the United States, began to face a herculean onslaught from those newly converted to the same-sex marriage cause.

The Church Stands Up for Traditional Marriage 197

The newly converted relished calling the Church backward, antiquated, hypocritical and, of course, bigoted. The same people who 16 years ago couldn't care less about the issue were now committed to any cause that would bash the Church. The attacks ranged from the sublime to the ridiculous. Sports writer Mike Lupica, who seems to flaunt the fact that, unlike most sports personalities, he's not conservative, told Archbishop Dolan that, since His Excellency came from out of town, he shouldn't lecture New Yorkers on the subject.[1]

First of all, Lupica lives in Connecticut, and, secondly, Archbishop Dolan's job is to proclaim the Church's teachings. Lupica, a graduate of Boston College, should know better. It seems Lupica is more a Fr. Drinan Boston College man than a Dr. Peter Kreeft Boston College man. Fans of ESPN's *The Sports Reporters* often grate at Lupica's pontificating style and self-absorbed persona. Perhaps he's jealous of the popularity of Gotham's new, high-profile prelate.

Liberals tend to believe that Christ cared little about the sins of the flesh. They point to the passage in the Gospel of John when Jesus forgives a woman caught in the act of adultery (see John 8:1-11). This was nothing new, though, for Jesus always recommended forgiving sinners. This is a personal thing we all have to do, lest we let revenge against sinners dictate our lives. However, Jesus also told the woman to "go and sin no more." For many in our present culture, nothing two consenting adults can do could possibly be sinful. Remember, Jesus also used the analogy of the sins of and punishments for Sodom and Gomorrah throughout the Gospel. Everyone in Jesus' day knew what happened in those two cities and the destruction that followed because of their sins.

All of the world's major religions, including Judaism, Christianity, and Islam, have always taught against homosexuality. Catholicism had been one of the more liberal religions in that it taught that some people are same-sex attracted and, though they should not act upon these feelings, they should be loved and encouraged, as this is their cross. The Catholic Church has long taught that every human being is meant to carry a cross in this world. As I've previously mentioned, there is an organization for those who are same-sex attracted called Courage, with many chapters and members.[2] For many years, some religions took the Catholic Church to task for being too liberal; some said the Church should tell those who act on their homosexual feelings and do not repent that they are destined for hell. Now the Catholic Church is catching it from those on the Left who say the Catholic Church is engaging in hate speech for saying those who are same-sex attracted shouldn't act out their feelings.

Recently a profile was done in *The New York Times* on same-sex attracted Eve Tushnet, the Ivy League-educated Catholic daughter of Harvard Law School professors.[3] She has chronicled her growth in Catholicism and the logic of the Church's teachings on sexuality, teachings exemplified in a recent letter on the subject from the prelate of Phoenix, Bishop Thomas Olmsted.[4]

For the Church to change her teachings would be to deny not only what Christ said in Matthew 11:20-24 but also his apostles, not to mention St. Paul's lengthy discourse on the subject (see Romans 1:26-28; 1 Corinthians 6:9-10.) Today, St. Paul would be called a homophobe and subjected to hate speech prosecution. Is the very man God knocked off his horse on the way to Damascus only to spread the Gospel farther and wider than anyone in the Early Church wrong? The thought is sheer madness, and yet some gay activists point to St. Paul as a homophobe.

In addition to the apostles, there is a rich history of saints writing on the subject, particularly the Early Church Fathers (St. Augustine, St. Justin Martyr, St. Basil, St. John Chrysostom) as well as Church intellectuals like St. Thomas Aquinas, St. Albert the Great (the greatest scientist of his time), along with mystics like St. Catherine of Siena. In other words, every one of these great religious minds, as well as almost every political mind until about the year 2000, would have to be wrong for same-sex marriage to be right.[5]

Many who disagree with the Catholic Church tend to forget that homosexuality was much more common and approved of by the Roman government in the early Christian era than it is in 2012. Many in the upper echelons of Greek and Roman culture experimented with all sorts of sexual practices. It would have been far easier for Jesus, the apostles, the saints, and the popes to approve of this conduct than to disapprove of it. Christianity might have grown at a faster pace. However, there was a reason for this swimming against the tide, and the faithful accepted it. From a theological point of view, homosexuality does not allow for procreation, which was man's main charge given by God in the context of a marriage between a man and a woman. In addition, from a medical perspective, there is a whole host of diseases that result from homosexual sex acts that do not exist in a heterosexual relationship.

Often one hears the newly converted who favor same-sex marriage claim that their thinking has "evolved." One is tempted to ask: "Evolved into what?" Truth is truth; it does not change or evolve. The Church's admonition against immorality (homosexual and heterosexual) did not end in the biblical age. It has continued in the writings of saints and theologians until the present day. Actually, the punishments for the sins of the flesh were very stern in the Bible, in both the Old and New Testament.

One only need read the account of Sodom and Gomorrah in the Old Testament and St. Paul's moral outrage at the immorality (both homosexual and heterosexual) he came across in his travels to understand this point. Even the adulteress whom Jesus confronted repented for her sins, and Jesus responded by telling her to sin no more.

It's not that the sins of the flesh couldn't happen to anyone—they can. It was none other than the famed G.K. Chesterton who said, "A man who knocks on the door of a brothel was probably a man who was seeking God but got hopelessly lost along the way." Loneliness and emptiness often lead to sins of the flesh. It is really a sad thing to behold, and yet our modern world seems to encourage it, as if by sinning in this fashion by sticking a finger in God's eye, one should celebrate. In our modern era, too many people feel they must act upon every urge and whim. If one falls for that belief, one will also probably fall for one of Satan's oldest lies: If you don't think you're sinning, you aren't.

Another fact lost on those in the mainstream media and popular entertainment outlets pushing for same-sex marriage is the little-reported fact that very few homosexuals have stated any interest in marriage. While many homosexual activists claim that 5 to 10 percent of the populace is homosexual, many other experts on same-sex attraction put the number far lower. However, even if the higher percentages are conceded, we are talking about a very small percentage with no push being made for marriage in the hundreds of years of years that homosexuality was allowed to openly exist in the days of the Roman Empire.

Fast-forward to 2012, and we see that an issue that had no relevance to the homosexual community some 20 years before now is a civil rights, make-or-break issue. Like many of you, I have friends who are same-sex attracted; some of my friends live a celibate life and some embrace their same-sex feelings. One friend of mine who is same-sex attracted told me that 20 years ago anyone in the gay community who spoke of same-sex marriage was considered on the Far Left fringe. This person told me that the overwhelming majority of those in the gay community will not get married and have no real interest in the issue outside of the fact that it will push the gay agenda.

Even if 5 to 10 percent of the population is gay (and many think this number is exaggerated), should there be such a push for same-sex marriage even though most people who are gay will never get married and, until recently, it was an issue that was not even on the homosexuality activists' radar? The answer is very clear: It is a push to normalize the gay lifestyle on the general population. There is a long list of saints, popes, historians, academicians, secularists, and atheists who have voiced their opposition to the homosexual lifestyle through the centuries. Yet we are throwing that all out for the latest societal whim. Why?

To conclude, has anyone who lashes out against the teachings of the Catholic Church and every other religion (remember, until a few years ago every organized religion disapproved of homosexuality) ever considered *why* the Church is opposed to the homosexual lifestyle and same-sex marriage? Do they really think that everyone in these religions, including God himself, has some sort of bias against those who are same-sex attracted? Could it possibly be that through the centuries there has existed a loving approach to those who were same-sex attracted? Until 1973, the American Psychiatric Association labeled homosexuality as disordered as well. Yet, the Church has always called on the faithful to love everyone, including those who are same-sex attracted.

Maybe, just maybe, those who opposed the homosexual lifestyle were using the same approach that one might use toward someone who is an alcoholic. Another person I know to be same-sex attracted pointed out to me that this is what finally hit home for him. For example, when professional golfer John Daly was disowned and dropped by his sponsors after going back to gambling and drinking, he infamously stated: "Gambling and drinking is in my blood." Commentators from various political persuasions said Daly was being a terrible role model; it was just something he would have to deal with and conquer. There seems to be a great deal of hypocrisy among those who attack Daly and those who feel any sexual desire between adults should be pursued.

Though some may scoff at telling someone what they don't want to hear, it doesn't mean that you don't show concern for them; it may be just the opposite. While some attack religion in general and Catholics in particular for not changing their stance on the homosexual lifestyle, it may be because the faithful truly care for the very people who are attacking them.

TEN

THE CATHOLIC CHURCH KEEPS GROWING AND THE MEDIA CAN'T SEE WHY

It had become all too much for *Newsweek's* former religion editor Kenneth Woodward. *The New York Times* was once again bashing the Catholic Church. The victim *du jour* was Pope Benedict XVI, and the story dealt with a priest who had abused male students at a school for the deaf in the Archdiocese of Milwaukee. Woodward remembered well how the Old Gray Lady's editor Bill Keller repeatedly bashed the Church and wistfully admitted that he himself was a "collapsed Catholic."

Now Keller's paper was doing it publicly underneath its famous motto, "All the news that's fit to print." In response, Woodward penned an article for the left-of-center Catholic magazine *Commonweal* that took the *Times* to task for its outrageous bias.[1] This was all the more revealing when one considers that Woodward is hardly a conservative. He isn't Catholic, either. He is, however, a principled journalist who couldn't stand by and see the nation's most famous newspaper betray the journalistic standards he was taught to uphold.

Sadly, this sort of principled stand wasn't adopted by *Times* columnist Maureen Dowd, who is Catholic. Judging by her work, it is hard to imagine another person in our culture who is seemingly so angry at life. What makes it hardest to understand is that she, a journalist, works at such a citadel of journalism (at least it once was). Dowd seems to find a way to blame and take out all of her life's frustrations out on the Catholic Church by attacking it on any and every issue. She also seems to take glee in trashing any and everything she deems conservative. Conversely, there is one group in the Catholic Church that Dowd seems to relish defending: dissidents or the self-proclaimed Future Church. For instance, Dowd spared no venom in defending dissident nuns who were facing an official Vatican visit.

What Dowd and her like-minded friends don't realize is that, outside the enclaves of Manhattan, Cambridge, Hollywood, San Francisco, and Berkeley, few really pay any attention to what these folks think, which is demonstrated by the *Times'* junk bond status. It would appear that this doesn't matter, however. Give 'em a soapbox, and they'll take advantage of it. As a result, it looks as though those in the news media who want to do a hit piece on Pope Benedict need to take a number.

The latest to engage in this yellow journalism was CNN. In 2010 the self-described "network of record" dispatched reporter Gary Tuchman to do its dirty work, once again regarding the school for the deaf sex-abuse case in the Archdiocese of Milwaukee.

CNN had been advertising its hit piece on Pope Benedict XVI as if he was already guilty of some sort of cover-up, even though during the sex abuse scandal, many in the media praised then-Cardinal Ratzinger for tackling the tough problems.

What tough problems did he tackle? The most notable example was the situation with Fr. Marcial Maciel, founder of the Legion of Christ. Maciel became one of the few prominent faithful priests caught up in the scandal. There had been rumors for years, even accusations, but looking at the wonderful fruits being produced by the Legionaries and its associated lay ecclesial movement, Regnum Christi, who could believe such things about the founder of such terrific organizations?

However it happened, Cardinal Ratzinger saw through the façade, and he took on Fr. Maciel at the height of his power and popularity. One might recall that Fr. Maciel was quite close to Pope John Paul II. So from this example, we can see that His Eminence was not going to kowtow to someone just because the Pope liked them. He was a man who showed no favorites and pulled no punches, and he still is.

Once the allegations were confirmed, the Legionaries were shaken to the core. In the wake of the scandal, many good priests such as Fr. Jonathan Morris and Fr. Cliff Ermatinger, both well-known authors, left the order to become diocesan priests, and many laypeople in Regnum Christi gave up their consecrated vows. Despite the assets possessed by the Legion—both material and human—Pope Benedict XVI removed its leadership and installed his own, a move that could have backfired and was hardly the work of a timid man.

The CNN piece was perhaps even more despicable than the *Times*' because, in the interim, much of the *modus operandi* of the Old Gray Lady had been exposed. Still, CNN used the same material as the newspaper, and yet the network had the nerve to claim it had something new.[2] But, no, there was nothing new. The crux of its argument comes from material provided by Jeffrey Anderson, the attorney who Woodward said has made $60 million off the scandal. Anderson says he is on a mission to "reform the Church." What kind of reform would that be? Some Catholic dioceses have been forced into bankruptcy, which means that the poor whom the dioceses assisted through their social programs are left in the cold. For all his concern of "reform," Anderson hasn't provided a penny of that $60 million to these poor.[3]

In addition, the other source for the *Times* piece (and likely the one by CNN) was the disgraced Archbishop-emeritus Rembert Weakland of Milwaukee. The retired prelate made his disdain for Pope Benedict XVI's ecclesiology no secret. Indeed, he laid it all on the line in a memoir that was largely hailed by the liberal media who reviewed the book.[4] Both the *Times* and CNN stories claimed Weakland had not known of the abuse case in question until 1997. He told the times that when he reported his discovery to Cardinal Ratzinger, His Eminence acted as if the situation wasn't his problem. Actually, the archbishop had known of the allegations since 1977, and the situation really wasn't the Cardinal's problem, because the

CDF, which he served as prefect, did not get responsibility for sex-abuse cases until 2001. A review of these and other facts in the case make one really wonder if Archbishop Weakland wasn't doing whatever he could to make himself look good in the case. Hey, CNN and *The New York Times* bought it, right?

The only time mass media favorably reported on the Holy Father occurred when they believed he said something he did not. Case in point: the fallout over the interview Pope Benedict XVI gave to the German journalist and former atheist Peter Seewald, who often interviews the Pope while the Holy Father is on his summer vacation. What happened concerned a very fine theological point made by the Holy Father that is not easily grasped at first glance. The remark concerned the AIDS crisis and condoms, and some interpreted his statement as allowing condom use in sexual relationships where one of the partners has AIDS. That would indeed mark a radical change in the Church's teachings. There was just one problem, however: This is not what Benedict was saying. When the error was cleared up, many in the media returned to business as usual: Discredit the Pope at every turn.

What do those who do hit pieces on Pope Benedict XVI and the Catholic Church hope to gain? Saul Alinksy and other mentors of the radical Left spoke about first attacking the head and then the body. What better primary target than Catholicism and its established hierarchy? After all, if one can successfully damage the Church, then other churches and Communions will become easier targets for those who scorn the teachings and beliefs of Christianity.

It won't stop there, either. Orthodox Judaism would likely be the next target and so on, until religion is nothing but a social club animated by leftist political activism. With the Judeo-Christian ethic destroyed, the radical Left can impose their ethos.

Does this sound outlandish or farfetched? Conspiratorial, maybe? Possibly, but before making up your mind, read the writings of those who started the French Revolution, that oft-praised but little understood event. Consider what they did to hundreds of bishops, priests, religious, and laymen simply for being faithful Catholics who would not reject the Church. Read also what those who attempted violent revolution in the 1960s believed. After doing so, then ask, "Was that author being conspiratorial or paranoid—or not alarmed enough?"

So the agenda is to diminish the role and respectability and thus influence of faith in society. Given that, the sex-abuse scandal was a gift-wrapped Christmas present that for roughly six years kept giving to those who wanted an easy bludgeon to wield against the Church. The scandal was legitimate news, and the media's breaking the story was something of a backhanded blessing in that it finally got the hierarchy to take seriously the situation.

Nonetheless, considering the over the top and much overdone coverage that was given to the subject, one has to wonder if many reporters were all too willing to keep alive a news story that might have died or faded away much sooner. The reason for this speculation is that poll after poll has shown that journalists are at least five times more likely to have a dim view of religion in general, and the Catholic Church and Evangelical churches in particular. These men and women of the Fourth Estate simply do not like historic Christianity's conservative views on sexuality. This puts these denominations in the crosshairs of those who hate them.

Before I go any further, and because I don't want anyone to think I'm minimizing the situation, I want to elaborate on the terrible toll wreaked by the scandal. When I was a Catholic grade school- and high-school student in the 1970s and 1980s, our little Rust Belt parish had two priests pass through who would later be kicked out of the priesthood for molestation. In perfect justice, both spent a good deal of time in prison. One of them caused by far the biggest compensation my diocese ever paid out to victims of abuse.

Sadly, I knew some of the victims of these evil men. Fortunately, I was not one of them. I take this scandal very seriously and, having lived through it, know more than I care to know about the make-up of these men and their *modus operandi*. The following will make some uncomfortable and likely to accuse me of engaging in some type of phobia. However, believe me, statistics bear this out.

Eighty-one percent of the victims were male. Whether that was because as altar servers or the like, pederasts had more access to them or because the abusers were homosexuals or were so emotionally immature as to not have a clearly defined sexual identity, many opinions exist.

Furthermore, according to a 2004 article in *America* magazine, Some 149 priests—3.4 percent of the 4,392 priests accused of misconduct in the US—were responsible of 10 or more acts of sexual assault each. Thus, these men accounting for 2,960 or roughly 27 percent of the 11,000 instances of alleged abuse. Fifty-nine percent had only one allegation against them. Still, one allegation—assuming it is true—is one too many, is it not?

Another thing: Fr. Maciel notwithstanding, the overwhelming majority of these abusers made no secret about how their vision was to help promote the idea of the Council as a rupture with the past and tradition (both in terms of Sacred Tradition and pious customs). As young as I was, their agenda was strikingly clear: Change the Church.

Yet too many in the press would have you believe that the majority of these evildoers were pre-Vatican II types: overly pious, bitter, old, and sexually repressed. As I indicated above, nothing could be further from the truth (although it is true that most graduated from seminary just before or just after the end of the Council). The John Jay Report does indicate that the overwhelming number of abuse cases occurred between 1965-1985. As a matter of fact, since 2000 the number of abuse cases is less than 1% of the total from 1950 to the present day.

Another truth about the scandal that is often too little talked about is the way some bishops handled it. It's not that reporting some bishops being asleep at the switch or bishops moving abusive priests from one place to the next didn't get the notice all of this deserved. No, it is just how much the bishops—not just this or that one but as an entire conference—put more faith in psychoanalysis rather than the Church's own faithful psychiatrists, for it was the secular world's psychiatrist who said serial molesters could be cured. The Church's own psychiatrists often thought there was something amiss here. One wishes they had acted on the recommendations of world-class scholars in the field such as Dr. Conrad Baars and Dr. Anna Terruwe, who addressed the 1970 Synod of Catholic Bishops about how to prevent a crisis in the priesthood. In their presentation to the Synod Fathers, they "warned that priests and religious with emotional repression and love deprivation could lead to disaster in the Church."

Afterward, they wrote a book expanding on what they had told the prelates titled *The Role of the Church in the Causation, Treatment and Prevention of the Crisis in the Priesthood*. As reported in the *National Catholic Register*, the book described something called "emotional deprivation disorder." This condition "is the deprivation of the innate human need to be loved for oneself. It is a frustration or a lack of fulfillment of a natural process. People grow physically, intellectually, and spiritually, but emotionally their growth does not keep pace.... Symptoms include a difficulty in relating emotionally with other adults, whether through friendships and other relationships or in marriage.... People with the disorder may have feelings of inferiority, inadequacy, insecurity, and uncertainty.... They can be brilliant and accomplished academically or professionally, but emotionally they're immature."

One wonders what would be had Drs. Baars and Terruwe's talk and balk had received a response that went beyond, "Hmm. Interesting," and actually been acted upon. One wonders why the American bishops listened more to those whose psychiatric perspective came from something other than a Catholic worldview. Of course, that might not have mattered as much had they, instead of shuffling abusive priests from parish to parish, simply listened to their own consciences, canned these men, and worked with authorities to bring them to justice. Instead, they listened to folks such as Kinsey acolyte Dr. Fred Berlin, who in 1985 told the bishops what a bad idea it would be to remove the predators from priestly ministry. Today, Dr. Berlin is recognized as an expert ... and he speaks at conferences sponsored by groups such as B4U-ACT, which "advocates the decriminalization and tolerance of persons who have a lifelong attraction and desire for sexual contact with youngsters." He also "still remains actively opposed to reporting sex offenders to the civil authorities, although all major psychiatric and mental health organizations and professional associations have strongly supported mandatory reporting for decades."

This all goes back to what I wrote in an earlier chapter about those who became bishops in the 1960s and 1970s who may have been too consumed with putting the Catholic ghetto and anything associated with it behind them in favor of respectability of academia and other parts of the culture at all costs, which Pope Leo XIII actually called a heresy. It's name? "Americanism."

In any event, getting back to the question at hand, if the country elected the most liberal presidential ticket and Congress in the nation's history, why have our culture's elite become so annoyed with politically conservative, religiously observant people, even if they are active in the public square? Wouldn't they just dismiss such people as a dying breed or even relics of a bygone age? Hadn't the 2008 election results proved this? In this observer's opinion, the answer appears quite simple: Those who believe in "that old-time religion" are the last line of defense. Once they (or at least their influence) are removed, those who long for radical change will have an unfettered hand to change our society.

When the Jesuits were kicked out of France before the French Revolution, a gleeful Voltaire opined that the next step was doing the same with the entire Catholic Church. In turn, this would make eliminating Christianity in general that much easier. Voltaire didn't live long enough to see the horrifying results of the Reign of Terror, when thousands of French Catholics, both peasant and clergy, were hauled off to the guillotine or left to rot on prison ships for their religious and cultural views. Oddly, the elites who funded the radicals who perpetrated these crimes in France, and who later bankrolled their successors during the Russian Revolution were the very persons who often lost their family and friends to the violence enabled in part by their financial help.

Case in point: In 1916, when Leon Trotsky, a cofounder of the Soviet Union, planned to return home to aid the revolution, President Woodrow Wilson arranged for him to have a US passport, which essentially amounted to a "get out of jail free" card. On the eve of his departure, the radical told a mass meeting that the revolution would overthrow Russia's provisional government and end Russia's part in World War I. Who stood to benefit from this? Germany.

The only problem with Trotsky's plan was his arrest the next day by Canadian authorities during a stopover in Halifax. The record of his arrest shows he carried with him roughly $197,800 in today's dollars, which historians think likely came to him from the German government. At the time, Great Britain ruled Canada. Had authorities continued to hold Trotsky as a POW (which is how they booked him, given his comments the night before), the war might have taken a substantially different turn.

Instead, an intermediary between President Wilson and the head of the British Secret Service in the US told the latter how much president wanted Trotsky released. Shortly, thereafter, Trotsky was back on a ship sailing to Russia. (At this point, America was not a combatant in World War I, although the UK most certainly was, making their acquiescence to the president's request incomprehensible.)

Outside of this incident, a political cartoon from the period shows the world's richest men—J.P. Morgan, J.D. Rockefeller, Andrew Carnegie, and Theodore Roosevelt, who by then had left the GOP to head the Progressive Party—happily shaking hands with and slapping the back of Karl Marx. With the backing of these American tycoons, supporters of the Bolshevists had set up what amounted to their own branch of the Red Cross.

The War overwhelmed the Red Cross, so when these wealthy, respectable men offered to handle the organization's outreach to combatants, the aid group gladly agreed. This front was then used to help fund the revolution. J.P. Morgan himself chipped in $100,000. He later gave an additional sum that equated to $1 million in rubles.

Another wealthy American who financed the communists, particularly Leon Trotsky's activities, was Jacob Schiff, who gave $20 million to the revolutionaries. It is impossible to know if the dollar figures given here have been adjusted for inflation. If they have not, however, the $100,000 would equal $1.98 million today, the $1 million would equal $19.8 million, and the $20 million would come out to $395.6 million.

A French witness to the Bolshevik Revolution wrote in his account of the Marxist overthrow of the Tsar that Alfred Milner, a British lord, provided 21 million rubles to finance the Russian revolution. This perfectly illustrates what Lenin supposedly said: "The Capitalists will sell us the rope with which we will hang them."

The Situation Today

In our modern times, some in the cultural elite are deeply concerned that the great liberal experiment in Washington is fast unraveling. The hoped-for liberal blossoms never really bloomed and the conservative blossoms never faded, try as some have to make that happen. However, whereas their grip on political power may wax and wane, there is one part of our society where they seem to have a lock: the entertainment industry.

The Left has always wanted control of culture. Don't believe me? While the 1950s hearings of the House Un-American Activities Committee (aka, HUAC) are in many ways justly infamous, their purpose was perfectly legitimate. After all, it is a matter of historical record that one way the Soviets wanted to undermine our society was through the culture.

Do you remember how much television has changed in the last 25 years? In the 1950s and even through much of the 1960s, programs featured intact families, strong male figures, and fathers who not only had authority and were firm, but who were also wise and kind and offered a gentle, guiding hand to their children. And even though by the 1980s and 1990s things had changed so that fathers and parents in general had become dupes or worse, this period still had programming with some value.

However, when was the last time you saw a show such as *Eight Is Enough, Full House, Family Ties, The Cosby Show,* or anything remotely similar? How often is that Hollywood really invests in making a really well-done family film? Not often, and one has to wonder why—because when, by some act of God, a fun, entertaining, quality, family friendly movie gets made, it does boffo business at the box office. Think *Cars, The Incredibles,* the *Toy Story* series, and the like.

Hollywood knows this. But knowing this, does it—an industry predicated not on edifying the culture with the true, the good, and the beautiful, but with making as much filthy lucre as humanly possible—produce more of such fare, knowing it will get unimaginably rich in doing so?

At the end of January 2012, just two movies in the Top 12 were unquestionably OK for all ages, and one of those was a 3D release of the Disney gem *Beauty and the Beast* (and these two films were likely the only family friendly flicks in release at that time).[4] At the end of February, the same thing: two kid-friendly movies, although one, *The Lorax,* was a poorly made paean to an environmentalist agenda that made many parents uncomfortable.

So, in any given month, you will see roughly one to two movies that Mom and Dad can take their kids to see. And let's not forget black auteur Tyler Perry's films. Talk about through-the-roof box office numbers! Sure his films are often gritty and full of clichés. Nonetheless, they are entertaining, treat universal themes, regard faith in Christ as a good thing, and hold up virtues and the values that spring from them as the difference between leading a happy life and an unhappy one. And remember where you will see his films and other good, family-friendly films: in the Top 12. They are moneymakers! Therefore, why we don't see more of them?

Considering all of this, is the disappearance of family-friendly fare is an accident? And keeping your answer to that question in

The Catholic Church Keeps Growing... 213

mind, what do you think popular culture would be like if the Left was in total control? What if we weren't so blessed by God with countervailing forces such as Tyler Perry, Sherwood Pictures (producers of *Fireproof* and *Facing the Giants*), Metanoia Films (producers of *Bella*), and graduates of programs such as Act One, which bills itself as the "premier training program for Christians pursuing a career in the mainstream entertainment industry," founded by Catholic screenwriter Barbara Nicolosi?

We are blessed to have these companies and individuals, and if it pleases God, we'll have even more of them very soon. The reason: God always gives us the hope of more light, especially when times seem the darkest.

The Print Media

Do you recall any major newspaper giving any great degree of coverage to Pope Benedict's objectively triumphant visit to the United Kingdom? What about the story of the many Anglican clergy and laymen who were so distressed about the direction their Communion has taken since the 1970s that they begged the Vatican for a special provision to enter the Church en masse?

In the first story, we have a Catholic Pope not only visiting the nation that was formerly called "Our Lady's Dowery," but given not a banger's chance against a hungry English Bulldog of making the trip a success, and having that visit end in the nation's prime minister essentially tell him, "Wow. You've left us dumbfounded." In the second, you have well over 1,000 people saying, "Help! We can't take it anymore! We want to come home!" And what is the Church's response? Well, like the father in the Prodigal Son parable in Luke 16, she welcomes these people with open arms. These are two pretty big stories. And while some outlets gave them decent coverage, for most they hardly raised an eyebrow.

We've spoken about how great the WYD in Madrid was in 2011.[5] Sadly, the BBC's coverage was so outrageous that even the liberal journalists at the *Guardian* found it appalling. However, Johann Hari's opinion piece at the Independent, "Catholics, It's You This Pope Has Abused," really raised the stakes in the hate fest directed at the Church—all because young people in Madrid were seen showing support for their Catholic faith and engaging in debates with leftist groups hurling vile insults at them while they were walking, praying, etc.[6] Then we have the tired old stories of how the Vatican systematically covered up the sex-abuse scandal (with then-Cardinal Ratzinger up to his shoulders in the mess, of course), when nothing could be further from the truth.

Under the heading of, "With friends like these…" here in the US, we have Maureen Dowd, *The New York Times* columnist and a Catholic, who jumps at the chance to defend those in Catholic Church who have possibly entered into heresy. However, when it comes time to stand up for the Vicar of Christ, the Successor of Peter—especially when it is her employer that is on the attack—she doesn't lift a finger.[7]

To his credit, Michael Sean Winters of the liberal *National Catholic Reporter* said that *The New York Times* piece on Pope Benedict XVI was an article filled with animus and lies. Couldn't the likes of Dowd have at least mentioned that the *Times* praised then-Cardinal Ratzinger for his role in uncovering the scandal? No, she spent her time applauding these muckrakers and cheering them on in a column, saying a nun as pope is needed.[7] It seems they not only have little care for the pope's soul, but virtually none for their own.

Maybe Dowd is simply a product of the years in which she came of age. After all, she entered high school in the fall of 1966, just as the counterculture and its rejection of the "Establishment" gathered full steam. The summer following her freshman year was the culture-shifting Summer of Love. A Washington, DC, native, Dowd graduated from that city's Immaculata High School in 1969, which means she closely witnessed, maybe even firsthand, the theological rebellion sparked by *Humanae Vitae* led by Catholic University of America professor of Theology, Fr. Charles Curran.

Four years later, she matriculated from this same school, and it is likely that in her theology and philosophy courses—and probably on-campus or local parish Masses—she was fed a diet of dissent against the Church's timeless teachings. Those, she must have surely been told (just as practically everybody was being told back then) were soon to be jettisoned. It was just a matter of time.

To the degree this speculation about her early days of adult womanhood is correct, her story is probably typical of many in her generation, male and female. This was the formation she received. To an extent, this was the formation all of us received, whether we were making felt banners in our First Communion classes or were in our middle-aged years hearing homilies detailing all the reasons why all the things we had known as "Catholic" all our lives were all wrong.

Hopefully, she—hopefully all of us, for pity's sake—will be cut a break for any bad witness we have given for our faith. God only knows the true effects of how the bad formation we of the last 40-60 years received has played itself out in the lives of others.

However, what should all of this cause us to worry about?

Nothing.

Nothing? you might ask, incredulous. Consider all the damage this is doing ... that it has done!

Undoubtedly, it has done some damage. It may continue to do some damage or it may continue to do much more. What many aren't considering, however, is that despite all these rotten tomatoes being thrown at us and our holy Faith, our *Mater et Magistra*, things are on the upswing.

Through Peter's Pence, American Catholics are the reason why the Catholic Church can have a budget that occasionally goes into the black now and then. (Boy, wouldn't that be nice if we could say the same for our own country?) We contribute great amounts to Catholic Charities, which is there to lend an indispensable hand when disasters strike or when a single mother with three children is about to lose power during the dead of a subfreezing winter.

The likes of Dowd may not understand that vocations in the Catholic Church are increasing. Or maybe they do and the prospect of more theologically traditional priests coming to the local rectory and faithful women religious coming to a nearby convent deeply troubles them, even if some won't be ordained or take their final vows for roughly a decade.

And for a religion that is supposedly so backward, medieval, benighted—insert your favorite pejorative—keep in mind that when Pope Benedict XVI came to Britain in September 2010, the crowds were much larger than expected, and many commented on the fact that the British thought that the heavily German-accented pontiff had more to say than their own melodious Archbishop of Canterbury, Dr. Rowan Williams.

Why? Because whatever his personal beliefs, Dr. Williams has chosen to believe that the only way to keep the worldwide Anglican Communion from imploding is by kowtowing to the popular culture on any number of issues. Furthermore, the fact is, he agrees with many of those (women clergy, etc.). And yet it was Benedict to whom the British listened and whose words they considered carefully when he walked amongst them.

Dowd surely know the basics of the 2,000-year-old teachings of the Catholic Church. The successor to St. Peter is the Vicar of Christ on Earth. That man has the authority in the Holy Name of Jesus to bind and loose. Furthermore, Jesus promised those who deny him and his successors that he will deny them (see Matthew 16:16-20; Luke 10:16).

Dowd must know this, one would think. When she was in school in the 1960s, they taught from the *Baltimore Catechism*. If you've ever had the chance to read this solid catechetical series, you know that these points were definitely taught during that time. She and many like her know the truth, but they have chosen to believe it is not true. That is sad.

We must pray for them. (Before we do that, however, let us redouble our efforts to beg God's mercy upon our own souls, for we are sinners, too.) I pray for Dowd, her admirers, and those like her, for they are both very intelligent and gifted, and the gifts they could bring to building up the kingdom of God on earth, the Church, are lying fallow.

The Catholic Church Keeps Growing...

The secular world is grasping at straws, forever bouncing around on the endlessly drifting boat called the "dictatorship of relativism," and they never know why. I think that, often, those who attack the Church are really longing for the truth. The problem isn't even that they just refuse to knock on the right door (although that is sometimes the case). Rather, it's that they put blinders on to the fact that the door to truth is already open to them. They can't see that the truth isn't a thing but a Person, one whom they can easily access. Truth is not an *attribute* of this Person; rather it is his very *essence*. And anyone can access him so easily—just let the Catholic Church show the way.

There are responsibilities that come with claiming you believe something and then attacking it. It is quite simple: Either you believe in something or you don't, which is why it doesn't help matters when the likes of Dowd (with her snarky and borderline seething anger) attack the Church to which they claim to be faithful followers.

In late 2011, an activist professor at George Washington University, John Banzhaf, filed a lawsuit against Catholic University on behalf of Muslim students claiming that they should be accommodated with prayer locations devoid of crucifixes, images of Jesus, and various other Catholic iconographies that Muslims find offensive. On the surface the argument seemed ludicrous, as Catholic students, or students of any other faith, are not allowed to show public religious symbols of any sort in Saudi Arabia, the birthplace of Islam. (This came on the heels of a Colombian soccer player who, while awaiting his match, was shopping at a Riyadh mall. He was wearing a short-sleeved shirt that didn't completely cover a tattooed picture of Jesus Christ on his upper arm. He, along with his pregnant wife, was detained for questioning. This occurred in the wake of a Romanian soccer player who kissed his tattooed arm with an image of Jesus after scoring a goal. The scene caused much consternation in Saudi Arabia.)

However, the media tried to portray this as rigid Catholic ideology stifling religious pluralism. Even worse, most media outlets failed to report that, on further examination, no Muslim students came to Professor Banzhaf; he simply filed the lawsuit on their behalf. This prompted psychiatrist Dr. Keith Ablow to wonder about the psychological makeup of a man who claims to know what's best for those who never actually asked for his help. Where are Dowd and her followers here? Why aren't they defending their faith?

For all the negative news the mainstream media likes to put forth concerning the Catholic Church, it would be a nice surprise if positive developments like Catholics Come Home would at least get a mention, let alone a little coverage. The group headed by Tom Peterson has helped bring home fallen-away Catholics and converts into the Church by the tens of thousands in each of the various dioceses where it has been asked to help. Since its founding a few years ago, the group has helped to bring more than 300,000 back home to the Catholic Church. In the Diocese of Phoenix alone, some 92,000 Catholics registered in parishes after an extensive ad and personal visit campaign.

Catholics Come Home also launched compelling commercials on national television, including popular shows on the Fox Network and NBC's *Today* show. Contrary to popular opinion, many who left the Church did so not because of a particular theological beef with the Church. The reasons were more mundane, but many fortunately were grateful that they were being welcomed back with such open arms.

In the 1961 Dino De Laurentiis movie *Barabbas* (adapted from the novel of the same name), the fictional Roman procurator scratches out the symbol of Christ from Barabbas' medallion, which he secretly kept on the backside. After Barabbas, played by Anthony Quinn, tells the procurator that he tried to believe in Christ but couldn't, the procurator answers that it is better not to wear medallions of people of whom you don't believe in.

The world is looking for the truth in all the wrong places, and all the while some who claim to believe in the truth are attacking it at every point. It would do us all well to remember the words of Jesus, who said, "He who acknowledges me on earth, I will acknowledge in heaven; and he who doesn't acknowledge me on earth I will not acknowledge in heaven (Matthew 10:32-33.)

ELEVEN
CATHOLICISM AND ISLAM: AN INTERESTING HISTORY

It would stand to reason that when the "dictatorship of relativism" is allowed to control the hearts and minds of many in our modern world, as our brave but often ridiculed Holy Father, Pope Benedict XVI, has defined it, they are going to be deceived every time. The deception continues on with a false notion that our Christian, and specifically Catholic, forebears were bloodthirsty aggressors trying to rid the helpless Muslim world of their belief.

Actually, many more Muslim scholars, compared with Western scholars, are aware that this statement is falsehood. These same scholars probably saw the writing on the wall concerning the Arab Spring of 2011. They knew it was coming, and the Church probably knew it was coming. Both sides also probably knew that radical forces would do their best to prevent the Middle East and North Africa from reverting back to the way of life they enjoyed before the 1979 Iranian Revolution that brought radical Islam back to the forefront. Before 1979, women in veils and certainly burqas were hardly visible in the streets of Cairo, Tehran, and Kabul.

Before we delve more into the modern world, a refresher course of Catholic-Islamic history is in order. While much of the Western world salutes Saladin, the famous Islamic general during the Crusades, all too often academia denounces both the Catholic Church and the Knights Templar for their roles in the Crusades.

Each year, two momentous events in Western and Church history passed with hardly a mention. Actually, these events may be better known in the Muslim world than the Christian world: the Islamic army's desecration of St. Peter's in Rome, along with St. John Lateran and other churches in 846, and the stunning defeat of the Islamic military onslaught by Charles "The Hammer" Martel at Tours, France, in 732. Though these two events occurred more than 100 years apart, they do point out that, until the Ottoman-Turkish Islamic defeat in 1683 at the gates of Vienna, Europe was facing a never-ending threat from radical Islam. Yet, how is it that, according to the mainstream media, it was the fault of Christians, and specifically Catholics?

Ask most practicing Catholics, Evangelicals, and mainline Protestants who Martel was, and you will probably get blank stares. Perhaps a few young people might be under the false impression that he is some sort of up-and-coming professional wrestler. However, you would probably stand a better chance of having someone in the Islamic world tell you about Martel. The same might be true for the sack of Rome in 846 by Muslim forces, who disembarked at Ostia (the Tiber port) and marched right into Rome, desecrating holy sites like St. Peter's and St. John Lateran and leaving the Eternal City with their plunder. Many in the Western world might be surprised why they have never heard this and why those who reside in the Islamic world are better informed of these events than those of us in the Western World. Let us peer back into time to see what we can learn about the past and what it might mean for the future.

It is said that God can make the best out of the worst. As Martel grew older and realized that his mother was simply a consort of his regal father, Charles must have realized that he could have been abandoned to poverty or, worse yet, aborted (and if that had happened, Christianity might have been confined to Ireland!), Charles must have developed a thick skin and a courageous spirit that enabled him not to run at the first sign of trouble. Europe was in a state of near panic by 730, as the well-seasoned and professional Islamic army had laid waste to much of the Middle East and North Africa, leaving the homes of those past saints like Augustine in ruins. Europe was in the Dark Ages;

Catholicism and Islam: An Interesting History   221

armies were merely feudal in their makeup, a far cry from the type of regimented units needed to stop the largest invading armies that Europe had seen since the days when Rome ruled the world.

Martel wasn't above putting the fear of God into noblemen and clergy alike to make them realize what life would be like under Islamic rule. Finally, the Church and mayor agreed to give him the men he needed. Martel's battle plan was as crafty as it was strategic. "The Hammer" knew that he must attack the invaders head-on, along with planting the seed that the booty they had acquired in their previous conquests and left back at their base camp was not safe. Both plans worked, and Western Europe was saved in the latest rounds. However, this didn't mean that the banner of Islam would not be waved again over Europe.

A mere hundred years later, Islamic forces disembarked from their 73 ships at Ostia at the mouth of the Tiber. From there they marched to Rome, descrating old St. Peter's, destroying the altar and vandalizing various pontifical tombs, including that of the first pontiff, St. Peter. It didn't end there. St. John Lateran, the pope's actual cathedral, also was targeted, and the tombs of many other saints around Rome, including that of St. Paul, saw the wrath of this invading army.[1]

While most of Europe would be spared from Islamic rule, Sicily and Spain were the exception. Islamic rule in the agriculturally rich island of Sicily would last for some time. Western words like "assassin" were really Arabic words that became part of the Sicilian nomenclature. Another Sicilian tradition that would arise from the long stay of the Arab conquest would become known as the Mafia. Strong men would emerge who would do whatever was necessary to keep political control over a region; sometimes that meant making alliances with other important families, and sometimes that meant killing them.[2]

Spain saw the longest Islamic reign in European history. Islam's long hold over Iberian Peninsula wouldn't end until 1492, the same year that an Italian sailing under the Spanish flag would discover not a shortcut to India but the New World. The Reconquista of Spain took many centuries, and the lessons learned here could have wide-ranging implications in our modern world.

There is a belief that once a land has been conquered for centuries, there is no way to get it back to its cultural roots. Yet, in our own 21st century, we are seeing before our very eyes in Kosovo that the Christian presence via the Catholic Church is still strong; some have speculated that centuries after the Islamic conquest of much of Albania, there are many crypto-Catholics in the land that gave us Bl. Mother Teresa.[3]

Why is it that many Muslims both in the Western world and in the Middle East and North Africa know far more about their history and that of the Christian West than many Christians? I saw this first-hand in the small-town Catholic school I attended and at which I then taught. I also observed this in college. I can understand a greater degree of knowledge in college, but how do we account for this in a small Rust Belt town—a town, not unlike many small towns, where Muslim doctors send their children to Catholic schools?

I believe the answer lies in the strong beliefs of many Muslim families. They simply believe their faith more than what they are told by the education and media gatekeepers. Sadly, many Christian families, including Catholic families, have bought into the historical distortions or outright fabrications that they were taught in school or have seen on cable television, etc. I am specifically thinking now of the oftentimes brutal treatment of pilgrims to the Holy Land by Muslims and the relatively meek answer to that by the Christian West, known as the Crusades.

The West, particularly in Europe, has bought into the myths about overpopulation. As a result, with their many children, a large number of Muslim families in Europe resemble Catholic families of old, while most of those native to Europe are aborting and contracepting themselves into low birthrates that are historically unprecedented.

Protestant readers may be thinking, "Wait a minute, this Catholic objection to contraception has nothing to do with us." Actually, as already mentioned, not one Christian church allowed contraceptives until 1930. The Anglican Church was the first, and though Evangelical churches said they would never change, many of them did, just like some have on the same-sex marriage issue.

Many Christians, especially Catholics, have the mistaken belief that St. Francis was some sort of hippie, selling flower power, telling everyone, "Make love, not war," and "All is well." In reality, he was a very tough, determined saint. During the Fifth Crusade, he made his way to the Holy Land to try and persuade Sultan Malek al-Kamil and all of Islam to convert back to the Catholicism of their ancestors.

When the sultan replied that the only way he would meet with St. Francis was if the man from Assisi would walk through fire, St. Francis agreed. The sultan was so impressed—since he knew no imam who would do the same—that he did meet with St. Francis. Though he did not convert, the sultan gained a higher appreciation for Christianity after St. Francis' long journey.[4]

Even iconic explorers like Christopher Columbus have been demonized by academia. Columbus is often seen as either a bloodthirsty conqueror taking advantage of the sinless, peaceful Native Americans or some sort of Bible-thumping explorer bent on converting heathens to Catholicism. Both counts are hideously in error. The New World was plagued with the same sort of marauding tribes as were the parts of Europe that were pagan during the so-called Dark Ages.

Granted, Columbus was far from sinless, but because he was very devout in his Catholic beliefs, his treatment of Native Americans was far better than explorers such as Pizarro. Columbus named most of the islands he discovered for the various saintly titles ascribed to the Blessed Virgin Mary. A recent Discovery Channel show about Columbus conceded that he was more religious and pious than other explorers. However, one of the "Columbus experts" featured in the show described Columbus in such terms that one would think of him as a religious nut. The expert said he certainly was "a holy roller."

Why do Christians take this sort of abuse from academia when the Muslim world would object in the most strenuous terms to their famous ancestors being treated in this way? Perhaps the answer is twofold, and both parts lie in faith, with the first being the lack thereof in our modern world. Too many in the Western world's main ambition is to be liked and admired by the secular powers that be. Jesus foretold that this would happen and reminded us that we can't serve two masters. Unfortunately, it would appear that many in the West have decided to serve mammon and its secular masters rather than God.

The other possibility is because Christ told us to turn the other cheek, that we were blessed if were hated because of him, and that we would be persecuted for his name's sake, and because St. Paul told us to bless those who curse us, many of us do just these things. Rather than inciting riots, we pray for their conversion, for God's mercy ("Lord, forgive them for they know not what they do"), and for his mercy upon us, for we are sinners, too.

In any event, in 2010, Western intelligence obtained an al-Qaeda target list for Western Europe from the captured Ahmed Sadiqui. The presence of Paris' Notre Dame Cathedral on the list seemed a bit out of place, for every other target was secular in origin. The Eiffel Tower, the Brandenburg Gate, the Alexanderplatz TV tower in Berlin, or the United Kingdom movements of the British royal family—none of them had any religious value. Why did Notre Dame (which means "Our Lady" in French—i.e., the Blessed Virgin Mary) and not other churches such as St. Paul's in London or St. Peter's, or St. Michael's in Munich make the list, which has caused world governments to issue terror warnings and travel updates?

To understand this question, one has to understand the mindset of al-Qaeda. To the tried-and-true jihadist, Western Europe was almost under their control until two critical events occurred: the Battle of Lepanto in 1571 and the Siege of Vienna in 1683. In both cases, the Christian victors credited Our Lady's intercession for having stopped the Islamic armies in their tracks.

Catholicism and Islam: An Interesting History   225

The Crusades as Background

Some would falsely point out that the Crusades of the 11th and 12th centuries were Western victories and thus greater Islamic sore points. This is far from the truth. The Crusades actually were seen as a great victory in the Islamic world. Though we are now told by those in the mainstream media that the various Crusades over 700 years were heinous acts of religious thuggery, bigotry, and imperialism, they were in fact small defensive actions.

For instance, the first one was called in 1095 by Pope Bl. Urban II (1088-99). His reason was twofold. First, Christian pilgrims had for years been harassed, enslaved, robbed, beaten, scourged, and otherwise brutally treated for no other reason than that they were Christian pilgrims. Secondly, the infidels had dealt the Byzantine Empire a near decisive blow, and Emperor Alexios I Komnenos beseeched Urban to send him aid. Being convinced of the idea's efficacy, His Holiness traveled to the Council of Claremont in France and there challenged the nobility and royalty present from different parts of Europe to take back the city where Our Lord won for us our salvation.

Some participated not only because of a sense of resentment over the Islamic hordes' never ending assaults on Europe but what they had to done to lands that were formally under the sway of Christianity. Long before they were Islamic lands, the Middle East and North Africa were vibrant Christian centers populated by holy persons such as St. Augustine. Islam argues that Christianity obviously did not appeal to the masses, as evidenced by the conquered people's rapid acceptance of Islam. Left unsaid is that it's very easy to accept someone else's religion when it is offered to you at the point of a scimitar held against your neck and compelled by the need of the Islamic armies to have ever more military conquests.

To this point, others took part because they knew that if the Byzantine Empire fell (as it eventually did in 1453), it was only a matter of time until the Saracens came knocking on their city walls with battering rams. This made great sense given how the Islamic armies had invaded historically Christian lands for centuries.

To give a sense of just how terrifying the idea of a Muslim army showing up outside your city's gates in the early Middle Ages must have been, consider that by 550 AD under Emperor Justinian the Great, the Byzantine Empire (loosely corresponding to the eastern half of the Roman Empire) had reached its greatest extent. It covered almost all of northern Africa, southern Spain, all of Italy, Sicily, and surrounding islands, all of what is now the southern part of Slavic Europe, Greece, Turkey, Syria, Lebanon, Jordan, Armenia, Azerbaijan, parts of Iraq, and all of the Holy Land.

By 661 and the end of the Rashidun Caliphate, Islam controlled most of Turkey, all of Cyprus, Egypt, Jordan, Syria, Iraq, Armenia, Azerbaijan, and Lebanon, plus northern Africa up to the border of modern day Tunisia. By the end of the of the Umayyad Caliphate in 750 AD, the rest of northern Africa was under the green Muslim flag, as was all but a part of what is now Basque Spain. This list does not include other Asian lands that Islam put under its sword.

Using Spain as their base, the Moors launched attacks on France in 721 and 722. Each was repelled in a decisive fashion. However, they attacked again in 732 and again thereafter in 737, each time being repelled by Charles Martel (aka the Hammer). After Charles' son Pippin the Younger drove the Islamists out of Narbonne and his son Charlemagne established the Marches region in northwest Spain, the infidels never again made such progress into France.

They did, however, make great progress for a time into the Christian African kingdom of Makuria, which was the dominant power in what is today southern Egypt and northern Sudan. Not only did the Makurians eventually best the Muslims, though they even gained some ground on them before signing a peace treaty that lasted for 600 years. It only ended when, through intermarriage and immigration, Islam had supplanted the number of Christians. By this point, the kingdom's cathedrals had become mosques.

Catholicism and Islam: An Interesting History 227

Then there was the Moors' considerable progress into Italy. It took them 61 years to do so, but by 902, all of Sicily was a Moorish kingdom, which it remained for 189 years. Sicily, in turn, was the launching point for the Aghlabid Muslims' sacking of Rome in 846 and various incursions against Italian coastal towns.

In 820, the Muslims captured the Slavic nation of Georgia, and 10 years later, they controlled Crete (although they lost it in 961 and relinquished Cyprus in 965). The now Islamic Turkmen tribes helped give Islam incremental gains into what is now Turkey during the late 11th century. However, the most demoralizing and strategically important victory leading up to the First Crusade on August 26, 1071. This battle saw the Seljuq Turks decisively trounce Byzantine forces at what is now called Malazgirt, Turkey, as well as capture Emperor Romanos IV Diogenes.

This mêlée not only disheartened the Greeks, but it sent their economy into a tailspin. This in turn greatly compromised the empire's ability to pay for its defenses, much less launch a counteroffensive. The confrontation also led to severe political infighting, which only further compromised the Byzantines' ability to meet their foes should they come spoiling for another fight.

Indeed, when Muslim ruler Alp Arslan returned Romanos to Constantinople (now known as Istanbul), the emperor returned to such political discord that a civil war soon erupted. This ended in his defeat, exile, and extraction of his eyes, which was so brutally done that infection set in, and this eastern caesar died with a rotting face. Similarly, contemporary historians agree that while the Turks' conquering of the empire's heartland, the loss wasn't a decisive blow. However, it did signal the beginning of the end for "East Rome."

Thus, a history of mosquitoes-in-a-swamp pestering Christian lands by the Moors was a decisive factor for many who answered Bl. Urban's call for the First Crusade. Most who responded, however, did so out of a sincere piety, as witnessed by the historical record. Contrary to various black legends, what was not a motivating factor was the chance for participants to enrich themselves. Most who responded came back poorer than they could ever have imagined and even impoverished. Indeed, many had to build life anew, since traveling for battle to so far away a place required enormous capital. This meant that, to finance their participation, they had to sell their estates and all their worldly possessions. Their going also put tremendous strain on the finances for the families that a large number left behind.

Regardless, while the seven Crusades may have had a noble purpose behind them, to call some of the stupid things Christians did in them a comedy of errors would not be quite correct. A comedy of stupidity, avarice, pride, hunger for power, prejudice, and other numbers of vices and sins would be more like it. Thus, their successes were limited and ultimately ill-fated.

We Now Return to Our Regularly Scheduled Programming…

Getting back to the naval Battle of Lepanto and the Battle of Vienna, as previously noted, they were the turning points for Islamic military dominance and the beginning of a decline that would result in the collapse of the Ottoman Empire in 1922. After Lepanto, Moorish naval vessels would never again threaten European coastlines. After Vienna, Islamic armies would never again threaten the heart of Europe. Because of these two victories, the hoped-for world caliphate did not come to fruition. As a result, you and I don't bow five times per day toward Mecca or, worse, pay the *jizya* or live as *dhimmi*.

To the militant jihadist, it must have seemed as if defeat was snatched out of the jaws of victory.[5] For the faithful Christian, especially the faithful Catholic (since precious little, if any, help came from Europe's Protestant forces in these battles), the Islamic defeats were miraculous and seen as the hand of God the Father working through God the Son and by the glorious intercession of Jesus' mother, Mary.

Perhaps a brief recap of these battles is in order. In each instance, the Ottoman Turkish forces had superior forces, yet they somehow lost. The faithful Catholic sees the hand of Divine Providence and this has thus been celebrated as such for years. The Feast of Our Lady of Victory (October 7) and the Feast of the Holy Name of Mary (September 12) were once much bigger liturgical celebrations than they are now, but both are still observed because Catholics believe the divine hand of God worked through the intercession of the Queen of Heaven, with each resulting in a stunning defeat for the Turks.

At the Battle of Lepanto, a superior and more experienced Ottoman Turkish naval force was defeated by a mix of keen and innovative military strategy that changed the course of naval warfare and events that seemed supernatural. Pope St. Pius V asked for all Christians to pray the Rosary. He feared, with good reason, that were the Holy League allies defeated, the Turks would have a clear path to the Italian heartland and Rome itself. At the same time, Don Juan had each ship hold Masses and offer confession until the last man had his sins shrived, and every man on every vessel prayed the Rosary.[6]

Furthermore, on his flagship, the banner under which Holy League naval commander Don Juan of Austria sailed, was a reproduction of the Our Lady of Guadalupe tilma, the 40-year-old Mexican miracle that is the still the talk of Catholic Europe. Our Lady of Guadalupe's intercessory power was unquestioned. Before the apparition on Tepeyac Hill outside of Mexico City, few of the New World's indigenous peoples had accepted Catholic. Just a few years afterward, millions had converted.

The miraculous tilma (a cloak woven of cactus fiber) still exists, defying the laws of science that can't explain how a tilma that should have lasted less than 50 years still exists nearly 500 years later. In addition, scientific tests proved that the image of the Blessed Mother was not painted on the cactus cloth.

As for the battle, despite the brilliant innovations employed by the Holy League, some military tacticians still find the superior Ottoman navy's defeat perplexing. No mystery exists for Catholics, however. The Blessed Mother intervened and convinced her Son Jesus that a miracle from him was necessary. The Feast of Our Lady of the Rosary (Pope Gregory XIII changed the title from Our Lady of Victory in 1573), which is observed each October 7th, serves as a chance for us to give God thanks for saving Western civilization, and is thus a celebration of great importance.

The subsequent defeat for the Turks at Vienna came about only because of the last-minute arrival on September 11 and 12, 1683, of Polish King Jan Sobieski and his cavalry. He, too, had his men pray the Rosary before their lightning appearance. Their arrival so disoriented the Ottomans that they fled en masse, thus saving not only Vienna but, many feel, Western Europe from the Islamic advance.

As an historical side note, the Saracens already had an alliance with Prince Imre Thököly, and they promised the Hungarian Protestant rebel leader that if he joined forces with him, he and his men would receive some of the resulting booty. However, many doubted that the marauding Ottoman Turks would give any Christian leader a share of their wealth. Indeed, given that there was no booty to give him, they gave him what was left: blame for the defeat. Many viewed his cooperation as the highest treason against Christ.

For Thököly, however, it was not Ottoman versus Christian, it was who would allow him to practice his Lutheran faith in peace. Holy Roman Emperor Leopold I would not; Sultan Mehmed IV would, and he granted the prince lands and a small kingdom of his own, to boot.

In any event, Bl. Pope Innocent XI instituted the Feast of the Holy Name of Mary in 1684, placing it on the Sunday within the Octave of the Nativity of Mary (September 8). However, following the Council, the Servant of God Paul VI removed the feast from the General Roman Calendar since it fell so close to the Feast of Our Lady's Nativity. As a result, the celebration does not have as much renown today as in the pre-Vatican II Catholic Church.

An interesting aside to this story: It was revealed by First Lady Michelle Obama that her husband carries with him a Mary Help of Christians prayer card. This was given to him some time ago by the

Catholicism and Islam: An Interesting History 231

Salesians, a Catholic religious order that often works in the inner city helping the less fortunate. The Salesians have a special devotion to the Blessed Mother, who they believed saved European Christianity on those fateful days of September 11-12, 1683.

As you might imagine, for people who are so convinced God is on their side that they will fly huge airplanes into skyscrapers, government buildings, and farm fields, the defeats at Lepanto and Vienna seem inexplicable. As with their own failed attacks (the attempted assassination of Bl. John Paul II, the failed attempt at blowing up airlines after WYD '95, the respective bungled shoe and underwear bombings, the unsuccessful first attempt to bring down the World Trade Center buildings, etc.), they must wonder what went wrong those hundreds of years ago and feel they must go back into time to change what in their minds should have resulted in an Islamic Europe.

There is a school of thought that al-Qaeda plans its attacks to coincide with historical dates. For example, is it coincidence that the terrorist group's greatest success came in 2011 on September 11, the anniversary Sobieski's victory at Vienna? Was it vengeance?

Indeed, it was none other than a famed atheist, the late Christopher Hitchens, who advanced the idea that al-Qaeda uses historic dates in its attack planning scenarios. I am not saying a future attack will definitely happen on October 7 (of this year or any year), or on September 6 (Siege of Belgrade), August 5 (Battle of Petrovaradin), August 12 (Battle of Mohács), August 19 (Battle of Slankamen), January 26 (Treaty of Karlowitz), July 21 (Treaty of Passarowitz), or any other anniversary of a date where Christians bested the Moors, but I also would not rule it out.

As I noted in a previous article,[8] many al-Qaeda-planned attacks against the Catholic Church have religious significance, like the failed Christmas Day 2000 cathedral bombing plot in Strasbourg, France. However, there have been other plots that have been targets of convenience due to a papal visit—for example, the previously mentioned 1995 Bojinka World Youth Day plot in Manila.

Many Catholics believe that the Blessed Virgin Mary has had a history of reaching out to Islam in order to bring Muslims around the world to the Catholic faith. If true, this started around the same time the Battle of Lepanto took place and continued with the apparitions of Fátima and Zeitoun. The Catholic Church has approved both sets of apparitions as worthy of belief. The former appearance of Our Lady occurred in the only Portuguese town with an Islamic name, having been named for a Moorish princess who converted to Christianity, who in turn was named for Mohammed's favorite daughter. The year was 1917.

The latter apparitions took place at the Coptic Orthodox Church of St. Demiana between 1968 and 1971 in Zeitoun, a district of Cairo, Egypt, and therefore obviously located in a predominantly Islamic country. During the apparitions, which sometimes happened two or three times a week, many were healed of illnesses and ailments, including Muslims. As one might imagine, the apparitions—which were confirmed both by the Coptic Orthodox Church and the Cairo police—drew nearly one million people from all backgrounds and religions. They also attracted the famed Egyptian leader Gamel Abdel Nasser.

One wonders whether another Cairo resident came to see the miracle, perhaps a young man named Ayman al-Zawahiri. Young Ayman would become a physician like his father. However, unlike his moderate father, he would become an Islamic radical who was implicated in the assassination of Egyptian President Anwar Sadat. He would later, along with Osama bin Laden, become one of the founding members of al-Qaeda. If he had been a witness to these visions, it is too bad they didn't steer his life in a different direction. Regardless, perhaps Our Lady is reminding the Muslim world through these apparitions that before the Middle East and North Africa were Islamic, they were largely Christian.

At this point, it might be a good idea to address what some Protestant readers may be objecting to right now, which is all this focus on the Blessed Mother. After all, for the most part, she has little role in their particular theology.

You can almost hear the objection: "Dave, this shows why Catholicism will never convert Islam because it takes the focus off of the Lord Jesus Christ and puts in onto Mary, his mother, a mere human being. Now, Mary *was* a great woman, I'll grant you. But isn't thinking that *she'll* convert Islam to Christianity blasphemy, since Scripture tells us that Jesus—who through his 'once for all sacrifice,' as we read in Hebrews 9:28 and 10:10—is the only means by which people may be saved?"

While this is a typical misunderstanding of Mary's place in the economy of salvation (although it's becoming less typical in some circles), she does have a large role in the Catholic and Orthodox Churches and always has. And that role, just to be clear, never takes people away from her Son or focuses attention on her. Rather, the whole purpose for her existence was to be the vessel that would bring reconciliation between God and the world. She did so by her acceptance of the angel Gabriel's message to her in Luke 1, she did so by her faithful witness at the Cross, and she continues to do so in apparitions such as those we have discussed in this book. Her message is always the same: Draw closer to my Son, convert, repent, and turn away from any sin you may have in your life.

Furthermore, we see her throughout Scripture. For instance, the Church Fathers recognized Mary as "woman" in the Protoevangelium (Genesis 3:15) and as "the woman clothed with the sun" in Revelation 12. In addition, many Catholic theologians reason that Jesus never called Mary "mother" because she is the Blessed Mother of the entire world.

While one doesn't expect radical Islam to be familiar with Marian apparitions or Catholic eschatology, Islam of whatever stripe does take Mary very seriously and gives her great reverence. After all, they believe Jesus was the greatest prophet after Mohammed, they acknowledge the virgin birth (but not Incarnation), and they hold no other woman as high as she.

That aside, however, we have to look at the theology of the radicals. The rhetoric of al-Qaeda increasingly reflects an ever-more radicalized Muslim world. While the academics love to reminisce about Islam's cerebral side, the radicalized Islamic world quotes the more militant parts of the Koran. This is why, in addition to their seeing Christianity as an apostate faith, they also believe it is a failed religion. Therefore, they loved to remind the unbelievers of how Islam spread the faith with the sword further in one century than Christianity had with kindness and love for seven centuries.

Dr. Yossef Bodansky provides us with an interesting glimpse into this mindset. Dr. Bodansky refers to a January 7, 1994, speech given by former Iranian President Hashemi Rafsanjani. In it, he stated that Christ's message had failed because Jesus had been incapable of bringing man to God, so God had to send Mohammed to get the job done. In other words, the Islamic conquest of the Middle East, North Africa, and Southern Europe was necessary only because Christianity had failed.

This is an interesting statement because, although Rafsanjani is a Shiite and al-Qaeda is Sunni, the message is the same: Christianity failed and conquest—entailing bloodletting, death, war, enslavement, violence, mayhem, and the dehumanization and deportation of whole peoples—was needed to bring man to God. However, even in their defense of the Islamic conquest, these two radical wings of Islam are forced to admit that Christianity was alive and well in the Middle East and North Africa centuries before the arrival of Islam. One of the familiar themes on any al-Qaeda tape is the plea to remove the infidel from Islamic lands.

The radicals fail to mention the divisions in Islam. Some speculate that groups like the Mu'tazilah, who were rationalistic and seemed to take great pleasure in learning from the Hellenistic era, were eventually overtaken by a more deterministic group, whom some might describe as an Islamic form of Calvinism. The caliphate was never as strong as it was before the Mongols' sacking of Baghdad in the 13th century and the Lepanto fiasco in the 16th century. A few centuries later, Wahabism developed in the Arabian Peninsula; this was a belief so austere that it wanted Islam to go back to a life that existed at the time of Mohammed, before Islam and particularly Baghdad were far from their creative zenith. Had this school of thought developed in a remote part of the world, free from wealth and natural resources, it may have simply been academic asterisks. However, when oil was discovered in the Arabian Peninsula, the money it generated helped propel this radical belief system the world over. It became the driving force behind radical Islam.

Al-Qaeda raised money in the Arabian Peninsula by sheer bribery and guilt. Many a rich Saudi, who spent too much of his oil wealth on wine, women, and song in Beirut, Monaco, or some other lively locale, has been bribed or made to feel that giving to al-Qaeda might help settle the account. In turn, this money was used for planning and attacks. Providentially, many of the attacks, especially those directed at the Catholic Church, would never see the light of day as previously noted.

One of the mistakes of the Far Left or the Isolationist Right is to believe that if radical Islam is just left alone, it will do the Christian, Hindu, or moderate Muslim little harm. This is wishful thinking. Radical Islam has always been powerful when the West is weak. There have been countless waves of immigration to the Western world from Lebanon, Turkey, Syria, and Iran, which resulted from pogroms aimed at the non-Muslims. Radical Islam becomes nervous when, in our case, faithful Christians stand up for their faith. However, it becomes powerful when we do not stand up for our faith.

Al-Qaeda knows that the Catholic Church is the only international Christian body that is growing. In its adherents' minds, what better way to eliminate the threat than to terrorize the competition? They must have thought they had nearly won when the Anglican Archbishop of Canterbury, Dr. Rowan Williams, recently stated that Britain must accept the coming of Sharia law. The archbishop and his liberal religious counterparts have become media darlings for changing their respective church's doctrine to reflect the whims of the modern world. It might seem that the Anglicans and other liberal Christian bodies have little to worry about, since, to al-Qaeda, it would seem as if they have already surrendered. Fortunately, no such surrender is coming from Rome, and for that the Catholic Church the world over must pay the price. Yet, Our Lady looks on and pleads to her son, Jesus, to save the faithful as has been done many times in previous centuries. Let this time be another.

Perhaps Catholic-Islamic relations took a positive turn during the so-called Arab Spring of 2011. Young Arab people and intellectuals started their drive for democracy in Tunisia, which spread to Egypt—the largest Arab country—which in turn sparked movements throughout the Middle East. Those were heady days in Tahir Square, Cairo, along with Benghazi, Libya, and Hom, Syria, when courageous young people fought off the entrenched security forces, which pushed the military (in the case of Egypt) to intervene on the side of the reformers.

However, in Egypt and other budding democratic Middle East hot spots, idealistic young people were forced to see the obvious in their region: Islamic radicals under the umbrella of the Muslim Brotherhood were not going to go quietly in the night. A preview of this was seen in 2009, when Iran was rocked by a series of civil disturbances (which were virtually ignored by many of the West's cowardly leaders) that only led to more brutal suppression.

This was quickly seen in the fall of 2011 when Egypt, Tunisia, and Libya were pushed forward toward Sharia law by the newly formed political parties as the foundation of law in those lands. Where 40 years ago women strolled the streets of Cairo, Tehran, and Kabul with nary a headscarf in sight, now the complete opposite is seen. The forces of radical Islam have made their aims clear.

Perhaps the brutal methods of the Muslim Brotherhood, which predates their sworn enemy—the modern state of Israel, along with their ideological brethren al-Qaeda and the Taliban—have caused many Muslims to start to see the wisdom in the statements of Pope Benedict XVI concerning radical Islam.

TWELVE
A GERMAN POPE TRIUMPHS IN BRITAIN

In September 2010, a somewhat miraculous event took place in Britain. A few short years before, it would have been dismissed as sheer fantasy: an aging German pope arriving in Britain to the cheers and rapt attention of many, all the while his detractors were scorned as everything that is wrong with Britain and the modern world. St. Thomas More, Bishop John Fisher, and the rest of the English martyrs must be smiling in heaven. The English martyrs, both the well-known (Sir Thomas) and the unsung (St. Margaret Clitherow), would have found their views more often than not supported by the rank and file. However, the same rank and file didn't have the courage to make the stand as did these courageous men and women who were martyred. Though Catholicism was widely practiced, the fear of a bloodthirsty king left many too weak to fight the good fight. (If you don't believe me, read Eamon Duffy's *The Stripping of the Altars.*[1]

The truth will either set you free or convict you of false witness. It was the brutal King Henry VIII who began England's separation from Catholicism because Pope Clement VII wouldn't give him a divorce. The king later had two of his wives beheaded. This makes him a rather odd sort of person to start a church, but start a church he did. Starting in 1534, Catholics were killed and a legal Catholic Mass wasn't allowed to be celebrated in Britain or conquered Ireland for nearly 300 years. The creation of King Henry, the Anglican Church, would reach the far-flung corners of the mighty British Empire. As recently as 50 years ago, the Anglican Church in Britain had one of the highest rates of church attendance in the Western world. Her teachings were mirrored by those like C.S. Lewis. Fifty years later, her teachings are being mirrored by the likes of Elton John. However, to be fair to Sir Elton, even he is to the right of the Anglican Church on matters like welcoming Islamic Sharia law to Britain as the spiritual leader of the Anglicans, the Archbishop of Canterbury, recently did.

The Catholic Church has been derided and mocked by the mainstream media for some time. One might think that with all of this and the horrible sex-abuse scandal within the Church, it would be the Catholic Church that would be withering and not the liberal Anglican Church, which is modeling the whims of the modern world. Yet, the Catholic Church continues to grow—and even rapidly so in Africa and Asia (Christ told us this would be so in Matthew 16:16-20). The faithful aren't as ignorant as the militant secularists would like to believe. The religious faithful of all stripes are beginning to clearly understand what Pope Benedict XVI is saying about the dangers of the "dictatorship of relativism." It cannot work, as Jesus reminded us; we cannot serve two masters. Sadly, that is what modern Anglicanism and liberal Christianity have tried to do. The results have been disastrous.

Perhaps this is why, as British journalist and blogger Damian Thompson notes in his column, "The Pope in Parliament and Westminster Abbey: A Day That Shook the Foundations of Britain's Protestant Myth," that even in the liberal *Guardian* newspaper a story about "the unthinkable events" was published. In addition, from the *Sun*, the tabloid notorious for gossip and the infamous Page 3 Girls, came this: "Pope: Don't Let the PC Brigade Wreck Christmas." The world is looking for answers, and they can't be found in the lyrics of Lady Gaga or even the thoughtful Irish band U2. (I say U2 because the Anglican Church, especially in the United States where it's known as the Episcopal Church, is very proud of its U2 Charist celebrations. This is where one can receive the Eucharist while U2 songs are used for the Communion meditation.[2] While Bono, the

A German Pope Triumphs in Britain

Edge, and the rest of the band are great humanitarians, they would hardly consider their lyrics divine.

Yet this is what liberal Christianity has become. Its followers somehow think this will woo the thoughtful unbeliever. Perhaps the unbeliever may check out one of these services, but as the numbers indicate, they then move on to something else: a Lady Gaga concert or perhaps an edgy movie. In other words, they want to tune out from the truth and reality. The Gospel message is the last thing they want to hear and, try as liberal Christianity might to make it appealing, it can never be dressed up to appease the rebellious. It must first come to terms with its rebellion and submit to the love and teachings of Christ, which is hard for those who have humility in such short supply.

Karl Marx told the workers of the world to throw off their chains. He also stated that religion was the opiate of the masses. Marx and Friedrich Engels, along with their followers from Leon Trotsky to Saul Alinsky, ignored the obvious chains of sin and concentrated on the means of production. However, what they were producing was an alternative message to the New Testament. How ironic that some in the Christian world tried to dress up Marxism and incorporate it into various liberal Christian denominations! They even found elites with guilty consciences to come their way. Who would have thought that in the US presidential election of 2008, the very wealthy and trust-funders would vote for the most liberal ticket ever to be elected president and vice president? Yet the world, which so eagerly embraced this ticket, has seen what the US voters have seen: The oceans haven't listened to the pleas of the elites, the poor are still among us, and hostile nations haven't beaten their swords into plowshares.

The liberals' attempt at creating a parallel faith has failed, which is why the British so eagerly listened to the words of an aging, heavily accented German pontiff while all but ignoring the melodious tones of their own Anglican leader, Dr. Rowan Williams. Although a humanitarian he may be, the Archbishop of Canterbury's churches are empty. More Britons are seen in their respective mosques on Friday afternoon than in Anglican churches on Sunday morning.

Many Britons are asking what went wrong. In addition to saying we cannot serve two masters—the whims of the world and God—Christ also spoke of building his Church on the Rock. The Catholic Church was founded by Christ, who gave the proverbial keys to St. Peter and his successors. There was only one set of keys, not 40,000-plus different sets (the number of denominational and nondenominational churches that exist today in just the United States alone). This is hardly what Jesus had in mind when he stated there should only be one Church (see John 10:16). Jesus also said that those who will not listen to his successors are not listening to him; in essence they are rejecting him (see Luke 10:16). Perhaps now many of the faithful are beginning internalize these words.

Recently, while on a business matter, a man asked whether I could meet with him in his office. I had no idea that it would concern religion. Though currently Episcopalian, he came with several books: Steve Ray's *Upon This Rock*; Scott Hahn's *Signs of Life*; Mike Aquilina's *The Fathers of the Church*; and my own *The Tide Is Turning Toward Catholicism*. I sat there dumbfounded as he quoted from Ray's book concerning apostolic succession, from Hahn's book concerning the role of the sacraments, and from Aquilina's book concerning the early Church. He even quoted from my own book concerning the rise in vocations from the more orthodox or more conservative Catholic dioceses, as well as the shallowness exhibited by the many entertainment-style megachurches that dot the US landscape.

He stated that for some time he had been exploring Catholicism. At first, he said, his wife was rather hostile to the Church. She cited the sex-abuse scandal and the rules associated with Catholicism. However, this man gave an amazing witness of why the Church suffered through the scandal. He viewed it as the Church paying the price for allowing those the world said should be allowed into the priesthood. Fortunately, although many of these abusers tried to change the Church, they could not. In contrast, many of the liberal Protestant churches did change, though their own form of clergy abuse was barely reported.

His openness to Catholicism was far more than an intellectual exercise. He mentioned something that *Spirit Daily's* Michael Brown alluded to: the power of miracles and healings associated with the Church. John Cardinal Newman's beatification came about, as do all beatifications and subsequent canonizations, because of a miracle. The miraculous healing of an individual due to the intercessory help of someone—in this case Cardinal Newman, or in other cases in Britain, St. Thomas More, St. John Fisher, Bl. David Gunston, or any of the multitude of British martyrs killed for their refusal to renounce the Catholic Church—tells us this is of God. Miracles have to stand the scrutiny of non-believers and medical science, all the more reason why the Catholic Church's legitimacy as the Church Jesus Christ founded stands the test of time. When the faithful—and even the not-so-faithful who are at least open-minded—understand this, the Church flourishes.

Britain recognized this in the witness of an 83-year-old German pontiff who came to their shores much derided but who left victorious. He was victorious not because of any miraculous feats he performed, but by reminding those who were listening of the amazing things God has in store for us all. The instructions for this lifelong exercise can be found in sacred Scripture and Sacred Tradition; the problem is that our modern world wants to either omit or add to the sacred texts and traditions that God has given us. Perhaps St. Thomas More said it best, though he knew these words would cost him his life: "I am the king's good servant, but God's first."

THIRTEEN
THE IMPACT OF CATHOLIC MEDIA

For weeks, two young men were attending daily Mass in the same Hollywood Catholic Church but hadn't met; although since the churchgoing crowd was generally older, both men were aware of each other's presence. Eduardo Verastegui, a popular Latin film star who was dubbed to be the next American film star, was mulling over his future. He was tired of being stereotyped in "Latin lover" films and had no interest in being the next Brad Pitt, as he was being billed by US promoters. He felt called to a different life. Yet the more he felt called to use his cinematic talents for more wholesome purposes, the louder the crescendo grew from friends and associates telling him that he could make compromises and still be the Latin superstar.

Leo Severino was the other younger man at Mass. He, too, was tormented about where his life was going. Involved in film projects he didn't feel comfortable with, he delved into the Faith that he had long ago walked away from. He was praying for answers. Little did he know they would involve this mysterious younger man he would see at daily Mass. Severino's curiosity was piqued, however, so he wanted to know who this other man was. The two struck up a friendship, which led to the founding of Metanoia Films. Born out of despair, Metanoia Films would bring faith, hope, and love home to millions with its first release, *Bella*.

Shot on a shoestring budget scrapped together with loans from investors, the film went on to win the Toronto International Film Festival, a verdict that stunned Hollywood insiders who were expecting one of the other more secular yet highly acclaimed films to win.[1]

Verastegui spoke to me about his experiences and how he cannot go back to living a lifestyle that would embarrass not only his mother but the Blessed Mother. He told me that every project he agrees to participate in must meet the criteria of making his mother and the Blessed Mother proud.[2]

Verastegui currently is starring in a movie called *For Greater Glory*, which features a star-studded cast with the likes of Peter O'Toole, Eva Longoria, as well as up-and-coming stars like Karyme Lozano. The film focuses on a successful attempt to attack the Catholic Church in early 20th-century Mexico. A military dictatorship outlawed the physical presence of the Catholic Church outside the confines of church buildings. Priests were forbidden to wear their collars in public, a law that was strictly enforced until the good will that was generated by Bl. John Paul II in the 1980s allowed it to be relaxed. With this backdrop, a group of Mexican peasants fought against this military junta and between 1926 and 1929 the movement spread throughout Mexico. Many martyrs gave their lives for the Catholic faith, perhaps none more dramatic than Bl. Miguel Pro, who not only was executed but had his execution filmed in his executioners' hope that he would be seen begging for his life.

In fact, just the opposite occurred; when Fr. Pro was executed, he outstretched his arms in Christlike fashion. A picture of this was circulated throughout Mexico, and it became a rallying cry for the faithful. Though President Calvin Coolidge was in the White House during the Cristero War, an administration that was in the White House ten years earlier had a hand in this sad chapter. Evidence for this is widely available; a good reference point for this is the Central Intelligence Agency's website. In the library section is an article written by Mark E. Benbow, who outlines the anti-Catholic nature of some of the Wilson officials who were sent to Mexico.

Unfortunately, these same officials seemed smitten with the outlaw Pancho Villa, who would eventually raid a New Mexico town, killing several Americans. It would eventually take General John J. "Black Jack" Pershing and several thousand of his men to keep Villa at bay and prevent further attacks.

This new Catholic Hollywood's emphasis on movies with a message and morality, self-sacrifice, and discipline was in marked contrast to that of secular Hollywood's 40-year battle to tear down the importance and legitimacy of the Church. Starting in the 1960s, many classic films sought to awaken the general populace about what could be achieved without the Church. When Hollywood was happy with the Church, the Church was not growing or healthy; yet, now that the Church is growing in the Third World and seeing an uptick in vocations in the United States, all too many pop culture stars have come out of the woodwork to attack the Church.

However, secular Hollywood was not always against the Church. In many an old time Hollywood film where religion figured into the script, a classic-looking Catholic Church was featured. Even today when Hollywood uses religious imagery, it is that of a traditional-looking church, not a modernist one. Catholic religious imagery often touches even non-Catholic producers and directors. The director of *Rocky*, John Avildsen, stated in the film's 25th anniversary DVD re-release that he wanted to begin the film with a compelling image. The opening scene wasn't planned until Avildsen saw the image of Christ holding the Eucharist in a former parish gym that housed the opening boxing scene of the movie.

For years (1940s to early 1960s), Fr. Patrick Peyton headed the National Legion of Decency, which could easily squelch the success of any film deemed to be morally indecent. Directors and movie studios feared any negative publicity coming out of the decency board, or the Hays Code as some referred to it.[3] That board no longer exists. However, the Gay & Lesbian Alliance Against Defamation has replaced the decency board with one of its own, which causes the same feelings of fear for any film that would run afoul against the gay and lesbian agenda.

While Hollywood feature films were already thumbing their nose at society, it took television a little while longer. Even as late as the 1970s, there were iconic figures like *Hawaii Five O's* Steve McGarret (played by Jack Lord) who lived life by the straight and narow and expected those under his charge to do the same. He was portrayed as an almost suffering servant figure protecting the good citizens of Hawaii, which precluded him from having a family and indulging on past hobbies like golf. The 1980s introduced us to the new "Hollywood hero" in TV shows like *Hill Street Blues*. In that award-winning series, Captain Frank Furillo was the overworked police captain. However, unlike the noble McGarret, Furillo dumps his traditional, conservative-minded wife for the modern, sultry Joyce Davenport. It was a theme that ran over and over again: conservative minded people—dumb and boring; progressive minded-people—intelligent and exciting.

In the world of film, 1999's *American Beauty* truly broke the mold of anti-traditional values films. This Academy Award-winning picture managed to attack all the totems of traditional American society, but it seemed to take special pleasure at grilling the traditional family, the military, and a belief in entreprenuerialism. In the film, Kevin Spacey's character, Lester Burnham, is the sympathetic hero. Why? Because he quits his job, hates his entrepreneurial wife, and finally gets his "lust for life" back by trying to seduce his teenage daughter's friends. I could go on, but it would be too depressing, and if you haven't seen the film, I think you get the picture. Thankfully, Hollywood now has an emerging faith-filled group of filmmakers, writers, actors, and actresses who are trying to fight the good fight, despite being equipped with what appears to be at times a mere slingshot. However, we know the wonders God can work with slingshots.

The idea of California as a haven of liberalism is rather new. Fr. Peyton arrived in the 1930s, believing that Hollywood was the tool that could evangelize the world for the Catholic Church. Dubbed the "Rosary Priest" for his devotion to the Rosary and the power of its prayers to save a dying man like himself, Fr. Peyton cast a huge shadow over Hollywood. While in the seminary, Fr. Peyton was diagnosed with a terminal illness and told he would never be ordained.

He asked the Blessed Mother to intercede with her Son, because the future Fr. Peyton couldn't believe that he would have toiled for so many years at odd jobs before entering the seminary only to die before he was ordained. Miraculously, he was completely cured. He is said to have coined the term, "The family that prays together, stays together."[4]

In the 1940s and beyond, Fr. Peyton believed that Hollywood would be a great source of evangelization. Some might find these claims preposterous now, yet the group he started, Family Theater, has had a tremendous influence on Hollywood and still exists today. Fr. Peyton got the idea from hearing so many men and women talk about the hardships on the family caused by men who had fought a world war and returned home, which unleashed new tensions.

Many say Family Theater is stronger than it has been in years due to Fr. Willy Raymond's leadership and drive in helping films like *Bella* achieve popular acclaim. During its heyday, Family Theater produced many famous films and had a who's who of famous stars of the screen sing the praises of its production. Famed Hollywood stars and starlets like Bob Hope, Jimmy Stewart, Ronald Reagan, and Grace Kelly took part in Family Theater ventures.

Family Theater and the Congregation of Holy Cross, the order that assists Family Theater, aided other Catholic endeavors. For example, they held rosary rallies across the country. One of the largest occurred in San Francisco in 1961. Over 550,000 people attended the rally at the same place where a few years later the counterculture movement would promise the end of traditional religion and promote the ideas of every sort of inhibition. While it is widely perceived now that certain cities like San Francisco are always on the fringe and in concert with liberal ideas, the truth of the matter is that a few years before the Summer of Love began, many more participated in a true rally of love, a love of God, and a denial of self.

Art and film by their very nature can push the envelope, and push the envelope they did in the 1960s and beyond. Today, one is

The Impact of Catholic Media

rarely shocked by anything that comes out of Hollywood. However, militant and secular Hollywood is still shocked and outraged over the direction of society and the fact that a majority of Americans attend religious services regularly. Not only do these Americans believe in the existence of God but also in heaven, hell, angels, and miracles, let alone the principle belief of Christianity that Jesus Christ died for the sins of mankind and rose on the third day. Hollywood has a disproportionate amount of individuals who don't believe in God and attack the notion that religion might be the best way to worship him. After all, don't atheists get together for meetings, have fund drives and put together websites? Isn't that organized disbelief?

There are some avowed atheists in Hollywood, Jodie Foster among them, but many more claim no religious belief and believe instead in the power of other activities. Jack Nicholson, who was raised Catholic, has stated that he never had any use for religion. However, he is a follower of Wilhelm Reich, who taught and believed that enhanced sexual activity and long durations of it would cure societal ills. Even some Hollywood political conservatives like Kelsey Grammar don't seem to have much use for organized religion. At least there is hope for Grammar, since he does not participate in the sort of vile anti-religious and anti-Catholic activities that some in Hollywood do. Perhaps he is borrowing from his longtime role of Dr. Frasier Crane, featured in both television situation comedies *Cheers* and *Frasier*. In both shows, Dr. Crane was always searching for the truth while trying to assist others in his psychiatric practice and radio therapy show.

There are some who claim to be agnostic but yet hate religion, especially the Catholic Church. A good example is Bill Maher. One might recall Maher saying that those who believe in religion have a "neurological disorder." Maher was raised in a Catholic and Jewish home where neither faith was practiced. Maher seems to relish the opportunity to attack the Catholic priesthood and the Eucharist. He calls himself an "apatheist," which is an offshoot of atheism and agnosticism. The term is said to have been coined by French thinker

Denis Diderot, who when accused of being an atheist said that he simply didn't care if God existed or not.[5] This is somewhat different than an agnostic, who claims not to know. An apatheist seems the epitome of arrogance; they just don't care. I have long maintained that most atheists I have met may claim there is no God, but deep down they believe God is real; it is just their pride that won't permit them to believe there is someone better than themselves.

It seems all too often that atheists get caught up in rebellious events, unaware what it is they are rebelling against but glad to be a part of it. The 1960s were a great example of this, and San Francisco became its epicenter due to a grouping of universities near the city. The GI Bill permitted a large increase in the number of students able to attend college; because of this, an increasing number of professors were brought in to meet the demand. These professors by and large came from the Northeast, and they brought their liberal ideology with them. While not apparent at first, this mindset helped spark the student protest movement on the Berkeley campus of the University of California. The student protest, while hailed as a movement for free speech, basically centered on the use of foul language. It was hardly the type of human rights struggle that was going on in the American South.

Indeed, while the media and many filmmakers hail events like the Summer of Love, along with other countercultural events, there exists not one documentary on the rally that drew more than the countercultural protests, the San Francisco Rosary Rally of 1961. Even the archdiocese makes no mention of the historic event in the Archdiocesan History portion of its website. One could posit that the intense media scrutiny given these countercultural events led to these moving from regional events to national sensations. No such Catholic or religious rally of any sort was given near the attention that the Berkeley free-speech demonstrations of 1964 (which, when they began, were nothing more than a band of students who wanted the right to use profanity in public) or the Summer of Love alternative movement that began in the Haight-Ashbury district of San Francisco in 1967.

The Impact of Catholic Media

Contrast two iconoclastic moments, one from entertainment and one from religion. The concert at Woodstock in upstate New York in the summer of 1969 was a proclaimed seminal moment in pop culture history. The biggest names of rock music were there, and to this day the event not only has musical implications, but it has been assessed political ones as well. However, in many ways, the concert was a disaster. Poor planning led to lack of food, and poor security almost led to a riot as thousands tried to get into the event free of charge. Musically, few objective observers would say any of the marquee bands and individual acts gave memorable performances, mostly due to the poor quality of the sound system and the fact that the stage was still being completed while the concert was in progress. Also due to poor planning, headliner Jimi Hendrix didn't take the stage until Monday morning, when only 30,000 of the 500,000 were still in attendance. Years later, Billy Joel would comment that it was a big mess, which he couldn't wait to leave. Although the "Piano Man" wasn't alone in these feelings, few commentators would ever say the event wasn't an astonishing cultural success.

Contrast the event in upstate New York with the event outside of Denver some 24 years later—World Youth Day, dubbed by some the "Catholic Woodstock." Both events had the same number of attendees, but which would have the most lasting impact? World Youth Day was the launching point for a renewal of orthodoxy among the young. Countless vocations were a direct result of World Youth Day. While onlookers at Woodstock were given free access to verbally tell the world their countercultural views, those attending World Youth Day were peppered with questions proclaiming bewilderment for their "traditional views."

World Youth Day's lasting impact will be with us for years to come, as many of the young people who were there are now directly influencing the Church with their hearts, minds, and prayers.[6] Woodstock launched no new bands; it was a planning nightmare and yet was dubbed a success, so much so that there have been two reunion concerts. However, as perhaps a harbinger of things to come, the 1994 concert saw violence and arson that shocked even the most hardened alternative aficionado.

Oddly enough, when the veneer is pulled from these events, all too often one finds something far less than meets the eye. As I detail later, while some of the San Francisco protesters would go on to be productive citizens, many participants would drift through life trying to find the next cause to join. Some even became involved with the pornography boom that hit San Francisco some 10 years later. World Youth Day, on the other hand, would go on to lead many into faith-filled lives; for some it would be the spark that that a religious vocation was their true calling.

Sadly, without a vision, the people perish. These familiar words are from the Old Testament, yet we still see the truths they contain in our everyday world. I couldn't help but think of this while glancing through various articles and books written about famous pop stars who discuss their Catholic upbringing only to have it disappear into the mists of pop culture history. Somehow, though, elements of the faith seem to surface in subtle ways, perhaps even unbeknownst to them. One can hear flickers of it in the most obscure of places, from the longing and wistful lyrics of the Cars' Ric Ocasek to heavy-metal figures like Tony Iommi, the lead guitarist and brains behind the seminal heavy-metal band, Black Sabbath.

Iommi was raised Catholic in Birmingham, England. Interestingly enough, he notes in his book, *Iron Man,* that he remembers going to Mass only a couple of times in his youth. While his Italian immigrant parents had little use for faith, his grandfather went to daily Mass. Iommi recoils at the harsh memories of his abusive father while fondly recalling his early years spent with his daily communicant grandfather. One wonders what a different atmosphere, other than the doom and gloom of Birmingham's dying 1960s welfare state coupled with faithless parents, might have had on Iommi. Yet, it seems his grandfather must have had some influence because tucked away from the occultist imagery seen in many of Black Sabbath staple songs are others like "After Forever," which may be the most pro-Christian heavy-metal song ever recorded.

The same subtle Catholic imagery may be seen in, of all places, the lyrics of some Led Zeppelin songs such as "Ramble On," "The Battle of Evermore," and the iconic "Stairway to Heaven." Certainly Led Zeppelin has had such a dubious past with such infamous parties that I couldn't even begin to chronicle in a family-friendly book. In addition, guitarist Jimmy Page admits to having had a sinister fascination with the occultist Aldous Huxley. Yet, today Page and the rest of the surviving members of Led Zeppelin have renounced the wrong path they once chose. They much prefer now to discuss their interest in J.R.R. Tolkien. It may have been Led Zeppelin who first brought Tolkien to the attention of the 1960s and 1970s counterculture. Tolkien would later gain prominence in the new millennium after his various works made it to the silver screen in blockbuster fashion.

Tolkien's first major convert was C.S. Lewis, a colleague at Oxford with whom Tolkien often had a pint at the local pub. During pre-World War II England, Lewis was already considered by some to be one of the world's smartest men. Tolkien took it upon himself to aid in Lewis' conversion in whatever way he could, which often took the venue of the local pub. Tolkien was a Catholic from the old school and wasn't embarrassed to tell anyone so. His grandson remembers him still reciting the proper responses in Latin well after the Novus Ordo Mass was implemented. Yet, in Tolkien we see what is possible when one takes the time to evangelize through the spoken word—e.g., Lewis at the pub, or even through his science-fiction works that would later influence countless number of people who would have never even considered giving Christianity in general, and Catholicism in particular, a fair hearing.

Both during World Youth Day and the events for Pope Benedict XVI's visit to Washington and New York City, Catholic musicians figured prominently. Two of the biggest names were John Angotti and Matt Maher. Both cradle Catholics, they took an interesting road to become the budding stars they are. Angotti came from the hills of West Virginia, while Maher came from Newfoundland on Canada's

Atlantic Coast. He journeyed to Arizona and come under the tutalege of noted Catholic liturgical singer-songwriter Tom Booth.

Angotti's voice could almost be mistaken for that of Billy Joel, only even stronger, while Maher has not only a strong voice but one that seems perfectly scripted for the Christian rock scene, of which Catholic acts have had little presence. Maher is a ministry in and of himself, reaching out to an Evangelical world that by and large greets him with open arms, though the strident exceptions can easily be seen on Christian music message boards and the comment sections of the various YouTube clips of his performances and videos. Maher was evangelizing and dispelling age-old myths concerning Catholicism to an Evangelical world eager to embrace someone proclaiming the truth in an ever-increasing world of militant secularism and gimmick-oriented megachurches.

However, it was Maher's video with Catholic theological rock star Scott Hahn that went viral in the Catholic Web world in 2011 and 2012. Before performing at Franciscan University, Maher issued a challenge to the one-time teenage rock band member Hahn to join him on stage. Hahn eagerly hopped onstage before a raucous crowd in Steubenville.

Maher is hardly alone, as an ever-increasing number of new Catholic singers and songwriters were entering the world of contemporary Christian music; Audrey Assad is one such example. A twenty-something, highly acclaimed singer-songwriter originally from New Jersey, Assad has showed the world that Catholic young people from all backgrounds (Assad's father was from Syria) could adhere to the Church's teachings and sing about what it means to their lives in a revealing, personal, and remarkably beautiful style.

The tide was turning because events like World Youth Day raised the spiritual conscience of many, while events like the Summer of Love and Woodstock became pop culture icons whose lasting worth was truly in doubt. This is why figures like Dave Wang, a Canadian physics professor and the godfather of Catholic rock, may be known

The Impact of Catholic Media 253

to a relatively very small number of Christian musicians, yet his influence continues to live on in other musicians who bring the gospel truth to many. On the other hand, those caught in the ways of the world may be popular one minute, but their influence hardly registers in a world filled with a whim a minute.

In 2008 one of Hollywood's most celebrated and edgy writers had a reversion to Catholicism that stunned both the faithful and not so faithful. Joe Eszterhas, the man behind such erotic, dark, and suspenseful thrillers as *Basic Instinct*, *Sliver*, and *Jagged Edge* not only returned to the Faith but fully embraced her teachings, sacraments, and devotions. Though a book entitled *Crossbearer: Memoir of Faith* would come out in the fall of 2008, it was a August 23, 2008, interview with the *Toledo Blade* that first alerted the public to this Damascus-style conversion.

Eszterhas grew up in Cleveland but had been born in a refugee camp in Hungary. His first job was with the Cleveland's *The Plain Dealer* covering the crime beat, which he says gave him a window to life's dark side. Following a stint as editor of *Rolling Stone*, Eszterhas began his foray into Hollywood writing mainstream screenplays like *Flashdance*. Soon after, he started taking a dark, edgy, erotic path that earned him the kudos of the Hollywood glitterati. However, his own life was anything but settled. Finally, in the summer of 2001, facing a health crisis, Eszterhas pleaded for God's help—which stunned him more than anyone. Miraculously, his doctor reported great progress, and Eszterhas and his family moved back to the Cleveland area from Malibu, where they began attending Mass. Eszterhas was no longer in the mood to embrace the dark, edgy, erotic films that were his trademark. He began to work on projects that were edifying, with themes of faith and hope.

One could write an entire book on the many young—and some not so young—people who are faithful and are slowly but surely changing Hollywood one script, one performance, one episode, and one movie at a time—those like the good folks at the aforementioned Family Theater: Fr. Willy Raymond, Tony Sands, and countless others affiliated with this worthy endeavor. There are many others like screenplay writers Cary Solomon and Chuck Konzelman (the men behind *The Resurrection* film project), writers and directors like Barbara Nicolosi and Steve McEveety, and up-and-coming filmmakers like Tim Watkins and Christian Peschken. This is merely the tip of the iceberg—and a growing iceberg at that!

FOURTEEN
THE CATHOLIC CHURCH, AGNOSTICS, AND ATHEISTS

In the last decade or so, the number of atheistic writings has not only grown, it has become vigorous in its own brand of apologetics, the aim of which is to lead people away from faith. Several authors who have been branded the "New Atheists" have churned out books such as *Letter to a Christian Nation* by Sam Harris, Richard Dawkins' *The God Delusion*, and *God Is Not Great: How Religion Poisons Everything* by the late Christopher Hitchens.

However, it seems that whatever the virtues or lack thereof of these men's arguments (and it is, alas, mostly a lack), for many atheists, it appears from personal experience and anecdotal evidence that there is no great thought that goes behind the rejection of God. Indeed, one can easily judge the ad hominem attacks against religion masquerading as witty and urbane, and well-thought-out philosophy as banal, unimaginative, tired, and just plain ridiculous.

It goes to show what G.K. Chesterton is famous for saying (although he actually didn't): "When a man stops believing in God he doesn't then believe in nothing, he believes anything." That this quote is apocryphal is not the point. Rather, the point is that for people who pride themselves on their intellect and rational thought process, atheists will often accept the most amusing arguments against religion as something possessing the logic and airtight reasoning of Plato and Aristotle.

Furthermore, for people who find belief in an Almighty God unsophisticated, they sure do find the paranormal and New Age fascinating. In *Makers and Takers*, author Peter Schweizer notes that in one of America's biggest atheist and agnostic bastions, Berkeley, California, *Dell Horoscope* magazine has one of its highest subscription rates.[1]

Soon after the first phase of the Iraq War ended in 2003, the war became increasingly unpopular. Not only were our reasons for going to war questioned, but bigger questions were also asked. What was the nature of this war? Was it one of national interest, a war to secure a steady flow of oil for our vast military/industrial complex-driven economy (which worked out *really* well, if that was indeed the plan, don't you think?) or part of the larger War on Terror? Was it a war against the Islam faith?

Given that the coalition forces led by the United States laid out a strictly secular argument for initiating hostilities and even though most organized religions took positions on the war that ranged from ambivalent to outright hostility, that didn't stop some from equating the war against Saddam Hussein to a war on Islam. The media featured stories on this theme, while newspapers published editorials stating that religion had started all wars, it was responsible for this one, and therefore religion was responsible for man's woes.

This sort of thinking coincided with the aforementioned reinvigorated atheism. Its adherents soon launched an offensive the likes of which hadn't been seen since the heyday of the counterculture movement of the 1960s or perhaps since the French Revolution in the 1790s.[2]

Every movement needs a book or film to solidify its base and give its followers an image. Between 2004 and 2007, a plethora of atheist apologetics books came out at a furious pace, and even an underground movie that did quite well on the alternative film circuit. The film's director even posted on my website, *The Catholic Report* (www.catholicreport.org), his objections to my views on the film and those hired to assist in its production. Noted atheists like Dawkins and Harris made their way across the talk-show circuit.

The Catholic Church, Agnostics, and Atheists 257

Modern atheists have always professed a belief that there is no rational order to the universe (as the Catholic Church teaches in *Humani Generis* and other documents), but that everything has been governed by random chance since the world's inception. For instance, atheists believe that it was just random chance that caused the Earth to appear as it is. Thus, they reject the hand of God, its Creator. Originally attributed to Thomas Huxley—and later to a host of others, including Stephen Hawking, considered by some to be the smartest man since Albert Einstein—the infinite monkey theorem was put forth. This theorem states that monkeys playing on a typewriter could eventually produce a sonnet worthy of William Shakespeare. The idea even made the cover of several magazines, as one could see many monkeys pounding or beating on a typewriter while one diligent chimp in the corner was busy producing a great literary work.

With the advent of the laptop came an idea by a researcher to try out the theory: One zoo equipped its monkey population with laptops. Most of the monkeys were too busy swinging around their small jungle-like area to bother with the laptops. Some did, however, used the laptop as a bathroom and/or threw the keyboards all around the simulated wildlife area. A few monkeys actually did sit down to type. Now we are getting somewhere, the atheists must have thought. However, when the research project was done, the monkeys had not even produced one word, let alone a sonnet. The computer was filled with gibberish, but not even one word. Yet these atheists want to tell us that the planet Earth has just the right amount of air, water, temperature conditions, space, and food by random chance. This despite there not being one planet whose existence we know of that has even one of the aforementioned conditions that we on Earth possess.

Speaking of Albert Einstein, many atheists who attack religion somehow think Einstein must be on their side, since of course he was considered to be the smartest, if not the most interesting man in the world (with apologies to Jonathan Goldsmith and Dos Equis beer.) However, Einstein was fascinated by the Eucharist and Transubstantiation. In addition, he met with the Belgian priest Fr. Georges Lemaitre, considered to be the true pioneer in the view that the universe is expanding. He authored the Big Bang Theory, which is often falsely attributed to Einstein or Edwin Hubble. Then again, many athiests also may not be aware that the title "the Father of Science" once was given to St. Albert the Great, the 13th century saint and future Doctor of the Church. St. Albert set the stage for scientific inquiry in the coming Renaissance.

In order to glean more information about modern atheism, it might behoove us to understand Madalyn Murray O'Hair. Most believers usually cringe when her name is mentioned, for it was O'Hair who took school prayer to the Supreme Court and got it removed from the public schools of the United States. Just a few years before the court's 1962 decision, O'Hair had unsuccessfully tried to immigrate to the Soviet Union. The powers that be in Moscow wouldn't let her into the official land of Lenin, even though she journeyed on a ship from Baltimore to Europe in the hopes of entering the "atheist's paradise." O'Hair has been sympathetically portrayed by many in the media. Chances are you never knew that she tried to become a Soviet citizen.

In 1980, O'Hair's son William became a Christian and eventually a Baptist preacher in Texas. The doting mother had this to say about her son's conversion: "I repudiate him entirely and for all time…. He is beyond human forgiveness."[3] Apparently she didn't show a lot of love for her fellow atheists who worked at the American Atheist headquarters, either. One employee threatened to quit over her profanity; O'Hair didn't stop there. She constantly practiced deception and stole from sympathetic organizations. (Hey, if you are an atheist and you can deceive the cops, why not? O'Hair must have thought. Who else is going to bring you to justice?) Eventually an unscrupulous employee took advantage of his knowledge about these activities and murdered O'Hair and others in the organization with the hopes of pocketing several hundred thousand dollars in gold coins he believed they were to pick up.

Christians, especially Catholics, revere the life of Mary. When

The Catholic Church, Agnostics, and Atheists 259

today's believers hear "Behold your mother" in relationship to Mary, they think about her integrity that guided not only the early Christians but themselves. However, mouthing "Behold your mother" to an atheist in relationship to O'Hair, who financially ran modern-day atheism and was the group's visible leader, would prompt anything but feelings of warmth and love.

O'Hair's legacy didn't seem to dampen the atheists' enthusiasm for disbelief. However, while Christianity's early days were marked with the "joy of the Lord," atheism seems to believe in the "joy of the rant." Instead of enticing believers to the land of disbelief with kind words and reason, the "unholy alliance" of Richard Dawkins, Sam Harris and Christopher Hitchens seems to think it can bully, belittle, and badger believers into a state of disbelief.

Most movements appeal to the better angels of the hopeful converts—as well as one can imagine. Since atheists don't believe in angels, there is no need to proselytize their views in a kind and gentle manner. It was indeed a strange way to win converts. One can go to a host of atheistic sites and find stories belittling the faithful and commenters extolling their own intellect for not believing in religion. Ridiculing potential followers goes against every marketing plan. Yet, they seem to enjoy every moment along with the sarcasm they directed at believers of any sort.

Perhaps the life of Jack Kerouac provides hope to all of those concerned for those who are lost, ambivalent, and downright angry at God. The Beat poets have been celebrated by many in the alternative culture for their rejection of religion, family, country, and heterosexuality. It is hard to fathom that someone of the likes of William Burroughs could murder his wife and get away with it, but so it is with those who admire the Beat poets.

The unofficial leader of the Beat poets was Kerouac. After a life spent wandering, writing, complaining, and engaging in everything imaginable, Kerouac was the 1960s version of the Prodigal Son. Later in life, near his death in 1969, Kerouac was asked about the Beat poets. "I am a Catholic, not a Beat poet," Kerouac announced.[3] Kerouac spent his final days engrossed in traditional Catholic literature, as well as defending the United States and her unpopular foreign and domestic policies. It was quite a turnaround for the unofficial leader of the "Alternative Pack." Yet, with all the literature available on Kerouac, few talk about his latter days and the alternative lifestyle that he came to disown.

Perhaps because of stories like Keroauc spending his latter days thinking about what might have been, many younger Catholics turned to orthodoxy and rejected their rebellious peers who were off extolling the praises of atheists like Dawkins and Hitchens. These younger Catholics spent their days embracing orthodoxy, sometimes against the wishes of their liberal parents, priests, teachers, and/or professors. When their curiosity or intellectual pursuits took them to the subject of history, the young would find a recent history replete with the carnage of atheism.

While there had been skeptics and perhaps even private atheists before the French Revolution, the movement went into full swing after the effects of the siege at the Bastille were fully understood. The storming of the Bastille is celebrated by many outside France as some sort of continuation of the American Revolution, which it was not. Soon after the nobility was targeted, and the Catholic clergy and the outspoken laity were sent to the guillotines. And that's not all: The cathedral at Notre Dame was renamed the Temple of Reason, and a naked prostitute was paraded around the altar to rub salt in the wounds of the faithful. Pagan festivals sprang up across the country to replace Church festivals, which were banned. (As Jonah Goldberg describes in his book, *Liberal Fascism*, the Nazis would do the same thing some 150 years later.) From there Napoleon would take control, and his hatred of all things faith-filled could be easily noticed in the fact that he stabled his horses in Catholic churches. Along with conquering much of Europe, he also tried to dislodge the Holy See and take it over.

Much of the French Revolution and the goals of Napoleon were taken up again some 150 years later. As mentioned above, Hitler cop-

The Catholic Church, Agnostics, and Atheists

ied much of the secular plans and goals from the French Revolution to rid Germany of religion. Hitler not only lamented that the Christian missionaries succeeded in Germany but that the Islamic conquests of the seventh and eighth century weren't successful in their efforts to take the European continent.[4] The Christian ideals of loving one's neighbor, redemption, and assisting those in need were foreign concepts to Hitler, ones he wished were never introduced to Germany.

The Communist ideologies that took over the Soviet Union, Eastern Europe, China, Cambodia, Vietnam, and North Korea are well documented. However, that doesn't mean that at one time they were lionized or even denied. How many millions of humans beings killed at the hands of these barbarians are still unknown? In the former Soviet Union, China, Cambodia, and North Korea, we know their numbers are in the tens of millions.

The socialist offshoots of these movements in Portugal, Cuba, Venezuela, and Mexico would be somewhat ignored by the unknown forces that guide pop culture. Few movies or books were written about what these faithful people suffered, which may be why some Western youths seem to enjoy wearing Che Guevara shirts. Why anyone would glowingly wear the face of a psychotic murderer on their shirt points to their ignorance—we hope. Mexico in particular would see harsh repression of the Church, which would last until the end of the 20th century. Limitations were put on priests and their movements, while beautiful churches were whitewashed—some of which, especially the New World's first Catholic churches located in the Yucatan Peninsula—remain that way today. However, it is from these lands where miracles (Our Lady of Fátima and Our Lady of Guadalupe) and movements would spring up and forever change the Church and the world.

Perhaps because of that Catholic culture, some atheists realize that a culture influenced by the Rock of Peter is better than some other faith or man's whims. Oriana Fallaci was one such person. An Italian woman of great contradictions, Fallaci was raised Catholic but became an atheist as an adult. Together with Bat Ye'or, she coined the term "Eurabia" along with "dhimmitude" with regard to both the changing culture of Europe and the silence to which many Christians in the Middle East are forced to adhere. However, unlike many atheists, she often defended the Catholic Church as the guardian of Western culture. She pilloried Islam as the destroyer of cultures and women's rights. She received death threats and even lobbed insults at Pope John Paul II for becoming too cozy with Islam. However, in her dying days she asked for a deathbed meeting of sorts with Pope Benedict XVI, which was granted, and she continued to speak highly of the Church.

At her deathbed per her request was Archbishop Rino Fisichella, who at the time was rector of Lateran University in Rome. As a dying request, Fallaci had asked that she be given a room with a view of one her favorite sites: the dome of the famed cathedral Santa Maria del Fiore in Florence. By her seen actions (nobody knows what she privately thought, though Archbishop Fisichella did call her last hours beautiful), we see a woman coming to grips with the truth as all the while the end steadily grew near; and so it will be for all of us. Let us hope and pray that those who lived in rebellion of God's mercy may come to faith in their dying hours. It would appear that Fallaci did.[5]

FIFTEEN
"NON LATINE LICEAT HIC" ("NO LATIN ALLOWED HERE")

One often hears the Latin language described as a dying language. It is a language now mainly used only by pharmacists and scientists, and even there it is just used to describe certain products, diseases, or theories. High schools and universities often recommend Latin for students pursuing degrees in English and law, for it helps them understand the formation of the English language. A perception exists for some that those preparatory schools that require students to learn it are superior to those where it is not required learning. After all, how is one to read Ovid in the original or speak the language of Erasmus without knowing this tongue?

With this educational and genteel background, it was more than a little puzzling that, in 2007 when Pope Benedict XVI issued *Summorum Pontificum*, his *motu proprio,* as many put it at the time, "liberated" the traditional Latin Mass. Its release meant that no longer could certain recalcitrant or ungenerous bishops thwart those groups of Catholics who wanted to attend Mass in Latin according to the 1962 Roman Missal of Bl. John XXIII.

Given the firestorm of criticism that accompanied its release, one would have thought Latin was an insidious virus much like the Y2K bug that many feared would end life as we know it on January 1, 2000.

Of course, Latin used to be the Mass' only language. However, after the Council—and in spite of the Conciliar Fathers' explicit call for maintaining Latin as the liturgy's primary language—the local vernacular became the language of choice for celebrating Mass.

Despite this, many Catholics maintained a special devotion to the Church's history and tradition as exemplified in TLM. In the first years following the Council, it also became a refuge from the crazy liturgical abuses that priests claimed were now OK because they were in line with the "Spirit of Vatican II." Many who attended the TLM spoke of the piety, reverence, and holiness that they witnessed, unlike some Masses at a typical parish where one witnesses all manner of dress and behavior.

Now, it is true that many attendees took to heart the reservations of the man who headed what would later become the CDF, Alfredo Cardinal Ottaviani (1890-1979), the Council's most forceful conservative. In what became a best-selling book titled *The Ottaviani Intervention*, His Eminence and Antonio Cardinal Bacci (1885-1971) wrote a cover letter to a report of those aligned with the anti-reform movement, warning Paul VI of serious problems with the revised Missal draft currently in circulation at the Vatican. Many of these same people drew on a widely circulated and false interpretation of a papal bull titled *Quo Primum* by Pope St. Pius V (1566-72), thereby simply rejecting the Council's liturgical reforms as even being possible.

For others, the revised Mass just seemed too different from what they judged the Mass hould be. Others thought it seemed too Protestant. A persistent rumor has been that, given his great desire to see all of Christianity reunited, Paul VI requested that the *novus ordo* be crafted to appeal to Protestants. For many, it seemed like kowtowing to heretics whose understanding of the Mass' purpose (since they don't accept the Mass as an unbloody representation of Christ's once-for-all sacrifice) would be suspect at best.

Most, however, didn't (and don't) concern themselves with all of this. They simply wanted a beautiful, reverent liturgy where priests preached solid Catholic doctrine from the pulpit, confessors dispensed orthodox spiritual direction to help them become holy, and catechesis for their children that would be unquestionably good.

However harmless the reasons the vast majority of those attending had for assisting at the extraordinary form, many, including some in the Church, left no stone unturned to give the impression something very sinister was being brought back. Certainly, Rome must be concocting something *very* nefarious.

Dissident Catholic groups such as We Are Church said the Pope's move made them afraid that he and his henchmen had decided to jettison Vatican II (i.e., their understanding of it) and bring back the bad old ways. Neutral observers were often left to conclude that most Catholics opposed the Holy Father's wishes. Thankfully, many observers, even those of other faiths, spread the word that if the Pope's action raised such vociferous opposition, it couldn't be all bad.

Just how vociferous was the coverage? Well, no sooner had Pope Benedict issued *Summorum Pontificum* than the media began posting headlines such as this one from the *Los Angeles Times*: "Pope Elevates Latin Mass, Leaving Some Polarized—Benedict Authorizes Wider Use, Pleasing Traditionalists. But Others See an Erosion of Vatican II Reforms."[1] You just gotta love objective journalism.

The United Kingdom's liberal newspaper *The Guardian*'s headline groaned, "Pope's Move on Latin Mass a Blow to Jews."[2] Given that use of the extraordinary form had never fully died out, and considering Bl. John Paul II's mostly ignored *motu proprio* asking from bishops a more generous allowance for the TLM, this was a curious headline, indeed, as the move had nothing to do with Jews or Judaism.

True, some Jews were apprehensive about the traditional Latin Mass due to some both accurate and inaccurate things they had heard. For instance, there was one Good Friday prayer that was improperly translated for our times—as scholars such as Bl. Ildefonso Schuster, OSB (1880-1954), had noted over the years—some in Judaism even feared that the TLM condemned them.

This was not true. It only prayed for their becoming Catholic, which St. Paul predicted would happen, and which is a sign of our Savior's second coming. And while it is correct that the invocation called for the "conversion of the perfidious Jews," at the time the prayer was written, "perfidious" did not mean "deceptive" or "treacherous." Instead, as Schuster proved, it connoted "lost" or "unconverted."

On the other hand, many Jews, especially observant ones, had no trouble with the extraordinary form. As an observant Jew in Israel wrote on my website, "Why would any Jew have a problem with a Christian prayer imploring their salvation? I would be upset if a Christian came and told me what I could pray for and what I could not."

Regardless, to allay any fears, Pope Benedict even changed that prayer. However, the damage was done: The reaction of a small subset of Judaism obscured the Holy Father's goal for *Summorum Pontificum* and thus what should have been focus of the story. For decades, the Pope had made clear in ways large and small that the post-conciliar reform of the Mass had been ham-handed (his polite way of putting it was that it was not an "organic development"). He also clearly recognized that it had been marked by abuses great and little, and that these had become entrenched in certain places as a normal part of the liturgy. Therefore, the reform itself needed reform.

To this end, he looked to the extraordinary form. This was not, as some charged, to "turn back the clock on Vatican II." Remember, the TLM is all he knew from the day of his birth until sometime after 1965 (different countries' episcopal conferences or even individual bishops took it upon themselves to introduce liturgical reform before 1970, so it is hard to say just when this order of the Mass disappeared from Benedict's experience). Furthermore, for over 10 years, it was the only Mass he ever celebrated as a priest.

Additionally, the Holy Father has expressed on numerous occasions his devotion to and love and admiration for the beautiful things the Tridentine rite gave him during his formative years. And he believes the good and beauty it has offer will have a reforming effect on the so-called *novus ordo* (i.e., the post-1969 missal). He trusts that once people see the beauty, majesty, mystery, and (dare we hope) silence it offers, that they will either recognize the lack thereof in their parish's liturgies or request more of what they already have of these qualities from their pastors.

To date, there have been numerous reports of priests who only reluctantly learned the pre-conciliar rite of the Mass because a "stable group" asked them to celebrate it for them. After a time, however, this Mass became their favorite way of celebrating the Eucharist. Even if this isn't all priests' experience, many have found their presiding at the TLM has greatly enriched their priesthood and their way of celebrating the *novus ordo*. If *lex orandi, lex credendi* is true, the liberation of the extraordinary form promises extraordinary things such as a more reverent sacrifice of the Mass, and that can only be good news for the Church. This will produce *great* fruits, trust me.

In the weeks leading up to the *motu proprio*'s release, efforts to get people to accept it came from an unusual corner. Even if some Catholics avoid the *National Catholic Reporter* at all costs, they do read the weekly articles by its best reporter, John Allen, because he is perceived as fair and that rarest of rare beasts, an objective journalist.

Before it was issued, Allen wrote extensively about the *motu proprio*. This leading *Vaticanista* even did some heavy lifting for the Vatican by working to alleviate one reason why so many reporters do such a bad job when it comes to covering news of a religious nature. The problem stems from many journalists' complete lack of knowledge about Christianity in general and Catholicism in particular. Allen helped his colleagues by using sociological and psychological terms so they could understand why some Catholics would welcome the TLM.[3]

In a culture that has left religion at the curb, many Catholics, old and young, long for piety and a deeper, more profound sense of faith than is often available in a typical parish (of course, many parishes and their priests do a fantastic job). However, many in our age—not to mention many in the Church—openly mock piety and the devotions meant to help make people more pious. However, this ignores what our first pontiff, St. Peter, wrote:

> ... the greatest and priceless promises have been lavished on us, that through them you should share the divine nature and escape corruption rife in the world through disordered passion. With this in view, do your utmost to support your faith with goodness, goodness with understanding, understanding with self-control, self-control with perseverance, perseverance with *devotion,* devotion with kindness to the brothers, and kindness to the brothers with love (2 Peter 1:2-7; emphasis added).

What Peter says here is that if social justice ("kindness to the brothers") is a non-negotiable, then the best way to accomplish this is through pious devotion. Wouldn't that conceivably include "pious devotions" such as the Rosary? Today, many old and young (especially the young) answer "Yes," and the fruits this "Yes" is bearing—increased vocations, more people actually involved in charitable work, etc.—are beautiful to behold.

When they experience what he means by the term firsthand, many young Catholics rally around Pope Benedict XVI and his warning to reject the "dictatorship of relativism" that so clouds our age. Why, therefore, is it a surprise that they would cherish the TLM, which is possibly the most "unrelativistic" thing in the world? The great thing about the extraordinary form is that unless the priest is a real master at speaking Latin, he can't make things up as he goes along during Mass. Also, remember, this is a generation of Catholics that had to endure "Clown Masses" and other "hip" spectacles that left them less than impressed. After all, nothing turns off a young person more than an older person trying to be hip and fit in. Why do you think several of Frank Sinatra's singles of the late 1960s sold so poorly?

So, while these Catholics may be young, they have seen the wisdom of the saying, "There's no school like old school." The extraordinary form is age-old and tested. Therefore, when the TLM comes to their parish or a parish near them, they will give it a try and after a while (it takes five to seven times to get the hang of following a missal), they'll even attend regularly because they want something that strikes them as authentically Catholic.

Older Catholics have often experienced the pain of losing their children to another faith or to secularism's grasp. They look to the TLM of their youth as a bedrock foundation that provided awe, mystery, and comfort during some of the twentieth century's darkest times. Now that is once again available to them, neither they nor the young (and large!) families in the pews want to impose it on everyone (well, one or two here and there probably do, but that's a different topic). Rather, they simply want their wishes and that of the Holy Father's respected. It is so sad to hear, for instance, of someone whose last desire was to have their funeral Mass celebrated according to the preconciliar form only to have the pastor or funeral coordinator tell the bereaved survivors, "Sorry."

In one instance at a parish in northern Indiana, the refusal was almost comical. The coordinator told the woman's daughter, "We will do everything to make this celebration of your mother's life just as you want it."

"Great," the daughter replied, and she relayed her mother's wish for a TLM funeral.

"Oh," the woman replied, "we don't do anything but the Vatican II Mass here."

"Can we at least do something—the Gloria, the Sanctus, the Agnus Dei—in Latin?"

"No, I'm sorry. I'm afraid not."

"Well, my mom wanted Gregorian chant and these three traditional hymns sung."

"Oh, that is unfortunate," said the woman; "we only do the most modern and up-to-date liturgical music because we feel it is more relevant, and we don't want anyone feeling alienated when they walk through our doors."

"OK, well, then, uh... well, last but not least, my mother wanted to pray the Divine Mercy chaplet after the Rosary that we'll say during the wake."

"Oh, we don't believe in the use of private devotions such as the Rosary or the...what did you call it? The Divine Mercy...caplet? I'll check with Father and see if he'll allow one decade of the Rosary, but this thing you mentioned, it's definitely out."

So much for doing "everything to make this celebration of" this woman's life "just as [she would have] want[ed] it." And stories such as this exist by the hundreds. These devotions and rites made saints. They are testified to by what G.K. Chesterton called "the democracy of the dead." If they were good enough for our forbearers in faith, why not us? We hear so much about young priests not being "pastoral." How does treating people like this qualify as pastoral?

Our culture thrives on tradition, whether it is national celebrations like Memorial Day or the Fourth of July, or traditions in the fields of sports and the theater. I bet you if you thought about things that happen in your town, in your parish, throughout your life, you can see the truth in this. Who really needs to hear "Walking in a Winter Wonderland" or "Adestes Fideles" ever again at Christmas? I mean, haven't we heard them enough? No! Why? Because they're part of the tradition. Along with the prayers and rituals of Advent, the anticipation of Our Lord's birth and second coming, the sleigh bells, trees, mistletoe, eggnog, and all the rest, they're what help make Christmas *Christmas* for so many of us. But while those traditions get great (and due) respect, those of the Church are liable to be jettisoned at the first opportunity. This is pretty cynical, I know. It's cynicism, however, born out of frustration and bewilderment.

A steady stream of pronouncements followed the release of Pope Benedict's *motu proprio*. Even before it was released, the editor of

England's *Catholic Herald*, Damian Thompson, noted in *The Telegraph*, "My goodness, the jangling nerves in liberal circles over the return of the Traditional Latin Mass!"

Thompson then referred readers to Jeff Miller's *The Curt Jester* blog for some timely information. The witty Miller had written a cut-and-paste talking points column for those journalists who could admit to not being friendly to Catholicism but who couldn't come right out and say so, and who were therefore unsure what to say about the TLM. It covered all the bases about a Church in despair reaching for the past. Miller even gave advice for reporters on who and who not to interview. Certainly, keep away from young adults or the very old, but by all means quote anyone of a certain age, since many could be reliably be counted upon to them what they wanted to hear. While it was humorous, it had a sad and slightly sobering ring of truth to it.[4]

However, as if on cue, the very next day, *The Telegraph's* UK competitor, *The Independent*, ran a headline that read, "Church Split Feared as Pope Backs Return of 'Anti-Semitic' Latin Mass."

Had *The Independent* took Thompson's and Miller's jest to heart? Stories in other outlets spoke of angry Catholics who rejected the call to be dragged back to pre-Vatican II times when women, along with rest of the laity, were treated as chattel. National Public Radio referenced an AP story stating that not only would the TLM divide parishes and dioceses, but it could also split the Church. Its source for the contention was the dissenting group, We Are Church.

Of course, one expected such know-nothing hysteria about the TLM from the media or from those with an obvious agenda. Simply in the name of academic and intellectual honesty, though, one would have hoped for better from scholars. One would have hoped in vain. In *The Washington Post's* On Faith panelists' blog, Rev. Susan Brooks Thistlethwaite, president of the Chicago Theological Seminary, wrote that the Catholic Church was certainly out of touch with the laity; it was moving in a "reactionary direction."

She stated that the Catholic Church needed to spend all of its time dealing with the sex-abuse scandal and not worrying about Latin. According to Thistlethwaite, "The [TLM] was developed during the most reactionary time of the Catholic Church, the 'Counter-Reformation' ... The [extraordinary form] was a product of a reactionary time in the Catholic Church where it rejected many very necessary reforms and consolidated its power in the hierarchy. Today the reintroduction of the [pre-conciliar rite] signals to me that far from becoming open to the kinds of changes needed to protect children from abuse, the Catholic Church is once again circling the wagons, rejecting necessary reforms and consolidating power in the hierarchy."[5]

It is in moments such as these that one struggles with where to begin regarding comments such as this coming from the president of a theological seminary. First of all, the Mass was originally in Greek. It changed to Latin because, for most Christians, that was the vernacular. When Christianity spread beyond the limits of Rome's reach, Latin had a unifying effect (it still does if you attend a TLM in, say, Goa, India). All of this was in place even before Constantine permanently legalized it. We really should call it "the Mass of Pope St. Gregory the Great" (590-604), because in all its essentials, in its most basic form, this is the same Mass he celebrated. Some things were added such as the ringing of bells at certain points. However, if you transported someone from the seventh century to the 17th century and brought them to Mass, they would feel perfectly at home.

It most certainly was not an answer to the Protestant Revolution, which occurred nearly 1,000 years later. At least it wasn't in the sense that the Counter-Reformation created this liturgy out of whole cloth. Indeed, all the Council of Trent (1545-63) did was to codify the Mass. At issue was the fact that the Mass could be very different depending where it was celebrated. This led to liturgical abuses, which in turn led to muddied doctrine, which in turn led to fertile ground for the Protestant movement. Furthermore, the sex-abuse scandal has zero to do with language in which the Mass is celebrated.

Even if it did, one does not ignore the hole in the window or the fire on the stove just because there is a hole in the roof or a door with a missing lock.

It is slow going, and there is still an awful lot of resistance to *Summorum Pontificum*. However, the tide is turning toward the Latin Mass being respected and given an appropriate and (dare we say) pastoral place in most dioceses.

Also, let's not forget what a great example Pope Benedict XVI gave us through all of this. He had long ago learned that one needs to ignore criticisms and insults because there is nothing one can do to really stop them. Rather, one continues with the work one is called to do. The Bible mentions King Solomon being amazed at the industriousness of ants (see Proverbs 6). Someone or something plows into their hill, and they immediately begin to repair the damage. So it is with our Papa Benny. He had no illusions about how people would criticize, so he just went on doing what he does best: writing, explaining, and calmly exhorting the faithful.

Interestingly, the cause for the TLM was greatly enhanced by an event that had nothing to do with the Roman rite's extraordinary form: Pope Benedict's visit to the United States. Though he never mentioned the TLM during his visit, the Holy Father went about his papal duties, and by the love he showed, made believers of many who couldn't help but admire the beauty and pageantry of his visit and, most importantly, his love for all he sees. Is it a coincidence that beauty and pageantry are what one gets in spades at a solemn or pontifical High Mass?

Pope Benedict has made some other pretty gutsy liturgical moves. As noted in a footnote above, when the 1975 indult for Communion under both species (i.e., the Body and the Blood) expired in 2005, he did not allow for its extension. In 2007, he revoked the indult for non-clergy to purify the sacred vessels used in the consecration and distribution of Communion. Then in the spring of 2008, Pope Benedict XVI, without fanfare, said that any faithful who approached him for Communion could only receive on the tongue and while kneeling.[6] While some questioned or angrily complained about the move, many understood and appreciated the Holy Father's reason for doing. He wanted to restore a sense reverence and a deep desire for Our Lord's Blood, a sense of piety and holiness at Mass that comes from knowing that, at Communion, you do not receive mere bread and wine or simply a symbol of Christ, but the actual Body, Blood, Soul, and Divinity of Jesus. Like many actions of the Pontiff from Bavaria, the example of this man who lives the piety he teaches has brought him no little respect and has even won over some doubters.

The English-speaking world saw a new translation of the Mass come their way on the first Sunday of Advent 2011. The version of the missal in force since Advent 1969 had used a translation method called "dynamic equivalency," where some words and phrases were translated quite accurately, whereas others were approximated and even grossly paraphrased. Beginning in the late 1990s, a push came from such ecclesiasts as George Cardinal Pell of Sydney and Francis Cardinal George of Chicago to give a more accurate, theologically precise translation to the vernacular words we use at Mass. Change is never easy for anyone, and the "Spirit of Vatican II" crowd complained that this was yet another turning back the clock on the Council's reforms. Leading the charge against the new translation were, naturally, the *National Catholic Reporter* and those who agree with its editorial line, but also a prominent bishop from the Northeast, who vehemently protested the changes.

Their protests proved fruitless, however, and once the changes were implemented, the reports coming back indicated that all the fuss was much ado about nothing. The transition went off without a hitch (although it was mentioned as one point in a list of reasons/grievances why the leftist computer "hacktivist" group known as "Anonymous" broke into the Vatican website in early March 2012).

In the brouhaha leading up to the new translation's implementation, Fr. John Zuhlsdorf made an interesting observation (Father blogs as Fr. Z at What Does the Prayer Really Say, which itself was born out of the same bad translations of liturgical prayers that prompted the new Missal).[7] He outlined the militant secularists' agenda and then observed that it is practically indistinguishable from anything written by Satanists such as Alistair Crowley or Anton LaVey. As a result, one might reasonably conclude that militant humanism and "magick," the occult, Satanism, New Age, etc., are closely aligned.

The connection seems even stronger when one investigates how at the core of each seemingly unrelated side's agenda is the Mass, the unbloody representation of Christ's salvific sacrifice on the Cross, a rite that goes back to apostolic times. If you upset dark malevolent forces, concluded Fr. Z, then chances are you are on the right path.

Not Going Back to the Future but into a Brighter Tomorrow

The overwhelming majority of those who attend Mass probably attend it at their local parish and hear it celebrated in the vernacular. However, for those who like the 2,000-year-old tradition(s) of Catholicism and the Catholic Mass, it speaks well of the Church that she has given her offspring the opportunity to hear Mass in the language it was said for centuries.

Sure, some belittle and mock this. However, like the Pope, the faithful Catholic simply ignores the naysayers and does her or his best to become a saint by providing the best witness possible, taking an active role in their parish, and raising good, faithful, virtuous children in a world where that is increasingly difficult.

Obviously, the devoted people who attend the TLM do not represent a huge portion of the Catholic Church in the English-speaking world (or any place on the planet for that matter). But their often heroic striving to become the best Catholics they can be and their contagious love of the Faith is providing a powerful, attractive, and fresh witness.

In turn, this greatly helps promote the tide-turning movement that is furthering the growth of God's kingdom on earth.

SIXTEEN
THE CHURCH DRAWS FAMOUS ATHLETES AND COACHES

Do you ever wonder why athletes, even the famous and pampered, rarely attack religion—especially Catholicism? After all, the well-heeled in other fields, especially the militant secularists in Hollywood and their allies in the liberal churches, hardly seem immune to trashing Catholicism. Perhaps by the very nature of competitive athletics, we can understand and appreciate the reasons athletes admire Catholicism far more than those in other entertainment fields.

In competitive athletics, the cream rises to the top. There is simply no room for special treatment, favoritism, quotas, etc. Perhaps that is why the world is so sports crazy. It is one of the few areas left where merit is still rewarded. The testimony of athletes about their Catholic faith seems particularly gripping to many of the faithful, not just because they are famous—there are far more famous and educated people who could better testify about their faith. However, athletes and coaches are often better able to explain the faith in words that seem genuine and full of real-life experiences than can other well-intentioned folks. The perseverance of the faith and athletics go hand in hand. St. Paul said he had run the race, using the imagery of the marathon that was quite recognizable in the Apostolic Age.

It was very heartening to me that athletes and coaches embraced my first book with interviews and endorsements. Obviously, figures like ESPN commentator Dick Vitale and former Notre Dame football coaches Lou Holtz and Gerry Faust had never heard of me. However, they enthusiastically supported the book to the point of using their own time to help get the word out about *The Tide Is Turning Toward Catholicism*.[1]

In the Catholic world today, many athletes give of their time to help spread the "good news." Baseball players Mike Sweeney and Jeff Suppan constantly relate their faith to others through many forms, including EWTN and video. Sweeney, a five-time all-star for the Kansas City Royals, has been seen on EWTN's *Life on the Rock*, telling viewers of his family's dedication to Christ and his Church.

Sweeney spoke of the tremendous blessing he had when he and his wife, along with their young child, visited Vatican City. For Sweeney, seeing the catacombs of the early Christians gave him great hope and cause for rejoicing, as they suffered to keep the Faith alive so that future generations could understand Christ's message.

In addition, meeting Pope Benedict XVI gave Sweeney the visual of seeing St. Peter in action through the leadership of his successor. The words of Matthew 16:16-20 came alive for Sweeney. He had met the man who had the power to loose and bind and who served as the successor of St. Peter.

There are many other baseball players who live the Faith with whom Sweeney is able to share and grow in his faith during the long baseball season, when one is often away from one's family. Jeff Suppan is one such person. The former St. Louis Cardinal pitcher not only tells others of his faith but even got involved with a controversial pro-life television commercial for a 2006 Missouri ballot issue. He took some flak for his pro-life views but wore them as a badge of honor.

In 2007, a landmark video was made called *Champions of Faith*. The video featured the aforementioned Sweeney and Suppan, along with a host of other baseball players and managers talking about their Catholic faith. Stars such as Ivan Rodriguez and Mike Piazza told of their faith journey, the ups and downs of life under the microscope, and their daily faith walk.[2]

During the 20th century and especially through the 1940s, the mystique of Notre Dame football held sway over many Catholic sports fans, especially those who saw the rise of this institution as a beacon of hope for many in the immigrant Catholic ghetto. No one symbolized this rags-to-riches story better than the legendary coach of the Irish football team, Knute Rockne. He coached the Irish from 1919 through the 1930 season. He died in a plane crash shortly after that season. An immigrant from Norway, he worked after high school to scrape up enough money to fulfill his dream of being a scientist. He excelled in academics and athletics while a student at Notre Dame. However, he was a Lutheran, and it would be the faith life of his players that would propel him to become Catholic.

During his early years at Notre Dame, Rockne always kept a close eye on his players, not wanting them to stray too far off the reservation of good behavior—a lesson undoubtedly learned from George Gipp, the legendary player who would become known as "The Gipper" and whose dying speech ("win one for the Gipper") to Rockne would live forever in football and political lore. One morning, Rockne noticed several players slipping out of their dorms before sunrise. He subsequently followed them and noticed they went to Mass. Afterward Rockne quizzed these players. They told him that because of class and practice, they couldn't get to any other Mass except at 6:00 a.m. "It's that important to you?" quizzed Rockne. Yes, it is, the players responded, the Eucharist is that important. Rockne immediately began to read more about the Eucharist and why few in his church deemed it that important. Shortly thereafter, Rockne asked to be received into the Church—a lesson learned from those who weren't ashamed or too tired to practice their faith.[3]

In my previous book, I wrote of the faithful life of Gerry Faust, yet I only scratched the surface. Before he arrived at Notre Dame, he had prayed to Mary at the famed Notre Dame grotto while still coaching Archbishop Moeller High School in Cincinnati. The opportunity to coach a major college power straight from high school seemed ludicrous, and coaching Notre Dame seemed preposterous. Yet, shortly thereafter Faust was given this amazing opportunity.

Faust honored a commitment he made to the Blessed Mother that he would visit the grotto every day that he was in South Bend. Still today, long after he left South Bend, he visits and prays at the grotto every time he returns. Faust modeled faith to his players by always praying and preaching the Gospel 24 hours a day as St. Francis commanded, using words only when absolutely necessary.[4]

Faust's career at Notre Dame didn't end as a Cinderella story. He left five years after he came. The luster was off and another faithful coach, Lou Holtz, would take over and eventually win that coveted national championship. Yet, Faust is still greatly admired by Notre Dame fans. Then head coach Charlie Weis invited Faust back to address the team at the conclusion of the 2006 season. It seemed the man who modeled faith to his players also modeled faith to the entire university, including the vaunted Subway Alumni. Some wondered aloud why God would allow such a faithful man to lose, since he could have been such a great spokesman for the faith. However, the Almighty's wisdom was seen in the reverence for a man who never won the national title but whose example won many souls.

Often lost in the profiles of athletes are the religious narratives that make up their lives. While many may be aware that the athlete is a faithful person, often little else is revealed that would allow observers to realize how important their faith life is to them. However, we are all too often told of everything else about an athlete's personal life. A case in point is Tara Lipinski, an American figure skater and gold medal winner of the summer 1998 Olympics. For years Lipinski had a special devotion to "The Little Flower of Jesus," St. Thérèse.

The devotion came about during trying times for the Lipinskis. Four years before the Olympics, when Lipinski was just 11 years old, her mother, Pat, lost her faith after a series of family tragedies. The crisis of faith almost caused her mother to pull young Tara out of competitivie figure skating entirely. One dark night in Budapest, Hungary, young Tara looked out her hotel balcony to see a beautiful church with an image of St. Thérèse holding roses. Lipinski found out more about the saint, and her devotion began, complete with a medal given to her by a parish priest. Lipinski would wear the medal when she won the gold medal in 1998. Though athletes face constant media attention and scrutiny, it would not be until after the Olympics that the story of her devotion to St. Thérèse would become public.[5]

Tim Tebow became a hero to many people of faith during his college years of playing football at the University of Florida. Love for Tebow did not diminish once he joined the National Football League's Denver Broncos (and later the New York Jets), partly because it seemed a subtle campaign against Tebow was being launched by those in the secular media for his outspoken support of his Evangelical faith. In addition, his pledge of chastity has also drawn snickers from those in the chattering class.

However, a few years before Tebow burst on the scene, there existed a Catholic version who espoused the same social beliefs as Tebow. Philip Rivers grew up in northern Alabama, where Catholics were few and far between. He grew up having to know and defend his Catholic faith. After a successful career at North Carolina State, Rivers became a star for the San Diego Chargers. He appeared on EWTN and other television programs, speaking about his Catholic faith as well as his and his wife's personal experience with chastity.

In 2011, Rivers got off to an average start, far from his usual stellar performances. Oddly, some began to question whether his large family (by modern standards) of six children was too much to handle. It seemed an odd question, considering Rivers is hardly the first athlete to have six kids. Yet, in our modern society this hardly seems to fit the bill. Rivers has never been conventional; the fiery and temperamental performer on the field doesn't seem to fit the mold of a family man who speaks about chastity, his Catholic faith, and his devotion to the practice of Eucharistic adoration. Rivers has also set up an organization called Rivers of Hope, which helps children in foster care find homes through adoption.

In 2008, legendary college basketball announcer Dick Vitale was admitted to the College Basketball Hall of Fame. Vitale's enthusiasm, optimism, and energy are legendary. However, few remember his college

The Church Draws Famous Athletes and Coaches

and even NBA coaching days. These positive traits didn't come from the thin air; they came from years of being taught by his parents, teachers, priests, nuns, and coaches. Many credit ESPN's college basketball coverage of the 1980s as the catalyst for making college basketball the stunning success it is today. It would be inconceivable to imagine that success without Vitale. Though a celebrity, Vitale was more than generous with the time he gave me to ask some questions for my first book. Vitale even gave the book an endorsement, which I greatly appreciated.

Vitale told me the story of the faith life of his parents, which in turn greatly affected him. Though his mother had a stroke and paralysis on the right side of her body, she literally dragged her limping right leg to Mass every day to St. Leo's Church in Elmwood Park, New Jersey. Powerful visuals like this stuck with Vitale, who said he never misses Mass, though basketball season's travel schedule is brutal and many would find some excuse if they traveled as much as Vitale did. During his travels, Vitale is never without his rosary tucked in his right pocket, always at the ready for a quick prayer. Though he wouldn't admit to it, Vitale has been a great help to many successful charities, principally the The V Foundation for Cancer Research, named after former North Carolina State basketball Coach Jim "Jimmy V" Valvano. The fund has raised millions for cancer research, and few doubt it could have been the success it has been without the tireless fundraising of Vitale.

Vitale's optimistic and caring personality has rubbed off on others. While many would run from an encounter with the sometimes volatile former basketball coach of Indiana University and most recently Texas Tech University, Bobby Knight organized a campaign to support the efforts of those who wanted Vitale to be elected to the College Basketball Hall of Fame. Knight personally called every Division I basketball coach, totaling over 300, to make sure that Vitale received his just due. The living, faithful example of Vitale has propelled others to at least attempt to do the good they see Vitale doing—a great testimony for his Catholic faith.

SEVENTEEN
THE DISINTEGRATION OF LIBERAL CHRISTIANITY

Ever since the utopians felt they could intermingle God with radical social change, God became less and less important—so much so that for many of the modern-day liberal descendants, he simply doesn't exist. Yet, while two brave souls of the Unitarian Church rally the faithful to believe that God actually *does* exist (it was reported that as many as 50 percent of the liberal Unitarian Church were atheists),[1] most Catholics go about their business attending Church and even believing what goes on, much to the chagrin of some of the media's gatekeepers.

In the spring of 2006, the Episcopal Church in the United States (whose numbers are only a fraction of the Catholic Church's) and Protestantism in general would be given a great deal of favorable media publicity when a woman was named presiding bishop of the church. Dr. Katharine Jefferts Schori would become the first presiding woman bishop of any major church, and her comments about Catholicism, the state of religion, and the order of society would become a lightning rod. However, that favorable publicity helped put the spotlight on the Episcopal Church and the myriad imploding events that occurred shortly thereafter.

For some in the media, the joy of the election of the liberal Bishop Jefferts Schori was almost too hard to contain. ABC News reporter Dan Harris excitedly stated that she had made it past the "glass ceiling," as if God needed to be told who and what could lead churches. Harris went on to suggest that other women in the Catholic Church also want to be ordained, but they are excommunicated.² ABC also featured a story about a group of women in Pennsylvania who claimed to be priests. It seemed like a takeoff on the comedy film, *This Is Spinal Tap*, or a host of Monty Python films, yet a reputable news organization was somehow agreeing that a group of women who claimed to be priests were such because they said so.

Tim Graham of the Media Research Center illustrated a helpful analogy on MRC's website, NewsBusters: "If I decided to buy a microphone and a TV camera, and put ABC logos on them, am I an ABC reporter? Or does ABC think I don't need to be officially recognized as an ABC reporter before I go around town claiming to represent ABC?" It was all too much for Bill Donohue of the Catholic League, who stated: "Some at ABC News are obviously hyperventilating over the election of the first female bishop in the Episcopal Church, and that no doubt led them to package the story with a bogus account about women bring ordained as Catholic priests."³

In the fall of 2006, Bishop Jefferts Schori was interviewed by *The New York Times*. Her views on life, Catholicism, and society angered many Catholics, even though the mainstream media barely made mention of it. She suggested that the reason Catholicism was growing may have to do with the fact that Catholicism seems to value people more than the planet. "Episcopalians tend to be better educated and tend to reproduce at lower rates than some other denominations. Roman Catholics and Mormons both have theological reasons for producing lots of children," she said.⁴

Later in the same interview, Bishop Jefferts Schori was asked about Pope Benedict XVI's recent remarks about Islam during his talk at Regensburg, Germany. She was asked whether Muslims have a history of violence. She responded, "So do Christians. They have a terrible history.... I think Muslims are poorly understood by the West, and it is easy to latch onto that which we do not understand and demonize it." The Catholic blogosphere sprung into action, reporting on the comments and deluged by angry posts in their comment boxes. Had a Catholic bishop made a conservative comment such as this, one can only imagine the press coverage it would have received. Yet despite the plummeting numbers in the Episcopal Church, the media seemed to give Bishop Jefferts Schori a pass. Not only were Catholics upset, but so were many conservative Anglicans, who comprise the majority of the Anglican blogosphere's readership. One commenter on the popular conservative Anglican site, Virtue Online, noted that it was telling that Bishop Jefferts Schori referred to Christians in the third person.

Yet, she and the Episcopal Church would be beneficiaries of the "hear no evil, see no evil" approach of the mainstream media. Many in the mainstream media seem to enjoy the writings of the ultra-heterodox (many would say heretical) Bishop John Shelby Spong. He is most famous for what he doesn't believe. For example, the retired bishop of Newark, New Jersey, states that he doesn't believe Christ was born of a virgin, worked miracles, or rose from the dead. Perhaps it would be easier to tell us what he does believe.

However, that doesn't stop Spong from writing more books and giving more speeches, telling all who would listen that Christianity must change. What it would become, according to Spong, would only be a shell of itself. It seems that Spong was more passionate about defending gay marriage than defending the historical tenets of Christianity. Even though the Episcopal Church (and all liberal churches) are in a statistical free fall, it hasn't stopped the mainstream media from gushing over his ideas. One might expect that of *The New York Times*—but AARP? In its inaugural magazine, which came out in 2003, the AARP (formerly the American Association of Retired Persons) listed Spong as one of the 50 most innovative leaders.

For all his talk of diversity, Spong doesn't seem too interested in the views of the only part of the Anglican Church that is growing, the African church. In 1998, at the annual Lambeth Conference, when asked why the African church leaders were so much more conservative than Anglican leaders in the United Kingdom or United States, he stated that the African bishops were "only one generation removed from animism, and their brand of Christianity was superstitious."[5] One can only imagine the uproar that would have ensued had a conservative or orthodox-minded Catholic prelate made such a remark. Fr. Richard John Neuhaus noted that 98 percent of the African bishops had earned PhDs, compared with 50 percent of American Anglican bishops.

In April 2007, the recently retired Episcopal Bishop Daniel Herzog of Albany, New York, announced that he had been received into the Catholic Church merely a month after he had retired as an Episcopal bishop. He stated for the record that he had been opposed to much of the recent decisions taken by the Episcopal Church, which he deemed unscriptural and heretical. While there was gnashing of teeth at the largest website of orthodox Episcopalians, TitusOneNine, there was little if any mention of either the conversion or its aftermath elsewhere. Rather, he was just the latest high-profile convert to come into the Church to barely register a blip on the mainstream media's radar.

In June 2007, *The New York Times* ran a "civil union announcement" for two Episcopal priests. There was little or no coverage of this by any of the news channels. There also was no mention of God—or faith, for that matter—in the announcement made by the priests. The utter apostasy of this statement was not lost on many in the Catholic or Evangelical world. However, it seemed to be lost on the gatekeepers of information in society, the media.

What was all of this enlightened thinking costing the greater Anglican Communion (made up of Anglican Churches worldwide, which includes the American Episcopal Church)? The simple answer is plenty. Survey after survey, often done by the Anglican Church itself, showed a frightening decline in church membership in the Western world, home to all this progressivism. In the United Kingdom, half of all Anglicans stopped going to church all together from 1979 to 2005—a sobering statistic when one realizes that by 1979, the Anglican Church was experiencing a serious decline in the previous 26 years that preceded it.

The story wasn't much better in the United States or Canada. From 1961 to 2001, the Anglican Church of Canada experienced a 53 percent decline. So steep was the decline that *Christian Today* noted that if the trend continued, there would be "only be one person in the Canadian Anglican Church by 2061."[7] In the same article, Canadian Ted Byfield noted that liberalization of the Church is the main reason why the precipitous drop had occurred. Keith McKerracher told *Christian Today* that the Anglican Church of Canada is "in real crisis" but noted that the Church "talks things to death." Canadian Archbishop Andrew Hutchison said that he felt social justice and ecumenical cooperation would someday halt the slide. Statements like this were commonplace within liberal Christianity, where plummeting church attendance was greeted with the hope that someday the populace would be enlightened to see it their way instead of the 2,000-year-old way of Christianity that had existed before their arrival.

The story wasn't much better in the United States. Orthodox-minded Episcopalians were gnashing their teeth and expressing their exasperation on blogs and websites like TitusOneNine and VirtueOnline. It was all too much for these readers to see their religion crumble and yet to see such positive news coverage of their presiding leader, Bishop Jefferts Schori, and the openly homosexual leader of the New Hampshire Episcopal Diocese, Gene Robinson.

Bishop Robinson was at the heart of the struggle. It was because of his ordination that so many in the greater Anglican Communion wanted to break away or at least discipline the US church. His statements added more fuel to the fire, and yet little was made of it by the mainstream media. Upon hearing that Cardinal Ratzinger had become Benedict XVI, he seemed elated. "Pope Ratzinger may be the best thing to happen to the Episcopal Church." The controversial Episcopal bishop even called the Catholic Church's teachings on homosexuality "vile," although every Christian church and every other religion held the same views until the last few years. Bishop Robinson reasoned that because of the Catholic Church's stance against the gay lifestyle, the Episcopal Church would see growth. I interviewed him in June 2006, during which he made provocative statements on abortion and homosexuality in the New Testament. Against the bishop's

The Disintegration of Liberal Christianity 287

hope, it was the Catholic Church that grew because of the crisis; many Episcopalians left and joined the Catholic Church, so much so that a special Anglican ordinariate had to be set up by Pope Benedict XVI. So many orthodox-minded Anglican clergy and laity alike were heading for the Tiber that His Holiness had to set up a special process for those Anglican clergy who wanted to leave and continue their ministry in the Catholic Church.

The Episcopal bishop from New Hampshire also seemed to have his own take on various Scripture passages involving homosexuality. "The Bible was misinterpreted in order to reject gay people from the Church.... The Sin of Sodom had nothing to do with homosexual sex, but was rather a failure to care [of] the poor, the widows, and the orphans," he said.

After our interview concluded, there was a puzzling occurrence. Bishop Robinson promised to reveal to me a secret that would cause great scandal in the Catholic Church. He again slyly alluded to it in the second interview he granted me while I was covering the Episcopal General Convention in Columbus, Ohio, in June 2006. He told me that if I gave him my word not to say anything about it for two years, he would tell me about a Catholic bishop who allowed him to give a retreat to gay Catholic priests in this bishop's diocese. Bishop Robinson told me to call him in two years, and he would tell me everything because by then the heat would be off this bishop. Two years later I called the bishop's office, but my phone call was not returned. The same thing happened the next year. Who knows why?

Perhaps the most shocking statement made by Bishop Robinson concerned his "gay civil marriage," which took place in June 2008. He stated he had always wanted to be a "June bride."[8] The Anglican Church believes in apostolic tradition, and the thought that someone who considers himself (albeit falsely) a successor to the apostles would call himself a "June bride" is very sad.

It was incidents such as these that were responsible for 1,000 Episcopalian a week leaving for dioceses and parishes associated with the more conservative African Anglican jurisdiction. For all the talk of the Episcopal Church becoming the liberal alternative, it did not happen. Bishop Robinson expressed the hope that droves of homosexuals would come into the Episcopal Communion. Rather, its numbers continued to decline.

Sensing their prominence waning, liberal Catholics unleashed a torrent of anger at faithful Catholics. In his book *Makers and Shakers*, Peter Schweizer points out that Garry Wills, who is often dubbed a "devout Catholic" by admirers in the mainstream media, said this about the faithful following the re-election of President George W. Bush in 2004: "Can a people that believe more fervently in the Virgin Birth than in evolution still be called an enlightened nation?" Strange words from a man hailed as a "devout Catholic."[9]

Apparently the words from the "devout" Wills must have sent a signal to others, for Nicholas Kristof of *The New York Times* said the following on the subject of the Virgin Birth: "The faith in the Virgin Birth is becoming less intellectual and more mystical over time."[10]

It seemed with the aftermath of Hurricane Katrina, the continuing US presence in Iraq, and the rising cost of energy, liberals felt they could tie traditional religion with the sagging fortunes of the Bush administration. Liberalism sensed an opening the likes of which they had not had in years. Liberal Christianity pursued this perceived opening with reckless abandon. One book that caught the attention of many in late 2007 was *American Fascists* by Chris Hedges, a former correspondent for *The New York Times* and a Harvard Divinity School graduate.[11]

Hedges' book reads like a parody. Indeed, had an orthodox religious writer wrote what Hedges did about the Left, he would be accused of being rude and insensitive. Hedges asserts that those religious conservatives who live in Rust Belt states such as Ohio are sad characters indeed, not smart enough to move to more urbane locations. Nor are they up to the task of realizing their religious beliefs are being manipulated for political purposes. The author notes his fear that some "right-wing" Catholics have joined the American

The Disintegration of Liberal Christianity

fascists (i.e., Evangelicals). This, he claims, could result in a further setback for the American democratic process.

Politically, Hedges' book seems to assert, with little documentation, that the American democratic system is taking the same path that led to Germany and Italy falling under the spell of fascism during the 1930s. Hedges' book came out shortly before Jonah Goldberg's *Liberal Fascism*, which asserts just the opposite—that our Western political system, like that of Germany and Italy, is being influenced not by ideas from the far right but the far left. Hitler and Mussolini detested organized religion, Goldberg notes, specifically Catholicism. Both came under the sway of radical environmentalism and New Age, especially Hitler. Unlike Hedges, Goldberg uses meticulous facts and figures to point out his assertion that the fascists Hedges warns us about are coming from the Left, not the Right.[12]

Theologically, Hedges asserts, using famed liberal Pastor William Sloane Coffin as an example, that the writer of the Book of Genesis didn't realize the Earth wasn't flat, so anything contained within it should really not be believed. A rather remarkable revelation from a graduate of Harvard Divinity School, seeing how a Christian or Jew might actually believe that the text from the Book of Genesis was divinely inspired and not just the ramblings of some ancient nomad trudging through the desert with nothing better to do than to wax and wane about how life might have began.

The upheaval in Christianity had its roots in the 1960s. Christian leaders like Coffin, the Jesuit priests the Berrigan brothers, and Episcopal Bishop James Pike were cause célèbre for the mainstream media. Seminaries and universities were taken by their mixture of social revolution with the Gospel. However, their liberation theology would remain popular only in certain liberal enclaves. After their symbolic 15 minutes of fame were up, few were found in their churches or espousing their causes. However, that didn't mean the seeds they planted all died. They lived on in those of that era, whether they were ordained, taught in seminaries, or used their ideas through the political process.

While President Obama's former pastor Rev. Jeremiah Wright's interest in liberation theology is well documented, Secretary of State Hillary Clinton also came under the spell of religious social activists. In the 1964 presidential campaign, she was a proud "Goldwater Girl," the name affixed to many young women who supported the charismatic Senator Barry Goldwater, who received a thumping at the hands of President Johnson. America certainly changed from 1964 to 1968, and Secretary Clinton (then Hillary Rodham) was no exception. One may recall seeing her youth pastor from suburban Chicago being interviewed during the 2008 campaign. While coming across as a kindly, elderly man, Rev. Donald Jones would eventually lose his ministry for being too political.

In *Liberal Fascism*, Goldberg notes that Rev. Jones bought the young Rodham a subscription to *Motive*, a Methodist magazine, for her high-school graduation gift. It eventually folded a few years later, many having believed it went too far left even for that time. Yet, unlike President Obama, Secretary Clinton actually did meet Saul Alinsky through Rev. Jones. As we have already noted, the famous agitator must have made quite an impression on the young Hillary Rodham because in college, she wrote her senior thesis on Alinsky's tactics.[13]

Since liberal Christianity takes its cues not strictly from Scripture and Tradition but from people such as Alinsky, people who peddled a vision of Christ and social justice that sapped the soul out of the Christian faith, who peddled a Utopia that required no prayer or holiness or God to create, the remnants of that version of Christianity is withering on the vine. It's terribly tragic. Still, recall the idealism that seemed to permeate the age's atmosphere. There was a desire for peace, a belief that war was not inevitable, and a conviction that everlasting brotherly love between all peoples was within our grasp. Readers of a certain age may remember former Vice President Nelson Rockefeller's famous stump campaign line of "BoMFoG:" The Brotherhood of Man, the Fatherhood of God.

Although Rockefeller and so many others got the order tragically wrong, one can understand how and why, for at least a brief period of

The Disintegration of Liberal Christianity 291

time, many of today's leaders were enraptured by the often deceptive promises peddled by those who were sadly held up as leaders. Some of the students of these leaders found their way into various Christian church leadership positions during the 1980s and 1990s.

Not surprisingly, inspired by the naysaying of these acolytes-turned-masters, the drumbeat we heard for so much of the pontificate of Pope John Paul II was that his papacy and the Church were going in the wrong direction. It was a time when it seemed the news regularly featured every instance when then-Cardinal Ratzinger had the unenviable task of trying to reign in theologians and dissidents who taught heresy to students (or had taught people who were now in positions of power and influence). He had to put a stop to those who thought they were given free license to teach views contrary to the Church's teachings.

Cardinal Ratzinger's duties were born out of a frustration with the late 1960s. As someone who was at the Second Vatican Council and cheered on its ideas, then-Fr. Ratzinger was shocked as to how far some in the Church had gone by 1968. Some students who came to Europe's seminaries full of faith left the increasingly liberal seminaries for the barricades of Paris full of revolution and empty of faith. Being the prefect for the Congregation for the Doctrine of the Faith was not a laudable position, according to many in liberal Christianity and those in the media who admired them. Years later, as the Catholic Church would continue to grow because of orthodoxy and liberal mainline Protestant churches would decline because of their resistance to it, Pope Benedict XVI would be vindicated.

In 1990, then-Cardinal Ratzinger disciplined American theologian Matthew Fox for his heretical views about the nature of God, which actually sounded as if they were more Hindu in nature than Catholic. Afterward, Fox permitted his ego to take out a full-page ad in *The New York Times* with the words "I HAVE BEEN SILENCED" emblazoned across the page. Never was silence so loud.

The crux of these stories is that all of these liberal churches and ideas, especially within liberal Catholicism, came to a calamitous crossroads by the 1990s and certainly the first decade of the new millennium. In some ways the liberals had succeeded beyond their wildest dreams. They had convinced large segments of the spiritually curious population that religion was more about self, ideas, and activism than it was about Scripture, liturgy, and apostolic teaching. Because of this, large numbers of those who came to trust and be shaped by these ideas saw the Church as too defining and stagnant. They moved on to spiritual and personal quests and abandoned their churches, all of which made Catholicism seem more and more attractive to those in society that believed in Scripture, liturgy, and apostolic teaching.

The death spiral of liberal churches and the curious way some once-conservative Evangelical churches morphed into liberal churches, which basically rejected the majority of Christian doctrine, helped illuminate the 2,000-year-old consistency and clear teaching of the Catholic Church. At one time the Puritans were so conservative that mincemeat pies and colored clothing was banned. The present-day Unitarian Church is the modern-day descendant of the Puritans. Sadly, as noted before, by the Unitarians' own admission, nearly half of their members aren't sure God exists, and most don't believe that Jesus rose from the dead or performed miracles—the hallmark of Christian doctrine.

Sometimes churches that once carried a powerful message have been replaced by social activism and a forging desire to reach out to alternative communities and lifestyles. In doing so, their new message almost becomes parody. Recently while on a family trip, as we passed through Asheville, North Carolina, we saw a sign on a mainline Protestant Church that would undoubtedly make those who built that church some 100 years or so ago cringe; it read "Keep Asheville Weird."

Perhaps convert Fr. Dwight Longenecker said it best while commenting on a John Zmirak article concerning the problems of liberal heresy in the Catholic Church. In a few sentences he states more truths about what went wrong in the 1960s and 1970s than are written in many multiple-page articles on the subject:

The Disintegration of Liberal Christianity

> The reason is (with apologies to the Holy Father) the dictatorship of sentimentality. Catholics in English-speaking countries (and maybe everywhere else for all I know) have drifted into sentimentality because they are too afraid of embracing the full blooded, supernatural, dogmatic religion we call Catholicism, and the rot began with the clergy who came out of seminary full of the modernistic critical theories about the Scriptures and the faith.
>
> They couldn't believe that sort of thing in the modern age, so they concocted another gospel which was all about being friends with Jesus and hanging up felt banners with words on them, and making the world a better place and the church a happy fellowship sort of group therapy session. The music is a bad dream, but when you consider that the music matches the theology, the nightmare is even worse.[14]

Yet, unlike some church groups who have firmly planted their theological flag on the whims of the modern world, the 2,000-year history of the Church makes far more sense to many than the latest theological trends and trappings, thus demonstrated by her growth and vocations boom. Catholicism offers a rich history of Sacred Tradition that, coupled with the Scriptures, helps the spiritual curious to see the panoply of Catholicism. Jesus told us, "By their fruits you shall know them," which is why he stated the Church must have apostolic leadership, beginning when he gave Peter the keys to the kingdom. If Christianity were an orchard, many denominations would have few if any trees left. Yet the Catholic Church is ever present, trying to grow new trees, while never abandoning those who need much fertilization.

EIGHTEEN
THE PERILS OF THINKING WE KNOW BETTER THAN OUR PREDECESSORS

There is a small segment in American society that somehow believes that if the Mafia ran things, the country would be better off. There was one city—Newark, New Jersey—where the Mafia did indeed control much of the city. When their grip on power was done, the city was in tatters. The same could be said for liberals running religion.

Many a religious radical started out as a political radical (someone has to employ all of those radicals leaving graduate school with unemployable majors.) Once the political-radical-turned-religious-radicals realized that they couldn't take over religion, they began to embark on a scorched-earth policy that left some Christian denominations in tatters. (Point of personal privilege: In my opinion, there are two categories of liberals: utopians, who are by their very nature good-hearted people though lacking in reality; and elitist control-seekers, who use the misfortune and suffering of others to gain, consolidate, and hold power. The crux of references to liberals in this and most of my writings revolves around the elitists and not the utopians.)

Having worked for the Church for much of my adult life (I was born in 1964), I've always been struck by some of those in the religious world who came of age in the 1960s and seemed to desire a religious revolution to further a political and cultural revolution that they felt didn't go far enough.

Fortunately, these radicals seem to be fading into the sunset, replaced by younger women religious, priests, and bishops who are far more conservative in their theological, social, and political outlook. The liberal voices like Cardinal Dearden, Archbishop Weakland, Bishop Untener, Cardinal Mahony, and Auxiliary Bishop Gumbleton are out of ecclesiastical power now, being replaced by far more orthodox-minded prelates.

The religious Left reached their heyday in the early 1970s. However, a few years later, with the elections of Polish Cardinal Karol Wojtyła as Pope John Paul II, Ronald Reagan as US president, and the ascendancy of American Evangelicals such as Jerry Falwell, the left turned on religion.

The end result has left some Christian denominations in tatters. In the last 50 years, it is estimated that some communions have lost half of their adherents. Though the Catholic Church is growing worldwide (phenomenally so in Africa and Asia) and at a much smaller rate in the United States, some European Catholic countries have seen their numbers plummet as well.

In Canada, the most liberal province is Quebec. It wasn't always that way; up until the 1960s, the overwhelmingly Catholic province may have been Canada's most conservative province. Religious surveys show that in the late 1950s Quebec had one of the highest rates of Church attendance in the Western world, higher than that of the United States; this all changed in the political and cultural upheaval of the1960s.[1] Now Quebec is Canada's most liberal province and has one of the lowest rates of church attendance in the Western world; a sad end to the province that was to be the Catholic New World's New Jerusalem. In 1967 France's Charles de Gaulle helped ignite Quebec's Quiet Revolution by saying *"Vive Le Quebec Libre"* from a Montreal balcony. He had noted to his son-in-law, General Alain de Boissieu, that he felt he owed it to the memory of the Frenchmen his country left behind to die, starve, toil in English-controlled Canada, or be deported to Lousiana after the debacle of the French and Indian Wars. The end result was that Britain dominated North America and sent France and in turn Catholicism to exile for quite some time.

Perhaps Quebec's Quiet Revolution, when Catholic clergy were partnered with radical elements of Quebec's revolution, showed us what happens when we try to partner with those who hate religion: We lose. Those radicals had far less in common with the American Revolution than they did with the French Revolution. While the American Revolution was all about liberty, the French Revolution's goals of liberty, fraternity, and equality on the surface seemed very inspiring. However, within a few short years the French Revolution came to be nothing more than class and open warfare on religious believers. The French Revolution's real goals were quite simple: claim they are for the poor by killing the elites, and then tell the poor to toe the line or else suffer the same fate as the rich.

Consider that some believe the practice of the priest lifting the Eucharist high during the consecration began in France during the Middle Ages. This was done so the peasants working in the town square could report to others toiling in the fields that they had seen Jesus, every bit of good news was a help in those trying times. Sadly, a few centuries later during the French Revolution in the country that gave us so many saints, leaders of that movement desecrated the very churches and tabernacles that their countrymen had so revered.

In a nutshell, that was the French Revolution, though you would be hard-pressed to get many on the "professional left" or their friends in the mainstream media to agree with you. Few may want to realize that it was the elites of France, like Voltaire, who helped set in motion the chain of events that would lead to the revolution that he would not live to see. Voltaire once mused that within a few short years, Christianity, and the Catholic Church in particular, would be destroyed.

His followers did their best to accomplish this goal. Not only were bishops killed, but so were simple country priests and nuns; then simple Catholic peasants were killed. Even that wasn't enough; Voltaire's followers desecrated churches and the Eucharist, as well as paraded prostitutes around the altar at Notre Dame in Paris. They knew the Eucharist and the altar on which it is celebrated were not

The Perils of Thinking We Know Better... 297

symbols but the truth, and they tried their best to destroy God's truth—which, of course, no earthly or demonic power can do. The same turn of events occurred in Russia; some of the elites financed the very revolution that would kill many of their friends.

The elites were the very ones who influenced Karl Marx and Friedrich Engels. One only need read about the early Marxists, and even those beforehand who greatly influenced Marx and Engels, to see what kind of vitriol, hate, and even genuine kookiness were directed at the Son of God. Now it was the likes of Bruno Bauer who influenced up-and-comers like Marx and Engels. It seemed Bauer was under the impression that if you don't like somebody, all you have to do is just pretend they didn't exist. Some little kids have make-believe friends, while some angry leftists just pretend that those they wish didn't exist never did.

When there is no Church authority, a church can be destroyed. It is hard to fathom that the ultra-conservative Pilgrims, who thought colored clothing and mincemeat pies were too vain, eventually merged into the ultra-liberal Unitarian Church, which doesn't believe Christ rose from the dead or performed miracles. Two to four former presidents called Unitarianism their own (depending upon your source). By the 1990s, it was estimated that half of the Church's congregation was either agnostic or atheist. Two men, David Burton and Dean Fisher, have become evangelists in their own church, preaching that, yes, God does exist. One might ask the simple question: Why even attend if you don't believe or have serious doubts about God's existence? It would seem that some stay because of the shared liberal beliefs, beliefs that have robbed this religious body of half its believing members.

An interesting debate might be what is needed by our friends who are Protestant to see what was the true aim of the Reformation. Those on the religious and political left do have a point when they assert that the Protestant Reformation was the first left-wing political and religious movement. Their aim was to tear down the authority that existed (which Catholics believe Jesus gave to Peter and each successive pope). Indeed, the ultra-conservative Puritans did meld into the ultra-liberal Unitarians.

The secular view that religion must be demystified was embraced by many of the leaders of the Protestant Reformation, who believed that miracles didn't occur once the age of biblical revelation ceased around the year 100 AD. Now, this might be news to many Evangelicals (and many televangelists), who often speak of daily miracles. Let's take this one step further: If most Evangelicals have a problem with the mindset of those who started their churches, what does that say about their very beliefs?

One of the former mainstays of Protestant upper-class respectability was the Anglican Church. As late as the 1950s, it had one of the largest percentages of Sunday church attendance. By the early 1960s, while worldwide Anglican Communion was growing (especially in Africa) the British mother church was dabbling in political and cultural liberalism and thus beginning its inexorable decline.

During the 1960s in its American cousin church, the Episcopal Church, figures like Bishop James Pike came to the forefront. The famous Episcopal bishop, who doubted much of Christian orthodoxy, found himself receiving fawning news coverage and being featured on the cover of many a news magazine. Fast-forward 40 years, and the same could be said for the first openly homosexual bishop of this decade: Bishop Gene Robinson of New Hampshire. For all their glowing mainstream news coverage, the western Anglican Church has been in a complete free fall. It is estimated that more people attend Friday prayers at Britain's mosques than attend Anglican Church services on Sunday morning. Yet, it gets worse for the Anglican Church; for in addition to the laity, the Anglican Church lost a large amount of its clergy as well.

This development has led Pope Benedict XVI to approve a personal ordinariate that will allow Anglican male clergy who accept Catholic Church teaching to become priests in the Catholic Church. One would think that most Catholics would feel a certain pity for

Archbishop Rowan Williams, the leader of the Anglican Church. One might even think he might feel tempted to swim the Tiber himself. One by one, the old mainline Protestant denominations became enamored with the Spirit of 1968 (more on that later), which not only robbed them of their congregants but their clergy as well. In a business model this would have been construed as an unmitigated disaster, and yet the mainstream media became enamored with them. Despite the Episcopal Church's numerical free fall, the mainstream media became smitten when liberal Bishop Katharine Jefferts Schori was named the Episcopal Church's presiding US bishop in 2006. It didn't take her long to make some controversial comments. In one *New York Times* interview, she said Catholics had more children than Episcopalians because Catholics were "less educated" and perhaps because Episcopalians cared more for the environment. Her faux pas received little attention.

In April of 2008 the mainstream media, and in particular CBS News anchor Katie Couric and ABC religion reporter Dan Harris, seemed mystified as to why the "hard-line" Pope Benedict XVI with his "tin ear" received so much positive affection from Catholics when he came to New York and Washington. The two, among many others in the mainstream media, seemed bemused as to how could this be since the conservative Bavarian pontiff opposed many cultural hot button social issues like women's ordination and same-sex marriage.

Sadly for Catholics, too many graying employees in diocesan offices and seminaries held views to similar to that of Couric and Harris. Yet, those who held these views in positions of power within the Church saw their numbers fall, as the young and those being ordained into the priesthood and entering the convent had far more conservative beliefs, a fact which angered those who were nostalgic for the Spirit of 1968.

What was the Spirit of 1968? It was a turning point for the Church. All throughout Europe, radicals were not only gaining a foothold on the streets as evidenced by the leftist uprising and burning barricades of Paris in 1968, but this rebellion was also being witnessed in many seminaries and even dioceses throughout the Western world. This, after all, was the year that Pope Paul VI issued his famous encyclical *Humanae Vitae,* which cemented the Church's stance against birth control.

It didn't sit well with those clergy who had hoped the Church would mirror the culturally liberal movement taking place in the Western world following the invention of the birth control pill a few years earlier. Prophetically, the embattled Holy Father predicted the rise of not only of an extremely sexually permissive society, but abortions as well.

Some four years later, as radical priests and nuns were calling for "political revolution" and leaving their vocations, Pope Paul VI voiced the famous quote that the "Smoke of Satan" had entered the Church, which has bemused the religious left to this day. Yet, the same group shrugs off the implications of their hero Saul Alinsky's having penned an epigraph to Satan for his most famous book.[2]

While the Catholic Church battles her liberals and takes flak for not acceding to their wishes, the mainline Protestant churches have been taken over by liberals. In Mark Steyn's book, *America Alone,* Steyn notes that "most mainline Protestant churches are, to one degree or another, post Christian." He quotes fellow Canadian writer Kathy Shaidle, who says, "Secularism created the Euro spiritual/moral vacuum into which Islamism has rushed headlong."[3]

Europe has relinquished its religious authority to those who want authority, namely Islam. There are no major movements in Islam for the core of their faith to be changed; one either believes or one doesn't.[2] There are many secular Muslims who live in affluent or academic settings who wouldn't dream of telling their religious authorities that Islam must change with the times.

Steyn relates the sort of nuttiness one sees in liberal places when Christianity loses its hold. While in Vermont doing some Christmas shopping, Steyn (who lives in New Hampshire) overheard the following conversation:

The Perils of Thinking We Know Better...

"Thanks for the sweater, Mom. Kevin really liked his present, too," a daughter told her mom.

The mother bewilderingly replied, "But it's only the twenty-third."

The daughter retorted; "Mom, how many times do I have to tell you? We always open presents on the solstice!"[4]

This is where the secular Left has taken us. Yet, even on the left, some heroes are more celebrated in modern circles than others.

One would think that someone like Norman Thomas would be greatly admired by the political Left today. It was Thomas, the Socialist Party's standard-bearer for the 1928 election, whose 34-plank party platform became merged into the Democratic Party platform with the victory of then-Governor Franklin Delano Roosevelt in 1932. It was Thomas who first mentioned Social Security, voting rights, unemployment compensation, and, of course, socialized medicine, which became the last of his 1924 platform to be enacted into law in that most contentious of all bills, President Obama's healthcare legislation, which became law in 2010.

Yet Thomas was not a demagogue. He didn't believe in the deceptive and underhanded tactics espoused by the likes of Alinsky. Thomas was hated by the Communist Party of the United States because he believed in elections and denounced Soviet tyranny, which had not as yet taken over Eastern Europe; that sad fact would occur following the Second World War. This says a lot about what the Far Left in this country thinks about Alinsky, even though it was Thomas who effectively gave them what they claimed to desire. Perhaps what they really desired was absolute control—the kind of control that would only be seen in places like the former Soviet Union and later closer to home in places like Cuba.

Yet, it may have been the first Catholic presidential standard bearer, Al Smith, who warned us all of the dangers emanating from the Left. Though Smith lost to Republican Herbert Hoover in 1928 and to Franklin Delano Roosevelt at the Democratic Convention in 1932, he did support and campaign for his fellow New Yorker in the general elections against Herbert Hoover.[5]

However, it would not last long. Smith, along with other prominent conservative-oriented Democrats, would soon form the American Liberty League and travel the country while denouncing the aims of the Roosevelt administration as nothing more than a government takeover on par with the worldwide socialist movement. The chattering classes snickered at the idea of the hardscrabble Smith, with his hallmark New York working-class accent (Smith literally grew up in shadows of the Brooklyn Bridge as it was being constructed), lecturing the urbane and regal Roosevelt on anything, let alone America's future.

The same chattering classes would soon become enamored with one Saul Alinsky. During the Depression, Alinsky made inroads into Chicago's Catholic neighborhoods and parishes. His methods seemed subtle, but his underlying message was radical. It wasn't until 1971 that he released *Rules for Radicals,* outlining all of his tactics and techniques.

One of Alinsky's more masterful techniques was to befriend liberal clergy and escort them and their often-privileged congregants to the ghetto. The elite would see a side of America they could have never imagined existed in a major, prosperous city such as Chicago. Alinsky would then bemoan the fact that all their money couldn't help these people. The only thing that would really help them was to change the power structure.

Liberal guilt would then often compel these WASPy (White Anglo-Saxon Protestant) Republicans to become left-wing activists and leave behind all that they had known and been taught about what really helps the poor to become members of the middle and upper classes. Somehow these elites were goaded into thinking that state control was better for the poor than the freedom to use their God-given talents to forge a life of their own, not that of the state.

One such young woman who was enthralled by all of this was a

The Perils of Thinking We Know Better... 303

former Goldwater Girl named Hillary Rodham (later to become Secretary of State Hillary Rodham Clinton). Her Methodist youth minister, Rev. Donald Jones, would actually introduce the young Hillary, and many others like her, to the activist extraordinaire himself, Alinsky.

Though he never met Alinsky, a young Harvard grad named Barack Obama would come to walk the same South Side streets of Chicago that Alinsky once strode. Obama would meet those who actually were taught by Alinsky. The future president often boasts that much of his ideas about politics and the world were formed from his days as a community organizer in Chicago's South Side. Though he rarely met his famous Kenyan father, President Obama did say in his book, *Dreams from My Father*, that many on his father's side say they see the same vision in him that they saw in his anti-colonial father.

Alinsky was an avowed atheist, although his infamous 1971 book, *Rules for Radicals* was dedicated to, among others, Lucifer. This little known fact was seemingly ignored by almost everyone until 2008, when it came to the attention of many that Alinsky's book and beliefs greatly shaped the two principal frontrunners in the Democratic primary, then-Senators Clinton and Obama. The Left pooh-poohed conservative qualms about the book's dedication, as if there was a plethora of other authors who had also dedicated their book to Lucifer.

Increasingly in the last few years, a firestorm of protest erupted due to the influence that Alinsky had in some Catholic circles. Unbeknownst to the faithful, the Alinsky-inspired Catholic Campaign for Human Development and ACORN were receiving aid from some Catholic parishes and dioceses. Many bishops and dioceses chose to distance themselves from such groups once their modus operandi was disclosed. In addition, though Alinsky and those who subscribed to his beliefs were by and large atheists, they actually tried to change aspects of Christian teachings.

Some on the Catholic Left have fired back that if all of this is true about Alinsky, why did the famed French Catholic philosopher Jacques Maritain, who spent hours in Eucharistic Adoration each day, befriend the man? The Catholic Left often goes on to say, "Wasn't Jesus a radical just like Alinsky, stirring up trouble not only among the occupying Romans but among Jewish religious authorities as well?"

These are fair questions that need answers, for at least in the case of Jesus they have been bandied about for quite some time. However, the truth of the matter is that Jesus was a far cry from being anything like the Catholic or secular Left would have felt comfortable with had they been his contemporaries. One can only imagine their outrage directed at Jesus had they heard him talk about hell for lustful people or those using little of their talents, let alone saying, "The poor will always be among you." In addition, Jesus told the young rich man to go and sell his possessions and give them to the poor. Jesus didn't say sell your possessions and give them to the Roman tax collector or procurator (Big Government). It seems to be Jesus' way of saying that the Left will always use the poor to their political advantage, thus they will always be among us.

With regard to the Maritain question, is it really a scandal to try and dialogue with someone if your intention is to convert them from an atheist to a believer? Jesus dialogued with many non-believers. We must also keep in mind that Alinsky didn't write his infamous book until after Maritain had died. Alinsky would die one year after the book's 1971 release. Perhaps he was beginning to reveal a side of himself that no one really knew. The most troubling question is why would an atheist dedicate a book to God or, in his case, Lucifer—the Prince of Darkness—if he really didn't believe? Could it be that Alinsky really did believe, at least in evil, and thus tried to pull more people down with him?

In 1968, the cultural elites cheered on the likes of dissident priest Fr. Hans Küng as he tooled about the German university town of Tübingen behind the wheel of his trendy Porsche. Yet, they snickered at the old-school Fr. Ratzinger as he peddled through the same town on his bicycle. Shortly before the French Revolution, Voltaire voiced the opinion that since the indefatigable Jesuits had been thrown out of the country, the Church would collapse once the revolution and the guillotine swung into action. He was very mistaken. So it was with the 1960s elites who thought the Church of Fr. Ratzinger would be gone in 40 years.

Forty years later the bicycling Fr. Ratzinger would become Pope Benedict XVI, while the Porsche-driving, ascot-in-the-breeze Fr. Küng would become but an asterisk of past dissidents who disappeared into the mists of history. The tortoise of truth had passed the hare of relativism. The "smoke of Satan" was being wafted out from whence it came by the likes of Popes John Paul II and Benedict XVI.

Many in the Church seem oblivious to the turning tide of Catholic orthodoxy. A good illustration of this was one that I personally witnessed in April 2008 while in Yonkers, New York, awaiting the arrival of Pope Benedict XVI. The appearance was geared toward the young, and the thousands gathered were the epitome of the new, younger, conservative-oriented Catholic. This was lost on one of the local news anchors, who served as an emcee before His Holiness' arrival. While engaging in banter with the youthful Pennsylvania delegation, she asked who they were going to vote for in the upcoming Democratic primary, Hillary Clinton or Barack Obama. The crowd repeatedly chanted neither, yelling back that their stances on abortion and other issues were not in line with their beliefs. The news anchor seemed oblivious and was overheard asking what was going on.[6]

It was a continuation of a mistaken understanding of Catholic youth that stretched back to 1993. George Weigel describes a feeling of near panic as some in the US Church feared that no one would come to Denver to see Pope John Paul II for World Youth Day because many of their children or nieces or nephews had little interest in such an event.[7] While anecdotal, I am sure I am not alone in noting that I can't think of a single instance in which a liberal Catholic parent (who graduated from high school or college in the 1960s or 1970s) has a liberal Catholic child who still practices the faith after leaving home. I can think of many children of Catholic liberals who left the Church for another faith tradition, adhered to no faith at all, or have become an orthodox Catholic despite their liberal upbringing. However, I cannot think of a single liberal Catholic family where the children have stayed in the Church and continued on in the liberal Catholic tradition.

Perhaps some of these parents were in attendance at a lecture I attended at Ohio Dominican University a few years ago, when noted Catholic journalist and writer John Allen told the theologically diverse crowd that Third World Catholics did not share the views of Western liberal Catholic prelates and academics. This may have been a bitter pill to swallow for liberals, since Allen worked for the liberal *National Catholic Reporter.* For all their talk of diversity, some Western liberals, especially in the Anglican Church, have caused deep rifts over their assertion that Africans are culturally backward on issues like women clergy and same-sex marriage—so much for Western liberals embracing diversity. As a matter of fact, some conservative US Episcopal churches have broken away to align themselves with Anglican dioceses in Africa.

In Jonah Goldberg's book, *Liberal Fascism,* Goldberg illustrates the Far Left's agenda and their supposed fondness for truth and the dignity of the downtrodden, all the while mocking them and sometimes doing far worse. The Left has been in the forefront of the eugenics movement. With this in mind, it is baffling to hear Catholic politicians show their admiration for the likes of Margaret Sanger, who founded Planned Parenthood and was at the forefront of the movement. The modern-day successors of Sanger are admired by the likes of former House Speaker Nancy Pelosi. When a bishop does speak out on such matters, it is the prelate who gets an earful from Pelosi, Congressman Pat Kennedy, and their supporters, and not on the very views that brought on the rebuke.

The Catholic Church, with all of her dissidents, was being saved from demise because—as Canon Kendall Harmon, a conservative leader in the Episcopal Church, put it—the Catholic Church had "clear doctrine." In my 2006 interview with Harmon, he lamented what had happened in his Episcopal Church when, during the 1960s, a few radicals were allowed to gain power in a few key dioceses. That interview and the one I conducted with openly gay Episcopal Bishop Gene Robinson showed a church in utter conflict over what it believed and where it was going.[8]

It may be heard to believe, but the Catholic Church has been the only organized religious body to always oppose abortion. The Evangelical *Christianity Today* magazine issued a mea culpa of sorts, wondering how words like "therapeutic abortions" were ever used. Even the conservative Southern Baptist Church supported abortion, and it took several contentious meetings in the late 1970s, along with the rise of figures like Jerry Falwell, to end that stance. Dr. Mohler lamented, "The early Evangelical response to legalized abortion was woefully inadequate." Mohler even says Evangelicals have much to learn from *Humanae Vitae*.[9] Today, many mainline churches not only support abortion rights but also same-sex marriage.

For the orthodox-minded Catholic, the statement by Christ that the gates of hell would not prevail against his Church has given the Catholic faithful solace that what is happening in the Protestant world would not lead to the Catholic Church's demise. Though the liberal onslaught has caused much anguish, the future of the Church is the youth, and those 30 and younger who attend Mass regularly are not only the most pro-life of any age group but also the most supportive of the Church's teachings, more so than even their grandparents.

While liberal convents are strapped for cash because they haven't had a postulant in years, more conservative orders like the Dominican Sisters of Mary, Mother of the Eucharist in Ann Arbor, Michigan, are running out of room due to the large number of young professional women coming their way. Theirs is not the only conservative order growing; the Dominican Sisters of St. Cecilia in Nashville, Tennessee, among others, also are experiencing growing pains.

Younger liberals might be forgiven if they mistakenly believed the canard told by their elder comrades that 1950s Catholic leaders, especially bishops, were all right-wing conservatives who had no patience for the ideas of liberals but possessed the patience of Job for fellow conservatives. In his memoir entitled *True Compass*, published shortly after his death in 2009, the late Senator Edward Kennedy wrote that his famous father, the former ambassador to England, Joseph P. Kennedy, would often socialize with Richard Cardinal Cushing of Boston. Senator Kennedy wrote that his father always called the famous prelate by his first name.

In a revealing account, the late senator spoke of an incident in which his brother, Bobby, the future senator from New York, heard a controversial conservative priest at a Boston lecture, whose views about Protestant salvation were deemed very conservative. After Bobby's father made a phone call to "Richard," the priest was promptly booted from the archdiocese. Senator Edward Kennedy surmises that because of this incident, Bobby unwittingly played a part in bringing about Vatican II. As one can clearly see from this example, the right-wing Catholic hierarchy may not have existed as vividly as it did in some liberal's imagination.[10]

If conservatives were all about spending money, accumulating possessions, and not giving to charity, then liberals would truly have a point in stating that their beliefs were closer to Jesus. However, with the exception of a few spendthrift young Republicans, most conservatives are true to their name: conservative, which means to conserve.

The presidential elections of 2004 and 2008 blew away all the old stereotypes. It was the millionaires and the trust-funders who voted for Senators John Kerry and Barack Obama for president, and in 2008 enough of the elites convinced the poorest among us to vote their way, while the middle class by and large voted for the McCain-Palin ticket. An unusual alliance between the elites and the poor helped Senator Obama to become President Obama and Senator Joe Biden to become Vice President Biden. However, a cursory review of the charitable giving of the likes of Vice President Biden and former Vice President Al Gore shows that they, like many liberals, give but a pittance of their riches to charitable causes.

The agenda of the radical Left is to water down religion, making it become some sort of trendy self-help series infomercial that comes and goes with the rest of the Johnny-come-latelys. Many mainline American Protestant churches have lost nearly half of their members in the last 50 years; some went to Evangelical churches, some to the Catholic Church, and others stopped attending any church. It would appear that, in the latter case, they took the relativistic sermons they were hearing to heart and felt, like those delivering them, that they knew better than the teachings of orthodox-minded Christianity.

Sadly, among liberal Protestants and liberal Catholics, there are those who try to change or put words in the mouths of the divine. Bishop John Shelby Spong of the Episcopal Church has given us a list of what he doesn't believe: i.e., the virgin birth of Jesus, the miracles of Jesus, the resurrection of Jesus, and on it goes. Once again, it would have been easier to tell us what he does believe. The liberal Catholic writer Garry Wills (a *National Review* conservative in the early 1960s) is presumptuous enough to have entitled two of his books *What Jesus Meant* and *What Paul Meant.* Thankfully, it took a good rabbi to set the record straight when it came to Wills' scurrilous lies about Pope Pius XII. Rabbi David Dalin wrote the revealing book, *The Myth of Hitler's Pope,* which tells of the heroic work of Pius and his rescue of thousands of Italian Jews who were destined for various concentration camps.

Judaism is not immune to these kinds of problems. The Anti-Defamation League's Abraham H. Foxman has released several statements denouncing conservative Catholic and Evangelical leaders for statements they have made that hardly seem to fall into the category of anti-Semitism. This led to rebukes from the likes of Norman Podhoretz and Michael Ledeen. In the *National Review,* Ledeen wrote the following: "I want Foxman retired and replaced by somebody who fights for Jews and our friends."[11] The interesting tie that binds all of these stories together centers around the fact that, in whatever faith tradition, liberal activists seem to think they know better than the faith they claim to follow.

In 2011, the Far Left and their many allies in the mainstream media were all aflutter over the Occupy Wall Street movement. The protests quickly spread around the world and became violent, though one would be hard-pressed to hear or read about that in the mainstream media. Though the Oakland riots became the most reported on, there were others that had elements of violence, including one that occurred in Vancouver, Canada, where protesters attempted to take over the Catholic cathedral. They had the cathedral surrounded and were ready to march in when cooler heads prevailed. Some of the hotheads were apparently inspired by a Facebook page called Occupy the Vatican.

The violence in Oakland was a mob gone wild. Nothing was safe; the city's new Catholic cathedral, Christ the Light, was vandalized with spray-painted vulgarity too unseemly to mention here. Even Whole Foods, the organic and liberal-friendly grocery store, was attacked and damaged. However, it was the vandalizing of the popular Men's Wearhouse that was the most telling. Columnist and conservative commentator Mark Steyn noted that, in a bizarre twist, George Zimmer, the popular owner and pitchman for the discount clothing outlet, publicly supported the general strike called for by a group of anarchists and radicals. Zimmer even posted signs on the windows of his store, saying he supported the radicals. What did Zimmer get for allying himself with the violent, militant far left? The Men's Wearhouse was attacked, spray-painted, and had its windows knocked out.[12]

The unofficial leader of the Occupy Oakland movement, Boots Riley, whose most notorious song was entitled "5 Million Ways to Kill a CEO," said he was shocked that violence occurred. He sounded as if he were the disingenuous Captain Renault from the movie *Casablanca*, telling Rick (Humphrey Bogart) he was shocked that there was gambling in his establishment. Therein lies a powerful lesson: One can never befriend those on the Far Left who preach anarchy and the destruction of society and religion, for they eventually destroy even their supposed friends.

Catholic blogger Thomas Peters reported the following: "What's the Occupy the Vatican movement? It has about 3,500 supporters

The Perils of Thinking We Know Better... 311

on Facebook and is allied with groups such as STOP the Missionaries of Charity ('Holding Mother Teresa's charity accountable for their monumental medical negligence and financial fraud'), Freedom From Religion Foundation, Religion Poisons Everything, 'Hell Does NOT Exist—It Is a LIE to Control Victims With Fear' and hundreds of other angry lefty causes."[13]

In October 2011, an Occupy Rome march made news when a band of marauding protesters damaged a statue of Jesus and smashed to pieces one of the Blessed Virgin Mary. The smashed statue, seen on a Rome street being stepped on by many Rome protesters, was more than a little telling about the goals and mindset of the movement. The odd thing about all of this was that some in the mainstream media had incorrectly reported that the Vatican (through a document by the Pontifical Council for Justice and Peace) was calling for a worldwide central bank, which one might think the Left would applaud. It took days for the media to report (thanks to the likes of George Weigel) that this was not what the document stated. Nevertheless, while all of this was being sorted out, one might have thought that the Left might view the Church more favorably. Sadly, the violence spoke volumes. When truth becomes something one smashes and stomps on, it says a lot about what else the Far Left might have in store for Christianity in general and the Catholic Church in particular.

Those of us who have written about the French Revolution and the way it is often lionized in the West and how the horrid beheadings of the lowly religious in the Church hierarchy is often covered up have often been ridiculed by the liberal elites. However, none more than the fiery Ann Coulter, whose book *Demonic* greatly details the violence directed at the faithful during the French Revolution as well as the unspeakable desecration churches suffered during that violent time. Perhaps now Coulter's words of the Far-Left mob violence and pack mentality can be better understood by those like Zimmer, who seem to think it is a hip trend to which he can attach his name.

Though the Left appeared to be making strides in the social spectrum through social engineering and the changing of definitions of the family and marriage, many of their supposed icons appear to have had their doubts. For instance, in 2011, many were shocked to hear John Lennon's personal assistant speak of his late boss' admiration for Ronald Reagan and the conservative argument, a possible shift in ideology for the iconic rocker that seems to have begun in the late 1970s.[14] Perhaps it was Lennon's meeting with the future president on the set of *Monday Night Football* in 1974 that started the process.

By the late 1970s Lennon was heard complaining about Big Government. He began reading religious books, even calling Pat Robertson's *700 Club* help line to ask for prayers. It appears Lennon did so after being visibly moved while watching the Franco Zeffirelli miniseries, *Jesus of Nazareth*, which was broadcast around the world and shown on American television in April 1977 on NBC.[15]

It appears that Bob Dylan's revelatory Christian album *Slow Train Coming*, released in 1979, also had an impact on the former Beatle, making Lennon confront his own life and causing much emotion within him. Though the album is now hailed (even by liberals) for its directness, lyrics, and musicianship, it was panned and excoriated by the liberal music press when it came out in 1979. Perhaps those demonstrating against the general order of things, including religion's role in society, might want to ponder why, at some point in their lives, liberal icons like Lennon, Dylan, and Jack Kerouac (mentioned in Chapter 15) decided to take a more conservative path.

I will close this chapter with a couple of anecdotal stories. In the late 1990s, while attending a friend's party, I was introduced to a truck driver originally from East Germany. Knowing that my mother came from Germany (she met my dad there while he was in the US Air Force) and that I had studied for a short period of time in Austria, the host thought we had something in common. I am certainly glad the introduction was made because, in those few short minutes, I learned a great deal about the mindset of the Left.

The trucker, who graduated from an East German high school in the early 1980s, told me that the only students he knew that were enamored with the communist way of life were the bitter kids, those who didn't like sports, the theater, or those who weren't very sociable with the opposite sex. I told him that this description sounded something like "Revenge of the Angry Nerds." He chuckled and said that's exactly what it was. In my mind, I come back to this conversation from time to time, most recently during the Occupy Wall Street protests, for it tells us about the mindset of those who feel terminally aggrieved at the world and want to take power and property from those whose only crime may be that they worked hard and followed their dreams.

The following story I will relate could happen to any supposedly wise and well-read Catholic. While traveling to promote my book, *The Tide Is Turning Toward Catholicism*, I came across a group that was upset that Catholic orthodoxy was being embraced by many again, especially the young. This group took special exception with Pope Benedict XVI's phrase "the dictatorship of relativism." One person retorted, "What is this notion about embracing the truth as if anyone can possess the truth?" Finally, this person exclaimed, "What is truth?" I replied, "Do you know the person who is most famously credited for saying, 'What is truth?'" The person in question asked, "Was it Aristotle, or how about Plato?" I replied, "It was Pontius Pilate." Then the rhetorical fireworks really began, and I was treated to a variety of insults about the ignorance and hateful nature of conservatives. The diatribe spoke volumes about the goals and mindset of the militant leftist movement. Bereft of anything other than their own agenda, they heap scorn on the very belief system they claimed to represent.

Perhaps it's worth repeating: The interesting tie that binds all the data, anecdotes, and stories together centers around the fact that, in whatever faith tradition, liberal activists seem to think they know better than the faith they claim to follow. This has led to the tragic decline of those who once called themselves religious or faith-filled. Fortunately, there is a way out, a return to the religious tradition they once embraced, free of the modern-day relativism that has sadly left too many saying, "What is truth?"

NINETEEN
THE COMING CRASH OF THE MEGACHURCHES

"I blew out my flip-flop, stepped on a pop-top..." Ah, the sounds of Jimmy Buffett. One conjures up an image of a tanned man holding a cold beer while napping in his small boat somewhere near Key West, not a care in the world as his hammock sways in the breeze. In our fast-paced world, many long to live the carefree Jimmy Buffett lifestyle. Some churches' pastors even clad themselves in Buffet beach-style attire, including none other than the most famous megachurch pastor, Rick Warren.

However, Buffet crafts his image well. The truth of the matter is that Buffet is a workaholic, going from one project to the next. Yet the image plays well in an overly stressed world. Pastor Rick Warren, of the Saddleback Church in Southern California, is most widely known for his multimillion-dollar selling book, *The Purpose Driven Life*. However, for many megachurch pastors, his landmark book was *The Purpose Driven Church*, a book that looked at what worked in most non-denominational churches. It was all based upon a premise of giving people what they want, which often meant comfortable theater seats, refreshments at the church entrance, short sermons, and pop music.

This Burger King "have it your way" mentality was the bane of many a traditional Evangelical, and especially orthodox-minded Catholics. However, it played well in some quarters. At first, Pastor Warren was dismissed as a more upscale and hipper Bible-thumping conservative by the mainstream media. However, his Hawaiian shirts and laid-back, non-confrontational approach soon earned him favor among the mainstream media. He became a fixture on CNN's *Larry King Live*.

The Coming Crash of the Megachurches

There certainly was much even a traditional-minded Catholic could admire about Pastor Warren. He was welcoming and warm, and most importantly he reverse-tithed all of his proceeds from the *Purpose Driven Life*, meaning that he gave 90 percent of the millions he received to the less fortunate. However, there was something revealing about the man seen so often on Larry King; his sort of approach to faith was just like King's—something that would be quite the hit one minute and merely passé the next. In a sense, the megachurches, like talk show hosts and reality-TV shows, come and go with the times, while the uncool Catholic Church remains. I often joke that Catholic churches should put up signs to counter trendy megachurch signs that read, "The Catholic Church—under the same management for 2,000 years!"

In the first volume of *The Tide Is Turning*, I noted that the megachurches would be in serious decline by 2020. Even many who liked my book thought I took a serious misstep here. However, look what has occurred in five short years: the Crystal Cathedral, the very first megachurch, was sold to the Catholic Diocese of Orange, California (more on this in a page or two). The Crystal Cathedral is far from being the only example. Large megachurches that once had no problems have had to issue special appeals; even Pastor Warren has had to make special appeals for increased donations. Where once the megachurches seemed untouchable, they now are coming under increased scrutiny.

In 2011, Joel Osteen, who holds services in the arena where the Houston Rockets once played, was criticized by the head of the Southern Baptist Theological Seminary, Dr. R. Albert Mohler. He denounced Osteen's fumbling response to a reporter's question about homosexuality. Mohler stated that Christian leaders who didn't know and articulate the faith are of no service to the faithful.[1] Sadly, Dr. Mohler's comments didn't apply just to Johnny-come-lately preachers but to established ones as well.

In 2008, Pat Robertson raised eyebrows when he endorsed former New York Mayor Rudy Giuliani for president, someone who is both pro-choice and pro-same-sex unions. When the famous mayor from New York had what seemed to be an insurmountable lead in 2007, the eventual GOP nominee, Senator John McCain, was left to carry his own luggage on red-eye flights with no reporters in tow, while Giuliani led an entourage of staff and reporters. Rev. Robertson said that despite his qualms with Giuliani over his private life and views on social issues—including abortion, which Robertson is against—he eagerly endorsed the heroic mayor from New York. At the time, many were more concerned with safety than the economy, and the mayor seemed to be the prohibitive frontrunner due to his leadership during the dark days following the 9/11 attacks.

Giuliani didn't win the nomination; that honor went to another famous hero, John McCain, who survived years of torture in a North Vietnamese prison, infamously dubbed the "Hanoi Hilton." If his endorsement of Giuliani struck many as odd, some comments Rev. Robertson has made since 2008 have been downright bizarre for someone whose job it is to show what Jesus meant when he said Christians were to be in the world but not of the world. For instance, in 2011, Robertson said it would be OK for the faithful to divorce a spouse with Alzheimer's since they were practically dead anyway.[2] So much for better or for worse.

This exemplifies something at the heart of the Protestant Reformation. Personal decisions often are allowed to trump truth and religious authority. Protestantism is, after all, a religion that holds that every believer has the ability to interpret Scripture for himself without benefit of any external authority; as Luther put it, "Every man [is] his own priest."

I remember discussing with an Evangelical the reason why my wife and I didn't use in vitro fertilization during our bout with infertility. "Dave, you are a conservative," he told me. "Don't you want to make your own decisions? Isn't that what conservatism is all about?" "No," I replied. "Conservatism is not about me disregarding the truth and the authority of Christ through his infallible teachings *as guarded by his* personal representative on Earth, the pope. There is a difference between the role of government in our lives and the role of God. The less government, the better; the more we honor God through respecting his laws, the better."

Loss of the Sacred

Most Christians who value the sacredness of their faith have experienced some sort of religious service, all too often a wedding, in some sort of space that is far from sacred. All too often those who belong to such bodies think they are trendsetting and cutting edge; they are apt to tell everyone, much to the bane of the sacred-minded, that they are "thinking outside the box" and welcoming new people. This couldn't be further from the truth, as most who attend such places either go back to what they are doing before or move on to a more serious approach to faith. You don't see those houses of worship that pop up in a closed-down bank or Taco Bell in the same place a few years later. They inevitably go the way of the Big Foot Pizza or mini taco.

Many a Catholic and Evangelical has seen the seriousness of their faith watered down by those who think that by appealing to the worldly using worldly ways more will come to church and find Christ. Yet, the only time Jesus' used violence occurred when the Temple lost the reverence that the Bible said was necessary for faith to be taken seriously.

One only need look at the history of the United States to see how seriously the faithful took their worship. In Catholic American in the 1800s, not only did the urban poor build and finance the construction of large, beautiful churches, but in that same century Catholics in rural America, especially the Midwest, did the same in small towns. Still today one can drive through Ohio, Indiana, Illinois, Michigan, Wisconsin, and Iowa and see regal churches towering over cornfields in towns that in some cases aren't big enough to have a stoplight. These churches were designed to signify how seriously the flock took their faith.

Evangelicals also believed in proper decorum and reverence. No better example exists today than that of the historic Dunkard Church on the grounds of the Antietam Battlefield near Sharpsburg, Maryland. The thought of appealing to the world was the farthest thing from the faithful's mind, since Jesus had exhorted them to be in the world, not of the world.

Some who were "of the world" certainly made death conversion back to truth of Christ's words and his holy sacraments. We have this account from Alexander Hamilton's Episcopal parish (Trinity) in New York City. The architect of the US economy lay dying of his wounds suffered in that ignominious duel with Aaron Burr. It was readily apparent that Hamilton's internal wounds were vast and unable to be mended, at least by 1804 medical standards. Hamilton was a unique man, who unlike many of the Revolution was not born in the colonies, but in the Caribbean and was born into poverty at that. He was practically an orphan as his father left his mother and she subsequently died from an epidemic. At a young age Hamilton showed so much promise that the residents of Christiansted, St Croix (now the American Virgin Islands) took up a collection to send him to school in New England. As a child, Hamilton excelled at informal learning picking up on what he could from passersby and those who took the time to help him. In August of 1772, a great hurricane hit the Caribbean. Hamilton wrote about it in such vivid detail that it wound up being published in New York.

During and following the Revolutionary War, Hamilton had a meteoric rise through the corridors of power. Sadly his Anglican Church attendance suffered. However, he never stopped believing. Though Anglicans and Lutherans don't believe in transubstantiation as do Catholics, the Eucharist is still held in high regard. As he lay dying, the father of the US economy longed to reconnect with his faith. He immediately appealed to the Episcopal Bishop of New York (and President of Columbia University) Benjamin Moore for Holy Communion. The Episcopal leader of New York balked, Hamilton had not been a regular attendee of services and he was dying from wounds in a duel, which went against the beliefs of the Episcopal Church (and most other churches.) Hamilton even appealed to a local Presbyterian leader.

Many of the New World's glitterati were surprised at Hamilton's vociferous requests, though few may have realized that his wife was a very pious and religious woman and held in great esteem by the dying Hamilton. Finally, after second thoughts and some pressure from the faithful, the Episcopal Bishop relented and gave Hamilton Holy Communion on July 12, 1804. Hamilton, with little energy left, gratefully thanked the Episcopal Bishop of New York and then asked his wife to bring in the entire family. One by one, from his two year old son down the line, Hamilton kissed his family good-bye. He assured the well-wishers gathered outside of God's grace and mercy. He even went on to say that the only hate he possessed was for dueling, not Aaron Burr. He asked them to hold no ill will toward the Vice President, who was now fleeing to a safer location. Aaron Burr was never able to politically recover and always carried the guilt of the events with him. He mused that, "If only I had read less Voltaire and more Laurence Stern, I might have seen that the world was big enough for Hamilton and me."[3]

While Catholic churches seemed to have turned a corner from some of the hideous, modernist constructions of the 1960s, many in the Evangelical world are fighting against those who believe a church should make one feel comfortable and kick up their feet. They state it should resemble a theater, complete with plush chairs and cupholders for your latte. Some have been incensed that Joel Osteen doesn't have a cross in his church. Detractors point to surveys that show that younger less religiously include churchgoers that feel uncomfortable with the idea of Christ and suffering. They attend because of their children and like the Christian message of love and giving, but they don't want to ponder on Christ's death and resurrection.

Perhaps this is why in many modern homes where Christian symbols once abounded, there exists images of Buddha. One can see this on the plethora of home shows seen on television or magazines dedicated to sprucing up a home's look. The image of Christ and all that blood and suffering doesn't sit well with those who aren't religious and instead prefer a picture or statue of Buddha. They acquaint Buddha (who didn't have an easy life either, but few seem to be familiar with this) with a religious version of Dr. Phil, the popular television psychiatrist known for his supposed quick fixes of life's complicated problems.

A September 2008 *USA Today* article asserted that the megachurch phenomena indeed had peaked. The article stated that experts see more troubling concerns than slowing growth: no measurable inroads on overall church attendance and signs that many churchgoers are spectators, not developing a deeper faith. "You can create a church that's big, but is still not transforming people. Without transformation, the Christian message is not advanced," says Ed Stetzer, head of LifeWay Research in Nashville, Tennessee, which conducted the *Outreach* magazine study.⁴

In the spring of 2011, certain Evangelical circles were abuzz over Paul Smith's book, *New Evangelicalism: The New World Order*. The book took a look at the growing influence of certain business and self-help gurus in the world of Protestant Christianity. The author and many of his supporters were alarmed that churches were being set up according to business and personal-growth models, with the Gospel getting short shrift. Perhaps that helps explain the following stories, which must make faithful Evangelicals shake their heads. Catholics certainly have had to endure liturgical dance, but thankfully much of that seems to have gone the way of lava lamps and shag carpeting. Now it seems our friends in the Protestant world have to endure this sort of charade.

In 2012, the NewSpring megachurch in Anderson, South Carolina, scrapped plans for Sunday evening services on its five-campus site because they coincided with the Super Bowl. Lead Pastor Perry Noble explained the reason in his blog. "I've been in church work for over 20 years, and the one thing I can say is that attendance on Super Bowl Sunday night in church has always been awful (and… the people who are there are pretending to be looking at [the Bible application software] YouVersion on their phone…but they are really checking the score of the game)!" he wrote. The Evangelical *Christian Post* reported the story, which was greeted with frustration by some of the Evangelical faithful, but not complete surprise, as some churches seem intent on bending to the whims of the world. "Scripture teaches that the job of a pastor is to preach the Word. That doesn't matter if God sends two or 3,000 people, the job of pastor is the same," Evangelical apologist Chris Rosebrough said.⁵

Also in 2012, more eyebrow-raising events hit the megachurch world. Mark Driscoll, the Seattle pastor known for his testosterone-induced statements such as, "He couldn't worship a God that he could beat up," boasted about his bedroom prowess with his wife. However, Pastor Driscoll was topped by an Ohio pastor who brought a stripper pole into his church

The Coming Crash of the Megachurches

to illustrate the right and wrong approach to sexuality. The *Christian Post* reported on this event, which caused many a faithful Catholic and Evangelical to roll their eyes. Jesus warned us that we had to be in the world, just not of the world. These points illustrate an approach to Christianity that smacks of desperation and wanting to fit into a world that Jesus warned us would lead us to being shaped by that very world that we should shape.[6]

All of this pandering to whims of the world does have consequences. One can drive through the rural parts of the United States and see, as I have, the many mainline Protestant churches left in disrepair or abandoned in many small towns across our country. Unfortunately, they are the victims of those heading those church bodies who would rather appease the whims of the relativistic world than the mind of God. Their congregations vote with their feet and find their way to some church that will preach the truth. It is interesting to note when driving through these small towns, you rarely see abandoned Catholic churches; if anything, you often see that they have built additions.

The best way to close this chapter is to focus on one of the most powerful metaphors in the religious world to surface in quite some time: the bankruptcy of the Crystal Cathedral, the world's first megachurch and its subsequent purchase by the Catholic Diocese of Orange, California. It had come up in numerous conversations between Catholic film producer and director Christian Peschken and me as we were working on the *Non-Negotiable* TV talk show. Peschken was adamant that this was a sign of nearly biblical proportions.

The nation's first megachurch, the one that started a theological trend, was bought out by the Rock of Peter because it was built on a foundation of sand. Jesus warned us to remain as one and build our faith communities on Peter, not sand. St. Paul later chimed in that churches that wanted to appeal to the whims of the people would not last. He gave a grave assessment when he visited one church where people didn't believe in the Eucharist. He chided them, telling them it was no wonder they had so many sick and so many had died (see 1 Corinthians 11:23-31). The words of Jesus and St. Paul are as true today as they were 2,000 years ago.

TWENTY
THE CATHOLIC CHURCH MARCHES ON

It has been written that, for those who believe, no explanation is necessary; for those who don't believe, no explanation is possible. So it is with those who have made up their mind against the Catholic Church. Some are truly ignorant of the truth and have been spoon-fed misinformation about the Church through dubious sources, primarily militant liberal secularists or fundamentalists; strange as it may sound, they share a great deal in common. Catholic apologist and author Mark Shea is fond of saying, "Scratch an atheist, and you will find a fundamentalist." This unholy alliance is an old and stubborn lot with roots going back to Nero and other barbaric emperors. They share the same intellectual pedigree with those early heretics who raised the ire of St. Paul for not believing in the Eucharist. Their intellectual bloodline continues onward to those in the French Revolution who thought he Church would disappear by the year 1800, those in the Communist movement who thought the Church would die after World War II, as well as those modern militant atheists who become apoplectic every time data is released showing the worldwide growth of the Catholic Church.

St. Thomas Aquinas laid out the five proofs for knowledge of God, while the early Church Fathers and more recent intellectual heavyweights like St. Thomas More, St. Robert Bellarmine, and St. Ignatius of Loyola made the case for the Catholic Church to be the one true Church. Yet the disbeliever will not listen to whatever intellectual premise, facts, and statistics are laid out in front of them. God gave everyone the free will to believe or not. However, with that free will comes responsibility; each of us will be judged for what we did or didn't do, and what we believed and didn't believe.

The charge of the Catholic Church, which includes the ordained, professed religious, and the laity, is to learn, understand, and live the gospel message. One cannot simply walk away from the truth because it is too hard. Much like a successful athlete simply can't make up a false training or those under a doctor's care can't make up a false weight loss routine, so must the faithful live under the guidance and laws that Christ gave us through his Church.

Where did this all start? In 1529, shortly after the Protestant Revolt's start in 1517, Martin Luther was abruptly shown the door at the Marburg Colloquy when he became upset that some of his fellow doctrinal revolutionaries didn't believe in the Eucharist (some would later deny most of the miracles of Jesus).[1] Luther's ego was such that he thought all those who disagreed with some of the abuses of the clergy within the Catholic Church would naturally listen to his ideas. They didn't, and so the division that Jesus warned us about began in the West (see John 10:16) just as it already existed between East and West.

We must remember that even though he was tortured on the cross, our Lord didn't cry. Yet Jesus was moved to tears at the thought of his followers not being as one. The division caused by the Protestant Revolution would escalate in the Enlightenment ideas that found their full voice in the French Revolution. That is when thousands of the faithful, from simple peasants to Catholic clergy, would ironically meet their earthly end by the guillotine at the very hands who decried how persecutory and intolerant was the Catholic Church.

In turn, this led the radicals ideas of Karl Marx, Friedrich Engels, Sigmund Freud, Vladimir Lenin, Saul Alinsky, and so on. In the name of helping them, the poor would be used as a foil by those saw in them a way to grab power. As they progressively grabbed power through the centuries, the elites could now mold and shape the world into their warped image of rebellion and anger. They were not happy warriors but warriors of death and mayhem.

Where will it end? A hint may lie in their heirs' treatment of Pope Benedict XVI. As Joseph Cardinal Ratzinger, he was hailed for his action in putting an end to the sex-abuse scandal. However, now that he is the pope, *The New York Times* and CNN blame him for not doing enough.

The speed of the liberal churches' demise is happening at an alarming rate. Fifty years ago the Anglican Church of C.S. Lewis was the epitome of respect; rates of attendance at Anglican churches in Britain were some of the highest seen in the Western world. Today, the Archbishop of Canterbury has welcomed the establishment of some form of futuristic Sharia law for Britain, while there are more Britons attending Friday prayers in their respective mosques than Anglicans attending church services on Sunday morning.

These events didn't happen out of thin air. They occurred because, as the Servant of God Paul VI said, too many Christians put their faith and trust in "the first profane prophet who speaks in some journal or some social movement, and they run after him and ask him if he has the formula of true life." More than the Bride of Christ, they harken to subtle whims and whispers of modern world.

At an increasingly alarming rate, we have sold and are selling our birthright for a mess of relativistic pottage that says the demented rants of men like Voltaire, Marx, Engels, Lenin, Freud, and Alinsky are on par with and often superior to that of Jesus, Sts. Peter, Paul, Augustine, Thomas Aquinas, Teresa of Avila, Joan of Arc, and the popes.

In addition, many Christians forget not only the teachings and lives of these important men and women, but also the dates and events that made up their lives, not to mention the heritage and lives of all those today who call themselves Christians. We know this doesn't have to be. In places where the Faith hasn't been watered down, it is alive. We just have to decide which master we will serve.

The modern world has constructed a faux Jesus, one who doesn't call out sinful behavior. This is the "I am OK, you're OK" Jesus who goes through life offending no one and standing for nothing. Jesus warned us that this would happen, and so it has. The real Jesus could be nothing further from the truth. As a matter of fact, why was he killed? For the same reason he had to rise from the dead. He told the truth, and—in the words of the fictional Colonel Jessup in *A Few Good Men*—the world then and now "can't handle the truth."

Jesus called people out for their lust, greed, laziness, and wasting of the talents that God gave them. He attacked those who were serious about their faith and even used violence in the Temple courtyard to get his point across loud and clear. Yet, those in realm of religion who do the same today are called judgmental, narrow-minded, and bigoted. However, people of all political and theological stripes who like sports and the world of acting have no problem with demanding the best from their athletes, coaches, film directors, actors, and actresses. One could only imagine the firestorm of outrage that would descend upon a coach who tells the world that he doesn't want to push his players this year, doesn't want grueling workouts, doesn't mind if they challenge his authority and overrule his play calls, but instead wants his players to find their true selves, for they are more important than the team.

In the world of the silver screen and the theater, no actor, actress, or director wants to put up with someone who feels he or she is bigger than the film or play. Yet this is exactly what the world wants to do with religion and those who actually believe in something bigger than themselves. They are labeled ignorant, narrow-minded, and even bigoted. Shouldn't faith be more important than sports and the world of film and theater?

Slowly but surely, we are seeing through the number of converts coming into the Church that the Catholic Church is the world's only hope. Though most Evangelicals are conservative, they may be shocked to learn that the leaders of the Reformation were liberals. Like all liberals, they wanted to overthrow the leadership and take over from what God had given us. Like all liberals, they wanted to put an end to mystery, so they tried to dispense with the sacraments that Christ gave us.

As noted several times before, 1930 saw the Anglican Church become the first church to permit birth control. Evangelicals protested, but then joined the Anglicans.[1] Former President Theodore Roosevelt, who was not Catholic, said of birth control, "Birth control is the one sin for which the penalty is national death, race death; a sin for which there is no atonement."

While one may be surprised to hear this of the former Rough Rider, one may be astonished to hear Freud, an atheist, saying the following:

> The abandonment of the reproductive function is the common feature of all perversions. We actually describe a sexual activity as perverse if it has given up the aim of reproduction and pursues the attainment of pleasure as an aim independent of it. So, as you will see, the breach and turning point in the development of sexual life lies in becoming subordinate to the purpose of reproduction. Everything that happens before this turn of events and equally everything that disregards it and that aims solely at obtaining pleasure is given the uncomplimentary name of "perverse" and as such is proscribed.[1]

Whereas once believer and non-believer saw the wisdom in the Church's teachings, now even many believers disregard the truth. Historically, Lutherans and Anglicans scoffed at the notion of same-sex marriage, but polls now show many strongly support it. When the shepherd is struck, the sheep will scatter. There is a reason why Jesus made Peter the first pope and gave him the figurative keys to be passed down.

The world often laughs at the Catholic Church's stance on issues like birth control. However, the demographic nightmare is beginning to be seen in the world financial debt crisis that began in 2008. There are simply not enough people in the workforce to support those who are retiring. The chickens are coming home to roost from the 1930 Anglican Church's decision. Here we are in 2012 with 40,000 different denominations, when Christ told us to remain as one. In addition, we have a demographic crisis caused by the same rebellion of Christ's authority that has gotten us into trouble for the last few centuries.

The narcissistic *Sex and the City* lifestyle loved by too many in the West has its price, recently played out for all to see in the riotous streets of Athens, Greece, and soon to come to a city or country near you (if your are reading this in a western country.) The Greek debt crisis that has the Euro teetering on the abyss (as we know it) is the effect, and a free-spending, fast-living, and zero-birthrate Europe is the cause. The continent is veering towards a demographic nightmare far removed from once beloved retirements at age 45, 50, 55, along with endless summers on the beaches of southern Europe. The declining birthrate means that the young will eventually have to pay for a culture that aborted or contracepted itself into oblivion. The generous benefits can only last so long. As the old saying goes; "The problem with Socialism is eventually you run out of other people's money." The ancient Greek world gods who hailed narcissism and hedonism and whose lifestyle was proselytized by the Epicureans seem as irrelevant as ever as the pall of smoke (from a seemingly endless spate of economic riots) hangs over the Acropolis, a fitting metaphor for what the secular Left has done to Europe.

Fortunately, there is a growing number of Catholics who are tired of those who want to water down or leave the Catholic faith or push for changes in society and government that would want to either attack religious faith or end it all together. A growing number of Catholic writers, bloggers, and film directors are speaking out. They are bluntly defending the faith in a variety of ways. There are many Catholic apologists who defend the faith through scriptural means as well as other theological methods. Karl Keating and Patrick Madrid started the ball rolling, and they have been joined by the likes of Jimmy Akin and Dave Armstrong, among others.

While they prefer dialogue along the lines of "Evangelicals and Catholics Together," in the spirit of Chuck Colson and Fr. Richard John Neuhaus (both now deceased), they won't mind mixing it up a little while reminding all who will listen that the Catholic Church was essentially started when Jesus gave the figurative keys to Peter to be handed to every one of the 264 successive popes. For those fundamentalists who attack the teachings of the Catholic Church, it would be as if someone 1,517 years after the fact (3293 AD) stated that he had come across the real reason for the American Revolution, and it wasn't what we were told.

The same could be said today if someone proposed (some 1,500-plus years after the fact) an entirely different reason why the Roman Empire collapsed: perhaps something along the lines of a massive flooding of the Tiber River that engulfed Rome, or that the Barbarians had nothing whatsoever to do with her demise. Such a theory would be laughed at as sheer lunacy; yet, for years Catholics have been told that for centuries the Church got it wrong until Martin Luther came on the scene.

The same holds true for those who claim that religion is man-made. All we have to prove is essentially one miracle to be true when we have countless miracles, let alone St. Thomas Aquinas' five proofs for God's existence. It really defies scientific reason as to why anyone could definitively say that God doesn't exist. We all have met some who struggle with faith, but I am talking here about those who defiantly attack God and those who believe in him. Their defiance toward authority figures is so obvious that the most amateur of psychiatrists could see this coming a mile away.

It's the same with those who want to change the order of society and marriage away from the truths found in the Judeo-Christian ethic, which date back thousands of years, for theories that are the most recent of inventions. This is why so many hate the Catholic Church. Even though she is filled with imperfect men and women who have sometimes strayed from the truth, she stands on the side of truth. Indeed, the reason her core teachings cannot be changed is that they come from the deposit of truth handed down by Christ to his apostles and through their successors to us.

The fact of the matter is that those who want to so irrevocably change the world have little or no use for religion. We can wonder if God were to physically reveal himself whether they might rebel against him. Most Catholics and Evangelicals would most assuredly change if God personally instructed them to do so because they truly love the Lord. However, those who initiate measures into churches that will inevitably kill off religion and the family as we know it have little or no use for God. They, in effect, think they are God. It is a story as old as time itself.

Fortunately, the battle has been joined because, for 30 or so years now, many Christians have realized this faith-killing agenda for what it is. The Catholic Church has seen a small but steady increase in vocations. More marked is the number of tradition-minded prelates who have regained confidence as authentic Catholic teachers and thus their voice, thereby showing the faithful through clear teaching how we are live and the reasons for it. This has been enhanced by a return to devotions such as the Rosary and the knowledge that piety and humility are the way to God. Catholics have taken strong stances against those who try to defy the Holy Father's call for the return of sacredness in the liturgy and a return to the Rosary and Eucharistic Adoration.

However, the Church's role doesn't just end at the border of the theological, for Jesus told us to be in the world, just not of the world. We are called to assist those in need. Who developed the idea of giving people food and aid? The Church, and it was during the Roman Empire, at a time when the Church as an institution was still illegal. She also provided the first orphanages, pleading to Roman prostitutes to drop off their unwanted babies rather than have them murdered in or out of the womb.

All of this is still true today. Whether it is in rural Appalachia or inner-city America, Catholic agencies are there helping those in need. The same holds true in Europe, Asia, Africa, and Oceania. In my previous book, I noted how Catholic Relief Services is often the first agency the world's leaders call upon when a disaster of epic proportions hits. Though it doesn't have the sheer infrastructure and bureaucracy that the United Nations has, the CRS is, by many accounts, the most trusted name in the world when speed and perseverance are needed to reach those whose lives are on the line.

The Church is there for whomever needs her assistance, regardless of creed. This is in no way letting off the hook those who were responsible for the recent sex-abuse scandal or the many other scandals that have occurred throughout the history of Christianity. Nevertheless, while there have been some terribly sinful men and women in the Church, they only sullied her reputation; they didn't change her teachings. Catholicism's vineyard remains fundamentally intact even though some of the workers were corrupted by the ways of the world. As we can see from those who have done so, this would not have been the case had the Church completely changed its teachings of Christ to conform to the modern world.

In Deuteronomy 18:15-20, we read that those who try to change God's teachings will meet with death. Meanwhile, Jesus made the position of Peter as pope (see Matthew 16:16-20) and the role of his apostles absolutely clear when he said, "He who hears you hears me, and he who rejects you rejects me." Sobering words, indeed!

The Church continues to reach out to all so that we may heed Christ's tearful admonition to be as one. Sadly, on any given Sunday morning, one might find a higher percentage of Evangelicals than any other religious group, who truly love the Lord and would do anything they could or were made aware of to serve God. Yet, because they haven't been made aware of what most Catholics should know, they aren't aware of what they, in most circumstances, would truly relish: the unbroken authority of Christ present among us.

Bringing the Lost Sheep Home

Since many Evangelicals are lapsed Catholics, some have been working to change that. Starting in 2011, a series of compelling commercials by Catholics Come Home began airing on various networks. In one of those commercials we are reminded that the Catholic Church built the West's education and hospital systems. Indeed, while the commercials don't go into this, we should note that our holy faith is responsible in so many ways for making this world a better place. Wherever the Church has gone, she has uplifted the lives of those cultures with whom she came into contact. Yes, some missionaries have perpetrated abuses and on rare occasions even took part in abuses. These people, however, are less than a pinprick on the vast mural of good our faith has wrought.

On the other hand, ask women in those lands controlled by Islam who find themselves being married off as young girls or experiencing the painful practice of female circumcision whether that sort of experience is uplifting. The Catholic Church ended all of those practices when she came to town. Likewise, inhabitants of Central and Latin America believed in ritual sacrifice until Catholic missionaries arrived.

Fr. Robert Barron's highly acclaimed *Catholicism* series is another great tool for not only bringing Catholics home but for better forming those who are still in the Church, because it highlights all that is great and noble about our faith. It aired in the fall of 2011 on the PBS network in the United States and is being shown around the world in 2012 on various international networks.

Fr. Barron wanted to put forth a Catholic series much like the groundbreaking BBC series, *Civilisation*, which was broadcast in 1969.[1] Fr. Barron's production team traveled around the world to shoot the documentary. His unique insights as well as his erudite but—in the same breath—man-of-the-people style help explain the Faith to those who have a great knowledge about its teachings and history as well as to those who have very little of it.

Besides the acclaim that he received from all quarters in the Church, he made many media appearances as well, including the top-rated morning program, NBC's *Today* show. It was certainly a win-win for the Church, as many from other faiths or those with no faith at all hailed the series as a *tour de force* and saw in Fr. Barron a likeable and well-informed spokesman.

One great thing about Fr. Barron's series and documentaries like it is that they remind us of the great traditions of our religion, some of which are being rekindled in our age. Take, for instance, the Way of St. James, an ancient pilgrimage route, which typically requires pilgrims walking great distances to get to the earthly resting place of the apostle St. James at the Santiago de Compostela Cathedral in northwest Spain.

Data shows that in the last 20 years or so, the number of pilgrims has skyrocketed in supposedly overtly secular Europe. In 2010, some 272,000 pilgrims finished the journey, compared with 5,000 only 20 years earlier. The pilgrimage became a backdrop to a 2010 Martin Sheen movie, *The Way*, featuring not only Sheen but his famous actor son Emilio Estevez.

Don't Count Us Out Yet

As we have shown in many ways throughout this second edition, an aggressive and virulent humanism is trying to back Catholicism into a corner. What those who think this way don't realize, though, is that is exactly where our faith wants to be (see 2 Corinthians 12:9). Indeed, the Church has always been strongest when her back was against the wall. Many might want to shoot us on that wall, but even then we can draw on the strength and courage of countless saints, from the early martyrs to Sts. Joan of Arc and Thomas More to more modern examples, such as Bl. Miguel Pro.

While we face the menace of militant secularism, which has been with us since the French Revolution, we may face a far more insidious enemy, and that is apathy toward God. Think about it: How many people do we all know who, while being nice and pleasant to be around, have no time for God? They may come up with some canard that they have met too many hypocritical believers, thus turning them off from religion. In a way, we can understand their point. However, did hypocritical athletes ever turn them off from sports? Did hypocritical actors or actresses turn them off from watching movies or going to the theater? Do hypocritical food and travel critics turn them off from enjoying a favorite food or vacation spot? We all know the answer.

Also, let's be honest: How often do we ourselves not make the time we should? The true answer lies within all who turn their back on God, who don't have him as their sole focus and instead go ever more inward to reach new heights of self-absorption. Our world—a world all of us have helped make because we are all sinners—has become obsessed with self, vain beauty, and every feeling and whim that race through our minds. We often reflect on our intellect, accomplishments, beautiful homes, and travel getaways, then subtly pat ourselves on our backs for a job well done. Is it really to our credit alone that things are in our possession? How many of us have truly thanked God, who gave us the opportunity to acquire these things with the talents he has given us?

The Holy Spirit, God's mysterious comforter, is always gently nudging us to look deeper and see the truths of life. To do so, he often takes the most mundane circumstances and turns them into periods of stunning revelation. In my first book, I wrote that hours before I was to turn in my manuscript I was tearfully informed by my mother that a haunting mystery in our lives had been solved. My 16-year-old sister Renate had been killed in a traffic accident in 1985. For some 20 years my parents struggled with the idea that in her dying moments no one was there to comfort her as she lay along the roadside awaiting the paramedic's arrival. Then through a chance meeting at a local nursing home, where my mother often went to comfort the residents, she met the mystery woman whom some had seen comforting my sister in her final earthly moments. Somehow, someway, the Holy Spirit had arranged this meeting; the whys and wherefores it is not for us to know.

God is always present, nudging us to see and hear the truth and through the intervention of the Holy Spirit even in the most roundabout ways. The Holy Spirit uses the most secular and hedonistic people to show others these truths of his being in ways only they would understand. I found this to be true in the life of William Kurelek, the Canadian artist who lived through a most traumatic childhood—one filled with abuse and deep depression—in the 1930s in the western prairies of Canada, and yet he came to the Catholic Church in his adult life.

His famous artwork, *The Maze*, was featured in a cropped version on the rock group Van Halen's fourth album, *Fair Warning*. Though it was their least-selling album, it is often voted by the group's fans as their finest work. It certainly is my favorite Van Halen album. Not only did I literally wear out the grooves to the album, God only knows how many times I have listened to it on CD; at least enough that I had to buy a second CD. It was not the usual party album featuring the high-wire antics of lead singer David Lee Roth, but a more subdued, introspective look at life, especially at its excesses and the toll that comes from living in the fast lane.

For years I had no idea who Kurelek was, and it was only as an adult that I realized the significance of his life. I have been able to relate to those who suffered through horrible cases of abuse and mental illness, especially those who would be familiar with Van Halen and the turnaround in their lives that can occur through Christ's intervention, as evidenced by Kurelek.[5]

Through Kurelek's life and his insights into suffering, we can shape our own roles for not only helping ourselves through life's dark periods but helping others as well. God saw fit that Kurelek would meet a possible future saint, Catherine de Hueck Doherty. The wealthy Russian baroness had seen the devil's work close at hand, and thankfully few in this world has known the horrors she experienced. She witnessed massacres during the Communist revolution in her native Russia. Being a pioneer female journalist, she covered the Spanish Civil War and saw not only the lionized supposed "Democratic forces" (still hailed to this day by many in the West) killing Catholic peasants for their faith, but also the brutal rape of nuns and their subsequent torture. She saw the faithful being forced to witness the bodies of priests being exhumed and defiled. She saw the Eucharist desecrated. She even encountered the horrors of World War II, of which the Spanish Civil War seemed a precursor. Yet, in all of this depravity, she saw Christ present, living in those who suffered. She felt called to start a movement to make sure that nothing like this could ever happen again, and she did it through the auspices of faith, not man-made institutions.[6]

In his chance meeting with Doherty, Kurelek saw the culmination of his life's experiences—his nagging questions, his anger and his artistic work—answered through this mysterious woman, whom he believed God had allowed to survive in order that people like him could understand their role in this fallen world. Doherty (now called a Servant of God by the Church as her cause toward canonization moves forward) went on to start her own apostolate called the

Madonna House, a community of clergy, religious, and laity who help those who are enshrouded by the ravages of life. The Madonna House is alive and well in Combermere, Ontario, Canada.

While putting the finishing touches on this book, I was informed that Fr. Thomas Shonebarger had died. This priest, who once had been a secretary to Fr. Thomas Merton, an influential Catholic 20th century Catholic author, gave me one of the best quotes for my last book, and I think it is worth repeating.

I had originally asked him why church attendance was so high in the 1950s. He looked me squarely in the eye and took a firm hold of my shoulder, saying, "You were born in the 1960s, and you had no idea what it was like going through in the 1950s in the aftermath of World War II." He elaborated by saying, "In the 1940s and 1950s, too many children did not have a living father, and too many wives no longer had their husbands, and too many brothers and sisters no longer had a brother. How could this happen, and what did it mean? They took their concerns to the only place they could get an answer, their house of worship. I could remember going to Mass early on Sunday just so we didn't stand ... We had to make sense of the horror we experienced."

Then on the last day of looking at my editor's edits and my own tweaking, an amazing story that helped to cement my book's thesis appeared in all of things: the *Wall Street Journal*. The title of the *Journal's* article was, "Traditional Catholicism Is Winning."[7] The story lists growth in Catholicism worldwide and the United States in general. Of special note was the growth in vocations. It noted that when Cardinal Sean O'Malley arrived in Boston in 2002 to deal with the horrendous aftermath of the sex-abuse scandal that occurred under Cardinal Bernard Law's watch, many told him to close down the archdiocese's seminary. Ten years later there are 70 men studying there, and some had to be turned away to other seminaries for lack of room.

This amazing fact displayed what I had written earlier, that research has shown that young men and young women who were taught and pastored by the very people who caused the Church great sin took it upon themselves to right these wrongs. They did so by helping the Church get back to her true self, her true teachings and devotions that were so important to the Church before those who wanted to change tried to usurp the Church's truths. They wanted the Church to return to her beauty.[1]

True beauty is made by God, and our true gut feelings are very important to him and his plans. This is why the world was naturally ordered the way it was and why God gave us his Son to redeem the world from what it had become. God put his stamp on the Catholic Church when his Son gave Peter the keys to the kingdom to loosen and bind on earth and in heaven (see Matthew 16:16-20). God is love, as Pope Benedict XVI describes it in his encyclical *Deus Caritas Est,* and that love is forever present in the gifts Jesus gave us in the sacraments, which follow the rhythms of life. Yet, these gifts need to be used and not left collecting dust like some unused department store gift card. However, if we take advantage of God's gifts and leave the whims of self-absorbed love behind, what an everlasting gift we have!

In some ways, while religious believers are taking fire from many sides, one should remember that the Church can be viewed as a safe port in the storms of life. For centuries she held firm in the truth while coming under attack from ravenous barbarians and pompous secular elites, both wanting to destroy her in their own way. The image of the Barque of Peter (the Church as a ship guided by St. Peter and successive popes, under the command of Christ) has been a powerful icon in the 2,000-year-old history of the Church. While many imperfect men and women have served her, the Church has survived onslaught after onslaught, the results of which have only made her stronger.

We can feel safe in the knowledge that the whims of the world are destroyed when they fall over the precipice, while the truth God gave us is not a mere whim destroyed by the physics of this world. The truth we follow is Christ everlasting, and with him we shall reside if, as St. Paul's states, we work out our salvation with fear and trembling and continue fighting the good fight!

APPENDIX
A BRIEF INTRODUCTION TO BASIC CATHOLIC BELIEFS

What Does the Catholic Church Teach About God's Existence?

God created us so we might know, love, serve Him. God loves us more than we can imagine; hence He sent His only Son to save us. We know God exists by faith and reason. The desire for God rests in the human heart. However, by reason alone we cannot know all the truths of God, which is why we have Sacred Scripture and Sacred Tradition given to us by God so that we more fully appreciate Him and His truths.

St. Thomas Aquinas gave us five proofs for God's existence. They are loosely translated as follows: 1. Mover: Something was set into motion, such as the Big Bang that created the Earth. 2 Causation: Again, something started a chain of events, so what was that cause? 3. Necessary Being: Eventually everything cannot be contingent on something else because you run out of contingencies. 4. Greatest Being: If all things are in a state of being, what is the greatest of these beings and where did it come from? 5. Intelligent Design: How do so many random acts end rationally? There is an intelligent design to all of what we see and don't see. In effect, God is the mover, causation, necessary being, greatest being, and intelligent designer of us all.

What Does the Catholic Church Teach About Jesus Christ?

Jesus Christ is God's Son sent to redeem the world. After the fall of man in the Garden of Eden, God was already preparing for Man's redemption (Genesis 3:16.) Jesus' coming was foretold throughout the Old Testament. Jesus announced He was the Messiah, the Son of God, in no uncertain terms. He was verbally attacked for doing so on several occasions before the crucifixion. Perhaps the most telling statement of Jesus' revelation was using the words "I am." This phrase came from Exodus and would have been patently clear to any fellow Jew of the era. God had announced to Moses at Mount Sinai, "I am who am."

In addition, Jesus foretold his death and resurrection not only to His followers but to those of the establishment who cared little for Him or His ideas. When Jesus told all those who would listen that the Second Temple, which took decades to build, could be torn down by Jesus and rebuilt in three days, it seemed ludicrous and shocking at the time but was later understood to be His death and resurrection. Jesus came to forgive mankind's sin and redeem us. Heaven awaits those who follow Jesus and keep his to his teachings. A harsher outcome awaits those who knowingly reject God's love.

What Does the Catholic Church Teach About the Holy Spirit?

The Holy Spirit is One God in Three Persons. The Holy Spirit guides the Church and gives the faithful inspiration and wisdom to discern God's word. The Holy Spirit gives us many gifts. Grace is one such gift, and it is divided into two groups: sanctification and charisma. One should keep in mind that sanctification is the process of a believer becoming more holy, while charisma (in the faithful sense) is the out flowing of God's benevolent love via spiritual gifts.

When Did the Catholic Church Come into Existence?

The Church came into existence at Pentecost, and the early leader of the Church, Peter, addressed the crowd. Peter was the guiding force of the Church. Although Paul would travel much farther, Peter was the leader. He is named far more than any other disciple in the New Testament. Some might correctly state the Church began when Jesus gave Peter (and every other successive pope) the figurative keys (Matthew 16:15-20). Already in the Acts of the Apostles and Paul's letters, we see the words presbyter (priest) and bishop being used.

By the time the Roman Empire was winding down in the late 300s, most of the Church's dogma on Christ, the Trinity, and the Virgin Mary was already intact. The canon of the Bible came into being 382 AD when Pope Damasus I agreed with past Church councils and officially proclaimed the Bible complete. All of the early popes were martyred. In a telling example that shows the Church's authority in 90 AD while St. John was living off Greece on the isle of Patmos, the church at Corinth had a theological dispute, so they sent a letter to Pope Clement in Rome. Even at this time everyone knew that the Church's leadership was in Rome. The word "Catholic" in Greek means "universal."

In 107 AD while St. Ignatius of Antioch was being carted back to Rome to face his death, he penned one last letter to the faithful. He told them to have no fear: "Where the bishop is present, there is the Catholic Church." A common phrase that existed at the time with regards to disputes and their resolution was "Rome has spoken," which meant the matter was settled.

Why Does the Catholic Church Believe in Sacred Scripture and Sacred Tradition?

The Bible is the inspired and inerrant word of God. This doesn't mean that everything is literal but could be metaphorical. The Earth could have been made by God in six stages, which became translated into "six days." The flood in Noah's time could have lasted more than 40 days and nights, but the term "40" in the ancient world meant a long time. The books of the New Testament were written between the late 40s AD to around 100 AD. The final form or canon of the Bible was approved by various Church councils and Pope Damasus I in 382 AD. Though Protestant and Catholic Bibles have some differences in the Old Testament, the New Testament is exactly the same. Without tradition, the Bible could not have been compiled, which is probably why the Bible tells us to "stand firm and hold fast to the traditions that you were taught, either by an oral statement or by a letter of ours." (2 Thessalonians 2:15)

What Is the *Catechism of the Church*, and Who Came Up with It?

The Catechism of the Catholic Church is the Church' teaching instrument, using Sacred Scripture, Sacred Tradition, Church documents, and principles of faith gathered through the 2,000-year-old history of the Church to spell out God's plan for mankind.

What Does the Church Teach About Heaven, Hell, and Purgatory?

There are three possibilities for one's soul in the afterlife: heaven, hell, and purgatory. Heaven and hell are permanent, while purgatory is a temporary holding place for those not possessing the fullness of grace for heaven. No one in purgatory will go to hell; eventually all will go to heaven, and the duration of time in purgatory is in direct relation to the state of their soul while entering.

What Is the Role of the Virgin Mary in the Catholic Church?

The Virgin Mary was born without sin so as to be the vessel to bring Jesus, the Son of God into the world. Because of that, the Blessed Virgin Mary was conceived without sin (the Immaculate Conception), a fact that Martin Luther and most of the leaders of the Protestant Reformation believed all the days of their lives. In addition to being the Mother of God (Christ Jesus,) she is the Mother of us all, as explained by Christ on the Cross, and thus has a special role in the salvation of the world. It is important to remember that when the Angel Gabriel addressed Mary, he said, "Hail Mary, full of grace." The Greek word kecharitomene is used—a word of extreme importance used nowhere else in the Bible, thus signifying Mary's important role in God's plan (see Luke 1:28). References to her were made in the Protoevangelium Genesis 3:16 and in Revelation 12 (The Woman Clothed in the Sun).

What Is the Role of the Saints in the Catholic Church?

The saints were often simple people who lived exemplary lives, and they can be our guides through their struggles. As explained in Hebrews, the saints are "the great a cloud of witnesses" (Hebrews 12:_) who come to our aid. In addition there are references to the intercession of the saints in Revelation 3:4, as well as by early towering figures in the Church such as Hermas (80 AD), Clement of Alexandria (208 AD), and Origen (233 AD).

Why Does the Catholic Church Have Sacraments?

The sacraments are guideposts and stages of our lives during which God showers us with His Grace in order to reflect these important times. They are the outward sign of God's grace. The seven sacraments of the Church (as found in the New Testament) are: baptism, confession, Holy Communion, confirmation, matrimony, holy orders, and the anointing of the sick.

What Is the Eucharist and Why Is Holy Communion So Important?

The Eucharist is Christ bodily with us on Earth. His Bread of Life discourse on the Eucharist is the longest discourse in the Bible (see John 6). An overwhelming majority of his followers "walked away" because they found what he said too difficult. However, Christ refused to soften his stance because it was that important. Jesus repeated the importance of the Eucharist at the Last Supper (Luke

22:14-20), and it was already being practiced shortly after His death and resurrection as recorded in the Acts of the Apostles (see Acts 2:46). St. Paul became so upset that some believers didn't believe in the Eucharist that he bluntly told one group it was no wonder that many were sick and dying among them because of their disbelief (see 1 Corinthians 11:23-30).Catholics believe Christ is physically present in the Eucharist, it is not a sign nor symbol, but Christ Himself.

Why Is the Sacrament of Confession So Important?

The first thing Jesus did on Easter Sunday night when he appeared to the Apostles was to establish the sacrament of confession. This sacrament frees us from the perils of guilt and the baggage that it carries, (John 20:19-23). Too many must feel very comfortable in our modern world because far too few partake of the sacrament. However, that doesn't include those who are dying and those in the field of battle or about to go to the field of battle. There never is a shortage of these individuals receiving the sacrament.

Why Does God Allow Suffering?

God does not enjoy suffering but allows it to exist among us so that a greater good can come from it. Sin entered the world through man, not through God. We live in a fallen world. However, it was God who sent His only Son to redeem man, which gives us the chance of entering heaven if we believe and follow the path toward it. We must remember that we are our brother's keeper. Christ told us to pick up our cross for them, not monthly or yearly, but daily.

Why Does God Allow Satan and Evil to Exist?

God allowed free will even among the angels, and sadly one of them, Lucifer, led a band of angels (around one-third) to rebel against God. Some theologians speculated that Lucifer wanted to control man and, thus knowing that man would sin and God would have to send his only Son, Lucifer didn't think man was worth redeeming. Sadly, because of man's fall, the Seven Deadly Sins entered the world: pride, lust, greed, anger, sloth, envy and gluttony. Fortunately, we can avoid all of this, including Satan, if we trust God and follow Him.

Why Are There So Many Scandals in the Catholic Church?

There are sinful people in all churches, not only in the Catholic Church. As noted before, we live in a fallen world; even one of Jesus' disciples (Judas) betrayed Him. We have to realize that presently all on Earth are sinners, and we can never put trust in personalities but rather in Christ and His Church, which He established on Earth.

What Does the Catholic Church Say About Poverty?

Jesus said the poor would always be with us not because He wanted people to remain poor but because Jesus knew that some people would be greedy and some would be lazy. It is our job to help those in need. We should not think that other people or the government should help those in need. We are called to help our brothers and sisters in need.

What Does the Catholic Church Say About War?

War must always be a last resort. St Augustine's Just War Theory written over 1,500 years ago still stands as a benchmark for the use of arms by a nation. Jesus told us to turn the other cheek (see Matthew 5:9), which some speculate to mean that we should never seek revenge or employ violence. However, He also said; "Let him who has no sword sell his mantle and buy one" (Luke 22:36). While war often occurred in the Old Testament, Jesus wanted the chances of it reduced in the New Testament. However, Jesus was not a pacifist, as exhibited by his aforementioned quote in Luke and his violent outburst in Temple at the lack of reverence he witnessed.

What Does the Catholic Church Say About the Role of Government?

"Political authority must be exercised within the limits of the moral order and must guarantee the conditions for the exercise of freedom" (CCC, 1923). No one can command or establish what is contrary to the dignity of persons and natural law. It is imperative to remember that the Constitution specifically says that our rights are endowed by our Creator. These rights do not come from rulers but from God.

What Does the Church Say About Other Religions?

While the Catholic Church has never surrendered the belief that Christ established His one true Church on Earth, the Church has always taught, and most recently explained through the document "Nostra Aetate," that some who did not know of Christ or His Church could have experienced some truths within their own faiths. However, the fullness of truth is with Christ and His established Church.

What Does the Church Teach About Modern Miracles and Apparitions?

Throughout the 2,000-year history of the Church, certain Marian apparitions have taken place that help the faithful to better understand the deposit of faith (Sacred Scripture and Tradition.) However, they never replace Sacred Scripture or Tradition. The best way to sum this up is from the Catechism of the Catholic Church: "Throughout the ages, there have been so-called 'private' revelations, some of which have been recognized by the authority of the Church. They do not belong, however, to the deposit of faith. It is not their role to improve or complete Christ's definitive Revelation, but to help live more fully by it in a certain period of history. Guided by the Magisterium of the Church, the sensus fidelium knows how to discern and welcome in these revelations whatever constitutes an authentic call of Christ or his saints to the Church" (CCC, 66).

What Does the Catholic Church Teach About Abortion?

Since apostolic times, abortion has been seen as a great abomination. It was already written about in the Didache, which was written in the lifetime of the earliest of believers. Even in her underground days during the first three centuries, the Catholic Church was known as the place to go to drop off unwanted infants and children, which was often done by prostitutes in the Roman Empire. In the Old Testament God told Jeremiah, "I knew you before I formed you in the womb" (Jeremiah 1:5). Remember, too, that John the Baptist leapt in the womb for joy when the Blessed Virgin Mary, pregnant with Jesus, greeted his mother Elizabeth (see Luke 1:40-44).

What Does the Catholic Church Teach About Birth Control?

Birth control was also viewed in a very hostile manner—not only by the Catholic Church, but by every other church until 1930. The birth control pill has many side effects that are harmful to women. Pope Paul VI, in in his famous 1968 encyclical *Humanae Vitae,* stated that promiscuity and abortions would increase. In addition he predicted that women would be looked upon as objects of sexual desire and sexual gratification rather than beauty. The pope was laughed at by the secular world, since they assumed the opposite would happen. Prophetically, the Holy Father has been proved right. Even progressive secular leaders like President Theodore Roosevelt, psychiatrist Sigmund Freud, and women's rights activist Dorothy Day spoke out against birth control.

Why Does the Catholic Church Emphasize Natural Family Planning?

The Church teaches that married couples can choose the size and number of their family. However, it is immoral to allow this to happen by artificial means not brought forth by God. Natural family planning is viewed as God's way to plan your family and is not something antithetical to that process.

Why Does the Catholic Church Believe in Marriage Between One Man and One Woman?

Marriage was instituted in the Old Testament (see Genesis 2:24) and continued in the New Testament against a backdrop of many cultures who believed either in polygamy or free love. It was considered very important to the Old Testament prophets, Jesus, and His apostles along with the leaders of the Early Church. In Matthew 19:5, Jesus talks about a man leaving his father and mother and taking his wife; both becoming one flesh. Also, St. Paul on more than one occasion talks about the very harmful effects to the body and eternal soul resulting from homosexual relations (Romans 1:26-27; Timothy 1:9-10).

Why Are Some Called to Celibacy?

Some people are called to be celibate in this world: single people, those who are same-sex attracted, and those who take a vow of celibacy; priests, and nuns. We are all meant to carry a cross in this world. For those who are same-sex attracted, their sexual wishes are not in line with God's wishes as spelled out in the Bible. Priests and nuns are called to live celibate lives in order to spend their time helping the flock whom they are called to serve.

Why Does the Catholic Church Have Nuns, Priests, and Bishops?

Jesus established this hierarchy, and it later came to be perfected by those whom He left in charge so as to promote the Church, her teachings, and her mission through an orderly transmission. Jesus made clear that an established order would be left in charge to transmit the Church's teachings. "He who hear you hears me; he who rejects you, rejects me" (Luke 10:16).

What Is the Role of the Laity (the Faithful Who Are Not Women Religious or Clergy) in the Catholic Church?

The role of the laity is essentially to do the same thing that priests and religious are called to do without the leadership and sacramental duties left to their charge. We are called to help those in the faith and outside the faith realize God's love for them and by that love to realize their own vocation in this world, which will hopefully lead to their entrance into heaven. The main job of the Church is to save souls.

NOTES

Introduction

1. Jimmy Akin, "The Smoke of Satan Homily," jimmyakin.com, November 13, 2006.
2. John Michael Talbot biography, johnmichaeltalbot.com.
3. Tim Drake, "He Could No Longer Explain Why He Wasn't Catholic," *National Catholic Register,* May 29, 2007.
4. Scott and Kimberly Hahn, *Rome Sweet Home* (San Francisco: Ignatius Press, 1994).
5. George Weigel, *God's Choice: Pope Benedict XVI and the Future of the Catholic Church* (New York: Harper Collins, 2005).
6. Luis Lugo, Director; Brian Grim, Senior Research Fellow in Religion and World Affairs; and Elizabeth Podrebarac, Research Assistant, "Global Anglicanism at a Crossroads," *Pew Forum on Religion & Public Life*, June 19, 2008.
7. Ibid.
8. Frequently Requested Church Statistics from CARA website, cara.georgetown.edu.
9. John L. Allen, Jr., All Things Catholic blog.
10. John L. Allen, Jr., *The Future Church: How Ten Trends Are Revolutionizing the Catholic Church* (New York: Doubleday, 2009) pp. 38-39.
11. Jim Naughton, "Numbers: Episcopalians Who Join the Ordinariate, Catholics Who Become Episcopalians," The Episcopal Cafe blog, January 23, 2012.
12. "10 Questions for Katharine Jefferts Schori," *Time* magazine, July 10, 2006.
13. Deborah Solomon, "State of the Church: Questions for Katharine Jefferts Schori," *The New York Times* magazine, November 19, 2006.

Chapter 1

1. George Weigel, "How Benedict XVI Will Make History," *Newsweek*, April 21, 2008.
2. Ibid.
3. John L. Allen, Jr., *The Future Church* (New York: Doubleday, 2007).
4. Ibid.

Notes

5. Tim Montgomerie, "Cameron Says Religious Faith Is Not a Problem to Solve but an Integral Part of National Life," conservativehome.blogs.com/torydiary, September 18, 2010.
6. Fr. Richard John Neuhaus, "*Libertas Ecclesia*," *First Things*, April 18, 2005.
7. Bob Reeves, "Bishops Supporters Upstage the Critics," *Lincoln Journal Star*, May 31, 2007.
8. John L. Allen, Jr., "Five Reasons the Papal Trip to Africa Is Important," All Things Catholic blog, March 13, 2009.
9. Richard John Neuhaus, *Catholic Matters: Confusion, Controversy, and the Splendor of Truth* (New York: Basic Books, 2006) p. 195.
10. Ibid., pp. 228-229.
11. Archbishop Fulton Sheen, *Archbishop Fulton Sheen's St. Thérèse: A Treasured Love Story* (Irving, Tex: Basilica Press, 2007) pp. 153, 157-158.

Chapter 2

1. Peggy Noonan, "Something Beautiful Has Begun," *The Wall Street Journal*, April 11, 2008.
2. Mark Finkelstein, *Time* editor, "As Cardinal Pope Benedict Was Hatchet Man," Newsbusters, April 3,2008 Newsbuters.org
3. CDC, http://www.vatican.va/roman_curia/congregations/cfaith.
4. Tim Graham, "Couric Insists Pope's 'Extremely Conservative, Very Conservative,'" NewsBusters.org, April 15, 2008.
5. "US Birthrate Dropped for Third Straight Year," CatholicOnline News Consortium, November 20, 2011.
6. "US Birthrate in 2009 reaches record low amid recession woes," Catholic News Agency, August 29, 2010.
7. "There Will Likely Be Fewer Catholic Baptisms and Marriages Next Year...Again," National Vital Statistics Report, CARA, August 31, 2010.
8. "Catholic Ministry Formation Enrollment: Statistical Overview for 2010-2011," CARA, April 2011.
9. Ibid.
10. "Ordinations in the Archdiocese of Saint Louis," Rome of the West blog, May 29, 2010.
11. Jacqueline Salmon, "We Live It Every Day," *Washington Post*, April 9, 2008.
12. Rush Limbaugh, "Pope Benedict Speaks Truth," T*he Rush Limbaugh Show* archives, April 21, 2008.
13. Pope Benedict XVI, Homily of the Holy Mass, Nationals Park.

14. Ibid.
15. Deacon Keith Fournier, *Benedict in America: He Came, He Saw, He Conquered*, Catholic Online, April 21, 2008.
16. Fr. Thomas Rosica, CSB, *The Shadow of Peter Fell On America Last Week*, ZENIT, April 23, 2008.
17. "What the Pope Accomplished: Firm but Warm, Benedict Reached Out to American Catholics," The Daily Beast, *Newsweek's* weblog, April 20, 2008.
18. Deal Hudson, "The Face of Pope Benedict XVI," *Crisis Magazine*, April 21, 2008.

Chapter 3

1. George Weigel, *God's Choice: Pope Benedict XVI and the Future of the Catholic Church* (New York: Harper Collins, 2005).
2. Fr. Tony Oelrich, "The Catholic Gheto," Fr. Tony's Bridge Builders, July 22, 2009.
3. George Weigel, *Letters to a Young Catholic* (New York: Basic Books, 2004), pp 1-2.
4. See George Weigel, The Courage to Be Catholic (New York: Basic Books, 2002), pp87-116. Note: This is the author's summation of Mr. Weigel's treatment of the post-ghetto mindset of US bishops.
5. George Weigel, *God's Choice: Pope Benedict XVI and the Future of the Catholic Church* (New York: Harper Collins, 2005).
6. Ibid.
7. "Warning Considering the Writings of Father Teilhard de Chardin," Sacred Congregation of the Holy Office, June 30, 1962.
8. Russell Chandler, "Seattle Archbishop Stripped of Authority," *Los Angeles Times*, September t, 1986.
9. Interview with (then Diocese of Saginaw) Bishop Robert Carlson, *The Catholic Report*, May 1, 2006.
10. Article on Bishop Robert Baker, Wikipedia.
11. Fr. Richard John Neuhaus, *Catholic Matters*, p. 191-192, Basic Books, 2006.
12. Ibid.
13. Ibid.
14. "Archbishop Burke Opposes Sheryl Crow Concert Out of Pastoral Necessity," Catholic News Agency, April 26, 2007.
15. Peter Slevin, "St. Louis Prelate Aims to Bring Flock in Line," *The Washington Post*, May 29, 2007.

16. Diane M. Korzeniewski, OCDS, "Archbishop Burke 'Cans' Pro-Abort Sen. Claire McCaskill's Speaking Engagement at Catholic School," Te Deum Laudamus! blog, May 2, 2007.
17. "Majerus [sic] Abortion Rights Comment Gets St. Louis Bishop's [sic] Attention," Associated Press, January 24, 2008.
18. David Hartline, "Issues of Moral Weight: Interview with Archbishop Naumann of Kansas City," Zenit News, November 19, 2008.
19. Archbishop Joseph F. Naumann, "Governor's Veto Prompts Pastoral Action," *The Leaven*, May 9, 2008.
20. *Meet the Press* transcript, August 24, 2008.
21. Archbishop George F. Niederauer, "Archbishop Niederauer in Response to Comments Made by Speaker Pelosi on Abortion," *Catholic San Francisco*, September 5, 2008; "Clarifying Pelosi Misrepresentation Catholic Church Has Always Been Pro-Life," Catholics for the Common Good, August 26, 2008; "Bishops Respond to House Speaker Pelosi's Misrepresentation of Church Teaching Against Abortion," statement by the USCCB issued by Justin Cardinal Rigali, Chairman of the Committee on Pro-Life Activities and Bishop William Lori, chairman of the Committee on Doctrine, August 26, 2008.
22. Fr. Richard W. Gilsdorf, The Sign of the Times: Understanding the Church Since Vatican II (Green Bay: Star of the Bay Press, 2008) pp 139-157.
23. Benedict XVI and Peter Seewald, Light of the World (San Francisco: Ignatius Press, 2010) p. 34.
24. "The Future," unsigned editorial, *Commonweal* magazine, April 23, 1999.
25. "France: Statistics on the Number of Seminarians and Ordinations," Documentation Information Catholiques Internationales, March 9, 2012.
26. George Weigel, *Witness to Hope* (New York: Harper Collins, 1999) p. 658.
27. "Mainline Protestant," Wikipedia article.
28. Katharine T. Phan, "2011 Church Membership: Southern Baptists Decline; Jehovah's Witnesses Increase," *Christian Post*, February 15, 2011.
29. *Shepherds of Hope* newsletter for vocations, Diocese of Providence, Rhode Island
30. P.J. Kennedy & Sons *The Official National Catholic Directory* (New Providence, NJ: National Register Publishing).

Chapter 4

1. Robert Webber, *Evangelicals on the Canterbury Trial* (Morehouse, June 1989).

2. Sadly, Fr. Alvin (now Aidan) Kimel and his wife (whom he apparently married while an Episcopalian) have left the Catholic Church. He is now a Western-rite priest in the Russian Orthodox Church Outside of Russia (ROCOR).
3. Peter Gillquist, *Becoming Orthodox* (Conciliar, January 2001).
4. Tim Drake, "He Could No Longer Explain Why He Wasn't Catholic," *National Catholic Register,* May 29, 2007.
5. Fr. Frank Pavone, "The Conversion of Norma McCorvey," Priests for Life.
6. Roe No More website taken from *Texas Catholic.*
7. Julia Duin, *Bernard Nathanson's Conversion,* taken from June 1996 *Crisis* Magazine and reprinted by EWTN.
8. "First World Youth Day," Chronicle of World Youth Days, Vatican website.
9. Michael Barone interview, former producer for EWTN's *Mother Angelica Live* show, January 26, 2012.
10. Anna J. Wiersma, "Teenage Promiscuity in the United States," senior research paper published by Traditional Family Coalition.
11. Fiona MacRae, "Record Rise in Sexual Diseases Among Promiscuous Young Adults," *Daily Mail,* July 16, 2008.
12. J.M. Tuazon, "United by Plot, Pope John Paul II Rises, Bin Laden Falls On Same Day," *GMA News,* May 1, 2011.
13. "World Youth Days Seen as Life-Changing: Survey Reveals Positive Experiences of Participants," Zenit News Agency, July 20, 2011.
14. Michael Dubruiel, "St John Bosco Prophecy," Annunciation blog, August 18, 2005.
15. Linda Morris, "Final Message to the Faithful," *The Sydney Morning Herald,* July 20, 2008.
16. Don McClarey, "Spanish Civil War: Sadly Still Relevant, TheAmericanCatholic.com.
17. Ibid.
18. Milo Yiannopoulus, "Why Benedict Has Youth on His Side," *Catholic Herald,* September 1, 2011.
19. Tim Drake, "John Paul II: Missionary to the World," *National Catholic Register,* April 3, 2005.
20. "Archbishop: Church Must Learn Language of Youth; Says Liberty and Science Are Two Dominant Values," Zenit News Agency, July 21, 2011.
21. "Anti-Abortion Demonstration in Madrid," Demotix News, March 7, 2009, and "Big Anti-Abortion Rally in Spain," BBC, October 17, 2009.

22. "Spanish General Election 2011," Wikipedia article.
23. Mercedes De La Torre, "Young Spaniards Return WYD Marian Icon to Rome: Chaplain Expecting Abundant Fruits from Summer Event," Zenit News Agency, December 16, 2011.

Chapter 5

1. Mark Smith, Pierre Plantard Convictions 1953, 1956, Prioryof Sion.com.
2. Arius was an early fourth century priest from Alexandria, Egypt, and an early believer in *sola Scriptura*. (This is the heresy that Sacred Tradition has no place in Christian theology and thus the economy of salvation, and that we have everything we need to be saved and become holy/righteous/justified in Scripture alone [the Latin for which is *sola scriptura*]. It's most prominent proponents, however, were the sixteenth century leaders of the Protestant Revolt, Martin Luther and John Calvin.) Through his reading of Scripture and his use of "Scripture alone," he determined that Jesus Christ was not co-eternal with God the Father, that He came into being at some point in time, and was thus merely the highest of all the creatures God made. Arius' followers were known as Arians and their heresy was called "Arianism." Their modern day heirs are the Gnostics, Jehovah's Witnesses, and, to an extent, the Mormons, who are more aptly labeled "Semi-Arians."
3. R. Albert Mohler, "Deciphering the Da Vinci Code," AlbertMohler.com, April 12, 2006.
4. Catholic League news release, The Catholic League website, 2005.
5. April D. DeConick, *The New York Times* op-ed.
6. wikipedia.com.
7. Bloodline news, bloodline-news.blogspot.com.
8. Jimmy Akin, "Tomb of Jesus Nonsense," JimmyAkin.com, March 2007.
9. Jimmy Akin, "Pope Joan," JimmyAkin.com, December 29, 2006
10. Rabbi David Dalin, *The Mythy of Hitler's Pope* (Regenery 2005).
11. Jonah Goldberg, *Liberal Fascism* (New York: Doubleday 2008).
12. Margherita Marchione, *Pope Pius XII: Architecht of Peace* (Mahwah, New Jersey: Paulist Press, 2000).
13. Comments on Pope Pius XII, *Time* magazine article on Albert Einstein December 23, 1940.
14. Robert Moynihan, "The Passing of a Friend," The Moynihan Report, September 2011.

Chapter 6

1. Tim Stafford, "Abortion Wars," *Christianity Today*, January 22, 2003.
2. R. Albert Mohler, "Can Christians Use Birth Control?," AlbertMohler.com, May 8, 2006.
3. Ibid.
4. Tim Graham, "Newsweek's Abortion Debate: 'Hard Right' vs. 'Pro Abortion Rights Groups,'" NewsBusters.org, February 27, 2006.
5. San Francisco Family Rosary CrusadeRally, Christian Newswire, September 13, 2011.
6. John R. Diggs, Jr., MD, The Health Risks of Gay Sex, catholiceducation.org., 2002.
7. Katy Hudson review, TheFish.com.
8. Susan Sward, "Porn King Jim Mitchell Walks Out of Prison Today," *San Francisco Chronicle,* October 3, 1997
9. "Condom Failure Rate Fact Sheet," Human Life International.
10. "Condoms and Seat Belts: The Parallels and the Lessons," *The Lancet,* January 29, 2000.
11. "One in Four New Yorkers Have Herpes Virus," AP via Brietbart, June 9, 2008.
12. Brent Bozell, "Sex and the 'Glamour' Girl," Townhall.com, August 27, 2003.
13. G. Tracy Mehan III, "NYC: The Statue of Liberty or the Grim Reaper," *The American Spectator,* January 10, 2011.
14. Dawn Eden, "A Superhero for Choice" Rides Again, The Dawn Patrol blog, August 23, 2005.
15. Marc Eliot, *To the Limit: The Untold Story of the Eagles* (New York: Little Brown, 1998) pp. 128-129.
16. Roger Kimball, *The Long March* (Encounter Books, 2000) p.168.
17. Daniel Flynn, *A Conservative History of the America Left* (New York: Crown Forum, 2008) p. 253-255.
18. R. Albert Mohler, "Santorum Predicament," *Sign of the Times*, February 27, 2012.
19. Elizabeth Anscombe, "Contraception and Chastity,." OrthodoxyToday.org, 1972.
20. Tara Parker-Pope, "The Myth of Rampant Teenage Promiscuity," *The New York Times,* January 26, 2009.

Chapter 7

1. Mark Stricherz, "Goodbye, Catholics: How One Man Reshaped the Democratic Party," *Commonweal* magazine, www.thefreelibrary.com.
2. Fouad Ajami, "Obama and the Politics of Crowds," *Wall Street Journal*, October 30, 2008.
3. Roger Kimball, *The Long March*, p.248.
4. Anne Hendershott, "How Abortion Became Kennedy Dogma," *Wall Street Journal*, January 2, 2009.
5. John Fund, "From Mao to Obama," *Wall Street Journal*, October 21, 2009.
6. Words of Saul Alinsky reported on breitbart.com via a 1972 Playboy Interview. See note from chapter 7 footnote additions on p. 169
7. Scott Whitlock, "Chris Matthews Sneers: If You Are Really Anti-Gay, You Become Catholic Now," NewsBusters, February 12, 2012.
8. Larry Doyle, "The Jesus Eating Cult of Rick Santorum," *Huffington Post*, February 24, 2102.
9. Mark Oppenheimer, "A Gay Catholic Voice Against Same Sex Marriage," New York Times, June 4, 2010
10. "Is Obama Trying to Replace the Pope?" Daily Editorial, *Investors Business*, January 24, 2012.
11. "Seeing Red," Editorial, *New York Daily News*, February 25, 2012.
12. Tim Graham, "Hate Radio: Mike Malloy Wishes Cardinal George and Rick Santorum Would Drink Hemlock and Die," NewsBusters January 14, 2012.
13. Steve Ertelt, "Cardinal: Obama Admin Lectured Bishops on Catholic Teaching," LifeNews.com, March 6, 2012.
14. Michael Sean Winters, "The Politics of the "Accommodation," *National Catholic Reporter*, February 12, 2012.
15. George Weigel, "No Compromise," *National Review Online,* March 14, 2012.
16. Glenn Beck, "We Are All Catholics Now," *GBTV,* March 17, 2012.

Chapter 8

1. Andrew Rabel, "The Overseer of Justice," *The Vatican Insider*, June 2009.
2. David House, "Catholic Colleges 20 Years After "Ex Corde," Chronicle for Higher Education, September 10, 2010.
3. Donald McClarey, "Gutless Wonders, Petty Tyrants, and Chancery Dwellers," TheAmericanCatholic.com, October 27, 2011

4. Taylor Marshall, "St. Nicholas Punches Heretics in the Face!," Canterbury Tales blog, Dec. 6, 2010.
5. *The Newman Guide to Choosing a Catholic College*, Cardinal Newman Society, 2011.

Chapter 9

1. Mike Lupica, David Tyree, "Archbishop Timothy Dolan Wasting Their Breath Spewing Ignorance on Gay Marriage Issue," *New York Daily News*, June 22, 2011.
2. Courage Apostolate website, http://couragerc.net.
3. Mark Oppenheimer, "A Gay Catholic Voice Against Same-Sex Marriage," *The New York Times,* June 4, 2010.
4. Bishop Tomas Olmsted, "Marriage: A 'Hang Up' Or God's Plan?", *Catholic Sun,* August 10, 2010.

Chapter 10

1. Ken Woodward, "Church of the 'Times,'" *Commonweal*, May 7, 2010.
2. Matthew Balan, "CNN Hints Pope Guilty of Mishandling Abuse Case, Leaves Out Details," NewsBusters.com, September 23, 2010.
3. Tito Edwards, "Pope Benedict to be Deposed," The American Catholic, June 29, 2010.
4. Rembert G. Weakland, *A Pilgrim in a Pilgrim Church* (William Eerdmans Publishing, 2009).
5. Andrew Brown, "The Pope Draws 1,500,000 to Madrid—But That's Not News?" *The Guardian*, August 18, 2011.
6. Johann Hari, "Catholics, It's You This Pope Has Abused," *The Independent*, September 9, 2010.
7. Maureen Dowd, "A Nope for Pope," *The New York Times*, March 27, 2010.

Chapter 11

1. "The Muslim Sack of Rome," Roman Christendom blog, September 2007.
2. "Mafia Word Origins," SicilianCulture.com, April 2002.
3. Matteo Albertini, "Vatican's Growing Presence in Kosovo," Balkanalysis.com, April 14, 2011.

4. Frank Rega, *St Francis of Assisi and the Conversion of the Muslims*, (Rockford, Ill.:Tan Publishing, 2007).
5. Michael Novak, "Remembering Lepanto," National Review Online, October 7, 2006.
6. David Hartline, "As the September 11 Anniversary Nears, a Review of Al Qaeda's Little-Reported-On War Against the Catholic Church," The-American-Catholic.com, September 10, 2007.
7. Tito Edwards, "Zeitoun Marian Apparition 40 Year Anniversary," The-American-Catholic.com, November 24, 2009.
8. David Hartline, "At Marian Apparition Sites, Great Trials and Tribulations Often Occur Before and After," The-American-Catholic.com, August 23, 2010.

Chapter 12

1. Eamon Duffy, *The Stripping of the Altars*, (New Haven: Yale University Press, 1992).
2. Gary Stern, "Episcopal 'U2-charist' Uses Songs in Service," *USA Today*, October 25, 2006.

Chapter 13

1. John Jalsevac, "Toronto Film Festival Winner *Bella* Finds Major Distributor, Anticipates Opening October 26," LifeSiteNews.com, July 26, 2007.
2. "David Hartline interviews Eduardo Verastegui," *Catholic Report*, September 2007.
3. Hays Code, as posted on ArtsReformation.com.
4. Joseph Pronechen, "Pray Together, Stay Together," *National Catholic Register*, August 14, 2007.
5. Jonathan Rauch, "How to Be an Apatheist," Beliefnet.com, reprinted from *The Atlantic Monthly*.
6. Fr. John Flynn, "World Youth Day's Lasting Impacts," ZENIT, May 7, 2009.

Chapter 14
1. Peter Schweizer, *Makers and Takers* (New York: Doubleday, 2008) p. 176.
2. William Murray, *My Life Without God* (Eugene, OR: Harvest, 1982).
3. Mark Fellows, "The Apocalypse of Jack Kerouac," *Culture Wars* magazine, November 1999.
4. Jonah Goldberg, *Liberal Fascism* (New York: Doubleday, 2007).
5. John Allen, "The Deathbed Friendship Between a Bishop and an Atheist," *National Catholic Reporter,* August 24, 2007.

Chapter 15
1. Tracy Wilkinson and Rebecca Trounson, "Pope Elevates Latin Mass, Leaving Some Polarized," *Los Angeles Times*, July 8, 2007.
2. Catholic Report link to comments section on *The Guardian's* "Pope's Move on Latin Mass a Blow to Jews," July 8, 2007.
3. John Allen, Latin Mass Update, *National Catholic Reporter*, August 2007.
4. Jeff Miller, "Get Your Motu Running," The Curt Jester blog, July 2007.
5. Susan Thistelthwaite, "Keeping Secrets: The Laity, the Latin Mass, and the LA Settlement," *Washington Post's* blog On Faith, July 17, 2007.
6. "Aide: Pope Prefers Communion on the Tongue," ZENIT, June 26, 2008.
7. Fr. John Zuhlsdorf, "Dealing with McBrien on the New Corrected Translation," What Does the Prayer Really Say? blog, January 1, 2012.

Chapter 16
1. Book cover endorsements for David Hartline's *The Tide Is Turning Toward Catholicism,* Catholic Report, 2006.
2. Tom O'Toole, *Champions of Faith* (Lanham, Maryland: Rowman and Littlefield, 2001).
3. Tom O'Toole, "Saving Notre Dame: the Impact of Youth and Rockne," Renew America, March 31, 2009.
4. Dave Hartline interview with Notre Dame Coach Gerry Faust, Catholic Report, September 2005.
5. Ann Rodgers-Melnick, "Saint Inspires an Olympic Champion," *Pittsburgh Post-Gazette,* February 11, 2011.

Chapter 17

1. Dave Shiflett, Exodus: *Why Americans Are Leaving Liberal Churches for Conservative Christianity* (New York: Sentinel, 2005).
2. Tim Graham, "ABC's Dan Harris Touted Feminist Church Leaders, Mangled His Catholic Angle," NewsBusters, June 20, 2006,. 3.
3. Ibid.
4. Deborah Solomon, "State of the Church," *The New York Times*, November 19, 2006.
5. Mark Tooley, "Resenting African Christianity," *American Spectator*, May 21, 2010.
6. Daniel Blake, "Statistics Suggest Anglican Church of Canada in Huge Decline," ChristianToday.com, February 13, 2006.
7. Martin Beckford, "Bishop Gene Robinson to Marry Gay Partner," *Telegraph*, June 6, 2008.
8. Ibid.
9. Peter Schweizer, *Makers and Takers* (New York: Doubleday, 2008).
10. Nicholas Kristof, "Believe It or Not," *New York Times*, August 15, 2003.
11. Christopher Hedges, *American Fascists* (New York: Free Press, 2007).
12. Jonah Goldberg, *Liberal Fascism* (New York: Doubleday, 2007) p.319.
13. Ibid.
14. Fr. Dwight Longenecker, "Anglican Pioneers," from articles section of Fr. Longenecker's website, http://www.dwightlongenecker.com.

Chapter 18

1. Kurt Bowen, *Christians in a Secular World: The Canadian Experience*, Google eBook conclusion, (McGill-Queens University Press, 2005).
2. Saul Alinsky, *Rules for Radicals*, original edition (New York: Random House, 1971).
3. Mark Steyn, *America Alone* (Regnery, 2006) pp.91-101.
4. Ibid.
5. "Alfred E. Smith Dies Here At Age 70; Four Times Governor," *The New York Times*, October 4, 1944.
6. Dave Hartline, "Some Time in New York City, My Reflection on the Visit of Pope Benedict XVI," Catholic Report, April 2008.
7. George Weigel, *God's Choice* (New York: Harper Collins, 2005) p.65.
8. Dave Hartline, "Final Report from the Episcopal Convention," Catholic Report, April 2006.
9. R. Albert Mohler, "Can Christians Use Birth Control?," AlbertMohler.com, May 8, 2006.

10. Edward Kennedy, *True Compass* (New York: Grand Central Publishing, 2009) p.12.
11. Michael Ledeen, "Rush & the ADL," National Review Online, January 22, 2010.
12. Mark Steyn, "Occupiers Part of a Grand Alliance Against the Productive," *Orange County Register*, November 4, 2011.
13. Thomas Peters, "Occupy Vancouver Attempts to Invade Catholic Mass," Catholic Vote, November 2011.
14. "John Lennon Was a Closet Republican: Assistant," *Toronto Sun*, June 28, 2011.
15. Steve Turner, "An Excerpt from the Gospel According to the Beatles," *Christianity Today*, January 3, 2007.

Chapter 19

1. "Dragged Kicking and Screaming Into the Modern Age? Lessons From Piers Morgan's Interview with Joel Osteen," AlbertMohler.com, October 6, 2011.
2. Ravelle Mohammad, "Pat Robertson Alzheimer's Comments Carnal and Selfish, Say Christian Leaders," The Christian Post, September 15, 2011.
3. "The Last Hours of Alexander Hamilton," The Archivist Mailbag, TrinityWallStreet.org.
4. Cathy Lynn Grossman, "As Their Numbers Stall, Megachurches Seek 'Seekers,'" *USA Today*, September 9, 2008.
5. Brittany Smith, "New Spring Cancels Sunday Evening Services for Super Bowl," *Christian Post*, February 4, 2012.
6. Anugrah Kimar, "Ohio Pastor Puts Stripper Pole Next to Pulpit to Talk Sex," *Christian Post*, April 1, 2012.

Chapter 20

1. The Marburg Colloquy took place at Marburg Castle to see if a consensus could be reached over the Real Presence between Luther and Huldrych Zwingli. While Luther did not believe in Transubstantiation, he did believe in consubstantiation, a term that came under what he called the "sacramental union." Consubstantiation means that the Lord's Body and Blood are present at the same time the bread and wine are present. Zwingli and his camp, however, believed the bread

and wine were simply symbolic of Christ's Body and Blood. Phillip I of Hessen wanted the two to resolve their differences so that there could be a strong Protestant political alliance. However, the failure of the Colloquy and subsequent debates only resulted in each side sticking to the views it already had.
2. PBS television program, *The Pill*, PBS.org.
3. Patrick Fagan, "A 'Culture' of Inverted Sexuality," Catholic Education Resource Center, November 1998.
4. Tim Drake, "Groundbreaking Series on Catholicism to Hit PBS," *National Catholic Register,* September 9, 2011.
5. Michael O'Brien, "The Passion of William Kurelek," StudiObrien.com.
6. "Our Foundress, Catherine Dougherty," MadonnaHouse.org.
7. Anne Hendershott and Christopher White, "Traditional Catholicism Is Winning," *The Wall Street Journal,* April 12, 2012.

INDEX

A

abortion 19, 27, 41, 69, 70, 72, 73, 74, 88, 89, 90, 96, 132, 133, 134, 135, 144, 145, 146, 147, 148, 149, 150, 151, 157, 160, 166, 167, 168, 170, 173, 177, 193, 286, 305, 307, 316, 345
Abramowicz, Danny 30
   abstinence 142, 143

AIDS 21, 22, 137, 138, 142, 205
Akin, Jimmy 122, 123, 327, 348, 353
Alba, Fr. Ángel 111
Alinsky, Saul 165, 166, 168, 169, 239, 290, 300, 301, 302, 303, 304, 323, 324, 355, 359
Allen, John 14, 18, 19, 26, 267, 306, 348, 349, 358
al-Qaeda 97, 98, 224, 231, 232, 233, 234, 235, 236
American Catholic 2, 18, 39, 44, 45, 105, 356
Angelica, Mother 92, 93, 94, 95, 352
Anglican/Episcopalian Communion 16
Anglican Ordinariate 17, 20
Anglicans 13, 16, 17, 20, 235, 238, 284, 285, 324, 326
Angotti, John 362
Anti-Defamation League 309
Aquinas, St. Thomas 4, 5, 194, 198, 322, 324, 328, 337
Archdiocese of Baltimore 13
Archdiocese of St. Louis 46
Assad, Audrey 362
Ave Maria University 156, 173, 194

B

Baker, Robert 62, 74, 350
Barone, Michael 5, 93, 94, 352
Barron, Fr. Robert 331
Beat poets 259
Beck, Glenn 135, 188, 355
Beckwith, Francis 11, 87
Belmont Abbey College 194
Benedictine College 194

Index

Benedict XVI, Pope 1, 2, 7, 9, 15, 20, 23, 24, 25, 27, 33, 39, 41, 43, 45, 47, 49, 51, 52, 53, 55, 56, 57, 59, 69, 72, 87, 91, 99, 100, 102, 104, 107, 108, 109, 179, 202, 203, 204, 205, 214, 216, 219, 236, 238, 251, 262, 263, 268, 273, 277, 283, 286, 287, 291, 298, 299, 305, 313, 324, 336, 348, 350, 351, 359
BigPulpit 2, 18
birth control 43, 44, 45, 133, 141, 154, 155, 156, 159, 184, 185, 195, 300, 325, 326, 345
Blessed Mother 14, 192, 229, 231, 232, 233, 243, 246, 279
Bloomberg, Michael 166
Bojinka Plot 97
Boorstein, Michelle 56
Booth, Tom 362
Bosco, St. John 101, 352
Breitbart, Andrew 159, 160
Brokaw, Tom 74
Brownback, Sam 14
Brown, Dan 113, 158
Brown, Michael 5, 113, 114, 116, 158, 241, 354, 356
Bruskewitz, Bishop Fabian 32
Buddhists 35
Buffett, Jimmy 314
Burke, Raymond 62, 69, 70, 71, 185, 190, 350, 351
Bush, George W. 47, 164, 186, 288

C

Call to Action 32, 33
Cameron, David 28, 122, 349
CARA 13, 17, 46, 67, 79, 349
Cardinal Newman Society 191, 194, 356
Carlson, Robert 62, 79, 350
Catholic identity 18, 34, 63, 76, 78, 80, 107
Catholic League 116, 124, 283, 353
CatholicReport.org 4, 74
Catholics Come Home 218, 330
Cavins, Jeff 155
CBS *60 Minutes* 68, 124, 142
CDF 40, 41, 42, 43, 205, 264
Center for Applied Research in the Apostolate (CARA) 13
Champions of Faith 277

Chaput, Charles 63, 78, 79, 168, 185
Chesterton, G.K. 196, 199, 255, 270
Choby, David Bishop 63, 64
Christianity Today 133, 307, 360
Chrysostum, St. John 192
Clarkson, Kelly 52
clergy abuse scandal 286
Clinton, Bill 70, 165, 168, 171, 196, 290, 303, 305
Clinton, Hillary Rodham 70, 165, 168, 171, 196, 290, 303, 305
CNN 52, 156, 157, 203, 204, 205, 314, 324, 356
Colson, Chuck 134, 327
Columbus, Christopher 5, 80, 83, 223, 287
Congregation for the Doctrine of Faith (see CDF)) 40
contraception 41, 44, 67, 132, 133, 134, 142, 146, 150, 172, 177, 180, 185, 187, 222
Costas, Bob 69
Courage 174, 198, 350, 356
Couric, Katie 43, 299, 349
Crow, Sheryl 69, 350
Crusades, The 84, 223, 227
Crystal, Billy 69, 315, 321
Culture of Death 72, 73, 96, 134, 160
Culture of Life 7, 70, 85, 96, 132, 133, 135, 137, 139, 141, 143, 145, 147, 149, 151, 152, 153, 155, 157, 159, 160, 161
Cumbie, Michael 85
Curran, Fr. Charles 41

D

Dalin, Rabbi David 363
Da Vinci Code, The 113, 114, 116, 117, 119, 121
de Chardin, Tielhard 60
DeConick, April D. 117, 353
Dolan, Timothy 68, 79, 145, 168, 171, 177, 182, 183, 185, 188, 197, 356
Dominican Sisters of Mary, Mother of the Eucharist 80, 307
Dowd, Maureen 173, 176, 202, 203, 214, 215, 216, 217, 218, 356
Drake, Tim 109, 348, 352, 360
Dutton, Fred 163
Dylan, Bob 312

E

Early Church Fathers 198
Einstein, Albert 127
Encourage 174
Ermatinger, Fr. Cliff 204
Escriva, St. Jose Maria 113
Eszterhas, Joe 253
Eucharistic Adoration 32, 190, 304, 329
Evangelical Catholicism 18
Evert, Jason 139, 140
EWTN 1, 5, 52, 53, 62, 82, 83, 92, 93, 94, 95, 159, 277, 280, 352

F

Fallaci, Oriana 261, 262
Family Theater 6, 136, 246, 254
Far Left 165, 179, 200, 235, 301, 306, 310, 311
Fátima 128, 129, 130, 232, 261
Faust 276, 278, 279, 358
Fellowship of Catholic University Students (FOCUS) 35
Ferrara, Christopher 130
Fisichella, Archbishop Rino 110, 262
Forbes, James 120
FOX 52
Foxman, Abraham 309
Fox, Matthew 2, 149, 173, 175, 180, 218, 291
Franciscan University 82, 194, 252
French Revolution 164, 205, 209, 256, 260, 261, 296, 304, 311, 322, 323, 332

G

gay lifestyle 200, 286
George, Cardinal 1, 6, 16, 24, 47, 58, 59, 101, 163, 164, 184, 187, 217, 274, 278, 288, 305, 310, 311, 348, 350, 351, 355, 359
Georgetown University 13, 43, 184
Gilsdorf, Fr Richard 14, 75, 351
Gilsdorf, Fr. Richard W. 14, 351
Gingrich, Newt 172, 173, 178
Girls Gone Wild 140
Giuliani, Rudy 315, 316

God's Rottweiler 15, 27
Goldberg, Jonah 124, 125, 289, 306
Goldhagen, Daniel 124, 125
Goldstein, Gary 121
Graham, Tim 43, 283, 349, 354, 355, 359
Grammar, Kelsey 247
Great Britain 16, 17, 210
Grodi, Marcus 83, 84
Ground Zero 53, 54, 136

H

Hahn, Scott 12, 82, 240, 252
hard-liner 43, 52
Hedges, Chris 288, 289, 359
Hemmingway, Ernest 105
Hermeneutic of Continuity, The 1, 18
Herzog, Daniel 285
Hitler 27, 124, 125, 126, 127, 132, 170, 260, 261, 289, 309, 353
Hitler's Youth 27
Hoover, J. Edgar 105, 301, 302
Howard, Ron 115, 116
Howell, Dr. Kenneth 83
Hudson, Deal 56, 138, 141, 350, 354
Humanae Vitae 41, 72, 134
Hunt, Allen 14

I

Irenaeus, St. 117, 118, 119
Islam 120, 219, 220, 221, 222, 224, 225, 226, 227, 228, 230, 231, 232, 234, 236, 238, 261

J

Jefferts Schori, Bishop Katharine 20, 299
Jenkins, Fr. John 189, 190, 191, 192, 193
John Paul II, Bl. 9, 14, 15, 17, 23, 24, 26, 33, 36, 37, 39, 40, 49, 55, 56, 61, 75, 84, 86, 87, 91, 96, 97, 98, 100, 102, 104, 108, 109, 166, 170, 179, 203, 231, 243, 262, 265, 291, 295, 305, 352
John Paul I, Pope 14, 129
Jones, Alex 84, 85, 86, 165, 169, 170, 290, 303

Judaism 52, 115, 173, 183, 197, 205, 265, 266, 309

K

Keller, Bill 170, 202
Kennedy, Edward 71, 162, 163, 166, 167, 168, 186, 306, 308, 355, 359
Kennedy, John 71, 162, 163, 166, 167, 168, 186, 306, 308, 355, 359
Kennedy, Robert 71, 162, 163, 166, 167, 168, 186, 306, 308, 355, 359
Kerouac, Jack 152, 153, 259, 260, 312, 358
Kimball, Roger 153, 165, 166
Kimel, Fr. Al 84, 352
King, Karen 14, 71, 120, 146, 153, 230, 237, 273, 314, 315, 354
King, Larry 314, 315
King's College 14
Kinsey, Alfred 154
Konzelman, Chuck 364
Kreeft, Peter 135, 167, 197
Kresta, Al 127
Kristol, Irving 367
Kudlow, Lawrence 14
Küng, Fr. Hans 36, 41, 42, 304, 305
Kurelek, William 333, 334, 361

L

Lateran, St. John 220, 221, 262
Lauer, Matt 116, 122
Led Zeppelin 251
Legion of Christ 203
Lennon, John 367
Lewis, C.S. 12, 159, 238, 251, 324
Limbaugh, Rush 47, 181, 184, 349
Lipinski, Tara 171, 279, 280
Longenecker, Fr. Dwight 84, 292, 359
Lozano, Karyme 1, 6, 243
Lupica, Mike 197, 356
Luther, Martin 132, 146, 316, 323, 328, 340, 353, 360

M

Maciel, Fr. Marcial 203, 207
Madonna 140, 335

Madrid, Patrick 23, 30, 103, 104, 107, 108, 110, 123, 213, 327, 352, 356
Magisterium 39, 75, 83, 344
Maher, Bill 184, 247, 251, 252
Maher, Matt 367
Margherita, St. 126, 127, 353
Maritain, Jacques 304
Marley, Bob 152
Martel, Charles "The Hammer" 125, 220, 221, 226
Martin, Curtis 35, 76, 132, 146, 323, 328, 332, 340, 353, 359
Masons, the 129, 130
Matthews, Chris 174, 176, 184, 355
McBrien, Fr. Richard 25, 36, 37, 190, 192, 358
McClarey, Don 105, 352, 355
McCloskey, Fr. John 90
McCorvey, Norma 88, 89, 90, 352
McEveety, Steve 254
McGovern, George 162, 163
McKellen, Sir Ian 116
Men's Wearhouse 310
Merton, Thomas 335
Metzler, Brad 129
Mitchell brothers, the 136
Mohammad, Khalid Sheik 97
Mohler, Albert 114
Morris, Fr. Jonathan 180, 204, 352
Moynihan, Robert 130, 131, 353
MSNBC 40, 52, 174, 178
MTV 92, 150, 151, 171
Muslims 27, 125, 217, 219, 220, 222, 224, 226, 227, 232, 234, 235, 236, 356

N

Naked Archaeologist 122, 123
Napoleon 260
Nashville Dominicans 64, 80
Nathanson, Dr. Bernard 88, 89, 90, 146, 352
National Catholic Register 2, 5, 87, 109, 208, 348, 352, 357, 361
National Catholic Reporter 17, 65, 67, 186, 192, 214, 267, 274, 306, 355, 358
National Public Radio 43, 271

Natural Family Planning (see NFP) 151
Naumann, Archbishop John 71, 72, 73, 351
Neuhaus, Fr. Richard John 36, 53, 63, 285, 327, 349, 350
New Age 36, 64, 80, 255, 275, 289
Newman, Bl. John Henry Cardinal 12
NewsBusters 43, 283, 349, 354, 355, 356, 359
New Springtime of Evangelization 102
New York City 14, 51, 105, 120, 144, 182, 251, 359
New York Times 17, 22, 117, 126, 160, 170, 174, 198, 202, 205, 214, 283, 284, 285, 288, 291, 299, 324, 348, 353, 354, 356, 359
NFP 151, 152
Nicene Creed 18
Nicks, Stevie 149
Nicolosi, Barbara 213, 254
Nienstedt, John 64, 65, 66, 67
Noonan, Peggy 40
Norris, Michelle 43
Nostradamus 113

O

Obama, Barack 73, 91, 157, 159, 164, 169, 171, 172, 176, 177, 178, 179, 180, 181, 183, 186, 187, 189, 192, 193, 230, 290, 301, 303, 305, 308, 355
O'Brien, Cardinal Edwin 22
Occupy Wall Street 310, 313
O'Hair, Madalyn Murray 258, 259
Ohio Dominican University 19, 306
Opus Dei 90, 101, 113
Osteen, Joel 315, 319, 360

P

Pagels, Elaine 120
Palin, Sarah 178, 308
Paul VI, Pope 10, 41, 44, 55, 62, 67, 72, 133, 151, 179, 230, 264, 300, 324, 345
Pavone, Fr. Frank 89, 352
Pell, Cardinal George 101, 274, 352
Pelosi, Nancy 73, 74, 170, 306, 351
Perry, Katy 141, 212
Peschken, Christian 367

Peyton, Fr. Francis 29
Peyton, Fr. Patrick 6, 29, 136, 244, 245, 246
Pfleger, Fr. Michael 184
Pill, the 44, 45, 360
Pius VII, Pope 48
Pius XII, Ven. 60, 124, 125, 126, 127, 309, 353
Pius X, Pope St. 67
Planned Parenthood 145, 146, 147, 148, 150, 306
Pontifical College Josephinum 80
priesthood 35, 74, 78, 79, 109, 206, 208, 240, 247, 267, 299
Priests for Life 89, 352
Priory of Sion 113, 121
Progressive Party 210
Protestant Reformation 112, 132, 297, 298, 316, 340

R

Raymond, Fr. Willy 246
Ray, Steve 64, 85, 240
Regnum Christi 203
religious freedom 47, 185
Rivers, Philip 280
Robertson, Pat 312, 315, 316, 360
Roberts, Thomas 65
Robeson, Paul 105
Rockne, Knute 193, 278, 358
Roe v. Wade 73, 88, 133, 145, 151, 163
Romero, Jesse 30
Romney, Mitt 156, 176, 177
Rosary 6, 13, 29, 32, 136, 139, 190, 229, 230, 245, 248, 268, 270, 329, 354
Rosary Crusades 29
Rosary Priest 136, 245
Ryan, Paul 369

S

Saddleback Church 314
Salesians 231
Salmon, Jacqueline L. 56
same-sex attraction 200

Sanger, Margaret 146, 306
Santorum, Rick 155, 156, 157, 158, 167, 168, 172, 173, 174, 175, 176, 177, 184, 354, 355
satanists 131, 147, 275
Scarborough, Joe 40
Schlink, Edmund 60
Schneier, Arthur 51
Sebelius, Kathleen 72, 177
Second Vatican Council 9, 15, 44, 49, 61, 71, 77, 291
Selmys, Melinda 174
Severino, Leo 159, 242
sexual-abuse scandal 28
Sharpton, Rev. Al 145
Shea, Mark 5, 322
Sheen, Fulton 37, 349
Shiflett, Dave 20
Shonebarger, Fr. Thomas 335
Söhngen, Fr. Gottlieb 60
Solomon, Cary 370
Spears, Britney 140
Spong, John Shelby 284, 309
Stafford, James F. 15, 109
STDs 96, 150
Stengel, Rick 40, 349
Stone, Daniel 56, 253
St. Patrick's Cathedral 52
St. Peter's Basilica 34
St. Peter's Square 14, 23, 24, 87
Stravinskas, Fr. Peter 15
St. Thomas More College of Liberal Arts 194
Summer of Love 135, 136, 214, 246, 248, 252
Summorum Pontificum 33, 34, 64, 263, 265, 266, 273
Suppan, Jeff 277
Sweeney, Mike 277
Synod on the Family 14

T

Talbot, John Michael 11, 348
Tebow, Tim 280
Thatcher, Margaret 26

Theology of the Body 26
Thérèse of Lisieux, St. 37, 279, 280, 349
Third Day 52
Thomas Aquinas College 194
Thomas, Norman 65, 68, 151, 194, 198, 237, 241, 257, 301, 310, 322, 324, 328, 332, 335, 337, 350, 360
Time magazine 20, 40, 127, 348, 349
TLM 32, 33, 46, 264, 265, 266, 267, 268, 269, 271, 272, 273, 275
Today show 116, 142, 218, 331
Tolkien, J.R.R. 251
Traditional Latin Mass 32, 271
Tridentine 33, 266
Trotsky, Leon 210, 211, 239
Tushnet, Eve 174, 198

U

U2 238, 357
United Methodist Church, the 77
United States Conference of Catholic Bishops 15
USA Today 319, 357, 360

V

Vagina Monologues, The 141
Van Halen 333
Vatican 9, 10, 14, 15, 20, 32, 33, 34, 40, 43, 44, 49, 58, 59, 60, 61, 62, 66, 67, 71, 75, 77, 80, 94, 110, 127, 128, 129, 130, 131, 180, 190, 203, 207, 213, 214, 230, 264, 265, 266, 267, 269, 271, 274, 277, 291, 308, 310, 311, 351, 352, 355, 356
Vatican II 10, 14, 33, 59, 66, 67, 75, 94, 180, 207, 230, 264, 265, 266, 269, 271, 274, 308, 351
Vatican II, spirit of 10, 14, 33, 59, 66, 67, 75, 94, 180, 207, 230, 264, 265, 266, 269, 271, 274, 308, 351
Vatican Information Service 128
Verastegui, Eduardo 242, 243, 357
Vitale, Dick 276, 280, 281
Voltaire 164, 166, 209, 296, 304, 319, 324

W

Waldman, David 174, 175, 176
Warren, Rick 314, 315

Washington Post 40, 46, 56, 178, 271, 349, 350, 358
We Are Church 265, 271
Webber, Dr. Robert 83, 84, 351
Weigel, George 18, 24, 58, 59, 187, 305, 311, 348, 350, 351, 355, 359
White House 47, 167, 169, 172, 183, 184, 185, 243
Williams, Archbishop Rowan 20, 216, 235, 239, 299
Williams, Dr. Rowan 20, 216, 235, 239, 299
Wills, Gary 288, 309
Wojtyła, Karol 14, 295
women religious 35, 49, 53, 64, 76, 80, 106, 215, 295
Woodward, Kenneth 202, 204, 356
World Christian Database 16
World Youth Day 15, 23, 79, 91, 92, 93, 94, 95, 97, 98, 99, 100, 101, 102, 103, 104, 105, 109, 231, 249, 250, 251, 252, 305, 352, 357
Wuerl, Donald 61
Wyoming Catholic College 194

Y

Yankee Stadium 53, 54, 55, 56

Z

Zenit 71, 107, 111, 351, 352, 353
Zuhlsdorf, Fr. John 5, 274, 358